Sex, Lies and Ho

A Parent's Guide for Fighting Back

Help Teens Develop Personal Identity, Set Boundaries, Resist Peer Pressure, Embrace Abstinence and Prepare for Marriage and Family

Proceeds from the sale of this book benefit Heritage Community Services, a 501(c)(3) non profit serving adolescents, their parents, and their communities

Sex, Lies and Hook-Ups: A Parent's Guide for Fighting Back
Second Edition

Principles That Have Been Proven Effective

Heritage Keepers® is the only abstinence-until-marriage program recognized by the U.S. Department of Health and Human Services as having met the criteria for being listed as an evidence-based teen pregnancy prevention program http://www.hhs.gov/ash/oah/oah-initiatives/teen_pregnancy/db/

Primary Authors
Sally Badgley Raymond, Tammy Bryant, MSW, and Anne Badgley, MEd

Reproduction Section
Joshua Mann, MD, MPH
University of South Carolina, Family and Preventive Medicine Department
Preventive Medicine Division

Heritage Keepers® Student Workbook
Carrie Musselman, Tracey Casale and Tammy Bryant, MSW

Editors
Anne M. Badgley, MEd, Tammy Bryant, MSW, Mary McLellan, MS, Ami Williams, Jerry Raymond, Robert Swain, MS, HIA, and Anna Tello

Medical Accuracy and Referencing Review
The Medical Institute for Sexual Health
Note: Second Edition references are identical to First Edition references.

Anatomical Illustrations
Deanna Sink Walter

Heritage Keepers® Curricula Consultant
Paul E. Douthit, PhD, LMFT
Texas Tech University School of Medicine Department of Pediatrics

About the Primary Authors

Sally Badgley Raymond

Sally was set up with her husband, Jerry, for her Senior Prom in 1996 and they have been happily married since 1999. They are the proud parents of 4 beautiful children – three boys and a girl! As a sorority girl at Clemson University, she witnessed firsthand the harmful emotional and life changing effects casual sex can have. Right after graduating college ('00), she was employed by Heritage Community Services. She has the unique position of researching effective behavior change principles and applying that research to the *Heritage Keepers® Abstinence Education* program. She is also the co-author of *Heritage Keepers® Abstinence Education II*, the *Heritage Keepers® I-V Life Skills* series, *Sex, Lies and Hook-Ups: A Teen's Guide for Fighting Back and Sex, Lies and Hook-Ups, A Young Adult's Guide for Fighting Back*. Since becoming a parent, Sally has felt a strong need to take what she has learned and empower parents to impact their children on this important topic.

Tammy Bryant, MSW

Tammy grew up with parents that talked to her often about the value of saving sex for marriage. She quickly learned that most parents did not have the same conversations with their teens, mostly because they felt ill-equipped. Tammy spent her college years at College of Charleston witnessing the pain of the hook-up culture on her sorority sisters and other peers and was determined to combat the sexual culture with a message about avoiding sexual activity before marriage. After college in 2004, she married the love of her life, Dusty, and began working as an abstinence educator for Heritage Community Services. After spending some time teaching teenagers about abstinence, she developed some talking points to help parents feel more equipped to talk to their children about sex. As the current Chief Program Officer for Heritage Community Services, she is excited to be part of a team that has now developed formal trainings for parents and other adults based on years of research on creating positive behavior changes. Her hope is that parents will feel empowered and equipped to promote the healthiest sexual message to their teens—one that will help them avoid the pains of the sexual culture. Tammy and her husband are proud parents of two young boys with hopes of adding more children to the family soon.

Anne Badgley, MEd

Anne met her husband, Gordon, while a freshman at Roanoke College; they married soon after graduation in 1970. The Badgleys have two grown children, Sally and Gordon, Jr. - both of whom are married, and four grandchildren. Mrs. Badgley, who has a graduate degree in Clinical Counseling, founded the Lowcountry Pregnancy Center in 1985, a support ministry for women. After ten years of counseling young people in crisis, she founded Heritage Community Services in 1995 for the purpose of developing and implementing a scientific approach to teaching teens the benefits of protective boundaries for sexual activity. She has served as the Chairman of the Board for the Berkeley County Department of Social Services, as the Chairman of the Adolescent Risk Reduction Committee for the South Carolina Maternal and Child Health Council, as a founding member of the Board of Directors for the National Abstinence Education Association, and as a member of the Medical Institute for Sexual Health Advisory Board. Mrs. Badgley has been a keynote speaker and has provided workshops on Abstinence Education for various state and national conferences and has testified before the U.S. Congress on the effective use of Title V, Section 510 (Welfare Reform) Abstinence Education funds. Mrs. Badgley is co-author of the evidence-based (proven-effective) *Heritage Keepers® Abstinence Education* curricula and is the Chief Executive Office of Heritage Community Services.

Contents

IMPORTANT, PLEASE READ BEFORE CONTINUING

Program Components and Order of Use

Sex Lies and Hook-Ups: A Parent's Guide for Fighting Back includes this book, the accompanying Parent Video Series and a Student Workbook.

Videos will be listed at the end of the chapters with which they are compatible. The videos contain additional information as well as interviews with *Heritage Keepers®* educators and students that participated in the *Heritage Keepers®* program – so don't skip them!

Completing the book, the Video Series and the corresponding chapter questions will prepare you to go through the Student Workbook, which is at the end of this book, with your child.

To view the DVD series, please visit https://vimeo.com/album/3102808 and type in family fusion (do not forget the space between the two words). Because this is a password protected site, you will need to re-type the link each time you access it – do not follow an old link your computer browser recognizes, that won't work. It must be typed in, letter by letter, each time.

Heritage Keepers® programs are distributed by Heritage Community Services, a non-profit organization created in 1995 to empower individuals and families to pursue the characteristics of personal responsibility, honor and integrity through education and personal relationship building. It is the mission of this organization to strengthen the character of America's adolescents and our communities – one individual, one family and one institution at a time.

Please contact us at heritage@heritageservices.org for further information about other resources, including *Heritage Keepers® Abstinence Education I and II, Heritage Keepers® Life Skills Education I – V, Heritage Keepers® Media Spots,* and *Heritage Keepers® Theory and Methodology Training*.

Forward
Testing a Risk Avoidance Model

"What was missing from the class that you expected to hear? The "sex is bad" lecture!"

Male *Heritage Keepers®* student

"I learned a lot about what makes a good marriage and thought about the qualities I want to look for in a husband. My Mom and Dad have never had a good marriage and they recently got a divorce. As you can conclude, I haven't had that much experience with why marriage is good and what things make it good. I have always known what doesn't make a good marriage, but it was very important for me to find out what makes a marriage worthwhile."

Female *Heritage Keepers®* student

I enjoyed your class very much. It made me realize that a lot of people are virgins and I am not left out in the dark to wait till marriage. I really liked your class, it was fun and I learned more than last year. Thank you."

Female *Heritage Keepers®* student

America is known throughout the world as the land of freedom. An important aspect of freedom is learning how to balance between rights and responsibilities. In America's early years, many people faced death as they crossed the ocean and settled across the country. Even today, people are coming to America desperate to be a part of a country that offers freedoms unknown in many parts of the world. Some came here wealthy; some came looking for wealth. Others came as indentured servants or slaves. Some had no choice; others came with a dream of land or a desire to worship in freedom. Meanwhile, the natives of America had to make great adjustments as people poured into their country.

All of our ancestors deserve respect for their hard work and courage, which built this great country. They built a land full of opportunity with ideals that would eventually inspire the world. They reached for the moon—and then actually went there. Each generation accomplished something more than the generation before, and they accepted the sacrifices it took to achieve greatness. They provided future generations with opportunities that were unheard of in the history of man and comforts unknown to kings and queens of years ago. Some risked their lives to provide that freedom and those opportunities, and some died with only the hope of a better future for those left behind. Americans have the opportunity to form their family in a land where the future is so bright.

How people go about forming their families in large part determines the degree to which they will be able to take advantage of the opportunities America offers. Statistics reveal that children raised in a stable home with their married biologically related mother and father do better in almost every category of well-being. Yet, the percentage of single parent homes is increasing and the percentage of families with parents that are married and living together is decreasing. Why, when family structure is so important to the well-being of its members, are families becoming so increasingly chaotic and fragmented?

Our culture seems reluctant to discuss this important topic! The fact is, it all starts with sex; sex creates the next generation. The idea that "sexual freedom" can be had without having children came along about the same time as contraception. The problem is that most forms of contraception, whether it's pills or condoms, require self-management. Adults are not all that perfect at managing its use, much less teens.

Think about it. Sexual stimulation must have already occurred for a condom to be used and sexual stimulation causes the brain to shift into a different control mode. In *Predictably Irrational: The Hidden Forces That Shape Our Decisions,* by Dan Ariely, an experiment was conducted with college men. The author wanted to make the point that our decisions are not always as rationale as we would like to hope. These young men were asked to answer questions about what they would and would not do sexually, first without being sexually stimulated and then later while being sexually stimulated. The difference in their answers were shocking, even to the participants. Sexual stimulation puts people in a different frame of mind!

This may explain, at least in part, why the steps to correct and consistent condom usage might not always be the first thing on the mind of teens that are heavy into foreplay. Yet, sexual foreplay is exactly what many *safe sex* classes are all about – how to have fun and pleasure while avoiding pregnancy by using a condom. The idea of adults teaching children how to have pleasurable sex safely was published as a "fantasy" by the Sexuality Education Information Cooperation of the United States (SIECUS) in 1988. A former Planned Parenthood educator stated: "Colleagues and I have fantasized about a national 'petting project for teenagers.'...A partial list of safe sex practices for teens could include: ...Undressing each other...Masturbation in front of a partner...Mutual masturbation." SIECUS became the go-to agency for setting sex education standards across America.

Since normalizing the *safe sex* idea, sex without commitment has resulted in a skyrocketing percentage of fatherless families. Communities of adolescents that have never had the advantage of living under the care and direction of both of their parents have become common. Subsequently, the cost of the "entitlements" that take care of such families has exceeded the nation's ability to cope. Only by borrowing trillions of dollars has America been able to continue its aid to needy families.

Under Welfare Reform, an attempt was made by the U.S. Congress to turn the tide on the increasing percentage of dependent families that are formed outside of marriage. Funding was allocated to teach the benefits and skills related to avoiding risk by delaying sex until marriage, that is, by changing the behavior that is causing the problem. Teen pregnancy rates plummeted! Educational approaches that teach people to avoid risky behaviors is called "primary prevention" or "risk avoidance." Some would call them common sense approaches!

Primary prevention sets a sensible standard. Nutritionists, for example, do not sugar coat their message. They wouldn't advise diabetics to visit a bakery, sample the wares, and then take a pill. Advocates against smoking don't advise people to smoke just a little bit. They do all they can to help people resist the initiation of smoking, and if someone has already started, they help them stop – completely. When a high standard is set for behavior, it is more likely that people will strive to meet that standard. Conversely, when a low standard is set, people tend to sink to that lower norm. Children raised in communities where risky behavior is acceptable are at greater risk than those raised in neighborhoods that do not accept such behavior.

Do you believe that decisions adolescents make about sex can be influenced by the standards set by their parents and community? Are you open to the idea that *you* can influence *your children's standards for sexual activity*? By establishing boundaries, adults provide clear guidance for the next generation. They are paving the way for their children to succeed, regardless of their race, gender or sexual orientation! High standards and good character can trump most other barriers!

My, How Things Have Changed!

An educator began meeting with a group of girls in a once-a-week after-school program in the fall of 2008. On the first day of the program, the students' reception of the teacher could hardly be deemed welcoming. As the students were all on different sides of the tables provided, even the teacher's mere request to have them all face her seemed like a nearly impossible task.

However, after just a few months of being able to meet with these girls for both the *Heritage Keepers® Abstinence Education* and the *Life Skills* programs, the educator has been so pleased to see significant attitudinal and behavioral changes from many of the girls. One student, who for many weeks was the class leader in making distracting comments about anything the teacher had to say, became quite the advocate for abstinence... and, for that matter, all healthy lifestyle choices. For the past several weeks, she has made it a habit of expressing her appreciation for the program by making statements like, "Why does this class always have to end so early? " and "Y'all be quiet so I can learn!".

Do character-based abstinence programs have a positive effect on students today? The attitudinal changes, which in turn lead to behavioral changes, certainly seem to say so!

Heritage is a 501(c)(3) non-profit founded in 1995 to utilize science-based findings to equip people with the skills that enable them to avoid risk and reach their potential. Heritage has taught more than 250,000 young people about Healthy Family Formation concepts, with a focus on abstaining from sexual activity outside of marriage and faithfulness within marriage. *Heritage Keepers®* has been taught successfully in public schools, private schools, faith-based schools, juvenile detention centers, group homes, youth camps, college campuses, prisons, the US Navy – just about everywhere teens and young adults are available to be taught.

Stan Weed, PhD, Founder and President of the Institute for Research and Evaluation, has conducted research in the field of abstinence education for more than two decades, surveying more than 500,000 middle and high school students across thirty states, Central America and Russia.

He has evaluated the outcomes of abstinence education programs in more than 30 states and in the process has discovered that there are actually predictors of teen "initiation of sex." That is, if we know a young person's attitudes related to sex, we can predict with a high degree of accuracy whether that young person will likely initiate sex – or not. And these "predictors" can be influenced to increase the probability of delaying sexual activity!

Heritage incorporated these findings into the development, training, implementation, monitoring and evaluation processes of its approach to abstinence education. Ours is the first program to apply these findings to every phase of its abstinence and life skills education process, and was the first to document through peer-reviewed research a significant positive effect across all of the predictors - a necessary accomplishment for influencing young people to avoid the risks associated with sexual activity outside of marriage.

Later in our series, we will be helping you consider ways to have a positive influence on these predictors at home. But first, it is important to build your confidence that these can not only be affected, but can be affected to the extent that teens actually adjust their behavior! We know this works because extensive research has been conducted on our program that indicates strong and lasting positive outcomes!

The research on our program utilizes a survey Dr. Weed developed that has a high degree of validity and reliability. That means the questions measure what we are trying to find out, even when they are asked several different ways. We survey students before and after the program and then a year later. The behavioral outcomes are compared with similar non-program students. Two studies indicate the program is effective.

In Dr. Weed's first study of *Heritage Keepers®*, he found that program students initiated sex at a rate half that of similar non-program students.[1] In his most recent study of the Heritage program, he says that "Significant differences were observed between program and comparison groups in levels of sexual behavior one year after the program, and also in the amount of change in sexual activity over that time period."[2] A year after the program, *Heritage Keepers®* students initiated sex at a rate 67% lower than similar non program students. This study was with 2,215 middle and high school students in 41 schools across South Carolina.

Surveys indicate that adolescents participating in the Heritage program embrace this message. On average, 90 percent or more of the program teens report that they would recommend it to a friend. Since federal abstinence education funding increased under Welfare Reform, research has shown that now more than half of the students in American high schools are abstaining from sex.[3] In fact, one study showed that 58% of teens believe that sex in high school is not appropriate,

---

[1] Weed, S. E., Erickson, I. H., & Birch, P. J. (2005, November). An evaluation of the Heritage Keepers Abstinence Education program. In A. Golden (ed.) Evaluating Abstinence Education Programs: Improving Implementation and Assessing Impact (pp. 88-103). Washington DC: U.S. Department of Health and Human Services, Office of Population Affairs and the Administration for Children and Families.

[2] Weed, S. E., Birch, P. J., Erickson, I. H., & Olsen, J. A. (2011). *Testing a predictive model of youth sexual intercourse initiation.* Unpublished manuscript. Retrieved March 30, 2011 from http://instituteresearch.com/docs/IREPredictors_(1-17-2011).pdf (manuscript in preparation)

[3] Centers for Disease Control and Prevention. (2009). *Trends in the prevalence of sexual behaviors: National YRBS 1991-2009.* Retrieved February 9, 2011 from http://www.cdc.gov/HealthyYouth/yrbs/pdf/us_sexual_trend_yrbs.pdf

and more than 90% believe that being a virgin is a good thing.[4] The most recent data on trends among teens shows that 70% of 15-17 year olds are *NOT* having sex.[5]

Teens report that parents and teachers are the most important role models in the lives of young people. What you do and what you teach can have an ongoing positive influence on the values and behavior of your child. Adolescent brain research confirms the importance of providing direction and guidance for young people. Important decisions, such as whether to become sexually active or abstain, should not be left on auto-pilot. The parent's role in providing support and encouragement for teens to abstain from sexual activity cannot be overstated. If Dr. Weed's identified predictors can be so positively affected by a program at school, think of the positive effect you can have as a parent in the home.

When teens are confident of the benefits of abstinence until marriage, and of the benefits of healthy family formation, they are much less likely to behave in a manner that puts those benefits in jeopardy.

If, however, they have developed justifications for sexual activity that take priority over their goals for their careers, marriage and family life, they could be at risk for not just teen pregnancy and sexually transmitted diseases – but for wiring their maturing minds in a manner that may limit their ability to cope with adult opportunities and responsibilities.

Remember that when you, as a parent, are not providing clear guidance, someone else is always willing to step in. Too often, these are people who are not driven by the best interests of your child, but instead by a profit motive. When you are not influencing these predictors of behavior, others might well be preying on their minds and hearts.

The American College of Pediatricians states that adolescent sexual activity is "detrimental to the well-being of all involved."[6] They also state that adolescent sexual activity alone has been acknowledged as an independent risk factor for developing low self-esteem, major depression, and attempting suicide.[7] Sexually active girls have been found to be three times as likely to report being depressed and three times as likely to have attempted suicide when compared to sexually abstinent girls. Sexually active boys were more than twice as likely to suffer from depression and seven times as likely to have attempted suicide when compared to sexually

---

[4] Kaiser Family Foundation (2003, October). *Virginity and the first time: A series of national surveys of teens about sex* (Publication No. 3368). Retrieved February 14, 2011 from http://www.kff.org/entpartnerships/upload/Virginity-and-the-First-Time-Summary-of-Findings.pdf

[5] Abma J. C., Martinez G. M., & Copen C. E. (2010, June) *Teenagers in the United States: Sexual activity, contraceptive use, and childbearing, National Survey of Family Growth 2006–2008.* National Center for Health Statistics. Vital Health Stat 23(30). Retrieved February 11, 2011 from http://www.cdc.gov/nchs/data/series/sr_23/sr23_030.pdf

[6] American College of Pediatricians. (2010, October 26). *Abstinence Education.* Retrieved February 14 2011 from http://www.acpeds.org/Download-document/129-Abst-Ed-Oct26.2010.html

[7] Hallfors, D. D., Waller, M. W., Ford, C. A., Halpern, C. T., Brodish, P. H., & Iritani, B. (2004). Adolescent depression and suicide risk: association with sex and drug behavior. *American Journal of Preventive Medicine, 27,* 224-231.

abstinent boys. As we will discuss later, they go on to state that "this is not mere coincidence. Scientists now know that sexual activity releases chemicals in the brain that create emotional bonds between partners. Breaking these bonds can cause depression, and make it harder to bond with someone else in the future."[8]

Every child deserves a bright and healthy future. But, in order to empower teens to reach their full potential, parents must convey the skills they need to make wise decisions. The implications for our children, however, reach far beyond their own welfare. The consequences of a society without sexual boundaries effect generations of families and subsequently the culture as a whole.

Our founding fathers knew that allowing great freedom requires people to be willing and able to govern their own behavior. Freedom without self-control ushers in chaos. Chaos is an invitation to governmental oversight and control.

Unless parents find their voice on this issue, each generation will become increasingly dependent on the government.

> When men and women fail to form stable marriages, the first result is a vast expansion of government attempts to cope with the terrible social needs that result. There is scarcely a dollar that state and federal government spends on social programs that is not driven in large part by family fragmentation: crime, poverty, drug abuse, teen pregnancy, school failure, mental and physical health problems.
> Maggie Gallagher, Institute for Marriage and Public Policy[9]

Parents can help their children understand the benefits of living in America and can strive to preserve what has been provided by past generations and build upon it. Every citizen has the opportunity to further the grand American cause, to reach their full potential and to take care of their families and communities. American children need to be able to see beyond today and into the future, reaching for the promise it holds for each of them and for their nation.

Parents play a crucial role in this process. Teens need their parents to be the primary influence in their lives. Teens report that parents are the most important role models in their lives. This resource provides the necessary tools for parents to be an ongoing positive influence on the values and behavior of their children for a lifetime.

For more information, view the video ***Testing a Risk Avoidance Model*** *Evaluation of the Heritage Keepers® Abstinence Education Program.* (Go back to page 7 for information on how to access the video.)

---

[8] McIlhaney, J. S. & Bush, F. M. (2008). *Hooked: New science on how casual sex is affecting our children* (pp.77-78). Chicago: Northfield Publishing.

[9] Gallagher, M. (2003, July 14). The stakes: Why we need marriage. *National Review Online.* Retrieved March 28, 2011 from http://www.nationalreview.com/articles/207483/stakes/maggie-gallagher

Abstinence Teacher Makes a Difference

A Heritage instructor had the opportunity to talk to the father of one of his students. The phone call turned quickly into a "thank you" from the father for the Heritage educator's effectiveness in teaching his son abstinence education.

He told the teacher how the *Heritage Keepers® Abstinence Education* program had "opened the channels of communication between my son and I, and we have never talked so much about this very important topic before." He closed the conversation with one last "thank you." The Heritage educator returned thanks for the words of encouragement, which fuel his passion for teaching comprehensive truth to students who are negatively influenced by a sex saturated culture. Heritage educators experience a sense of fulfillment and gratification as they teach the message of abstinence and then see the impact on the lives of adolescents.

TESTING A RISK AVOIDANCE APPROACH

Do you believe that children who are raised in an environment of high standards and expectations are more likely to avoid risky behaviors than those who are not?

YES NO

Why?

Do you believe that the decisions adolescents make about sex can be influenced by the standards set by their community *and* by the expectations of their parents?

YES NO

Why?

Are you open to the idea that *you* can influence your child's standards for sexual activity?

YES NO

Why?

Stan Weed, PhD, of the Institute for Research and Evaluation, has conducted extensive research on *predictors* of adolescent initiation of sex. He has discovered that by asking teens questions about their *behavioral intentions, sexual values, self-worth, future orientation, peer independence* and *self-efficacy,* we can get an idea of whether they will be more likely to initiate sex or abstain from sex. Are you willing to work on improving your ability to be a positive influence on these *predictors* in your child's life?

YES NO

Why?

In many states, the law requires public schools to offer sex education. There are basically two approaches.

Comprehensive sex education is a term coined in the 80's and 90's, when public health officials disseminated condom-advocacy programs in response to the HIV epidemic. This approach, known as *risk reduction*, assumes teens will likely initiate sex. Such programs encourage teens to *reduce* the risks associated with adolescent sexual activity by using contraception when having sex. The standard is to teach teens behavioral skills associated with using condoms.

Abstinence education is a term that became better known when Welfare Reform programs set abstinence as the standard for school-aged children. This approach, known as *risk avoidance*, assumes that teens are capable of abstaining from risky behavior. Such programs encourage school-aged teens to *avoid* the risks associated with adolescent sexual activity by abstaining from sex. The standard is to teach behavioral skills associated with abstinence.

Do you know what approach to sex education is provided by your community's public education system?

YES NO

How will you find out? What will you do about it?

Explain, in your own words, the difference between sex education that emphasizes *risk reduction* and sex education that emphasizes *risk avoidance.*

During the era when public funding for *comprehensive sex education* increased, teen pregnancy rates reached historic highs. Many adults, who grew up during the sexual revolution of the 60's and 70's, assumed that teens will have sex. It was the expected standard.

During the first decade of the twenty-first century, when Welfare Reform was ushered in, funding for *abstinence education* increased. Teen births hit a historic low by 2008, and now less than 30% of 15 to 17 year olds report having sex.

Based on what you learned in this video, how confident are you that risk avoidance is a viable strategy to bring about a decrease in the proportion of young people initiating sex and to increase the proportion of young people that are willing to abstain from sex outside of marriage?

1 2 3 4 5 6 7 8 9 10 (1 is low, 10 is high)

Did you rate yourself high or low? Explain your rating.

How confident are you in pursuing this strategy with your own family?
1 2 3 4 5 6 7 8 9 10 (1 is low, 10 is high)

Did you rate yourself high or low? Explain your rating.

What kinds of messages have you given your child(ren) about sex, if any?

Have you been communicating a risk reduction or risk avoidance message at home?

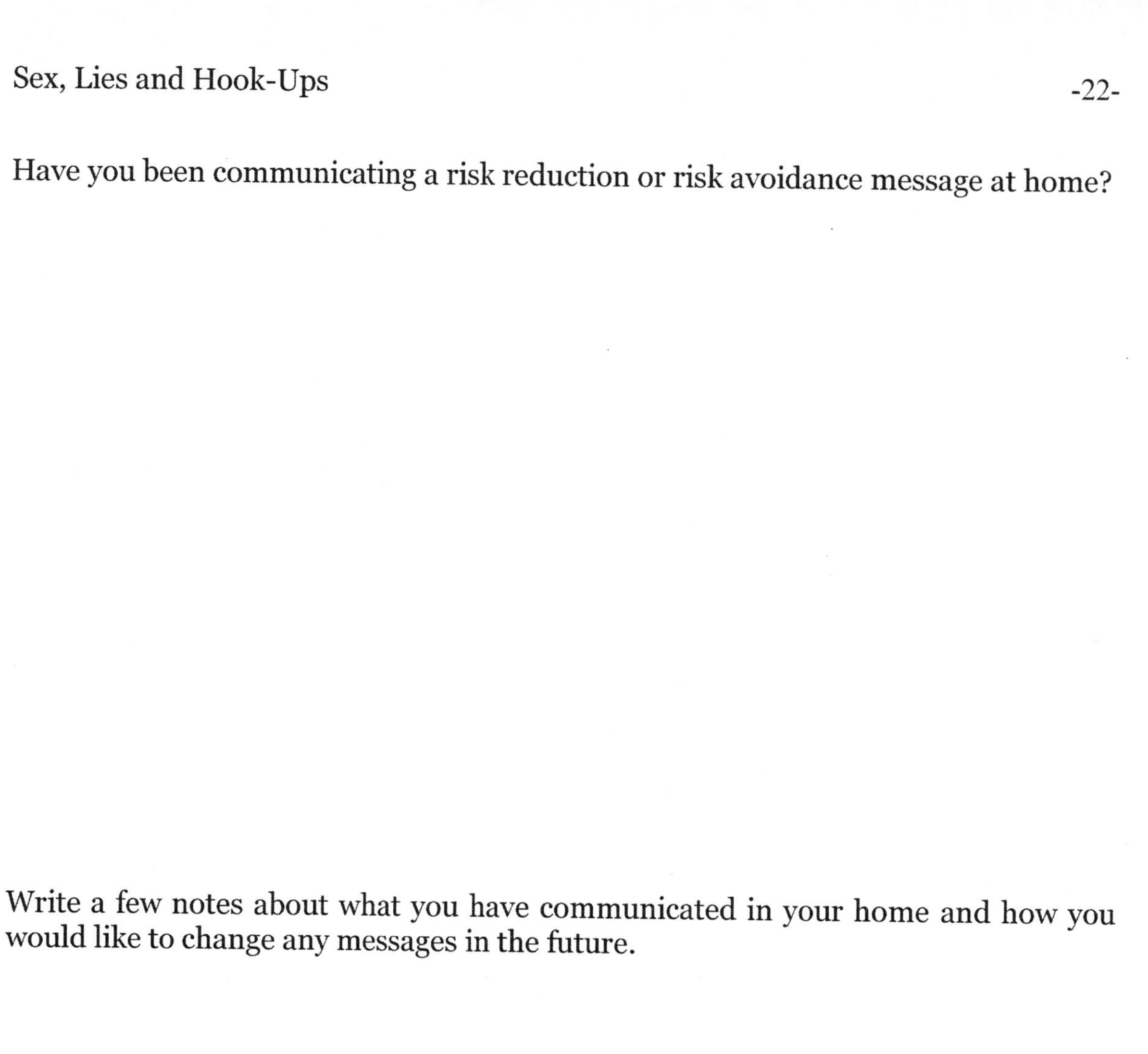

Write a few notes about what you have communicated in your home and how you would like to change any messages in the future.

Chapter One: YOU are the Key!

"My life has been changed by this class because now I know how to plan my life out. Keep sex within the boundaries of marriage, say no to sex, and stay abstinent. I also know what to look for in a guy and how to stay away from STDs. I also speak for my parents when I say thanks a million."

Female *Heritage Keepers*® student

"My life has been changed by this class a lot. Now I understand that it's ok to wait until you're married to have sex."

Male *Heritage Keepers*® student

Parents Were Right!

After the *Heritage Keepers® Abstinence Education* program, a young girl in the eighth grade approached the teacher regarding the information being taught. She told her teacher that her parents were very strict on her when it came to relationships and education. She didn't understand why they were so strict until she took our class. She told her teacher that everything discussed in the abstinence class were things her parents stressed at home. After realizing the realities of sexual activities outside of marriage and the benefits of forming healthy families, she decided to make a commitment to her future by staying abstinent.

She was instrumental in encouraging her classmates to also practice abstinence. Every time the Heritage educator sees this phenomenal young lady outside of school, the student credits the Heritage educator and message for her success in school and ultimately, in life.

Our kids are in a sexually saturated culture. When it comes to boundaries on sex, it seems that our society has been persuaded that there should be none. And yet, every culture in history has had boundaries on sex because the consequences are serious. In addition to disease, genetics, and child rearing implications, there are subsequent cultural impacts, such as the costs associated with subsidizing families that are unable to care for their own.

The lines have become blurred as to when adolescents should begin sexual activity and with whom. Our society is in a state of confusion about how to direct children on the topic of sexual activity. While most parents do not want their kids to have sex at an early age and know that the outcomes can be serious, many are convinced that the best they can hope for is *safe sex*.

When something is too stressful to even think about, the mind resolves the problem by pushing the thoughts so far out of the way that it becomes impossible to even consider them. That mindset is called denial. Denial is a mechanism that protects people from having to deal with something that is too painful to process.

Is America in denial about the need to set clear sexual boundaries for children? In his book, *Vital Lies, Simple Truths*, Daniel Goleman[10] explains how denial can set in, on the part of an individual or even an entire culture.

When the concept of *sexual freedom* (sex without boundaries) was first introduced, it was considered shocking. To reach the objective of normalizing sex outside of marriage, it was necessary to change cultural norms that make sex

---

[10] Goleman, D. (2005). *Vital lies, simple truths The psychology of self-deception.* New York: Simon & Schuster Paperbacks.

without boundaries appear to be acceptable. This was accomplished by targeting the next generation through federally sponsored programs. After several decades of systematically expanding such programs, which are increasingly sexually explicit and seek to normalize sex without boundaries, the shock has worn off. The collective sexual norm is to accept increasingly risky activity as the standard.

[For those interested in the history of the sexual revolution, *The War on Intimacy* by Richard A. Panzer and Mary Anne Mosack and *You're Teaching My Child What?* by Miriam Grossman, M.D. offer fascinating perspectives and documentation on how our culture was progressively led to where we are today.]

People like to be perceived as normal; it's only human to want to be liked. When an entire culture appears to have accepted sex outside of lifelong committed relationships such as marriage as normal, it can be stressful - even painful - to disagree with the perceived collective opinion. It may seem easier, at the time, to go along to get along. If, the mind may reason, teen sexual activity is justifiable and harmless, it may seem pointless – even wrong – to challenge the status quo. But, surveys show that when parents are asked in private what they really think about pre-marital sexual activity, they want their child to wait. Surveys of teens, as well, indicate that they agree that middle and high school students should not be involved in sexual activity.[11] According to a 2004 Zogby Poll, 90% of adults and teens agree that teens should be given a strong abstinence message.[12]

Denial provides a way out of the conflict between the perceived norms and that nagging inner voice that is saying something is wrong. A society can hold repressed information in common, denying that which makes them uneasy. Questions that cannot or will not be asked are a sure sign of societal denial. These "black holes" are "truths that are out of the line of sight of people in that culture, but they stand out as quirks to those from cultures that do not share them.[13]" Heritage asserts that when it comes to sexual activity outside of marriage and its repercussions, questions are not allowed; information is being repressed and there are "black holes" that must be acknowledged.

The way out of denial is to begin to create an avenue for information. Once there is a cache, or a place in the brain that stores and recognizes these concepts, it becomes not just okay, but actually essential to communicate that information to others. Thus, the evolution of *Sex Lies and Hook-Ups: A Parent's Guide for Fighting Back*, a resource designed to provide a way out of denial and towards communication about this topic. This book and video series enables the individual and the collective culture to process the serious issues associated with teen sexual

---

[11] Albert, B. (2004, December). *With one voice 2004: America's adults and teens sound off about teen pregnancy. An annual national survey.* Retrieved February 14, 2011 from www.thenationalcampaign.org/national-data/pdf/WOV2004.pdf

[12] United States House of Representatives, Committee on Government Reform. (2006, October) *Abstinence and it's critics.* Retrieved February 14, 2011 from www.acpeds.org/Download-document/105-Abstinence-and-Its-Criticx.html

[13] Goleman, D. (2005). *Vital lies, simple truths The psychology of self-deception* (p. 227). New York: Simon & Schuster Paperbacks.

activity and effective ways of teaching the next generation the benefits of waiting until marriage.

It is crucial to recognize the problems teens face on a daily basis. They are inundated with sexual images and are struggling to cope with the messages they are getting. No one is talking with them about these struggles. Many parents neglect initiating ongoing discussions with their teens about sex, thus allowing other influences to play a significant role in shaping their teens' sexual values. At the same time, Heritage educators hear from the students in middle school, high school and university level that they wish their parents would provide more guidance about sex. In fact, we credit the students for making this need so clear that we produced this series to help educate parents on how to talk with kids about sex – because, if you're not talking to your children about sex, who is?

You might be surprised to learn that mom, dad and teachers are the top three role models kids name. Your kids want guidance from you, not the latest top model, or recording artist, or movie star.[14] How empowering to know that your child really does want to listen to you and really does need your guidance! You are the key in so many ways to who your child will become. You will learn in this book that kids need direction and boundaries – it is an undeniable fact. Teenagers are not yet equipped to just be given information and then have the ability to make the right decision. You have to tell them what the right decision is; your kids need your loving guidance. In this book, you will learn that your children, as they develop through the maturation process, need you to tell them what is right and wrong (wow, what a concept in today's society, right?), and they need you to help them achieve the best for themselves and their future.

Did you know...

- 53 percent of high school students (14-18) have not had sexual intercourse?[15]
- 70% of 15-17 year olds are *NOT* having sex.[16]
- According to one survey, two-thirds of teens who have had sexual intercourse wish they had waited?[17]
- When parents tell their teenager they want them to wait, their son or daughter is more likely to wait?[18]

---

[14] Laippley, J. (2005, August 3). *Do the Right Thing: Educational Best Practices.* Paper presented at the meeting of the 9th Annual Abstinence Clearinghouse Conference, Hollywood, CA.

[15] Centers for Disease Control and Prevention. (2009). *Trends in the prevalence of sexual behaviors: National YRBS 1991-2009.* Retrieved February 9, 2011 from http://www.cdc.gov/HealthyYouth/yrbs/pdf/us_sexual_trend_yrbs.pdf

[16] Abma J. C., Martinez G. M., & Copen C.E. (2010, June) *Teenagers in the United States: Sexual activity, contraceptive use, and childbearing, National Survey of Family Growth 2006–2008.* National Center for Health Statistics. Vital Health Stat 23(30). Retrieved February 11, 2011 from http://www.cdc.gov/nchs/data/series/sr_23/sr23_030.pdf

[17] Albert, B. (2007, February). *With one voice 2007: America's adults and teens sound off about teen pregnancy. A periodic national survey.* Retrieved November 28, 2007 from http://www.thenationalcampaign.org/resources/pdf/pubs/WOV2007_fulltext.pdf

[18] The National Campaign to Prevent Teen Pregnancy, (n. d.). *Parent Power: What Parents Need to Know and Do to Help Prevent Teen Pregnancy.* Retrieved February 14, 2011 from http://www.thenationalcampaign.org/resources/pdf/pubs/ParentPwr.pdf

A 2014 survey[19] of young adults (18-24) showed:

There is tremendous support among young adults for waiting longer to have sex; virginity is widely accepted and respected among young men and women, including those who have already had sex.

- 66% of young adults think it would help teenagers wait longer if they knew less than half of their peers were sexually active.
- 86% of young adults say it's important for teens to know that "it's okay to be a virgin when you graduate from high school."
- 87% say it's important for high school freshmen to know that "sex doesn't guarantee a relationship will last."
- 86% say it's important for them to know that sex doesn't make you an adult.
- 69% among young adults say it is acceptable for someone their age to be a virgin.
- Of those 18-24 who have remained virgins, the majority are proud of that choice and say it was a choice, not because of circumstances.

Many young adults want the media to show more varied portrayals of those not having sex and they want the media to improve the way they portray young adults' sex lives.

- 85% of virgins wish TV and movies portrayed virginity in a more realistic way.
- 87% of non-virgins wish TV and movies portrayed virginity in a more realistic way.

Most young adults - men and women, some sexually experienced, some not- place a much higher value on romance and relationships than they do on sex alone.

- 72% of young adults say they could be happy in a romantic relationship that did not include sexual intercourse.

When they asked if they would prefer to have sex but not within a serious romantic relationship or if they would rather be in a serious romantic relationship that did not include sex,

- 78% opted for a relationship that did not include sex.
- 72% of those who had already had sex said they'd choose a relationship over sex.

If you choose to take a passive position on whether or not your child is involved in sexual activity, your children are left at the mercy of marketers, abusers and equally immature peers. They need you to set the standard and have on-going conversations about sex – not just one talk. How many times do you tell your child to clean their room, to not back talk, to sit up, to use manners, to do their homework - you get the picture. How many times a day does a TV show, movie, song lyric, magazine, etc. tell your child that sex outside of a lifelong committed relationship such as marriage is the expected norm? Asking teens to abstain from sex in a culture pushing them to

---

[19] Kramer, A. (2014). *Virgin Territory: What Young Adults Say About Sex, Love, Relationships, and The First Time*. Washington, DC: The National Campaign to Prevent Teen and Unplanned Pregnancy.

do just the opposite is going to take commitment. So, allow your mind to wrap around this concept for a few moments, and then we can move on!

You may be thinking, "I don't feel comfortable asking my child to abstain from sex; it is not what I did. How do I tell them to do something that I myself was not able to do?" There is a simple answer to that – simpler than you may think! This is not about you and the decisions you made – this is about what is best for your child in today's culture. So, for now, put aside thoughts about yourself – how this information could have impacted you, what you did or did not do – put it all away. Concentrate on your child and his/her future. As you become more confident in your stance on abstinence, you may or may not consider sharing personal consequences or regrets that you or others experienced related to sexual activity outside of marriage. You don't have to decide that now. Instead, what is important is to start an open, honest communication on this subject with your teen.

Believe it or not, your kids want to hear your expectations for them when it comes to sex! Whether you waited to have sex until marriage or not, your experiences, from an adult perspective, can help your child avoid living with the regrets you yourself, or others you know, may have.

From 4 parents.gov:

- 9 out of 10 teens (94 %) think that adults should let teens know they should wait to have sex at least until they get out of high school.[20]
- Nearly 9 out of 10 (88 %) teens say it would be easier to avoid early sexual activity and teen pregnancy if they were able to have more open, honest conversations about these topics with their parents.
- 6 out of 10 (59 %) teens say their parents are their role models of healthy, responsible relationships.[21]

Be empowered by knowing that YOU will make a huge difference in the decisions your child will make in regards to sex if you choose to take an active role. You can do it and we will teach you how!

Special Note about Dads of Girls

Fathers have a huge impact on their daughters' sexual decisions and attitudes about self. The research is clear about the impact fathers have on their children. We will be providing you with that research on page 30.

---

[20] Albert, B. (2007, February). *With one voice 2007: America's adults and teens sound off about teen pregnancy. A periodic national survey.* Retrieved November 28, 2007 from http://www.thenationalcampaign.org/resources/pdf/pubs/WOV2007_fulltext.pdf

[21] Albert, B. (2003, December). *America's adults and teens sound off about teen pregnancy. An annual national survey.* Retrieved January 28, 2009 from http://www.thenationalcampaign.org/resources/pdf/pubs/WOV_2003.pdf

Special Note to Single Parents of Girls

If you are single parent, work with the parent that does not live at home as much as possible, and share this book. If you are not able to involve the other parent and you are female, make sure there is a strong male in your daughter's life guiding her, preferably someone biologically related to her such as a grandfather, uncle, or a trust-worthy family friend that is a suitable role model.

Special Note to Parents about Boys

The research on the impact of parent connectedness on sexual decision making for boys is also prevalent. But more research has been done on the impact for girls because of teen pregnancy. Don't discount your role as a parent of boys just because there is more research in existence on girls. Boys in the *Heritage Keepers® Abstinence Education* program initiated sex at a significantly lower rate than similar non program boys.[22] Again, that is with just two weeks of program exposure – just think what you, the parent, can do at home as your child matures!

Abstinence Teacher Makes A Difference

A group home for male law offenders is not an easy place to teach abstinence from sex outside of marriage. However, a Heritage teacher found it to be one of the most rewarding teaching experiences he had ever had.

Most of the students were sex offenders and had been sexually abused. During the *Heritage Keepers® Abstinence Education* classes, the teacher was able to break through the hard and tough personalities that some initially displayed until they realized the Heritage teacher truly cared about their well being. As they began to respect the teacher they began to respect the message of abstinence. Many would question and challenge the Heritage teacher, but, by the end of class, the Heritage teacher could see their attitudes change.

Many of the boys talked to the Heritage teacher after class on an individual basis and thanked him for his time spent at the group home – he had won many of their hearts. They spoke of changed minds and a determination to live a better life when they leave the group home. The survey results from the group home confirmed what the teacher believed – they had made dramatic attitudinal changes regarding sex and marriage.

[22] Weed, S. E., Erickson, I. H., & Birch, P. J. (2005, November). An evaluation of the Heritage Keepers Abstinence Education program. In A. Golden (ed.) Evaluating Abstinence Education Programs: Improving Implementation and Assessing Impact (pp. 88-103). Washington DC: U.S. Department of Health and Human Services, Office of Population Affairs and the Administration for Children and Families.

Here are just a few stats to get you thinking: Father's Impact on Daughters: Research from *Strong Fathers, Strong Daughters*, Margaret J. Meeker[23]

- *Parent connectedness* is the number one factor in preventing girls from engaging in premarital sex and indulging in drugs and alcohol.
- Girls with doting fathers are more assertive.
- Daughters who perceive that their fathers care a lot about them, who feel connected to their fathers, have significantly fewer suicide attempts and fewer instances of body dissatisfaction, depression, low self-esteem, substance abuse, and unhealthy weight.
- A daughter's self-esteem is best predicted by her father's physical affection.
- Girls with a father figure feel more protected, have higher self-esteem, are more likely to attempt college, and are less likely to drop out of college.
- Girls with good fathers are less likely to flaunt themselves to seek male attention.
- Girls with involved fathers wait longer to initiate sex and have lower rates of teen pregnancy. Teen girls who live with both parents are three times less likely to lose their virginity before their sixteenth birthday.
- 76 percent of girls said that fathers influenced their decisions on whether they should become sexually active.
- Extensive research indicates that girls who have close, engaging relationships with their fathers start menstruation at a later age. Moreover, girls who live with an unrelated male (e.g., stepfather or mothers boyfriend) have menstruation even earlier than do girls living in a single mother household. Early sexual development, in turn, is associated with higher levels of premature sexual activity and teen pregnancy.
- 97 percent of girls who said they could talk to their parents had lower teen pregnancy rates.
- A daughter from a middle class family has a fivefold lower risk of out-of-wedlock pregnancy if her father lives at home.
- Girls who live with only their mother have a significant less ability to control impulses, delay gratification, and have a weak sense of right and wrong.
- Girls whose fathers provide warmth and control achieve higher academic success.
- Girls who are close to their fathers exhibit less anxiety and withdrawn behaviors.

Parents, hopefully you are feeling confident that you can influence your children. The fact is that if you're not talking to your kids about sex – plenty of other people are. How? Through television, the Internet, video games, the radio, music and magazines. There is wonderful potential for learning through technology but there is equal potential for harm. The ideas and possibilities for experimentation far outweigh the maturity level of adolescents. If you don't provide direction, clear boundaries and the skills for negotiating the maturation process, then your children

[23] Meeker, M. (2006). *Strong Fathers, Strong Daughters* (pp. 23-24). Washington: Regenery Publishing, Inc.

could believe whatever is thrown at them by professional marketing experts who do not have their best interests at heart.

There are many great things about technology. We like that we can type a topic into our computers and get an answer in seconds. It's very helpful. But the moment new technology is developed, it is corrupted – providing instantaneous avenues for the wrong messages and images that we never wanted to see ourselves, much less our sons and daughters or grandchildren.

Television

- Nearly every household in America has a TV, averaging 2.6 TVs per house.
- 25 percent of children under age two have a TV in their bedroom, yet, the American Academy of Pediatrics actually says that a child under the age of two should not get any exposure to television.[24]
- Children between two and seven years old watch TV without their parents 81 percent of the time, and that increases to 95 percent when the child is eight years old or older.[25]

Surveys indicate that when their parents are not around, children tend to watch different programs than they would under parental supervision. They hear you climbing the stairs. They hear you coming in the door and the channel gets changed quickly. The majority of teens have a TV in the bedroom. And if family members each have televisions in the bedroom, wanting to watch their own choice of shows, family interaction time can too often become alone time. With parents at work all day and television taking over at night, the time for learning from parents is much too limited, if not non-existent.

This takes away from accountability. If you can go behind a closed door and watch TV – or play with the Internet – and nobody is there to hold you accountable as to what you're watching or doing, there is no feedback to let young people know what is appropriate and what isn't. Having access to such technology behind closed doors, especially late at night, is not good. That's why many experts are advising parents to not provide a television or computer for their youngsters to use unsupervised.

- By the time adolescents graduate from high school, they will have spent 15,000 hours watching TV compared to 12,000 hours in the classroom.[26]
- Teens end up looking at a screen for approximately 40 hours per week.[27]

---

[24] Committee on Public Education, American Academy of Pediatrics (2001). Children, adolescents, and television. *Pediatrics, 107,* 423-426.

[25] Roberts, D. F., Foehr, U. G., Rideout, V. J., & Brodie, M. (1999, November). *Kids & media @ the new millennium.* Kaiser Family Foundation. Retrieved February 16, 2011 from http://www.kff.org/entmedia/upload/Kids-Media-The-New-Millennium-Report.pdf

[26] Committee on Public Education, American Academy of Pediatrics (2001). Children, adolescents, and television. *Pediatrics, 107,* 423-426.

[27] Walsh, D. (2004). *Why do they act that way? A survival guide to the adolescent brain for you and your teen.* (p. 162) New York, NY: Free Press.

Forty hours is a full-time job. Time in front of the screen is time not spent with family, playing sports and interacting with others – in general, it is time not spent learning how to cope with the adult world they are rushing toward.

But in addition to using much of their free time just sitting and watching a screen, they are also being exposed to dangerous content.

In TV land there are no consequences to sex outside of marriage, something you might want to point out during family time with your child. Unless trends drastically change, by the time the average child graduates from high school, they will have seen between 240,000 and 480,000 sexual acts or references to sex. Premarital sex outnumbers marital sexual situations 8 to 1.[28]

No wonder teens begin to believe this is the norm. They see it all the time. It can become difficult to tell the difference between make believe for entertainment and real life. Would you allow somebody to come in to your living room and have sex and let your child watch? Of course not. But so many people are allowing just that to happen on the TV screen.

A PBS documentary, *The Lost Children of Rockdale County*[29] tells the real life story of *laissez faire* parents who discovered their teens were having sexual orgies, copying the pornography they were seeing on television. The teens were riddled with sexually transmitted diseases, a fact discovered by the local health department when it became evident that syphilis was becoming epidemic among these upper middle-class youngsters.

When sex outside of marriage is presented as the norm, adolescents forget that sex can create new life that needs the love and care of a committed mom and dad – not just sexual partners.

When the norm is abstinence until marriage, the risk of our children growing up with disease in their reproduction organs, or of fathering a child before their adult life even begins, or of quitting school to raise a baby is dramatically decreased.

We don't want young people modeling their maturity after television. Twenty-eight percent of children's shows portray violent acts. The average teen will witness 200,000 acts of violence before he or she graduates from high school and this includes 20,000 murders.[30]

Studies have shown that 75 percent of teens say that media portrayals of sexual behavior influence their own sexual behavior and the sexual behavior of their

---

[28] Slane, C. (n.d.) US News and World Report compiled in *Why are kids so angry.*

[29] Goodman, R. D. & Goodman, B. (Producers). (1999, October 19). The lost children of rockingham county [1804]. In Fanning, D. (Executive Producer). *Frontline.* Boston, Public Broadcasting Service.

[30] Walsh, D. (2004). *Why do they act that way? A survival guide to the adolescent brain for you and your teen.* (p. 165). New York, NY: Free Press.

peers.[31] This is straight from the teens' mouths. They are saying that the media influences their decisions about sex. The media is also influencing their friends' decisions about sex.

The Public Broadcasting System published a documentary called *The Merchants of Cool.*[32] In this revealing piece, the public is given insight into the little understood world of those in the business of marketing to teens. In one scene, representatives of this world actually knock on the door of an unsuspecting youngster and go into his bedroom, look through his closet, and generally invade his brain looking for clues about what will get money out of his pocket into theirs. Trendsetters are paid to sit and talk about what they think is cool, and then that is sold to the rest of the millions of unsuspecting youth who are eagerly watching, listening and buying. And the message almost always is driven by sexual images.

What can parents do?

- Don't allow TV in your child's bedroom.
- Set standards for what programs and music will be allowed in your home.
- Be the example. Don't watch things you would be uncomfortable with your child viewing.
- Set boundaries for how much TV can be watched. The American Academy of Pediatrics recommends no more than two hours per day.
- Establish expectations regarding TV and schoolwork.
- Don't allow TV or music or video games to be your child's babysitter.
- Communicate with your child about why you set those particular standards.
- Get your children involved in activities that do not involve technology.

If you can teach them what you don't want them seeing or hearing, you are showing that you love them. You're also teaching them how to think for themselves. You are telling them, "We don't want you to watch this TV show because it portrays so many sexual acts outside of marriage with no consequences and that is not reality. And we don't want you to start believing that. And I think that it would be healthier for our family if you weren't exposed to those things."

Use television to your advantage by looking for teachable moments. They will come up. Explain the emotional consequences of what just happened on television. Take the time to talk about this during commercials and explain how the media exists for profit, not because they care about your child. Most programming is geared to sell, sell, sell. To sell, they must by definition infiltrate the mind of the viewer.

---

[31] Walsh, D. (2004). *Why do they act that way? A survival guide to the adolescent brain for you and your teen.* (p. 164). New York, NY: Free Press.

[32] Goodman, B. & Dretzin, R. (Producers). (2001, February 27). The merchants of cool. [1911]. In Sullivan, M. (Executive producer), *Frontline*, Boston, Public Broadcasting Service.

Internet

Seventy-two percent of teens use the Internet on a regular basis. The top uses of the Internet by teens are: sending and receiving e-mail, instant messaging, and My Space [and other social networking sites, such as Facebook].[33]

What do we know about social networking sites? Kids may have a picture of themselves on there, phone numbers, and even say where they live. People are looking through these – including sexual predators. Even with instant messaging, many teens put on a different persona when they are behind a computer. They pretend to be someone that they are not. Again, there is no feedback to let them know this is wrong. In fact, an entire Internet land where people can create alternative personas and lives is now available, where real life pales as the images on the screen take over.

Most people are somewhat aware that the Internet has made pornography uncomfortably available. Porn stimulates sexual curiosity derived outside of the bounds of a healthy nurturing relationship with a real person. It can quickly become a substitute for healthy relationships and be addictive. In fact, anything that takes the place of a healthy relationship can become addictive. If your child sees porn, more than likely it's something that will continue to spark interest unless you teach them how to say no and how to get off of the page. Statistically, nine out of ten kids stumble across hard-core porn on the Internet.[34] It's easy to find, and clever purveyors find ways to help youngsters into their world. The typical first exposure to porn is around age eight. The porn industry wants your child to see porn because they are hoping that if they see it, they will want to come back for more and become addicted, pouring money into their industry.

One in five kids will be solicited sexually while on the Internet.[35] You need to assume that your child could be a victim. We all want to assume that our child is going to be the four out of five that hasn't been solicited sexually. But if you assume that yours could be targeted, you will become a much more proactive parent.

A school-aged child spends about 25 hours per week watching the TV[36] and 44 hours per week on the Internet [now about 53 hours per week[37]]. Yet they report spending only half an hour alone with their father during the week and only two and a half hours alone with their mother – and only 2.2 hours per week doing

---

[33] Walsh, D. (2004). *Why do they act that way? A survival guide to the adolescent brain for you and your teen.* (p. 161). New York, NY: Free Press.

[34] Hagelin, R. (2005, August 5). *It's a Mad, Mad, Mad, Mad World: Home Invasion.* Paper presented at the meeting of the 9th Annual Abstinence Clearinghouse Conference, Hollywood, CA.

[35] Darkness to Light (n.d.a). *Realities, Not Trust, Should Influence Your Decisions Regarding Children.* Retrieved February 22, 2011 from http://www.d2l.org/site/c.4dICIJOkGcISE/b.6069317/apps/s/content.asp?ct=8575945

[36] Roberts, D. F., Foehr, U. G., Rideout, V. J., & Brodie, M. (1999, November). *Kids & media @ the new millennium.* Kaiser Family Foundation. Retrieved February 16, 2011 from http://www.kff.org/entmedia/upload/Kids-Media-The-New-Millennium-Report.pdf

[37] Rideout, V. J., Foehr, U. G.,Roberts, D. F. (2010, January) *Generation M2: Media in the lives of 8- to 18-year-olds. Kaiser family Foundation.* Retrieved February 24, 2011 from http://www.kff.org/entmedia/upload/8010.pdf

homework.[38] These top two numbers are too high. The time alone with the parents is way too low. Children are worth more than this minimal investment of time.

What can parents do?

- Don't allow access to the Internet behind closed doors.
- Monitor their instant messaging, phones and social networking sites.
- Limit the amount of time your child spends online.
- Enforce Internet boundaries.

Also, give serious consideration to taking advantage of Internet filters. These are designed to keep certain information from ever reaching your computer. Call your Internet provider and tell them you want a server-based filter. They can install it and update it for you and it is very strict on access. There are other filters available that require you to be more technical, but it pays to do the research. You can actually buy software that sends you an e-mail if any questionable site has been entered. The riskiest thing you can do is to do nothing.

Video Games

The Federal Trade Commission reported that 69 percent of unaccompanied 13 to 16 year olds were able to purchase M-rated video games from retailers. M is the mature rating. Most of the time kids are buying prohibited games with their parents' money. This is the equivalent of your child going to the movie theater and buying an R-rated ticket. A study of more than 2,000 8 to 18 year olds found that 83 percent of them have at least one video game player in their home; 31 percent have three or more video game players in their home; and 49 percent had video game players in their bedrooms.[39]

In that same study

- 21 percent reported that their parents set rules about which video games they can play
- 17 percent reported that their parents check warning labels or ratings on video games
- 12 percent reported they play video games they know that their parents don't want them playing.

If only 17 percent of parents are checking warning labels, that could be one reason kids are able to buy the M-rated video games. Nine out of ten teens play video games on a regular basis. There has been an increase in the ultra-violent first person shooting games. This is where the player actually has the ability to virtually shoot other people. It's very realistic. The players may steal cars, rob banks, shoot

---

[38] Ozretich, R. (2000). *TV and video games affect children, culture.* Parentingresearch.Org Retrieved June 2, 2011 from http://www.parentingresearch.org/papers/WalshTV1.pdf

[39] Roberts, D. F., Foehr, U. G., & Rideout, V. J., (2005, March). *Generation M2: Media in the lives of 8- to 18-year-olds.* Kaiser family Foundation. Retrieved February 24, 2011 from http://www.kff.org/entmedia/upload/Generation-M-Media-in-the-Lives-of-8-18-Year-olds-Report.pdf

policemen, sleep with prostitutes and buy drugs. In the extreme there is video game addiction, which is similar to gambling addiction. Players lie about how much they play. They forego social contact to play the game. They lose all concept of time. They play compulsively and some engage in dishonest behavior to support their habit.

What can parents do?

- Limit your child's playing time so it's not consuming all of their lives.
- Remove video game devices, computers and smart phones from the bedroom.
- Require that homework and chores be completed before playing.
- Discuss priorities with your child. Provide guidelines.
- Consistently enforce the rules that you have set and monitor the content of video games, especially not allowing first-person shooter games.
- If all else fails and they don't listen to your rules, get rid of the games.

Music

Sexual intimacy is prevalent in about 60 to 70 percent of songs.[40] Many times the emphasis is on sexual contact without commitment, violence, and the devaluing of women. We know how much our teenagers are listening to music and these are the messages that they are receiving. It is obvious why they believe that premarital sex is okay. They're being inundated with those messages constantly. *Pediatrics* magazine reports a strong correlation between teens listening to degrading sexual lyrics and their sexual activity.[41] While the study doesn't claim causation (and it is almost impossible to prove causation), it stands to reason that the media influences behavior. If your child is listening to these sexual lyrics, you should be concerned. Many of these songs center around carrying guns, violence, racial degradation, oral sex, drug use, exploitation and degradation of women, and are therefore inappropriate for children.

What can parents do?

- Screen music selections.
- Check out parental music ratings.
- Monitor your child's technological devices.
- Teach them to listen to music with an active mind, help them evaluate the messages to determine if they're consistent with their personal values.
- Listen to the song with them. Ask them if they know what the songs mean? What is being portrayed? Do they agree with the message?
- Check out the lyrics – look up the artist in question.
- Use the technology to your advantage as a parent.
- Educate them about recognizing the nuances of music.

---

[40] Escobar-Chaves, S. L., Tortolero, S. R., Markham, C. M., & Low B. J. (2004, January 30). *Impact of the media on adolescent sexual attitudes and behaviors.* (p. 25). Austin, TX: The Medical Institute for Sexual Health.

[41] Martino, S. C., Collins, R. L., Elliott, M. N., Strachman, A., Kanouse, D. E., & Berry, S. H. (2006). Exposure to degrading versus nondegrading music lyrics and sexual behavior among youth. *Pediatrics, 118,* e430-e441

Magazines

A study by *the Medical Institute for Sexual Health* found that teen girl magazines include an average of one to six articles per issue on sexual topics. Content analysis indicates that magazines aimed at teenage girls, even young teens, provide messages that girls should be beautiful and plan their lives to attract a man. They depict girls as sexual objects.[42] Most girls want to read magazines for fashion advice, but it appears they're getting much more than that.

What can parents do?

- Help your adolescent find some current and relevant magazine alternatives, which promote healthy and wholesome living.
- Set the standard by refusing to buy magazines that promote the same inappropriate standard.
    - Mothers, if you are reading the magazines that are fairly trashy, you need to know that your daughters are watching you.
    - Fathers, if you're constantly looking at magazines that have girls portrayed as sexual objects, two things: your sons and daughters are watching you and they will believe it's okay to view women as sexual objects. Your daughters may believe they must be sexual objects in order to get a man's love and attention.

This is not to be confused with overprotection. We know that eventually the children are going to walk out of your house and they're going to be exposed to the world and all it has to offer, good and bad. But your home should be that safe haven for them where they can escape the over-sexualization being thrown at them by the world of marketing.

Your first responsibility is to be the parent, not to be your child's friend. You have to set those rules and help them understand them as they mature. You are not here to impress your child or try to win their approval as though you are a peer. The love you convey in your concern for their welfare comes through clearly when you provide the balanced direction they need to develop into caring accountable adults.

Your responsibility is to stand strong in your values; don't back down. As they strive to figure out how the world works, they are looking to you to provide guidance.

Children thrive when they clearly understand expectations with appropriate boundaries about what is allowed and what is not. They want a clear sense of what is right and wrong. If someone else is setting that standard, competing with you for the role of the parent, the rules can become unmanageably confusing.

Don't put your children on auto-pilot, expecting them to raise themselves.

---

[42] Escobar-Chaves, S. L., Tortolero, S. R., Markham, C. M., & Low B. J. (2004, January 30). *Impact of the media on adolescent sexual attitudes and behaviors.* (p. 27). Austin, TX: The Medical Institute for Sexual Health.

Also, you should be concerned about the information that they are receiving in school. Find out what they're learning and either reinforce it or negate it. If they are learning that sex outside marriage can be risky, you need to reinforce it. If they are learning that there are no consequences of sex outside marriage, then you need to negate it. Ask them what they are learning in all aspects of their life.

You need to communicate through example. Be the role model for love, fulfillment and happiness. Don't be in denial – premarital sexual activity can have serious consequences. Again, if you don't give your child a clear standard, then all they are getting is what marketers, abusers and/or their equally immature peers are selling them.

> "Today's technology offers wonderful and amazing potential, but there is a dangerous side, and we need to learn how to use this marvelous new tool sensibly. Kids are being confronted with situations and materials beyond their years. They need to be equipped to handle choices wisely."
>
> Web Wise Kids

For more information, view the video ***Recognizing A Problem.*** *(Go back to page 7 for information on how to access the video.)*

You Are The Key

Do you believe parents can have a strong influence on their child's sexual behavior?

YES NO

Do you think our society gives kids clear messages as to when the appropriate time to start having sex is?

Do you think our society, as a whole, fully acknowledges the risks associated with sexual activity and that kids clearly get that message?

In this chapter you learned that parents have a great impact on their kids' sexual decisions and that teens want their parents to talk to them about sex. Were you surprised by anything you learned? Write some of your thoughts.

What is the current television situation at your home: How many televisions do you have? Where are they located?

Are you and your kids accountable to each other in regards to what is watched by each of you on television? If not, what are three specific ways you could hold each other accountable?

What are three things your family could do to ensure your kids are not getting an unhealthy sexual message from watching TV?

Premarital sexual situations outnumber marital sexual situations 8 to 1 on television. The consequences of sex outside of marriage are rarely portrayed in the media. If your child is watching shows that portray extramarital sex as the standard, how do you plan to communicate a different message about the realities of teen sex and the benefits of abstaining until marriage?

Do you research movies before you let your teenager go see them? If not, write a plan here for researching movies before you let your child watch them. What will you allow? What will you absolutely not allow? How do you plan to communicate and enforce these boundaries to your teen?

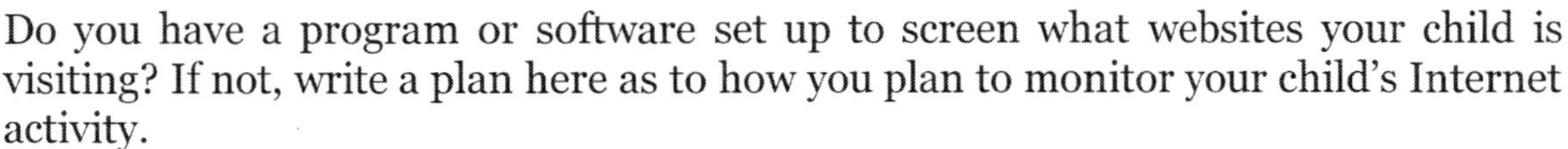

Do you have a program or software set up to screen what websites your child is visiting? If not, write a plan here as to how you plan to monitor your child's Internet activity.

What are some standards your family could set in regards to computers and Internet use? Have you communicated to your family these expectations and boundaries regarding Internet use? If so, how are you enforcing these boundaries? If not, write a plan to communicate and enforce these boundaries for your teen.

Do you check your child's social networking sites to see what others are saying to them and what they are saying to others, as well as the pictures they post of themselves? What will you allow? What will you not allow? Have you communicated and enforced these boundaries and expectations?

Where are computers located in your house? Are there any computers behind closed doors or in bedrooms? If so, where can you move them in order to increase accountability?

Have you talked to your teen about pornography? What are three things you could tell your teen about the negative effects of pornography?

Have you set up a boundary to protect your child from any online sexual solicitations? Have you also talked to your teen about how to handle an online sexual solicitation if one were to happen? If not, write your plan here for addressing these things.

How much time do you spend alone with each of your kids each week? If they are spending more time in front of the TV or computer than with you, what are three things you can do to change that?

How much time do you spend each week positively interacting as a family? If your family interaction time is lacking, what are three things you can do to increase the time with your family and decrease other distractions?

If your family has video game players (Xbox, Wii, PlayStation, etc.) where are they located? Are there any in bedrooms or behind closed doors? If so, where can you move them in order to create more accountability?

Have you set rules for your teenagers about which kinds of video games they are allowed to play, buy, and rent? What are they allowed to play and what are they not allowed to play? Are you monitoring and enforcing those rules? If not, how could you?

Do you understand the warning labels on video games, and do you check those that you buy as well as those that may be in your child's possession?

YES NO

Have you set time limits for how long video games can be played each week or month? If so, how do you monitor and enforce those limits? If not, what might be some good limits and how do you plan to communicate and enforce those standards?

Do you know what music (songs and artists) your child listens to? Have you communicated standards for what music you will allow and not allow your child to listen to? What are those standards? If you have not developed standards yet, write some here.

Have you researched what the lyrics of these songs actually mean? If not, write a plan here for finding out your child's musical interest and for researching lyrics. What is your plan for talking to your kids about what lyrics actually mean and negating any negative messages?

What magazines do you allow in your home to be read by you or any other family member? Do all of these magazines represent viewpoints that communicate the best possible messages to your teen? What kind of changes regarding magazine selection does your family need to make based on your teen's vulnerable mind?

What does "garbage in equals garbage out" suggest about media selection and behavior?

Children thrive when they clearly understand expectations, with appropriate boundaries about what is allowed and what is not. They want a clear sense of what is right and wrong. If someone else is setting that standard, competing with you for the role of the parent, the rules can become unmanageably confusing. How are you planning to ensure that your expectations and boundaries are clearly communicated and understood, especially when all of these other sources are trying to edge their way into your child's day? How are you making your home a safe haven from the world's invasions into your child's mind and heart?

Reflect on what this statement means to you, and reflect on whether or not your relationship with your child could use some changes:

"Your first responsibility is to be the parent, not to be your child's friend. The love you convey in your concern for their welfare comes through clearly when you provide the balanced direction they need in order to develop into caring accountable adults."

Chapter Two: Connecting Risk Avoidance to Healthy Family Formation

"It helped me realize all the STDs I could catch. And that there is no such thing as safe sex."

Male *Heritage Keepers*® student

"I knew having sex made it possible to get a disease even if I used a condom, but I never really thought about how if I got one it could change my life forever. Or how it could affect my goals."

Female *Heritage Keepers*® student

"My life has changed about having sex all the time because there are so many diseases out there that I didn't even know about. It made me slow down. Now I don't want to have sex with every girl I see in some short-shorts. This class made me a man."

Male *Heritage Keepers*® student

There are two important facts to keep in mind throughout this chapter.

- The information provided represents statistical averages. It is not necessarily true for every person, but when referring to the entire United States of America, it represents clear trends.
- The information provided should not be taken personally unless you determine that it is applicable and personally helpful. Personal history cannot be changed. The focus for this series is the future of your child and what is best for him or her.

If some of the information in this chapter hits home in a personal way, make a conscious effort to not become upset and to not dismiss it. It may provide a chance to process personal issues, but that is not the core purpose of this reference. Rather, consider the information for how it can help you empower your child to establish values and standards that will enable him or her to avoid risk and reach his or her potential in life.

Now that personal issues are addressed, what is meant by *Healthy Family Formation*?

Healthy Family Formation is the concept of waiting to form a family when the time is optimal to ensure the health and well- being of the people within the relationship and the children that are formed within that relationship.

Though we are living in an era when contraception is readily available, many babies are still being conceived within uncommitted sexual relationships, in spite of the couple's intention to avoid pregnancy. This is the harsh reality for many children being raised by struggling single parents. If a couple is sincerely determined to wait to form their family with someone to whom they are committed for life, and with whom they intend to raise any children conceived, the indication is to wait on sex until marriage. Healthy Family Formation means waiting until a young man and woman are so sure that "this is the one" that they have already made the legal and public commitment to "tie the knot" and to work together to care for any children they may have.

Statistics have proven that children (who are typically born out of sexual unions) are emotionally, financially, academically, physically and mentally better off when their biological parents are married and stay that way, because this means that both Mom and Dad are more likely to be present and actively involved in their lives. Though clearly not all couples that have sex outside of marriage have a child, many do. Unless the parents of those children decide to marry, the couple often drifts apart, leaving the child minus one parent.

Whether you had your child within or outside of marriage is not the point here. The focus, remember, is on teaching your child healthy family formation for his or her future family.

Why is abstinence outside of a lifelong committed relationship such as marriage an important concept to teach your child? Your child may be at risk for STDs, untimely pregnancy or emotional pain and regret. It is important to be able to convey those risks in a manner that does not frighten your child, but also in a way that he or she understands that there can be serious potential consequences. But keep in mind that scare tactics hardly ever are effective. Why? Because knowledge about risks will not change behavior. Your child needs to know deep inside why not having sex outside the legal and public commitment of marriage is the best decision for him or her and will give them the best opportunity for their future family's success. When given an opportunity to give consider to how they will form their family, teens respond in a thoughtful, positive manner. They care, a lot.

A brief overview of physical risks is provided, with references to reputable web-sites for additional information. Be well informed, but do not conclude that this information alone will change your child's behavior or completely influence their decision about the initiation of sexual activity.

Two of the most serious physical consequences of sexual activity outside of marriage are sexually transmitted diseases and untimely pregnancy.

She Didn't Know

Some venues offer a challenging environment for Heritage's abstinence education program, and this charter school was no different. With a high rate of teen pregnancy at the school, the Heritage teacher was determined to make a difference.

As the week progressed, students made several references to an absent student desperately needing the information. Understanding the dynamics of small towns and teen gossip, the teacher made it clear they needed to focus on themselves as individuals.

The student they referenced attended the Heritage class the following week. After a review of the previous week's lessons and a presentation of medical slides, the new student began weeping. The student said, "No one told me I could get it (an STD) that way, why didn't anybody tell me...I would have stopped."

The student was grateful that someone finally told her the truth about the consequences of sexual activity outside of marriage. Fortunately, her STD test results from her doctor's office were negative. The student continues to stop by the Heritage classroom to let the teacher know that she carries her SAFE card as a reminder, but most important, is still practicing abstinence.

[The SAFE plan will be discussed in detail on page 137.]

Sexually Transmitted Diseases (STDs) and Sexually Transmitted Infections (STIs)

STDs among teens and young adults are much more common than most people realize. Because so many are undiagnosed, experts can only estimate that there are millions of new STD infections among Americans each year in the United States.

STD Data[43]

- There at least 25 different STDs.
- STD infection is the most common infectious disease in the U.S. Nineteen million Americans get a new STD infection each year.[44]
- About 9.1 million teens and young adults (aged 15-24) got an STD in 2000.[45]
- Most teens do not think they are at risk of an STD.[46]
- Teen girls' cervixes are not fully developed and the cells are especially susceptible to STDs.[47]
- There are three types of STDs: parasitic, bacterial and viral. Parasitic and bacterial STDs can be cured with medicine. But damage or scars from these infections can be permanent. Some viral STDs never go away, while some viral STDs, like herpes, can be treated to reduce symptoms. Some go away on their own with time, but some viral STDs can never be cured.
- If treated early, many STDs will not cause lasting damage. But if they are not treated early, STDs can cause many problems. These can include sores that come back again and again, some types of cancer, damage to the liver, damage to reproductive organs, and weakening of the immune system. Some STDs can cause infertility in females and males.

---

[43] 4Parents.gov. (2009, July 24). *Common sexually transmitted diseases (STDs).* Retrieved February 15, 2011 from http://www.4parents.gov/sexrisky/stds/common_std/common_std.html

[44] Centers for Disease Control and Prevention. (2000) *Tracking The Hidden Epidemics: Trends In STDs in the United States 2000.* Retrieved February 11, 2011 from www.cdc.gov/std/trends2000/Trends2000.pdf

[45] Weinstock, H., Berman S., & Cates, W. (2004). Sexually transmitted diseases among American youth: Incidence and prevalence estimates, 2000. *Perspectives on Sexual and Reproductive Health, 36,* 6-10.

[46] Clinton, B. (1995, December 6). *The White House Conference on HIV and AIDS, Washington.* [Keynote address] Retrieved February 11, 2011 from http://clinton4.nara.gov/ONAP/youth/youth4.html

[47] U.S. Department of Health and Human Services. (2000, November). Sexually transmitted diseases. In *Healthy People 2010: Vol 2.* (2nd ed.). Retrieved February 13, 2011 from http://www.healthypeople.gov/2010/Document/pdf/Volume2/25STDs.pdf

Bacterial STDs[48]

Bacterial Sexually Transmitted Diseases				
Common STDs	**Chlamydia**	**Gonorrhea**	**Syphilis**	**Trichomoniasis (Parasite)**
Where is it found?	Vagina, cervix, urethra, throat, discharge from penis, and rectum	Vagina, cervix, uterus, urethra, throat, and rectum	Genital area, mouth, skin, anus, and rectum	Vagina, cervix, and urethra
How can it be spread?	Oral, anal, and vaginal sex; mother to child	Oral, anal, vaginal sex; mother to child	Oral, anal, and vaginal sex; contact with sores; mother to child	Vaginal sex
What are the possible symptoms and complications?	May not have early symptoms, burning or pain with urination, discharge from penis and vagina, chronic low abdomen pain, pelvic inflammatory disease (PID) and infertility may result (mostly in females)	Males: often have no symptoms; may have burning or pain with urination. Females: often have no symptoms. May have vaginal discharge, may lead to pelvic inflammatory disease (PID) or infertility	Painless sore, untreated can spread to brain and/or heart, flu-like symptoms, damage to major body systems if untreated, can cause rash on infants' skin, birth defects and other problems with organs or possible stillbirth	Vaginal discharge and itching, burning during urination, males may have no noticeable symptoms but can cause temporary irritation in penis, may cause early delivery and low birth weight babies
Prevention	Abstain from sex; faithful marriage or mutually monogamous relationship with an uninfected partner; condoms used correctly and consistently reduce but do no eliminate the risk; testing and treatment	Abstain from sex; faithful marriage or mutually monogamous relationship with an uninfected partner; condoms used correctly and consistently reduce but do no eliminate the risk; testing and treatment	Abstain from sex; faithful marriage or mutually monogamous relationship with an uninfected partner; condoms used correctly and consistently reduce but do not eliminate the risk; testing and treatment	Abstain from sex; faithful marriage or mutually monogamous relationship with an uninfected partner; condoms used correctly and consistently reduce but do not eliminate the risk; testing and treatment
What are the treatments?	Antibiotics (permanent damage may have occurred prior to treatment)	Antibiotics (permanent damage may have occurred prior to treatment)	Antibiotics (permanent damage may have occurred prior to treatment)	Antibiotics (permanent damage may have occurred prior to treatment)

[48] 4Parents.gov. (2009, July 24). *Common sexually transmitted diseases (STDs).* Retrieved February 15, 2011 from http://www.4parents.gov/sexrisky/stds/common_std/common_std.html

Viral STDs[49]

Viral Sexually Transmitted Diseases				
Common STDs	**Genital Herpes: Herpes Simplex Virus**	**Human Papillomavirus (HPV)**	**Hepatitis B**	**HIV/AIDS**
Where is it found?	Genitals and/or rectum	Vagina, cervix, penis, vulva, anus, scrotum, and other genital areas	Blood, semen, and vaginal fluid	Blood, semen, cervical and vaginal fluid, and breast milk
How can it be spread?	Oral, anal, and vaginal sex; contact with infected skin; rarely mother to child	Anal and vaginal sex; contact with infected skin; rarely mother to child	Oral, anal, and vaginal sex; IV drug use; mother to child	Oral, anal, and vaginal sex; IV drug use; mother to child
What are the possible symptoms and complications?	Often no symptoms are present, painful blisters or sores, fever, and swollen glands may occur, symptoms can recur throughout life, rarely serious infection can occur when passed to newborns	Most have no symptoms, but some can get genital warts, can cause cancer of the cervix, vulva, vagina, anus and penis	Often there are no obvious symptoms; jaundice, abdominal pain, loss of appetite, fatigue, joint pain; can lead to liver cancer and liver failure	No early symptoms or some flu-like symptoms that are often not noticed; rash; weakens immune system; multiple severe infections
Prevention	Abstain from sex; faithful marriage or mutually monogamous relationship with an uninfected partner; condoms used correctly and consistently reduce but do not eliminate the risk; testing and treatment	HPV vaccine (for some strains of HPV); abstain from sex; faithful marriage of mutually monogamous relationship with an uninfected partner; condoms used correctly and consistently reduce but do not eliminate the risk	Hepatitis B vaccine; abstain from sex; faithful marriage or mutually monogamous relationship with an uninfected partner; do not share needles; condoms used correctly and consistently reduce but do not eliminate the risk; testing	Abstain from sex; faithful marriage or mutually monogamous relationship with an uninfected partner; do not share needles; condoms used correctly and consistently reduce but do not eliminate the risk; testing
What are the treatments?	Symptom control that can help reduce recurrences, but no cure	No cure for infection, but medications can remove visible genital warts; regular Pap testing and follow-up medical treatment may deter development of cervical cancer.	Chronic infection can be treated with medication. No cure.	Symptom control with AIDS medicines (antiretroviral drugs); lifetime treatment is required; no cure

[49] 4Parents.gov. (2009, July 24). *Common sexually transmitted diseases (STDs).* Retrieved February 15, 2011 from http://www.4parents.gov/sexrisky/stds/common_std/common_std.html

The more sexual partners and the earlier sexual activity is initiated, the more likely a young person will acquire a STI.[50,51,52] If they choose to abstain from sexually activity until marriage, marry someone who is uninfected, and are faithful to one another, they do not have to worry about STDs and their consequences.

In the classroom, we conduct two activities with the students to help them understand the consequences of STDs and the ease in which they spread. Follow up to these activities are also in the *Heritage Keepers® Abstinence Education* Student Manual provided at the end of *Sex Lies and Hook-Ups, A Parent's Guide for Fighting Back.*

Below are the two activities we conduct within the classroom that you can modify with your child(ren). Preferably, you would want a group of young people to make these activities effective.

Dice Game Activity[53]

- *Give each young person one die and explain the rules:*
  - *The dice represent the risks of having sex outside of marriage.*
  - *The number a student rolls represents the number of the particular consequence resulting from the student's choice to have sex outside of marriage.*
  - *Point out that the statistical probabilities in the game are not indicative of those in real life.*
- *Have all young people roll at once and ask one or two to read the consequence they rolled, and to share their values and goals. (see page 91)*
- *Relate the negative consequence specifically to each person's values and goals. Cover as many of the consequences as time allows.*
- *Give them time to fill out the Rolling the Dice section of the student manual.*
- *Take time to have a brief discussion with them.*

Comments/Questions to Ask During the Rolling the Dice Game

- *You're going to play a game, called Rolling the Dice. Remember the number you roll, because there will be consequences.*
- *What is your number?*

---

[50] Kalmuss, D. S., & Namerow, P. B. (1994). Subsequent childbearing among teenage mothers: The determinants of a closely spaced second birth. *Family Planning Perspectives, 26,* 149-153.

[51] Pergamit, M. R., Huang, L., & Lane, J. (2001). *The long term impact of adolescent risky behaviors and family environment.* Chicago: National Opinion Research Center, University of Chicago. Retrieved September 6, 2007 from http://aspe.hhs.gov/hsp/riskybehav01

[52] Albert, B., Brown, S., & Flanigan, C. M. (2003). 14 and younger: *The sexual behavior of young adolescents*: Summary. Washington, DC: National Campaign to Prevent Teen Pregnancy. Retrieved September 5, 2007 from http://www.thenationalcampaign.org/resources/pdf/pubs/14summary.pdf

[53] Lickona, T. (1991). *Educating for character: How our schools can teach respect and responsibility.* New York: Bantam Books

- *As I call out negative consequences, is there one you are hoping for?*
- *Why wouldn't you want any of the negative consequences?*
- *What consequence was associated with your number?*
- *How would it make you feel if, in the game of life, it was a doctor telling you this consequence instead of me pretending?*
- *Consider the people you value. How would each one take the news if it related to you?*
- *Consider the things you value – especially your family now as well as the family you want to have in the future. Write a few ways that the consequences mentioned could affect the people and things you value, now and in the future.*
- *Consider your immediate goals, one by one. Write how each goal could be affected by the consequences of sexual activity outside of marriage.*
- *Consider your long term goals. Describe how a few of the consequences discussed could affect you and your goals.*
- *Having sex outside of marriage is gambling with your future. Don't take the risk! You could have avoided the consequences if you had abstained, if you had refused to roll the dice. Don't play games with your life, even if your friends do.*[54,55,56]
- *Resist the temptation to go along with risky behaviors, even if others try to get you to give in. It's your values that matter. Your goals, health, feelings and future are important. Don't give in – go for the best. You are worth it.*[57,58,59,60,61,62,63]

---

[54] Begley, E., Crosby, R. A., DiClemente, R. J. Wingood, G. M., & Rose, E. (2003). Older partners and STD prevalence among pregnant African American teens. *Sexually Transmitted Diseases, 30,* 211-213.

[55] Miller, H. G., Cain, V. S., Rogers, S. M., Gribble, J. N., & Tuner, C. F. (1999). Correlates of sexually transmitted bacterial infections among U.S. women in1995. *Family Planning Perspectives, 31,* 4-23.

[56] Tiller, C. M. (2002). Chlamydia during pregnancy: Implications and impact on prenatal and neonatal outcomes. *Journal of Obstetric and Gynecologic, and Neonatal Nursing, 31,* 93-98.

[57] Bearman, P. S., & Bruckner, H. (2001). Promising the future: Virginity pledges and first intercourse. *The American Journal of Sociology, 106,* 859-911.

[58] Brady, S. S., & Halperm-Flesher, B. L. (2007). Adolescents' reported consequences of having oral sex versus vaginal sex. *Pediatrics, 119,* 229-236.

[59] Cooper, L. M., Shapiro, C. M., & Powers, A. M. (1998). Motivations for sex and risky sexual behavior among adolescents and young adults: A functional perspective. *Journal of Personality and Social Psychology, 75,* 1528-1558.

[60] Mirowsky, J., & Ross, C. E. (2002). Depression, parenthood, and age at first birth. *Social Science and Medicine, 54,* 1281-1298.

[61] O'Donnell, L., O'Donnell, C. R., & Stueve, A. (2001). Early sexual initiation and subsequent sex-related risks among urban minority youth: The reach for health study. *Family Planning Perspectives, 33,* 268-275.

[62] Rector, R. E., Johnson, K. A., & Marshall, J. A. (2004, September 21). *Teens who make virginity pledges have substantially improved life outcomes.* The Heritage Foundation Center for Data Analysis Report #04-07. Retrieved October 25, 2007 from http://www.heritage.org/Research/Reports/2004/09/Teens-Who-Make-Virginity-Pledges-Have-Substantially-Improved-Life-Outcomes

[63] Rector, R. E., Johnson, R. A., & Noyes, L. R. (2003). *Sexually active teenagers are more likely to be depressed and to attempt suicide.* The Heritage Foundation Center for Data Analysis Report #30-04. Retrieved October 25, 2007 from http://www.heritage.org/Research/Reports/2003/06/Sexually-Active-Teenagers-Are-More-Likely-to-Be-Depressed

Having sex outside of marriage puts you at risk for lots of things. Here are some of them:

- ***HIV*** *If you have sex outside of marriage, you may be infected with the Human Immunodeficiency Virus, the virus that leads to AIDS (Acquired Immune Deficiency Syndrome). If you have enough money, you can take expensive drugs to prolong your life, but there is currently no cure for AIDS.*
- ***Herpes*** *If you have sex outside of marriage, you may become infected with the Herpes Simplex Virus, which can cause painful genital ulcers. Outbreaks can be treated, but the virus cannot be cured. Even when an infected person has no visible ulcers, they can spread the disease and may break out at any time.*
- ***HPV*** *If you have sex outside of marriage, you may be infected with the Human Papilloma Virus. HPV can cause genital warts which may be too small to be noticed or so large that they should be surgically removed. HPV is also associated with the development of cervical cancer, oral cancer, cancer of the penis and other genital and anal cancers.*
- ***Untimely Pregnancy*** *If you have sex outside of marriage you may get pregnant or get your partner pregnant. While every baby is a beautiful gift, a pregnancy outside of marriage changes the lives of the parents forever. Becoming a mom or dad means that you are responsible for the needs of your child. You might have to put off your education to work, to provide food, clothes, shelter and medical care, or to stay at home caring for your baby. Young people that have a child at a young age can make it, but statistics indicate that life may be harder for you and your child if you have a child outside of marriage.*
- ***Infertility*** *If you have sex outside of marriage, you may get an infection that could make it difficult for you to have a child naturally. For example, a man or woman infected with chlamydia may not have obvious symptoms, but may infect his or her partner without ever knowing about the infection. If the infection is not detected and treated quickly, damage to the reproductive organs can occur. A couple might not find out one of them has damage to their reproductive organ(s) until years later when they want to get pregnant. This can make it more difficult or even impossible to have a baby naturally.*
- ***Emotional pain*** *If you have sex outside of marriage, you might be deeply hurt by the experience. Some teens who have sex outside of marriage say they feel bad about the decision and wish they had not had sex.*[64,65,66]

---

[64] Albert, B. (2007, February). *With one voice 2007: America's adults and teens sound off about teen pregnancy. A periodic national survey.* Retrieved November 28, 2007 from http://www.thenationalcampaign.org/resources/pdf/pubs/WOV2007_fulltext.pdf

[65] The National Campaign to Prevent Teen Pregnancy. (2000,, June 30). *Not just another thing to do: Teens talk about sex, regret, and the influence of their parents.* Washington, DC: National Campaign to Prevent Teen Pregnancy. Retrieved February 8, 2011 from http://www.thenationalcampaign.org/resources/pdf/pubs/NotJust_FINAL.pdf

[66] Hallfors, D. D., Waller, M. W., Bauer, D., Ford, C. A., & Halpern, C. T. (2005). Which comes first in adolescence-sex and drugs or depression? *American Journal of Preventative Medicine, 29,* 163-170.

Pink Water/STD activity: *(You will need a group for this to work; remember Heritage usually does this activity within a classroom.)*

- *Prepare one clear plastic cup, 1/3 full of clear ammonia before beginning the activity. This is the "contaminated" cup and should be used by you.*
- *Before beginning the activity ask one participant to discreetly abstain from swapping with anyone.*
- *Give each participant a clear plastic cup, 1/3 full of water.*
- *Demonstrate how they should swap fluids by taking a participant's cup, pouring his water into your ammonia, swirling it around, pouring the mixture back into the participant's cup and handing the cup back to that participant. Repeat the process twice with other participants to dilute the odor of the ammonia, targeting students in the left, right and center of the room.*
- *Instruct participants to swap fluids with three other people.*
- *After all participants have swapped (except the one abstinent participant), reveal that one cup was "infected" before the swapping began and that everyone will find out who has been "contaminated" by the one "diseased" cup.*
- *Place one drop of phenolphthalein in each cup, and explain that a change to pink indicates the cup was "infected." Most cups will turn pink. Emphasize that sexually transmitted diseases are just as difficult to detect as the ammonia was; no one can tell whether a person has a STD just by looking.*
- *Disclose the identity of the one abstinent participant and note that his cup is not "contaminated."*
- *Discuss how they felt about getting "tested" (they will probably report mild nervousness or anxiety) and make the point that the abstinent participant had no worries about the results of his test because he had not placed himself at risk.*
- *Disclose that your cup was the one "infected" cup and note that by direct contact with only three people the "infection" has spread through much of the group.*

Questions/Statements for the Pink Water Game

- *Describe your reaction to the Pink Water Game. What did you learn?*
- *The fact is, sexually transmitted diseases are spreading at an alarming rate among young people. All forms of sexual activity can spread sexually transmitted infections (STIs). Statistically, half of all new STIs occur in 15-24 year olds.*[67,68,69,70]
- *Even if you have only one sexual partner, and he or she had only one sexual partner before you, you could still get a sexually transmitted infection that can become a disease with lifelong implications.*[71]
- *But, if you decide you are not willing to subject yourself to this risk, you are truly taking control over your own body and your own future. With that control comes the power over when and how you will form your family. That means you can work on reaching your potential in life so that your future is full of hope and possibilities.*

"Never Too Late"

While delivering the *Heritage Keepers® Abstinence Education* program it was revealed to the Heritage teacher that approximately half the students were already first time mothers. During the program the students were respectful but said very little regarding the information presented, and the teacher sensed tension in the classroom.

Upon completion of the post survey and on the last day of class, a group of students approached the teacher. One girl, a recent mother, spoke for the group saying, "We wanted to say thanks. Nobody has ever really cared enough to talk to us about the choices we were making." Another girl in the group went on to tell how she had decided to recommit to abstinence for the best interest of her and her children's future. She also said she had a new view of marriage – that it was a worthwhile and attainable goal. Another student who was in the early stage of pregnancy said, "I thought it was too late for me. I'm due at the beginning of next school year. Everybody's been telling me the obvious, I know I messed up. But, at least now I know it's not too late for me to change."

---

67 Alexander, L. L., Cates, J. R., Herndon, N, Ratcliffe, J. F., American Social Health Association, & Kaiser Family Foundation. (1998,December). *Sexually transmitted diseases in America: How many cases and at what cost?* Rerieved October 12, 2010 from http://www.kff.org/womenshealth/1445-std_rep.cfm

68 Begley, E., Crosby, R. A., DiClemente, R. J. Wingood, G. M., & Rose, E. (2003). Older partners and STD prevalence among pregnant African American teens. *Sexually Transmitted Diseases, 30,* 211-213.

69 Miller, H. G., Cain, V. S., Rogers, S. M., Gribble, J. N., & Tuner, C. F. (1999). Correlates of sexually transmitted bacterial infections among U.S. women in1995. *Family Planning Perspectives, 31,* 4-23.

70 Tiller, C. M. (2002). Chlamydia during pregnancy: Implications and impact on prenatal and neonatal outcomes. *Journal of Obstetric and Gynecologic, and Neonatal Nursing, 31,* 93-98.

71 Liu, L. (1999, September). Do you have HPV? *Mademoiselle,* 112.

Pregnancy

From The Medical Institute for Sexual Health, www.medinstitute.org:[72]

> Currently, more than 700,000 teens become pregnant every year. Based on this statistic, a teenage girl has a three in ten chance of getting pregnant at least once before the age of 20.
>
> Most teen pregnancies are unintended. Recent studies report that this is true in more than 80% of cases.
>
> Teenage mothers are more likely than older mothers to experience:
>
> - Serious health and emotional problems
> - Poverty
> - Less education
> - Single parenthood
>
> Fathers of children born to teen mothers are more likely than other fathers to experience:
>
> - Decreased earnings
> - Less education
> - Depression
>
> Compared to older fathers, teen fathers are
>
> - less likely to have plans for a future job
> - more likely to have anxiety
> - more likely to be homeless or in an unstable household
>
> Children born to are more likely than other children to experience:
>
> - Health problems
> - Abuse and neglect
> - Poverty
> - Less education
> - Incarceration

---

[72] Shuford, J. A. (2008 October). *What is the impact of nonmarital teenage pregnancy?* Retrieved February 14, 2011 from http://www.medinstitute.org/public/118.cfm

Real Choice

During the *Heritage Keepers® Abstinence Education* program, a sixteen year-old student announced to the class that she wished she had been introduced to our program sooner. This student was bright, beautiful, an honor student, a cheerleader and ... a mother. She explained to the class that if she had only been exposed to the information in the *Heritage Keepers® Abstinence Education* class earlier she might have made a different choice. She said she no longer has time in her life for proms, football games and parties. Those activities have been replaced by late night feedings, visits to the pediatrician and trying to maintain a 4.0 GPA on very little sleep. She continued on to say that these experiences are not what being a teenager is about and waiting to have sex until you are married is the best decision for teens and their future families. She encouraged the girls in the class to wait and to choose the best for themselves.

Teenage pregnancy is an all too common problem seen all over the United States today. Letting teenagers know they do have a choice to remain abstinent, and that it is possible, is a great way to begin to set a standard that will help our young people avoid risky behavior and reach their potential in life.

Condom Efficacy

It is the responsibility of every parent to consider what information will be given to their child(ren) about sex. There are basically two schools of thought – risk *reduction* and risk *avoidance*. Risk reduction focuses primarily on teaching young people the benefits and skills associated with using a condom and birth control while having sex. Risk avoidance focuses on teaching them the benefits and skills associated with abstaining from sex until they are in a lifelong committed relationship, commonly known as marriage.

During the 80s and 90s, when the fear of HIV was foundational to most sexual risk reduction programs, sex education was focused on condom usage. The assumption was that teens were going to have sex, no matter what the adults said. The problem is that during that era, teen pregnancy and STD rates skyrocketed to unprecedented highs.

It wasn't until Welfare Reform allocated Title V, Section 510 funding to teach young people the skills associated with abstinence that teen pregnancy rates began to plummet. When standards for teaching abstinence education were made clear under Welfare Reform, teen pregnancy rates fell nationwide. (See charts referring to drop in teen birth rates and percentage of teens having sex on next page.)

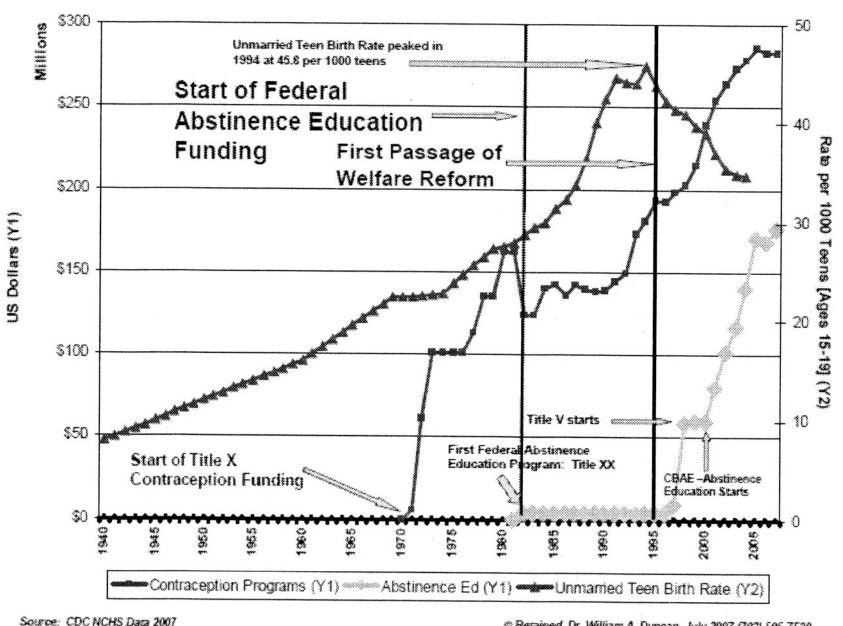

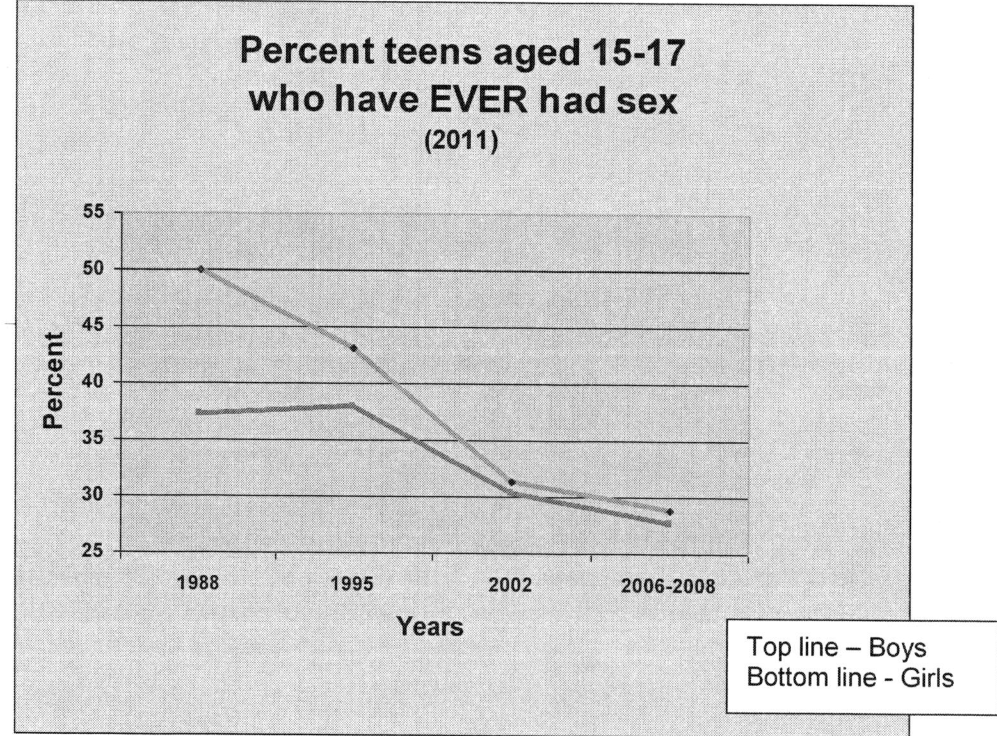

73 Abma J. C., Martinez G. M., & Copen C.E. (2010, June) *Teenagers in the United States: Sexual activity, contraceptive use, and childbearing, National Survey of Family Growth 2006–2008.* National Center for Health Statistics. Vital Health Stat 23(30). Retrieved February 11, 2011 from http://www.cdc.gov/nchs/data/series/sr_23/sr23_030.pdf

As was noted earlier, from 4parents.gov, when parents tell their children they want them to wait, their son or daughter is more likely to wait, and 9 out of 10 teens think that adults should let teens know they should wait to have sex at least until they get out of high school.[74] 76% of girls said that fathers influence their decisions on whether they should become sexually active.[75] The CDC reports that 70% of 15-17 year olds have not had sex.[76] The message matters.

During adolescence, the brain is undergoing massive pruning as young people learn what is important in life and what is not. If parents are teaching and emphasizing the skills associated with abstinence, their brain focuses on abstinence. If parents are teaching how to use a condom, and the attitude towards abstinence is skeptical at best, they may get the message that the parents expect them to have sex and to, hopefully, use a condom in the process.

The focus of this book is to enable parents to focus on building the skills associated with abstinence. There is a wealth of additional information on condom and birth control usage available from a number of sources, including the Centers for Disease Control, for parents who are interested.

Be sure to explain the difference between risk reduction and risk avoidance to your child. Risk reduction means the risk is still there, but reduced. As you consider the serious risks, also consider the state of mind any person is in during sexual arousal. Carefully consider possible consequences, if your son or daughter forgets to use a condom, decides to not use a condom, or uses a condom that fails.

CONDOM EFFICACY
from the Medical Institute for Sexual Health, www.medinstitute.org:[77]

> Condom breakage and slippage is estimated to occur 1-4 percent of the time. This is known as method failure.
>
> By far the most extensive research on condom effectiveness has been done for HIV. A number of authors have performed meta-analyses (summaries) of other studies. These meta-analyses show that with 100 percent consistent condom use, condoms reduce the risk of HIV transmission by about 85%. Condom effectiveness against transmission of bacterial diseases like gonorrhea, chlamydia

[74] Albert, B. (2007, February). *With one voice 2007: America's adults and teens sound off about teen pregnancy. A periodic national survey.* Retrieved November 28, 2007 from http://www.thenationalcampaign.org/resources/pdf/pubs/WOV2007_fulltext.pdf

[75] Meeker, M. (2006). *Strong Fathers, Strong Daughters (p.24)*. Washington: Regenery Publishing, Inc.

[76] Abma J. C., Martinez G. M., & Copen C.E. (2010, June) *Teenagers in the United States: Sexual activity, contraceptive use, and childbearing, National Survey of Family Growth 2006–2008.* National Center for Health Statistics. Vital Health Stat 23(30) (p. 23). Retrieved February 11, 2011 from http://www.cdc.gov/nchs/data/series/sr_23/sr23_030.pdf

[77] Shuford, J. A. (2008 October). *How effective are condoms in preventing sti's?* Retrieved February 14, 2011 from http://www.medinstitute.org/public/126.cfm

and syphilis is significantly lower than for HIV. Conclusive evidence is lacking for condom effectiveness against transmission of several other specific STIs, such as HPV and trichomoniasis, which each affect over 5 million people annually. Finally effectiveness is seriously limited for the many STIs which are transmitted through skin-to-skin contact, since condoms do not cover all the areas of the body which may be the source of transmission.

The major factor affecting condom effectiveness is not method failure, over which the user has no control, but user failure - the incorrect and inconsistent use of condoms during sexual acts.

STEPS TO CORRECT CONDOM USE

According to the Centers for Disease Control and Prevention (CDC), condoms must be used correctly and consistently to be effective in reducing the spread of STIs. The following steps are required to correctly use a condom:

- Use a new condom with each sex act (e.g., oral, vaginal, and anal).
- Carefully handle the condom to avoid damaging it with fingernails, teeth, or other sharp objects.
- Put the condom on after the penis is erect and before any genital, oral, or anal contact with the partner.
- Use only water-based lubricants (e.g., K-Y Jelly™, Astroglide™, AquaLube™, and glycerin) with latex condoms. Oil-based lubricants (e.g., petroleum jelly, shortening, mineral oil, massage oils, body lotions, and cooking oil) can weaken latex.
- Ensure adequate lubrication during vaginal and anal sex, which might require the use of exogenous water-based lubricants.
- To prevent the condom from slipping off, hold the condom firmly against the base of the penis during withdrawal, and withdraw while the penis is still erect.

Almost no studies actually measure correct condom use. In a study of college males, more than a third reported major errors in condom use over a three month period, despite having received instructions on correct use.[78]

---

[78] Shuford, J. A. (2008c October). *I heard that there are 6 steps to correct condom use. What are they?* Retrieved February 14, 2011 from http://www.medinstitute.org/public/124.cfm

When you see all the steps required for correct condom use, you can imagine why there is inconsistent and incorrect use, particularly among teens.

Incorrect use can lead to condom slippage or breakage, thus diminishing their protective effect. Inconsistent use, e.g. failure to use condoms with every act of intercourse, can lead to STD transmission because transmission can occur with a single act of intercourse.

Condoms provide different levels of protection for various sexually transmitted diseases, depending on how the diseases are transmitted. Because condoms block the discharge of semen or protect the male urethra against exposure to vaginal secretions, a greater level of protection is provided for the discharge diseases (HIV, gonorrhea, chlamydia, trichomoniasis).

A lesser degree of protection is provided for the genital ulcer diseases (syphilis and genital herpes) or HPV because these infections may be transmitted by exposure to areas, e.g. infected skin or mucosal surfaces that are not covered or protected by the condom.

Latex condoms, when used consistently and correctly, are highly effective (85%) in preventing the sexual transmission of HIV, the virus that causes AIDS, but not 100%. Latex condoms, when used consistently and correctly, can reduce the risk of transmission of gonorrhea, chlamydia, and trichomoniasis.

Genital herpes, syphilis and HPV infections can occur in both male and female areas that are covered or protected by a latex condom, as well in areas that are not covered. Correct and consistent use of latex condoms can reduce the risk of genital herpes and syphilis only when the infected area or site of potential exposure is protected. While the effect of condoms in preventing human papillomavirus (HPV) infection is unknown, condom use has been associated with a lower rate of cervical cancer, an HPV-associated disease.[79]

Contraception Efficacy and Abstinence

Young people who start having sex at an early age tend to have more sexual partners than those who wait. Additional partners increase the probability of pregnancy and disease.

Contraception, when used consistently and correctly can *reduce* - but not eliminate - the chance of pregnancy. Different methods have varying effectiveness/failure rates. Most methods, other than condoms, aim at preventing pregnancy and do not provide *any* protection from sexually transmitted diseases. The surest and most effective way to avoid pregnancy and sexually transmitted diseases is to abstain from sexual activity and other health compromising behaviors.

---

[79] Centers for Disease Control and Prevention. (2010, December). *Fact Sheet: Genital HPV.* Retrieved February 11, 2011 from http://www.cdc.gov/std/hpv/stdfact-hpv.htm

Sexual activity is safest in a mutually faithful marriage relationship with a partner who has been tested, who you know is uninfected, and where both marriage partners do not participate in other health compromising behaviors.

Correct and consistent use of the male latex condom can reduce the risk of STD transmission. However, no protective method is 100 percent effective, and condom use cannot guarantee absolute protection against any STD. That is why abstinence is so important.

In order to achieve any of the protective effects of condoms, they must be used correctly and consistently.

Two weeks of Heritage Changes the Rest of One Young Girl's Life

On the first day of teaching *Heritage Keepers® Abstinence Education*, the instructor noticed an exceptionally eager and anticipatory group of young ladies. It was obvious that the girls were more than excited to talk about sex. In one particular class there was a set of eyes that stood out above the rest. This young lady was very respectful and interested in everything the instructor had to say but rarely spoke up in class. The instructor was aware that she was listening intently, but the student never gave any verbal feedback throughout the majority of the program. On the next to last day of the *Heritage Keepers®* program the student walked up to the instructor and said "My boyfriend has had sex with other girls and I am a virgin. It's all that he seems to talk about. Before you came to this school and told me I am worth the wait, I didn't know what to do about being with him. If you had come into this classroom and taught us about condoms and contraceptives, then I would have probably never realized that I am truly worth the wait." She then continued to say at least five times, "This program really works," and "I love this program so much that I wish it were in every school." Again at least four to fives times she kept saying, "I now understand that I am worth the wait." The next day the student came back to class with two thank you cards in hand and said, "I broke up with my boyfriend because I realized that I was worth waiting for and I want to be with someone who thinks the same." She also said, "I told my mom that I was committing from this day forward to wait until marriage to have sex, and she told me that she was so excited and wanted to buy me a purity ring." The young girl was glowing with confidence and the understanding of her self-worth. It took a lot to break up with an older boyfriend, but the revelation that she was "worth the wait" had been transferred from her mind into her heart. She told the instructor that she had already told her friends that went to other schools, and they were interested to hear the same message even though some of them were already sexually active. The young lady also said that she wanted to do the same thing the instructor did when she graduated college because she was truly changing people's lives. The student looked the instructor in the eye and said, "Thank you so much for coming here and teaching me how to understand my worth," and walked out the door, grinning from ear to ear.

There are growing concerns about the effectiveness of programs that focus on the promotion of condom usage for teens. Probably one of our greatest concerns is that once sexual foreplay begins, even adults struggle with using condoms correctly and consistently, and sexual stimulation is necessary for using a condom. Teens are not as aware of the seriousness of possible consequence. They are already challenged by fluctuations in growth hormones and their brains – as well as their minds, hearts and bodies – are simply not yet fully developed. Age old wisdom acknowledges that when you play with fire, you are more likely to get burned.

Aside from acknowledging these common sense perspectives, the shortcomings of programs once touted as being "proven effective" are becoming public knowledge. In the era of international information highways, it is more difficult to keep information under cover. From food to sex, Americans are learning that research has too often been used to promote ideology over problem solving. As such, it is crucial that parents take the time to investigate what is being taught to their children at school or in any other setting.

For example, the authors of condom promotion curricula have long claimed that their programs increase condom usage and therefore prevent teen pregnancy and disease. Marketed as Comprehensive Sex Education during the 80s and 90s, federal funds and endorsements for such risk reduction programs are funneled through federal and state health and education systems. Considering the seriousness of the issue, for teens and their families, the actual outcomes of these programs deserve a closer look. On March 25, 2011, Dr. Stan Weed, of the Institute for Research and Evaluation, sent a letter to Paul Ryan, US House of Representatives Committee on Budget, providing scientific justification and documentation that federally supported Teen Pregnancy Prevention programs are "standing on thin ice with regard to their scientific support..."[80]

You, as a parent, have a right and a duty to look into programs being promoted by the government that affect the health and well-being of your child. Dr. Weed calls into question assumptions that have been perpetrated upon the public. In a meta-analysis of Comprehensive Sex Education (which is recognized in the field as sex education programs that promote condoms to adolescents), the Institute for Research and Evaluation found little evidence of effectiveness in school-based settings. In the following selected excerpts from another of Dr. Weed's papers on sex education programs, he challenges the scientific-sounding claims made in various condom advocacy publications. The following are highlights from the paper he sen to Representative Ryan, entitled “Misconceptions about Sex Education

[80] The Institute for Research and Evaluation (2010, December 31). *Federally funded teen pregnancy prevention programs: Not what they claim to be* Retrieved March 28, 2011 from http://instituteresearch.com/docs/IRE_Critique_of_28TPP_Programs_(12-3110).pdf

Effectiveness."[81] Other studies indicate that these type curricula typically have little-to-no information or skill preparation related to abstinence.[82]

> There is limited evidence of success for Comprehensive Sex Education (CSE) in school settings. *Emerging Answers 2007,* a review of 115 studies covering 20 years of sex education research, provided little evidence of CSE effectiveness in school settings. Of the 32 school-based studies:
>
> - No school-based CSE program demonstrated a decrease in teen pregnancy or STDs for any time period.
> - No school-based CSE programs were shown to increase the number of teens who used condoms *consistently* (i.e., every time) for even six months after the program ended. Note: *Consistent condom use* is necessary to achieve the partial protection from STDs that condoms can provide.
> - Only three of these [115] programs increased *frequency* of teen condom use (but not *consistent condom use)* for at least one year for the target population.
>
> A Centers for Disease Control meta-analysis of sex education studies found a lack of effect by CSE programs in schools.
>
> - A member of the meta-analysis study team reported in the Washington Post, November 7, 2009, that: "The analysis actually shows that *comprehensive sexual education programs in schools do not significantly increase teen condom use, or reduce teen pregnancy or STDS*...This is an important finding because the school classroom is where most teens receive sex education...Further-more, the data indicated that many types of [comprehensive sex education] programs do not work, even in non-school settings."
>
> *What Works 2010: Curriculum-based Programs That Help Prevent Teen Pregnancy* also showed little evidence of school-based Comprehensive Sex Education (CSE) effectiveness. The National Campaign to Prevent Teen and Unplanned Pregnancy published this list of 30 programs it designated as "effective." Of the nine programs that were school-based CSE:

---

[81] The Institute for Research and Evaluation (2010b, December 3). *Misconceptions about sex education effectiveness.* Retrieved March 28, 2011 from http://instituteresearch.com/docs/Misconceptions_About_Sex_Education_Effectiveness_(IRE,_12-3-10).pdf

[82] Martin, S., Rector, R., and Pardue, M.G. (2004) *Comprehensive sex education vs. authentic abstinence: A study of competing curricula.* The Heritage Foundation. Retrieved June 8, 2011 from http://thf_media.s3.amazonaws.com/2004/pdf/67539_1.pdf

- None of the nine school-based CSE programs demonstrated a reduction in teen pregnancy or STDs.
- None of these nine programs showed an increase in *consistent* condom use by teens for even six months.

The 2010 federal *Teen Pregnancy Prevention (TPP)* initiative found little Comprehensive Sex Education (CSE) success in schools. Federal *TPP* funding was approved for 28 sex education programs "proven" to be effective; but only three of these were school-based CSE programs that showed long-term effects on the target population:

- Only two [of the 28 "proven" programs] showed a significant long-term (one year) increase for the intended population (not a subgroup) in rates of teen abstinence and only one in frequency of teen condom use.

However, Dr. Weed points out in this same paper that the scientific evidence for the success of abstinence education in school-based programs is being ignored by condom advocates, who initiated – and have long controlled – sex education in America.

Research shows evidence that school-based Abstinence Education (AE) can reduce teen sexual activity.

- The *Heritage Keepers®* AE curriculum reduced teen sexual initiation by about one-half one year after the program.
- To date, no studies have shown that an AE program reduced teen condom use [even by sexually active teens].

A more recent study by Dr. Weed indicates that a year after the program, *Heritage Keepers® Abstinence Education* students reported initiating sex at *a rate 67% lower* than similar non-program students.[83] The program and the non-program students were matched not only by demographics, but also according to their scores on predicators of sexual activity before the program began. Sophisticated analysis indicates that nearly the entire difference between the behavioral outcomes of the program and non-program students, as measured a year after the program, are statistically attributable to the *Heritage Keepers® Abstinence Education* program.

Again, no school or community program can be as effective as caring and consistent guidance from a parent, over the years. But, it is also important to know what is being taught to your child by others. Are your values being backed up or

[83] Weed, S. E., Birch, P. J., Erickson, I. H., & Olsen, J. A. (2011). *Testing a predictive model of youth sexual intercourse initiation.* Manuscript in preparation. Retrieved March 30, 2011 from http://instituteresearch.com/docs/IREPredictors_(1-17-2011).pdf

challenged? Are the skills you are teaching being reinforced or torn down? And, is your child's commitment to abstain from risky behaviors being lauded or compromised?

Those who have already had sex can recommit to abstinence from sexual activity and other health compromising behaviors and begin immediately eliminating the risks associated with sex outside of the marriage commitment. It is important for them to be tested for sexually transmitted diseases and, for females, pregnancy as well. Those who have not yet had sex can commit to abstaining from sex until they are in a lifelong committed relationship such as marriage and can choose to not participate in other health compromising behaviors. Sexual activity is safest in a mutually faithful marriage relationship, where both partners are uninfected and both marriage partners do not participate in other health compromising behaviors.

The Benefits of Marriage

Each One, Teach One

While teaching *Heritage Keepers® Abstinence Education*, I encountered a sixth grader that told me that he was ready to be a father because his parents would care for the baby. His words were "that's what grandparents are for." No man had ever challenged him to think about all of the responsibilities of fatherhood and how teen parenthood contributed to the cycle of poverty. We discussed the many risks of sex outside of marriage and the real meaning of manhood. His classmates also contributed to the discussion by talking about how difficult it was for their own mothers (mostly single parents) to raise children and how much of a struggle it can be for grandparents who have to raise young children. By the end of the class, the student told me that he wasn't "ready for fatherhood or sex" and that he could see how waiting until marriage would be better for everyone involved.

In this section we will talk about the benefits of forming and maintaining a healthy marriage.

In a healthy marriage both spouses have a lifelong legal commitment to each other, to any children or extended family involved, and to actively supporting the physical, emotional, and spiritual growth and maintenance of all parties without fear of violence or infidelity.

It is vital that the adults who are participating in this series – parents, teachers, faith leaders – understand that the information is provided to enable them to empower their child(ren) with skills that will help them form healthy families. This is not a self-help book for adults who want to resolve issues from their own past or current and future relationship issues. While certainly much of the information can be useful to adults who may want to explore the benefits of establishing sexual boundaries outside of marriage, and the benefits of faithfulness within marriage, the focus here is on providing the next generation with the skills they need to negotiate through their teen and young adult years.

The authors recognize that the personal backgrounds of the adults using this series vary. Some are single parents, others are cohabiting, some are divorced, others are remarried, and some are married and living with the father/mother of their child(ren). While some of the information may be personally beneficial, it is vital for those using this series to realize that learning the benefits of sexual boundaries is about the next generation, not their own. For decades, the idea of sexual boundaries has been mocked and ridiculed. So, the skills associated with setting and defending sexual boundaries, for both males and females, have to some degree been lost. If you were not taught the value of abstaining from sex outside of marriage, you are not alone. If you were taught those values, chances are you didn't get a lot of support from the culture around you. Whatever your history, you can learn how to teach your child the benefits and personal skills related to healthy family formation.

This is a tool to help you become aware of data that has been accumulated by social scientists and researchers about how the body and mind work in relationships so you can provide the best direction for your son or daughter. When young people are provided with this information by someone who loves them, and who is passionate about their future, they believe it and it changes their behavior.

We want to repeat, over and over, that a year after students were in the school-based *Heritage Keepers® Abstinence Education* program, they initiated sex at a rate 67% lower than that of similar non-program students. In Dr. Weed's most recent study of *Heritage Keepers®* he says, "Significant differences were observed between program and comparison groups *in levels* of sexual behavior one year after the program, and also in the *amount of change* in sexual activity over that time period". A year after the program, *Heritage Keepers® Abstinence Education* students *reported initiating sex at a rate* 67% lower than similar non program students.[84] If an in-school program can have that much of an effect on the behavior (and ultimately the lives) of students, we are confident that you, their parents, have an even greater and more lasting positive influence.

This book and video series is designed to help you increase the likelihood that your children will have the skills to avoid risky behavior and to form the healthy relationships that build a foundation for a healthy marriage and family. Understanding the benefits of marriage, which are well documented by the social sciences, provides a framework for teaching your child the value of establishing and maintaining sexual boundaries.

---

[84] Weed, S. E., Birch, P. J., Erickson, I. H., & Olsen, J. A. (2011). *Testing a predictive model of youth sexual intercourse initiation.* Manuscript in preparation. Retrieved March 30, 2011 from http://instituteresearch.com/docs/IREPredictors_(1-17-2011).pdf

If we are encouraging young people to abstain from sexual activity until marriage, but they are not aware of the benefits of marriage, this could appear to be an unreasonable expectation. In a culture that appears to value marriage less than it used to, it is important to make the next generation aware that an increasing body of data indicates children being raised within a healthy marriage are statistically better off. Entire generations have been led to believe that cohabitation is "just as good" as marriage, but the statistics don't agree. What will we tell the next generation – a generation that has been raised in a culture that is greatly conflicted about family values?

A lot is at stake for our children – in particular, the well-being of their own future families as our culture struggles to determine what the standards for sex should be. Adolescents need direction during the maturation process and certainly their sexual choices are a major aspect of their lives that parents should not ignore. But, if we are telling teens to abstain from sexual activity until marriage, we must also take seriously preparing them for a rich and rewarding life-long commitment. Your child's future family is worth fighting for and worth your time and effort now.

The benefits of marriage are well documented by social sciences researchers from a variety of persuasions. *A Case for Marriage*, by Linda Waite and Maggie Gallagher,[85] points out what used to be considered obvious. Marriage is a unique institution that sets a married couple apart. There are expectations for married folks, among family, friends, the community and the State. Legal rights and responsibilities are well recognized by the courts. When two people make vows to one another, we still expect them to be faithful to one another and to take care of their children together. They tend to enter into long lasting agreements, like buying a home together, and we are saddened if they mistreat one another or are unable to keep those vows.

A wealth of data can be found on the web sites of think tanks concerned about the costs of broken and never-married families, both in human suffering and in costs to their fellow citizens. The Brookings Institute, The Heritage Foundation, The Hudson Institute, and The Urban Institute are great sources for charts and facts about adult and child well-being and risk as related to this ancient institution.

But perhaps one of the easiest references available that clearly explains and documents the benefits of marriage can be found in *Why Marriage Matters: Thirty Conclusions from the Social Sciences*.[86] This booklet organizes the data on marital benefits – to both adults and children – into easily understood categories that speak to the mind, the heart, and the pocketbook.

---

[85] Waite, L. J. & Gallagher, M. (2000). *The case for marriage.* New York: Broadway books.

[86] Institute for American Values (2005). *Why marriage matters: Twenty-six conclusions from the social sciences.* (2nd ed.). NY: Institute for American Values.

Family

1. Marriage increases the likelihood that fathers/mothers have good relationships with their children.
2. Cohabitation is not the functional equivalent of marriage.
3. Growing up outside an intact marriage increases the likelihood that children will themselves divorce or become unwed parents.
4. Marriage is a virtually universal human institution.
5. Marriage and a normative commitment to marriage foster high quality relationships between adults as well as between parents and children.
6. Marriage has important biosocial consequences for adults and children.
7. Children are most likely to enjoy family stability when they are born into a married family.
8. Children are less likely to thrive in complex households.

Economics

9. Divorce and unmarried childbearing increase poverty for both children and mothers.
10. Married couples seem to build more wealth on average than singles or cohabiting couples.
11. Marriage reduces poverty and material hardship for disadvantaged women and their children.
12. Minorities benefit economically from marriage also.
13. Married men earn more money than do single men with similar education and job histories.
14. Parental divorce (or failure to marry) appears to increase children's risk of school failure.
15. Parental divorce reduces the likelihood that children will graduate from college and achieve high-status jobs.

Physical Health and Longevity

16. Children who live with their own two married parents enjoy better physical health, on average, than do children in other family forms.
17. Parental marriage is associated with a sharply lower risk of infant mortality.
18. Marriage is associated with reduced rates of alcohol/substance abuse for both adults/teens.
19. Married people, especially married men, have longer life expectancies than do otherwise similar singles.
20. Marriage is associated with better health and lower rates of injury, illness, and disability for both men and women.
21. Marriage seems to be associated with better health among minorities and the poor.

Mental Health and Emotional Well-Being

22. Children whose parents divorce have higher rates of psychological distress and mental illness.
23. Cohabitation is associated with higher levels of psychological problems among children.
24. Family breakdown appears to increase significantly the risk of suicide.
25. Married mothers have lower rates of depression than do single or cohabiting mothers.

Crime and Domestic Violence

26. Boys raised in non-intact families are more likely to engage in delinquent and criminal behaviors.
27. Marriage appears to reduce the risk that adults will be either perpetrators or victims of crime.
28. Married women appear to have a lower risk of experiencing domestic violence than do cohabiting or dating women.
29. A child not living with his or her own two married parents is at greater risk for child abuse.
30. There is a growing marriage gap between college-educated Americans and less-educated Americans.

Marriage is an important social good, associated with an impressively broad array of positive outcomes for children and adults alike. It is also an important public good, associated with a range of economic, health, educational, and safety benefits that help local, state, and federal governments serve the common good.

In Maggie Gallagher's *The Stakes: Why We Need Marriage*,[87] she says, "When men and women fail to form stable marriages, the first result is a vast expansion of government attempts to cope with the terrible social needs. There is scarcely a dollar that state and federal government spends on social programs that is not driven in large part by family fragmentation: crime, poverty, drug abuse, teen pregnancy, school failure, mental and physical health problems."

However, in spite of these documented benefits to the family and the culture, divorce rates continue to spiral.

- 50 percent of marriages end in divorce.
- 60 percent of divorces involve children[88]

---

[87] Gallagher, M. (2003, July 14). The stakes: Why marriage matters. *National Review Online*. Retrieved March 28, 2011 from http://www.nationalreview.com/articles/207483/stakes/maggie-gallagher

[88] Forehand, R., & Long, N. (n. d.). *How parents can enhance their child's adjustment during and after parental divorce.* Retrieved February 22, 2011 from //www.aboutourkids.org/articles/how_parents_can_enhance_their_child039s_adjustment_during_after_parental_divorce

- 70 percent of all second marriages fail [The chance of a first marriage ending in divorce over a forty-year period is 67%; some studies find that the divorce rate for second marriages is as much as 10% higher.[89]]
- There are lower marriage rates, and young people are marrying later in life or not at all and have higher cohabitation rates.[90]
- Non-marital childbearing is increasing, with 52 percent of all children born to cohabiting parents.[91]
- One third of children do not live with their biological father[92]; in such situations, there is too often a lack of father involvement and child support.

Children want to belong to their parents. Regardless of how the family is broken, the child will often feel rejected. While we cannot control everything in our lives – poverty, prejudice and injustice sometimes seem to be insurmountable – this one thing we can control: how we form our families. It's not about you or me. It's about our children, the next generation. Are you giving them hope when it comes to marriage and family or failing to encourage them in this important future aspect of their life? It's important to note that social sciences have shown that cohabitation is not like marriage statistically. It is not just the presence of two adults in the home that help and protect children.

- Children with cohabitating parents and step-families are statistically at greater risk of problems than those living with their married, biological parents.[93]
- When couples live together outside of marriage, the relationships are weaker, more violent, less equal and more likely to lead to divorce.[94]
- The divorce rate of women who live with their partners before marriage is 80 percent higher than the rates for women who do not.[95]
- People who live together before marriage experience significantly more difficulty in their marriage with adultery, alcohol, drugs and independence than those who do not.[96]

---

[89] Gottman, J. M. (1999). *The seven principles for making marriage work.* New York: Three Rivers Press.

[90] Popenoe, D., & Whitehead, B. D. (2002). *Should we live together? What young adults need to know about cohabitation before marriage.* Retrieved February 22, 2011 from http://www.virginia.edu/marriageproject/nextgenerationseries.html

[91] Child Trends (2010). *Percentage of Births to Unmarried Women.* Retrieved February 23, 2011 from http://www.childtrendsdatabank.org/sites/default/files/75_Births_to_Unmarried_Women.pdf

[92] National Fatherhood Initiative, (n.d.). *The father factor.* Retrieved February 24, 2011 from http://www.fatherhood.org/Page.aspx?pid=403

[93] Thomson, E., Hanson, T. L., & McLanahan, S. S. (1994). Family Structure and Child Well-Being: Economic Resources vs. Parental Behaviors. *Social Forces, 73,* p221-242.

[94] Popenoe, D., & Whitehead, B. D. (2002). *Should we live together? What young adults need to know about cohabitation before marriage.* Retrieved February 22, 2011 from http://www.virginia.edu/marriageproject/nextgenerationseries.html

[95] Bennett, N. G., Blanc, A. K., & Bloom, D. E. (1988). Commitment and the modern union: Assessing the link between premarital cohabitation and subsequent marital stability. *American Sociological Review, 53,* 127–138.

[96] Newcomb, M. D., & Bentler, P. M. (1980). Assessment of personality and demographic aspects of cohabitation and marital success. *Journal of Personality Assessment, 44,* 11–24.

- Married biological parents strengthen children's claims to economic resources, love and affection, nurturing and social capital of both parents, and access to the resources of extended families.[97]
- Parents at high risk of poverty who are married experience less economic hardship than parents with the same characteristics who cohabitate or do not live together.[98]
- Married couples tend to pool their resources and receive assistance from family and friends.
- Married men typically work longer hours and earn more than their similar unmarried counterparts.
- Many single mothers may find themselves poor because they view the unemployed and undereducated father of their children to be unattractive as a marriage partner. For those who do marry, chronic economic hardship, lack of child care, bad housing and violent neighborhoods produce added stress on the relationship and could lead to divorce. Money is a factor in forming and sustaining marriage.
- Married families are five times less likely to be in poverty than are single-parent homes.[99]

Youth still do value marriage.

- A majority of high school seniors agree that married people are happier than those who go through life without getting married. While the percentage of women who believe this has decreased slightly since the mid '70s, from 60 to 58 percent, the percentage of men who agree with this statement has dramatically increased since then, from 63 to 72 percent in the mid '90s.[100]
- Most people still want to marry some day. Similar percentages of whites and African Americans say they want to marry. But again, more men say they want to marry than women. Among whites, 72 percent of women say they want to marry, but 79 percent of men do. Among African Americans, 72 percent of women want to marry, but 81% of men do.[101]

---

[97] Institute for American Values (2005). *Why marriage matters: Twenty-six conclusions from the social sciences.* (2nd ed.). NY: Institute for American Values.

[98] Institute for American Values, et al., (2005).

[99] McLanahan, S., & Sandefur, G. 1994. *Growing Up with a Single Parent: What Hurts, What Helps.* Cambridge: Harvard University Press.

[100] Axinn, W., & Thornton, A. (2000). The transformation in the meaning of marriage. In L. Waite, C. Bachrach, M. Hindin, E. Thompson, & A. Thornton (Eds.), *Ties That Bind: Perspectives on Marriage and Cohabitation* (pp. 147-165). New York: Aldine de Gruyter.

[101] Tucker, M. B., & Mitchell-Kernan, C. (1998). Psychological well-being and perceived marital opportunity among single african american, latina and white women. *Journal of Comparative Family Studies, 29,* 57-72.

The children of intact families are at less risk in many categories that indicate well-being.[102] Girls who grow up apart from an intact married household are more likely to have premature sexual activity.[103] Premature sexual activity often results in an increased number of partners, and teens having sex with more partners puts them at increased risk for sexually transmitted diseases and early pregnancy. An increasing proportion of children seen in clinical mental health settings from single parent families seek counseling, experience mental illness, experience chronic economic distress, and undergo frequent residency changes.

- 75 percent report serious conflict with parents.
- 55 percent report conflict between parents.
- 45 percent (up from 17 % only ten years ago) displayed assault behavior.

There is an increase in

- 7threatening and intimidating behavior,
- Scores on inventories of emotional and mental disturbance,
- Impulsive, isolative, withdrawn behavior, and
- Attention deficit disorders, oppositional disorders, anxiety and conduct disorders.[104]

What can you do?

If you are married:

- Work to make your marriage stronger.
- Fight to improve your marriage and to make it work unless there is a threat of violence and you are in danger. We want to emphasize the importance of a HEALTHY marriage.

Whether married or not:

- Help teens understand that there are benefits to marriage.
- Remember that you are their most important role model, and that they learn from you by observation, imitation and repetition.
- Recognize that cohabitation and marriage are not the same thing.
- Paint a realistic idea of marriage versus an unrealistic fairy tale. What attitudes are you passing along to your children about marriage?

Fireplace Illustration

Help your child begin to understand the concept of the lifelong commitment of marriage by using a fireplace as an example. The fireplace is made up of bricks or stones, built one on top of the other.

---

102 Institute for American Values, et al., (2005).

103 Meeker, M. (2006). *Strong Fathers, Strong Daughters* (pp. 23-24). Washington: Regenery Publishing, Inc.

104 The Commission on Children at Risk, (2003). *Hardwired to connect, The new scientific case for authoritative communities.* New York, Institute for American Values.

Intellectual Union

One wall of the fireplace is the intellectual union, which has to do with the mind and involves getting to know one another. Shared values, goals, interests and ideas are important aspects of the intellectual union. Help your adolescent understand that premature sexual activity doesn't often place importance on the value of building an intellectual union. And the intellectual aspect of the adolescent brain is undergoing tremendous change during the teen years.

Social Union

Another wall of the fireplace might be built with bricks representing the social union of marriage. The marriage union becomes known to the community through announcements of the intent to marry, wedding invitations, a solemn public ceremony in the presence of family and friends, the exchange of vows and the accountability of the couple not just to one another but to the rest of the community as a couple.

Emotional Union

The emotional union involves loving, honoring, cherishing and comforting one another. You share the feeling for and take care of each other, help and respect one another, shield one another from the difficulties of life. When two people decide they are uniting emotionally, there must be a lot of commitment, give and take, and ability to understand, build rapport, and in many ways help each other be the best version of them. This is a big commitment, one that adolescents would likely find difficult to keep.

Familial Union

Finally, there is the familial union. Two families join to make one. The couple lives together as a new and recognized family unit. They live together in one household and share the same name. Children born to the couple will be part of the new family and the couple shares finances.

Cement = Commitment

What is it that makes the fireplace a safe place for a fire? It is the cement that holds the bricks or stones in place. It is the mortar that keeps them from slipping and sliding apart. In the marriage union, the various parts of the fireplace can also slip and slide apart unless a lifetime commitment is taken seriously. That commitment is the difference between marriage and sex outside of marriage, the difference between marriage and cohabitation. It is the difference between children growing up in a never-married or divorced family or a married intact one. Commitment, a lifetime commitment, is what will be there when your own parents have grown old and passed on – but your family unit, your marriage, your family, is there for the long run. It is the lifelong legal and moral commitment of marriage that makes it a unique institution in cultures across the world. The lifetime commitment is the difference that makes sexual activity safe. It is faithfulness within that lifetime commitment that protects from emotional betrayal, infidelity, and simply walking out when times are challenging. It is keeping that lifelong commitment that makes a family.

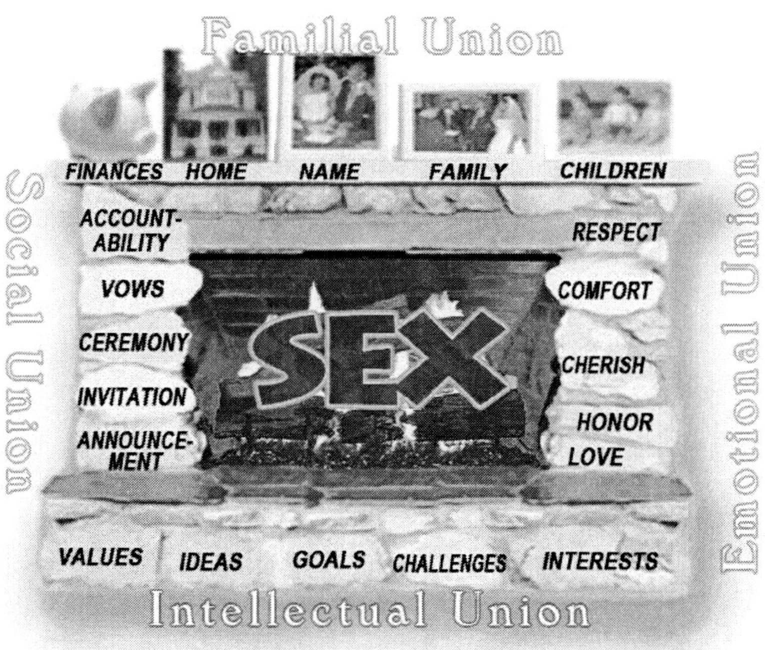

What are you teaching your child about marriage, through example or through your genuine effort to help him or her to prepare for a lifelong relationship, where their children – your grandchildren – will have the best chance of protection and success?

Marriage is worth fighting for, both in our culture, for ourselves and for our children. It is the institution through which we conceive, bear and raise the next generation. Forming our families within a healthy marriage, and encouraging our children to form their families after they have made the commitment and gone through the vows to stay makes all the difference. The next generation deserves to understand and respect the benefits of marriage.

After all four types of unions are established (social, familial, emotional and intellectual) and a lifelong commitment is made, sex is then within its safest context. If a fire is put into a fireplace that is missing a side or missing cement, it can break through causing chaos. In the same way, if sex enters a relationship before all types of unions and lifetime commitments are established, it can also cause chaos. Therefore, the physical union is the very last thing that should be introduced into a relationship. It just makes sense, like waiting for a fireplace to be completely built before building a fire.

In summary, we understand that, while there are benefits to waiting on sex until marriage, that doesn't always work out for everyone. There will always be hurtful situations for some, which end in betrayal and even divorce. And we also know that some couples are able to work out meaningful long-lasting relationships outside a formal marriage. It isn't that we are unaware of all those possible outcomes, but rather that we are not convinced that the next generation has been given a chance to seriously consider that decades of studies indicate that there are substantial statistically-backed benefits for those who wait and for those who commit to and are able to work out their marriages – and not just for those in the relationship, but for any children they may have, as well. The probability of emotional scars, children being raised by a single struggling parent, and the spread of sexually transmitted diseases are dramatically reduced when young people chose to reserve sexual activity for the person they marry.

For more information view the video ***The Benefits of Marriage.*** *(Go back to page 7 for information on how to access the video.)*

Connecting Risk Avoidance to Healthy Family Formation

What did you learn about STDs? Did anything surprise you?

In this chapter we mentioned that knowledge of STDs is important, but it will not change behavior, and that using scare tactics can actually backfire. What will you teach your child about STDs?

How will you go about playing the Dice Game and the Pink Water Game with your teen(s)? (While both may be more effective with groups, each can be used with just you and your teen to illustrate risk.)

Have you ever talked with your child(ren) about teen pregnancy? What are some things you could share with your teen(s) about this prevalent issue?

What did you learn about the effectiveness of condoms? Were you surprised about any of the information?

What did you learn about the effectiveness of "comprehensive sex education" programs? Were you surprised by any of the information?

What are you going to do to find out about the sex education programs being offered in your community? Don't just think about your own child – but also about how these programs are impacting the entire community.

The vast majority of Americans still believe in marriage, and for good reason! Men, women, children, and society benefit from marriage. Yet, these benefits are not often shown in popular media. If we base our perceptions on sitcoms, 24-hour news programming, reality shows, or the Internet, we might think marriage is on the way out. But the social sciences tell a different story. Ask yourself the following question about your perceptions. Are there benefits of marriage? YES NO

Name one of the benefits of marriage for each of the following:

For men –

For women –

For children –

For society –

Do you believe cohabitating is a good way to test a relationship before marriage?

YES NO Why or why not?

Do you believe cohabitation is a good substitute for marriage?

YES NO Why or why not?

What will you tell your child, right now, about marriage vs. cohabitation?

What will you tell your child regarding benefits of marriage?

In Maggie Gallagher's The Stakes: Why We Need Marriage, she says,

> *"When men and women fail to form stable marriage, the first result is a vast expansion of government attempts to cope with the terrible social needs. There is scarcely a dollar that state and federal government spends on social programs that is not driven in large part by family fragmentation: crime, poverty, drug abuse, teen pregnancy, school failure, mental and physical health problems."*

Why do you think family fragmentation (unwed child-bearing, cohabitation, divorce, etc.) is a major contributor to other social issues such as: crime, poverty, drug abuse, teen pregnancy, school failure, and mental and physical health problems? Have you ever considered that family fragmentation may be the source of some of these social issues? Write your thoughts here:

Brainstorm reasons that may explain why "*the divorce rate of women who live with their partners before marriage is 80% higher than the rates for women who do not*" and that "*people who live together before marriage experience significantly more difficulty in their marriage with adultery, alcohol, drugs and independence than those who do not*?" Write your thoughts here:

What attitudes are you passing along to your children about marriage? Write them here:

Brainstorm ways that you personally can better communicate the benefits of marriage to your own children in the future. What specifically do you need to do to improve upon what you have communicated about marriage in the past? Write your thoughts here:

A fireplace is used as an illustration because of how it's constructed and because of the cement that holds it all together, making it a safe place for fire. This analogy is used to help explain the construction of a marriage and the lifelong commitment that makes marriage a safer place for a sexual relationship than sexual activity outside of marriage. Sex is like fire! It needs boundaries in order to be safe.

The fireplace in the illustration has a foundation, two sides and a mantle. The four sides represent some of the foundational unions of marriage: intellectual, social, emotional and familial. These are summarized on the next page.

An intellectual union involves shared

- values,
- goals,
- interests, and
- ideas.

A social union becomes known through

- wedding announcements,
- a solemn public ceremony,
- the exchange of vows, and
- the accountability of the couple.

An emotional union involves

- loving,
- honoring,
- cherishing, and
- comforting one another.

In a familial union,

- two families join to make one,
- the couple is a recognized family unit,
- they share a household and name,
- children born to the couple will be part of the new family, and
- the couple shares financial income and obligations.

What is it that makes the fireplace a safe place for a fire? It is the cement that holds the bricks or stones in place. It is that mortar that keeps them from slipping and sliding apart. What does this cement or mortar represent? It represents the lifelong commitment to one another, not just a temporary commitment. It is what keeps a marriage and family together, just as the mortar holds the bricks together. A legal and ethical lifelong commitment is foundational to the definition of marriage, as dating and cohabitation relationships do not typically require any such widely recognized "contract." It is that legal and ethical lifelong commitment that makes sexual activity safe within the boundaries of a relationship.

Think through how you will explain the differences between sex outside of marriage and sex within marriage, considering what you have learned in this section. Write, on a separate piece of paper, a summary in your own words that you can use when you talk with your child(ren). Include benefits of marriage and risks of cohabitation. Practice talking about the difference between sex outside of marriage and sex within the legal and ethical commitment of marriage. Is this something you will be comfortable discussion with your child(ren)? It may be a topic you will want to talk about with your spouse or a trusted friend before you begin a discussion with your child(ren). Remember, you want to provide clear guidance. If you are somewhat unclear about what you think and how you feel, it is important to give substantial consideration to the topic before you provide direction for your child(ren).

You may want to list the benefits of marriage described in *Why Marriage Matters: Twenty-six Conclusions from the Social Sciences*, and reflect on the practical reasons why a couple and their children are likely to benefit from marriage in each category below. (Refer to pages 71 and 72.)

Family Benefits –

Economic Benefits –

Physical Health and Longevity –

Mental and Emotional Well-being –

Crime and Domestic Violence –

Finally, label the stones making up the fireplace drawing on the next page with the components of an intellectual union as the foundation for the fireplace, the components of an emotional and a social union as the sides of the fireplace, and the components of a familial union as the mantel of the fireplace. Only after the fireplace has been built and the mortar filled in with commitment should you add the physical union, the fire, into the fireplace. Continue to practice drawing this illustration until you can do so without referring to your notes, above.

The objective of these exercises is to equip you to be able to speak comfortably with your child(ren) about the benefits of marriage. When you have mastered this portion of the Parent Series, proceed to the next.

Chapter Three: Life Goals and Healthy Family Formation

"I learned that it is better to wait until you are married to have sex. Having sex as a teenager could end up ruining your future goals in life if you have a little kid to take care of when you are in high school."

Male *Heritage Keepers*® student

"I would like to thank ya'll tremendously. Right before this class my boyfriend and I were talking about sex. I have always said I wasn't going to do it until I was married, but I thought about changing it for him, but this class made me realize that what I think and believe is all that matters. This class gave me the extra boost I needed to wait! And even though I thought my boyfriend would leave me, he didn't and he totally understands and respects me. I would just like to thank both of y'all! You have done a lot for me! Thanks!"

Female *Heritage Keepers*® student

"I'm starting to plan out my life. And I'm taking sex more seriously. I understand the obstacles I have to cross. I know what I need to do now and I'm gonna stick with it."

Female *Heritage Keepers*® student

Healthy Family Formation

In order to help the next generation to avoid risk during adolescence and to build a foundation for forming healthy marriages and families, we are equipping parents to teach their children to abstain from sexual activity outside of marriage.

For a long time, the idea that teens will "just know" when to start having sex has been the cultural standard. But they don't "just know." Adults, who have lived longer and whose brains are more mature, struggle with this issue. Adolescents, whose brains are still developing and who have seen much less of life and its consequences, don't have all the necessary experience to discern who or when is "right." If there is any topic for which they need direction from you, it is this. Teens should not be left on auto-pilot about sexual values. They need clear guidelines.

We define abstinence as "not participating in any sexual activity outside of marriage." There are several key parts in this definition. The most crucial word is "not." Also, another key phrase to understand is that abstinence involves avoiding ANY sexual activity, not just sexual intercourse. Finally, it involves avoiding all sexual activity OUTSIDE of marriage—when married, keep it in the marriage rather than venturing outside of the marriage and avoid it before marriage. Abstinence means not just abstaining for the moment, or until you find someone you really like, but actually saving all sexual activity for marriage. Why do we believe you should teach your child to abstain until marriage? First and foremost, your child is worthy of real love and commitment. Your child has phenomenal potential to make something out of his/her life, but if your child(ren) choose to participate in sexual activity outside of marriage, their future may be at risk.[105]

A Life-Changing Day

While delivering the *Heritage Keepers® Abstinence Education* program, the educator was having trouble reading the reaction of a particularly silent class. The classroom dynamic was clearly dominated by a girl the teacher had dubbed in her mind "the queen bee," due to her evident popularity and social influence. The rest of the class had been following her lead of silence until one day when everything changed. As the bell was ringing and the students left the room, she approached the educator. "I just want you to know that the first day of class was a life-changing day for me," she said. She went on to describe how she and her boyfriend had decided to recommit to an abstinent relationship. The program had made such an impact that she and her boyfriend were both taking the initiative to address their youth group with the abstinence message. Not only were these two influential teenagers inspired to change their own decisions, they were inspired to spread the word and change the world around them for the better.

---

[105] Whitehead, B. D., Pearson, M. (2006). *Making a Love Connection: Teen Relationships, Pregnancy, and Marriage.* Washington, DC: National Campaign to Prevent Teen and Unplanned Pregnancy. Retrieved April 9, 2008 from http://www.thenationalcampaign.org/resources/pdf/pubs/MALC_FINAL.pdf

Teach your child to *wait* for the real thing, the commitment of a life-long relationship such as marriage, if you want him or her to have the very best chance for success for themselves and their future family. Setting a standard for your child should not make you personally feel bad if you made decisions in the past that are not consistent with the standard you are setting for your child. This is about your child's future, based on information our culture has accumulated during the era of the sexual revolution. Furthermore, if your child has already had sex, tomorrow is a brand new day. If your teen is already a parent, these standards will help him or her understand the benefits of waiting in the future. Remember, they deserve the respect and benefits of a lifelong commitment. When they understand their immense value and the opportunities they can pursue, and if they have the skills to negotiate the cultural pressure to be involved in casual sex, they are more likely to avoid those risks and reach their potential.

It is important for you to realize as a parent that, depending on the age of your child, they may have different levels of sexual experience.[106]

- *Those who are committed to abstaining from sexual activity outside of marriage.**
- *Those who are delaying sex and do not currently intend to initiate sex.*
- *Those who anticipate initiating sex.*
- *Those who have had sex one time.*
- *Those who have had sex with one partner more than one time.*
- *Those who have had sex with more than one partner.*
- *Those who were forced or were pressured to have sex.*[107,108]* Encourage your child to tell you if they believe they are the victim of unreported sexual assault or abuse. Let them know you want to get them help and stop the abuse.[109,110]

* *These categories were added by Heritage Community Services®*

Be ready to present the concept of recommitting to abstinence to your child. Abstinence is always an option no matter what a person has done sexually in the past. The abstinence message applies to and is valuable for every child. Anyone can start over and return to an abstinent lifestyle. This means "physically, mentally and emotionally recommitting to saving sex for marriage."

---

[106] Miller, K. S., Clark, L. F., Wendell, D. A., Levin, M. L., Gray-Ray, P., Velez, C. N., & Webber, M. P. (1997). Adolescent heterosexual experience: A new typology. *Journal of Adolescent Health, 20,* 179-186.

[107] Finkelhor, D., & Browne, A. (1985). The traumatic impact of child sexual abuse: A conceptualization. *American Journal of Orthopsychiatry, 55,* 530-539.

[108] Van Bruggen, L. K., Runtz, M. G., & Kadlec, H. (2006). Sexual revictimization: The role of sexual self-esteem and dysfunctional sexual behaviors. *Child Maltreatment, 11,* 131-145.

[109] Sorensen, T. & Snow, B. (1991). How children tell: The process of disclosure in child sexual abuse. *Child Welfare, 70,* 3-15.

[110] Summit, R. C. (1983). The child sexual abuse accommodation syndrome. *Child Abuse & Neglect, 7,* 177-193.

- ***Physically*** recommitting means that they wouldn't put themselves in physical situations where they might be tempted to cross their boundaries.
- ***Mentally*** recommitting to save sex for marriage may mean that they need to set their mind to make a commitment to abstinence, not constantly thinking about sex and avoiding messages that might have a negative effect on their thinking about their recommitment.
- ***Emotionally*** recommitting to save sex for marriage may mean that they need to honestly recognize and evaluate how they felt (their emotions) as a consequence of previous sexual activity.

Respect Yourself

A female student said that before taking the *Heritage Keepers® Abstinence Education*, she engaged in sexual activity two to three times a week. She said she lacked self-worth and did not value herself. During the class, her self-efficacy greatly improved as she learned the skills needed to demand respect for herself and her body. She has recommitted to sexual abstinence - physically, mentally, and emotionally. She learned the difference between love, lust, and infatuation. This teenager, like many others in her school, thought that sex was supposed to be a part of every relationship. She believed that sex is a significant sign of true love between a guy and girl. On the last day of class, the *Heritage Keepers®* educator received a heartwarming letter from the young lady thanking the teacher for making a difference in her life.

The student's regular classroom teacher also expressed her gratitude to Heritage Community Services for taking the time to schedule their school. She said she observed changes in attitudes and that she saw a turn around in self- esteem in the females who participated in the program.

After completing *Heritage Keepers® Abstinence Education*, the female middle school student – who had been having sex two to three times a week - said, "*I will not feel obligated to have sex as a way to express affection in my relationship. And just because it seems everyone is having sex, this does not mean I have to.*"

Remember, all forms of sexual activity can have serious health risks, including those forms of sex that are not actually intercourse.[111] Be ready to talk to your child about all sexual activity, not just intercourse.

If you want your child to abstain, it is important that first you help them set Healthy Family Formation as a personal value and goal.

[111] Begley, E., Crosby, R. A., DiClemEnte, R. J. Wingood, G. M., & Rose, E. (2003). Older partners and STD prevalence among pregnant African American teens. *Sexually Transmitted Disease, 30,* 211-213.

Help your child determine what they value, set boundaries for themselves and think through their future goals. You should keep these in mind, and as your child struggles with normal teenage issues, help them stick to these values and goals. The values of a young person establish his or her sense of identity.

Psychologist Stan Weed, PhD, Founder and Director of the Institute for Research and Evaluation, puts it this way:[112]

> In working with the concept of Personal Identity, that is, one's sense of identity -- how they see themselves, what they stand for, where they're going with their lives, and what constitutes their responsibility to others -- I have found that one's sense of identity is foundational to how one responds to the stimuli that come into their lives.
>
> When young adults are provided with an opportunity to carefully examine their personal identity, they are able to identify where they believe themselves to be in regard to certain dimensions of their lives and where they would like to be. They begin to recognize whether there is a gap there.
>
> When they consider where they are now and where they would like to be – as a man or woman, in their career, as a husband or wife, a father or mother – this exercise in self-examination helps them identify not just who they are, but subsequently how they want to live. They ultimately decide that certain behaviors will violate their own sense of identity – not only as currently defined, but how they want it to be in the future.
>
> This is a fundamental paradigm shift from how we typically address risk behavior. When we study young people that don't engage in risk behavior, what we find is that they have a healthy self-concept (not to be confused with self-esteem) that they do not want to violate. By providing young adults with support for recognizing and restructuring their sense of identity, we provide them with a whole new avenue for considering the benefits, to themselves and those around them, of healthy behavior.

[112] Personal Communication, January, 2011

A poem written by a student who participated in
Heritage Keepers® Abstinence Education

A Shining Pearl

"Girl, let me tell you, you wouldn't believe
The things he did, what he did to me.

You have got to get with it! You're so way behind.
Shoot! I was 15 when I gave up mine.

You're 17 years old, quickly approaching 18,
Graduating in June to live the 'College Dream.'

Come on Virgin Mary, it's not such a big deal;
If you let him do it, love you? He will!

So, tell me girl, tell me please!
Why not join the crowd, be a little tease?"

"I tell you now my body's a pearl;
It will shine alone without the world.

No need for love if love is just pleasure,
For my 'Love' is golden, only a 'Marriage's Treasure.'

I'd rather wait ten years for an unknowing mistake
Than give up my innocence from a bad choice I make.

I'd rather study books than cater to a baby
And let us not forget, that STDs are traveling daily.

So, call me what you want as Virgin Mary I may be;
Just note: My pride in my self respect is never taken lightly."

When you work with your child using the Student Manual, he or she will be considering who and what they value in life. The following are some of the questions your child will be considering. Review these in preparation for helping them through these exercises in their manual.

Right now, you may feel overwhelmed while you read this information – but the following exercises are foundational to your child's journey towards abstaining from sexual activity until in a committed relationship such as marriage. Review this information, so that you have a solid foundation in your mind as you read further. Don't actually do these activities with your child until after you have completed all videos, this book and the follow up questions at the end of each chapter. The exercises in this book are also presented in the Student Workbook. The concepts will come together for you by the end! Don't fill this out now, just skim over it. Space will be provided for you to actually fill these questions out, based on your opinions, not discussions with your child, in the questions section of the chapter. Remember, when you finish this series, you should do these activities again with your child. For now, just read these over and consider how your child might answer.

Who do I really value? Who makes a difference in my life?

Mother, Father, Grandmother, Grandfather, Aunts, Uncles, Sisters, Brothers, Friends, Religious Leaders, Coaches, Teachers

Is there anyone else your child values that is not on the list?

What do I really value? What really matters in my life?

Family, Education, Success, Friendship, Respect, Serving/Helping Others, Justice, Fun, Religion, Truth, Fitness, Love

Is there anything else your child values that is not on the list?

What character traits do I value? What kind of person do I want to be? I want to be...

Kind, Respectful, Generous, Trustworthy, Honest, Well-respected, Loving, Fun to be with, Dependable

Encourage your child to add to each section!

Your child will be considering what other character traits he or she values. Values are the standards by which you measure the worth of everything else. Our actions and opinions are based on what we really believe is important—our values. Every time we make a decision, we are weighing our values against the situation. After your child has determined who and what they value, you will be asking him or her to consider how risky behaviors might compromise those values.

It is important for your child to understand that in order to integrate their values into their lives, they must decide whether their actions – each decision – will be consistent with their values or compromise them. It is the responsibility of parents to help their child through this process as they learn how to cope with all that will impact them and their futures. They need your help.

As your child matures, he or she will gain the understanding that living consistently according to high standards "costs" them in "time and effort" and makes them the person they want to be. You want them to learn that investing their time and effort in directions that are not consistent with their sense of identity –

how they see themselves and their future – changes them, too often in a way that can have serious consequences for them and the people they value.

When there is inconsistency between the way one spends their time and effort and what they say they value, they must either change how they spend their time and effort or admit that they are not who they see themselves to be. This honest assessment helps them realize that it is their sense of identity – their sense of who they are and the kind of person they want to be – that provides guidance for how they spend their time and energy each day. This exercise provides a framework for establishing boundaries, which will help keep them safe from risky behaviors.

Boundaries

Help your child set personal boundaries in regards to sex, alcohol, drugs and violence. Setting clear boundaries establishes a way for them to protect their sense of identity – who they are and what they hope to become in life. Start by explaining the value of boundaries.

Begin by exploring with them their understanding of the concept of boundaries. For example, ask about the boundaries on a map. Why do states and countries have, and need, boundaries? You might suggest that different states and different countries have different values, laws and leaders. Boundaries establish the framework for where those values exist, and how they are protected and who protects them. On a smaller scale, what boundaries do pets or farm animals need, and why? What kinds of boundaries are there in sports, and why? There are boundaries for every aspect of life.

Ask your child about what boundaries are important to him or her. You may be surprised by how quickly they pick up on this concept. This paves the way for you to guide him or her to expressing the need for personal boundaries.

People absolutely need boundaries so they can live together in ways that keep them healthy, happy and productive. Establishing and respecting acceptable boundaries is one of the secrets to success in life. As your child develops, you are responsible for setting boundaries for your child because he or she cannot yet understand the dangers they might encounter. As your child matures, he or she will become increasingly able to understand the reasoning for the boundaries you have set. It is, however, quite possible that they will not fully appreciate the firm boundaries you have provided until they have experienced more of life. Until they can comprehend the serious and often lifelong consequences of sexual activity, they may not be able to personally understand your guidance. Early pregnancy, sexually transmitted infections (some of which lead to cancer and/or infertility), emotional scars, and financial burdens are just some of the issues you do not want your child to have to face.

What kind of boundaries do teens need today? What are some of the boundaries you, as a parent, want to set for your child to keep them safe and protected? A curfew? Dating standards? Telephone, TV and Internet monitoring?

Decide what is important to you and come up with appropriate boundaries. Post them in your house. Getting your teens involved in setting boundaries will help them be more eager and willing to accept the rules.

When you work with your child on the Student Workbook, you will be asking your child to write down boundaries for themselves in several risky behavior categories. Carefully think through appropriate boundaries for each so you are prepared to help your child through this exercise in the Student Workbook. Jot down your thoughts about boundaries you want to help set for your child in each category when you fill out the questions section of the chapter.

You may have thought through boundaries for drugs, alcohol, smoking and violence for your child, but this may be the first time they and you have given a lot of thought to sexual boundaries. Here are some examples to help you get started in this thought process:

- Don't let anyone touch me where a modest bathing suit covers.
- No fooling around, such as roaming hands, making out, and sexy talk.

Help your child understand that there are psychological and physiological reactions to sexual foreplay, which can lead to a decreased ability to resist increasingly risky sexual activity. When they know where to draw the line, they are more likely to be able to protect their boundaries.

Remember that if you, as the parent, have not given careful thought to all this, chances are your child has given less thought to it. Their brains are still developing and their life experiences are limited. It is up to you to provide them with clear guidance, and this series is designed to help you prepare to enable your child to think through these important life decisions.

Goals

Help your child set personal goals – both short-term and long-term. When you start with lifetime goals, you begin to realize that these are accomplished by establishing and accomplishing daily, monthly and yearly short-term goals.

Lifetime goals

These are the things they want to accomplish over their entire life. Owning a home, having a family of their own, a professional career - all are examples of lifetime goals. You will be asking your child to consider their lifetime goals. Certainly, they will not be able to list everything they hope to accomplish, but helping them verbalize some of their goals early will help them focus on the more immediate goals they will need to accomplish.

Educational and Career Goals

Educational and career goals represent what they want to learn and what sort of work they want to do. Graduating from high school, getting A's and B's, becoming a military officer - all are examples of educational and career goals. They may have no idea what kind of work they might want to do as an adult, but this provides an introduction into exploring what kinds of work interests them. Too many young people discover that they did not take the courses in high school, or even college that would have helped them work in a field they enjoy. Thinking about the kind of jobs they might want to pursue to help them understand the connection between education, strong work ethics and career.

Health and fitness goals

These goals, if set early in life, provide a foundation for a lifetime of health and fitness. Learning the value of eating well-balanced meals and snacks, hydrating, and enjoyable exercise is vital to a healthy family life and career. Protecting their physical and mental well-being is an important aspect of health and fitness. Being involved in risky behaviors, including sex outside of a lifelong committed relationship such as marriage, can have serious implications related to physical and emotional well-being. Children are never too young to realize that taking risks with their health and fitness can have lifelong consequences, sometimes making their lifelong goals more challenging – if not impossible. Developing and maintaining personal boundaries and goals are first steps to health and wellness.

Goals for this year

It is important to also have short-term and immediate goals, ones that are worked on this week and throughout the year. They might include goals related to education and career, family and friends, as well as health and fitness. It is helpful to work with your child to develop boundaries and goals for each category, short and long term. Think through how you will talk with your child about this process, so you are prepared when these topics are addressed in the student manual.

The social sciences have more than enough data to show that young people who get involved in risky behaviors are more likely to struggle later in life. In regard to sexual activity, the younger someone begins sexual activity, and the more partners they have, the greater the likelihood that they will struggle in the most important aspects of their lives in their future. Helping your child establish clear and constant values, a healthy sense of identity and sensible boundaries and goals are all key to him or her eventually forming and maintaining a healthy family life.

LIFE GOALS AND HEALTHY FAMILY FORMATION

When your child goes through the *Heritage Keepers® Abstinence Education* Student Manual, they will be filling out the My Values Worksheet. For now, YOU fill this out *the way you think your child will answer* these questions. When your child actually does this activity, you can compare how you thought they'd answer with how they actually answered!

Who do I really value? Who makes a difference in my life?

Mother, Father, Grandmother, Grandfather, Aunts, Uncles, Sisters, Brothers, Friends, Religious Leaders, Coaches, Teachers

Is there anyone else your child values that is not on the list?

What do I really value? What really matters in my life?

Family, Education, Success, Friendship, Respect, Serving/Helping Others, Justice, Fun, Religion, Truth, Fitness, Love

Is there anything else your child values that is not on the list?

What character traits do I value? What kind of person do I want to be? I want to be...

Kind, Respectful, Generous, Trustworthy, Honest, Well-respected, Loving, Fun to be with, Dependable

How can you help your child integrate these values into their personal identity as well as their daily actions?

Name some possible boundaries you could set for your child in regards to the following categories:

Drugs –

Alcohol –

Smoking –

Violence –

Sexual activity outside of marriage (you might want to include dating) –

What are some of the goals you think your child has? At the end of the series, ask them and compare.

Lifetime goals

Educational and career goals

Health and fitness goals

Goals for this year

How could emotional pain, STDs or pregnancy effect these goals? How will you help your child be goal oriented instead of present oriented?

Chapter Four: Teenage Brains and Bodies

"I really appreciate everything you taught me to stay abstinent. Looking up to you has helped me decide that my thinking of sex was way off and that if you can wait until marriage, then I know I can. This has helped me in so many ways with my morals. I was lost for a while but I have found me again. Keep doing what you're doing because people like me hear and listen. I like being who I am and not what my friends tell me is "okay, fun, or cool". I am holding myself until marriage. Thanks for letting me look up to you! P.S. look for me as a celebrity in the future."

Female *Heritage Keepers*® student

"I have changed a lot over these last few weeks. You really changed how I feel about having sex. You see, before, all I wanted to do was have sex and never really thought of all that could come from it. You made me see 30 minutes of pleasure is not worth a lifetime of regret."

Male *Heritage Keepers*® student

Young Woman Changes Mind

While teaching the *Heritage Keepers® Abstinence Education* program, the teacher met a young lady that was obviously a true leader. She battled every statement the educator made regarding the importance and benefits of a lifestyle of abstinence until marriage. Her challenges were valid and intelligent; however, they were also based on a society that lacks true understanding of the benefits of abstaining from sexual activity outside of marriage. The teacher was concerned about her effectiveness and wondered if anyone was receiving our information. However, to her surprise, on the very last day of class she received a letter from this young lady. The student stated that in the beginning of the class, she did not want to hear anything that the teacher had to say about abstinence. Although the student was a virgin, she was adamant that she would not remain a virgin until marriage. However, she expressed that after attending the class her mind had been changed. The student made a personal commitment to remain abstinent until marriage. Not only did she express her feelings in a letter, she also openly thanked the teacher on behalf of the class. The teacher was happy to have reached this particular individual, because she was equipped with a gift of leadership, and she is the kind of young lady that will influence other young ladies.

In this chapter we'll discuss adolescent brain research as presented by David Walsh in his book *Why Do They Act That Way,*[113] as well as how our brains interact with those around us, as presented by Daniel Goleman in his book *Social Intelligence.*[114] The following information will help you better understand the teen brain and body, and why parents need to provide clear guidance for their adolescents throughout the maturation process. For too long, parents have been lead to believe that adolescents are just younger versions of adults. Brain research now indicates this is far from the truth. Rather, as adolescents mature, their brains are busy developing the neural pathways that will largely determine their future as adults. There is good reason they are considered legal minors, and as such, in need of you – the parent – to provide them with clear direction. They have not had the life experiences you have had and are lacking the cognitive abilities adults possess. By the end of this chapter we will make clear why it is not a good idea to leave your child on auto-pilot during their important maturation years. They are not ready to negotiate the problems they could face as a consequence of early sexual activity and other risky behaviors. The physiological and financial challenges associated with bearing and raising a child outside of marriage are well documented. The heartbreak of sexually transmitted infections, from those causing HIV to those leading to cancer, are rampant. And the emotional consequences of premature sexual unions are only beginning to surface in research.

---

[113] Walsh, D. (2004). *Why do they act that way? A survival guide to the adolescent brain for you and your teen.* New York, NY: Free Press.

[114] Goleman, D. (2006). *Social intelligence: The new science of human relationships.* New York: Bantam Books.

The brain undergoes amazing transitions during the teenage years. If you as a parent can understand those changes, you will better be able to understand your child and help them through this transitional period.

The following section is indented because the concepts are from Dr. Walsh's book *Why Do They Act That Way.*

> I suspect some of you may have heard the following quotation: "Our youth love luxury. They have bad manners, contempt for authority, they show disrespect for their elders and love chatter in place of exercise. They no longer rise when elders enter the room. They contradict their parents. They chatter before company. They gobble up their food and tyrannize their teachers."
>
> Perhaps many of you have felt this way. Here's a little insight: this quote came from the 5th century BC by none other than Socrates. Each generation of adults has worried about the next crop of adolescents. Mood swings, temper tantrums, and infatuation with the word "no" isn't just for toddlers! Yet, adolescence can be much like the terrible twos all over again, with a few major differences.
>
> Adolescents are much bigger, much smarter, and can be much more challenging to deal with! And the trouble they can get into can be very serious, even altering their lives forever.[115]

Do you remember being a teen? Try to recollect the challenges you faced.

Parents of teens often see rapidly fluctuating moods from their children. In a moment your happy and energetic child may become angry and defiant. Teens have a lot to deal with. While their minds and bodies are maturing, they are simultaneously dealing with enormous changes in our culture and in their worlds. In the nineteenth century, the first signs of puberty were seen around age seventeen; today, the average age is twelve. The end of adolescence is fuzzier. Adolescence may be prolonged through a long period of formal education, delaying the responsibilities other generations had to carry earlier in life. And teens today must negotiate the pressures exerted by media marketers who do almost anything to lure teens into buying their music, movies, television shows, gadgets, and Internet connections. Using sexual images is at the top of their list. As your child personalizes the values that will see them through their preparation for the adult world, they need your guidance more than ever.

---

[115] Walsh, D. (2004). In *Why do they act that way? A survival guide to the adolescent brain for you and your teen.* (pp. 6-7). New York, NY: Free Press.

The Adolescent Brain

The following sections are indented because the concepts are from Dr. Walsh's book *Why Do They Act That Way.*

> Ninety-five percent of the brain's structure is formed by the age of six. But the brain doesn't stop growing until a child reaches 10 to 12 years. The teenage brain weighs the same as the adult brain: about three pounds. Because the teen brain looked similar to the adult brain, teens were expected to be able to collect information, weigh the pros and cons, and make wise decisions based on all the evidence. However, new evidence about the development of the adolescent brain reveals that it may not be completely realistic to assume teens are simply younger versions of adults. In fact, while the size of the teen brain and the adult brain are about the same, research indicates that there are important differences between the adolescent brain and that of a mature adult.
>
> Inside the brain there are potentially one quadrillion connections happening in the brain at any moment. To give you some perspective, this is more than all of the Internet connections in the world. Just for comparison, a developing baby has only about 17 percent of their neurons wired together. In the weeks, months, years and decades that follow, the rest of their neurons get wired together by two forces: genetics and experience. Nature and nurture both affect the brain's ability to interact with and respond to the environment.[116]
>
> Dr. Walsh points out the importance of realizing that "neurons that fire together wire together." Genetics are what provide the hard wiring of the brain. The DNA coding determines the connections of certain neurons. This is what we're born with, the hardwiring. Experiences are what provide the soft-wiring of the mind. So, any kind of experience is also going to shape the way that the brain forms.
>
> Language is a good example of this. A baby is born with the DNA, the hardwiring, to make a sound. But which of the 3,000 languages in the world they are going to speak is based on their experiences.[117] So we need both genetics and experiences. This actually takes away the nature versus nurture argument. You have to have both in order to shape who you are.

---

[116] Walsh, D. (2004). In *Why do they act that way? A survival guide to the adolescent brain for you and your teen.* (p. 28). New York, NY: Free Press.

[117] Walsh, D. (2004). In *Why do they act that way? A survival guide to the adolescent brain for you and your teen.* New York, NY: Free Press.

A researcher named Jean Piaget identified stages of human development, the last stage occurring between 11 and 16 years old, which he called formal operational thinking. He was originally concerned with the ability to reason because teenagers can reason and do algebra. Because teens could reason, and do complex tasks like algebra, he assumed the brain was fully developed in teens. Now, we know it isn't!

Today, we look at key processes of brain development:

- Use it or lose it
- Blossoming and pruning
- Windows of opportunity
- Windows of sensitivity
- Myelination[118]

The following section is indented because the concepts are from Dr. Walsh's book *Why Do They Act That Way.*

> What we already knew is that brain gray matter was overproduced in early development in the womb and for about the first 18 months of life. The brain becomes "the brain" through this process of overproduction and selective elimination, or pruning. But we now know that a second wave of gray matter overproduction occurs just before puberty. There is a thickening of gray matter that peaks around age 11 in girls and age 12 in boys, and the pruning process continues into the mid-20s, around age 25. So the teenage brain is not the same as the adult brain. It actually won't have fully developed until about [age] 25.[119]

Use it or lose it – The brain cells have to be fired in order to become wired. Remember, neurons that fire together are wired together. So, what are neurons? They are the building blocks of the brain. They conduct electrical signals. The possible number of configurations in the brain, it is guessed, could exceed the amount of atoms in the known universe. During adolescence, experiences and relationships are shaping the maturing brain. The neurons that don't get used will actually wither away. However, if neurons are being wired together by video games, questionable movies, use of drugs and alcohol, and sex outside of marriage, teens are not just at risk for sexually transmitted diseases and untimely pregnancy, they may be failing to develop essential brain circuitry necessary for transitioning into responsible adulthood.

Blossoming and pruning – As the process of blossoming and pruning takes place, older, weaker connections are eliminated in order to strengthen the stronger

---

[118] Walsh, D. (2004). In *Why do they act that way? A survival guide to the adolescent brain for you and your teen.* (p. 32). New York, NY: Free Press.

[119] Walsh, D. (2004). A guided tour of their brains. In *Why do they act that way? A survival guide to the adolescent brain for you and your teen.* (pp. 26-38). New York, NY: Free Press.

connections. This is no time to allow a rush of compromising influences into your child's life. Because experiences are what prune the circuits of the brain, the messages that they are receiving through the media (that premarital sex is not just okay, but the norm) is what they are learning. Those are the neurons that are used. Those aren't being pruned back. Conversely, however, with this knowledge comes the understanding that these years of maturation offer tremendous opportunity for influencing young people positively.

Windows of opportunity – During the brain maturation process, there are windows of opportunity. This window of opportunity is actually opened widest during the first three years of life. It is the window of time when the brain has the most potential to learn because neurons are rapidly firing and wiring together. An example is the finding that teenage literacy can be traced back to the first three years of life, and how often parents or other caregivers had a one-on-one conversation with their child or read to them during those formative years. Researchers are saying that this period provides the largest window of opportunity to shape your child's literacy ability. It is really because children learn in those first three years of life how to listen, how to enunciate, how to really communicate. However, we now know that there are also windows of opportunity later on – during adolescence.

Windows of sensitivity – There is also, particularly during the first few years of life, a window of sensitivity when the brain is especially vulnerable to adverse experiences. This can explain why children that have been abused continue to suffer later on, because during their window of sensitivity, they had negative experiences. However, there is also a window of sensitivity during the teenage years. So, if teens are watching violent scenes on the television or watching movies or hearing song lyrics about sexual activity outside of marriage that ignore the physical, emotional and familial consequences that may happen, these experiences are shaping their maturation process. They are particularly sensitive to what is being pumped into them, shaping who they are becoming and what they will do with their lives.

The following section is indented because the concepts are from Dr. Walsh's book *Why Do They Act That Way.*

> The last stage is myelination, the white substance that insulates the axon. There are electrical charges that travel 100 times faster on a myelinated neuron versus a non-myelinated neuron. Some circuits are still being myelinated during adolescence. And one of those that is definitely being myelinated (and is not finished) is the circuit for emotional regulation. This can help explain why teens experience such a wide range of emotions, because their neurons haven't completely myelinated. This is why you can have a tired teenager and then an energetic teenager and then an angry teenager and then a happy one and then a defiant one. It can all

happen at a wide range because their neurons are not completely myelinated. They are very impressionable in this stage.[120]

In both sexes, hormonal fluctuation can put adolescents at the mercy of extreme impulses that they may have difficulty controlling. The centers responsible for judgment are not fully myelinated until the mid-20s.

Pruning is as important for brain development as growth, even though the brain loses gray matter during this time. In gardening, pruning off dead growth enables healthy tissue to grow. So it is as the brain develops during adolescence, and what teens do or don't do can affect them the rest of their lives. According to Walsh, "If a teen is doing music or sports or academics, those are the connections that will be hardwired. If they are lying on the couch or playing video games or watching MTV those are the cells and connections that are going to survive."[121] Experiences influence the brain and actually change the fundamental structure of the brain. What experiences are you allowing your children to go through? We offer a strong word of caution against allowing the uncaring media – which is, remember, simply convincing teens to buy their products – to train your teen to give them money.

The Prefrontal Cortex

Teenagers often do not act rationally. Their ability to think through problems and challenges hasn't matured. Adults, especially parents, must help young people by giving them clear direction as the centers in the brain responsible for planning ahead and decision making develop.

As we discuss adolescent brain development, remember that the brain is made up of three distinct parts that are wired together to function as one.

- The brainstem is responsible for unconscious physiological functions like breathing and the heartbeat, as well as involuntary responses. It keeps us alive.
- The limbic brain is the seat of emotion. A lot of teen impulsiveness comes about because of the limbic brain. The limbic brain is made up of the amygdala, the seat of fear and anger; the hippocampus, which encodes memories; the hypothalamus, which is the master center for the body's hormone system; and the ventral striatal, the circuit involved in motivation.
- The cortex, what we actually mean when we refer to the brain, contains gray matter, which gives us conscious thought and reason. It is the higher brain, responsible for calculating, planning and language. The cortex takes up about 80 percent of all brain mass in humans.

---

[120] Walsh, D. (2004). A guided tour of their brains. In *Why do they act that way? A survival guide to the adolescent brain for you and your teen.* (pp. 26-38). New York, NY: Free Press.

[121] Walsh, D. (2004). A guided tour of their brains. In *Why do they act that way? A survival guide to the adolescent brain for you and your teen.* New York, NY: Free Press.

In the area behind and above our eyes, these three systems come together in the orbital frontal cortex, or the OFC. It is here that what Daniel Goleman calls the high road (or the smarter part of the brain) and the low road (or the more emotional part of the brain) work together. It is here that the ability to quickly make judgments about social situations – and in the case of our youngsters, about behavior that could either help them reach their potential or put them at great risk, takes place. And it is here that parental training – or the lack thereof - begins to shape both the firing and wiring of the brain, and the maturation process.

Realizing how the brain matures, how daily firing and wiring takes place, it quickly becomes clear that the role of parents in shaping the maturation process is undeniably crucial. This wiring of the adolescent brain *will take place* – it is physiologically inevitable. The question is, who and what will most influence that process? Who or what will they be mirroring? If parents and other caring adults fail to provide direction for teens during maturation, leaving them essentially on "auto-pilot," they are completely vulnerable to anyone who comes along to sell them an idea or a product.

Why? Neuroscience has discovered that our brain's very design makes it sociable. A newly discovered class of neurons, spindle cells that act the most rapidly of any, guide what Dr. Daniel Goleman describes as "snap social decisions" for us. A different variety of brain cells, mirror neurons, sense both the move another person is about to make and their feelings, instantaneously preparing us to imitate that movement and feel with them. It is vital that parents realize how quickly others can influence your children and that you monitor their maturation as you provide guidance and direction.

Essential to what Goleman calls *emotional* and *social intelligence* is the degree to which we are trained to control the low road of our emotions, by the quick intervention of the high road, the smarter part of our brains. And it is our prefrontal cortex that performs much of this task for us. The prefrontal cortex is the brain's executive center, which is responsible for planning ahead, considering consequences and managing emotional impulses–important functions that can drive parents to distraction.

And here is the interesting news. It appears that the prefrontal cortex begins growing again just before puberty, and is then pruned back during the entire period of adolescence, which lasts into the twenties. Clearly, this region of the brain is not yet fully wired in teens. Knowing this helps us better understand the risk taking, disorganization, distractibility, conflict seeking and lack of impulse control that teens can experience. In fact, the prefrontal cortex – the smart part of the brain, is the last part of the brain to reach cognitive maturity. Becoming aware of the changes going on in the teen brain enables parents to realize the importance of being involved with their teens in a daily, on-going relationship, providing guidance through these important years and protecting adolescents from influences that are not in their best interest.

The Major Changes of Adolescence

Dr. Walsh explains that during adolescence there are rapid physical changes such as growth spurts, voice changes, hair growth, skin problems, the development of sexual organs, and breast development in girls. There are also changes in both the intensity and volatility of emotions and a shift of influence from parents to peers. Dr. Walsh says that during this time there is a search for identity as they consider who they are and who they want to be. It is this sense of identity, as explained by Dr. Weed on pages 88-89 that will determine what they will or will not tolerate.

The following sections are indented because the concepts are from Dr. Walsh's book *Why Do They Act That Way.*

Hormones

> As most parents of adolescents will agree, teenagers have a tendency to anger quickly, take risks, have poor impulse control, and may even be rude, but why? There are major internal changes going on that can explain many of these qualities. As we have mentioned before, first, and probably most important, the adolescent prefrontal cortex can't always distinguish between a good decision and a bad one, no matter how intelligent the teen might be. This part of the brain is not fully wired until the mid-twenties. Unfortunately, at the same time the prefrontal cortex is not quite able to sift through and control impulses at the very time when teens are dealing with the onslaught of powerful urges, intense mood changes and confusing new feelings.
>
> Hormones regulate all sorts of bodily functions for all ages of people. At the beginning of puberty, messages are sent to the pituitary gland, which secretes hormones and regulates and controls other hormone-secreting glands and many body processes. This initiates physical maturation in boys and girls, including the three main growth hormones, testosterone, estrogen and progesterone. Each are present in both boys and girls during early childhood but their concentration in both sexes changes dramatically with puberty.[122]

Boys

> The main growth hormone, testosterone, can surge five to seven times a day. By the end of puberty, boys can have 1000 percent the amount of testosterone in their bodies than they had before and twenty times more than girls. Testosterone has a powerful effect on

[122] Walsh, D. (2004). In *Why do they act that way? A survival guide to the adolescent brain for you and your teen.* (pp. 61-62). New York, NY: Free Press.

> the amygdala (the seat of fear). It can trigger surges of anger, aggression, sexual interest, dominance and territoriality. Testosterone is geared towards quick tension release which leaves boys prone to follow impulses that may relieve stress. The amygdala is rich in testosterone receptors. Boys need to practice learning to manage their feelings, including anger.[123]

Physical activity, such as that required for physical work and/or many team sports, as well as individual activity such as running, builds serotonin and can help boys deal with aggression. Therefore, boys need to be encouraged to regularly partake in physical activity in order to increase their self-control. Your son needs your help and guidance, and skill building, as he learns how to negotiate the maturation process, and particularly as he determines how to cope with his increasing sexual awareness.

Girls and Neurotransmitters

The following sections are indented because the concepts are from Dr. Walsh's book *Why Do They Act That Way.*

> The two important growth hormones for girls are estrogen and progesterone. Estrogen is responsible for the development of breasts, widening of the pelvis, and the onset of the girl's period. For girls, throughout puberty and into adulthood, both estrogen and progesterone are present in the body. But the balance between them fluctuates throughout the menstrual cycle. As the level of one hormone shifts, so does the level of the other.
>
> These hormones have a powerful influence over neurotransmitters – norepinephrine, dopamine and serotonin, which carry impulses from one cell to another and amplify moods. Norepinephrine energizes and prepares the body for a *fight or flight* response; it also plays an important role in storing memory. Dopamine makes people feel good. Serotonin stabilizes mood, helping people feel relaxed and confident; a lack of it can make us depressed or aggressive. So, fluctuation in the hormones that affect neurotransmitters can result in dramatic, sudden mood swings. A seemingly small detail can blow an emotional reaction way out of proportion.[124]

Again, physical activity, such as that required for physical work and/or many team sports, as well as for individual activities like running, increases serotonin and helps stabilize mood. Encourage your daughter to regularly participate in physical activity

---

[123] Walsh, D. (2004). In *Why do they act that way? A survival guide to the adolescent brain for you and your teen.* (p. 62). New York, NY: Free Press.

[124] Walsh, D. (2004). In *Why do they act that way? A survival guide to the adolescent brain for you and your teen.* (pp. 63-64). New York, NY: Free Press.

to help neutralize large mood swings. Your daughter needs your help and guidance, and skill building, as she learns how to negotiate the maturation process, and particularly as she determines how to cope with her increasing sexual awareness.

Hormonal Fluctuations

In both sexes, hormonal fluctuation puts adolescents at the mercy of extreme impulses that they are not always capable of controlling. For boys, this can be aggression and anger. For girls, this can be an amplification of a wide range of emotions. Many adolescents may be surprised by these intense emotions, as are the adults around them.

Too many parents begin to let go during the process of maturation when, in fact, this may very well be the time of your child's life when they most need your love, strength and direction. According to Dr. Walsh, "Just when adolescents need it most, the prefrontal cortex's ability to act rationally and think through problems and challenges breaks down. Even though the teen prefrontal cortex is much closer to being mature, it is no match for overwhelming hormone-driven impulses." As such, help your adolescent avoid situations that challenge them beyond their ability to cope.

Not only are teens ill-equipped to handle media and peer pressure, but they are even less able to handle the potential consequences of sex outside of a lifelong committed relationship such as marriage. Gone are the days when young men and women worked alongside their mature parents and other relatives, learning the skills they need for coping with daily trials while being mentored in a trade and home making. Though our culture may not have yet caught up with the gap that has developed because of increasingly longer periods of time spent in school with their peers rather than family, you can make sure your adolescent has the benefit of your guidance. Don't forsake them in their hour of greatest need!

Though hormonal fluctuations can cause teens to act irrationally, adults should not view such behavior as inevitable and acceptable. Each time there is an emotional outburst or irrational action, adults have a responsibility to help train the teen mind in self-control and rational decision-making processes. When adults view erratic teen behavior simply as normal and explainable by hormones yet do nothing to train the teen in healthy behaviors, they may be enabling the teen to continue acting in this manner and to possibly stay immature. Rather, these moments should be used as ways to move towards wiring their pre-frontal cortex to respond, taking charge over the amygdala's initial reaction. We will talk more about this concept, which is considered emotional coaching, in Chapter Five.

A Silent Cry

During the *Heritage Keepers® Abstinence Education* program, the class became a bit rowdy and anxious to find out the teacher's purpose. The teacher noticed one young lady in particular that entered the class with a very nonchalant persona. She looked as if she were saying "Whatever. I'm just here." While many of the students were engaged and asking dynamic questions, the young lady sat in silence. The teacher thought to herself, "A penny for her thoughts."

After about the third day of class, the young lady approached the teacher after school and asked, "How can a person talk to her parents about sex?" The student went on to tell the teacher that she lives with her father, a police officer, and finds it difficult to talk to him. As the class continued she remained silent, not asking many questions and not very involved. On the very last day of class, she presented the educator with a personal letter. She stated, "Although I did not say much, I am very glad that you came and I learned a lot."

The teacher was grateful to have had the opportunity to provide this young lady with information she needed and for the opportunity to provide support for her, and for her father, as she enters into adolescence.

[NOTE: *Heritage Keepers®* school- based program now provides take-home discussion starters for parents!]

Miscommunication and the Teenage Brain

The adolescent brain interprets emotional expressions differently than the adult's brain. According to Dr. Walsh, adolescents tend to misread emotional signals, often mistaking fear or surprise for anger, because they rely on the amygdala instead of the prefrontal cortex. The amygdala, which is located at the rear base of the skull, is a much more *primal* part of the human brain than the smarter prefrontal cortex, in our foreheads. Located closer to the parts of the brain that receive messages from our five senses, the amygdala has a memory and is the seat of the *fight or flight* instinct.

It is through constant training, from birth on, that humans learn to control themselves so that we are not subject to the amygdala's more primal reactions.

Another part of the body that is not talked about much is the "gut." Sandra Blakeslee, an award winning science journalist with the *New York Times,* writes about the link between our gut and our brain, "Have you ever wondered why people get butterflies in the stomach before going on stage? Or why an impending job interview can cause an attack of internal cramps? And why do antidepressants targeted for the brain cause nausea or abdominal upset in millions of people who take such drugs? The reason for these common experiences is because each of us literally has *two brains* – the familiar one encased in our skulls and a lesser-known but vitally important one found in the human gut. Like Siamese twins, the two brains are interconnected; when one gets upset, the other does, too."[125]

This so-called second brain is called the *enteric nervous system,* and it consists of neurons, neurotransmitters and messenger proteins embedded in the layers or coverings of tissue that line the esophagus, stomach, small intestines, and colon.

While we talk about a *gut* feeling, or ask, "What does your gut tell you?", we don't teach children much about how to deal with their gut reactions, or with their primal reactions that originate in the amygdala. As an adolescent matures, with training, their more primal reactions will be mitigated by the smarter prefrontal cortex. Until then, the adolescent brain may react first and ask questions later.

Teens can overreact because they misinterpret a comment as a threat or insult, but given time to reconstruct and rethink, they are able to sort it all out.

It is essential to be involved with, and to provide direction for, your child during this important process of brain maturation so that he or she can learn properly how to interpret their surroundings without relying solely on the amygdala.

The following sections are indented because the concepts are from Dr. Walsh's book *Why Do They Act That Way.*

> Dr. Walsh provides helpful suggestions for effective parenting. He calls on parents to provide firm rules, firm enforcement, limited negotiation, stable leadership, balance and respect for their youngster. A permissive style consisting of few rules, few consequences, endless negotiation, limited leadership, and an emphasis on individuality does not provide sufficient structure. An authoritarian style, consisting of rigid rules, strict enforcement, no negotiation, and an emphasis on conformity does not allow the teen to practice self-discipline. A structured style, that is an authoritative style, cuts the teen reasonable slack so that every transgression does not turn into a battle, but draws the line when it comes to unacceptable behavior. When dealing with teens, listening is important. Listening attentively communicates respect. This sets a positive tone and lowers defensiveness.[126]
>
> When a teen is talking with you, establish eye contact but don't stare. Don't interrupt. Use short phrases, which encourage the

---

[125] Blakeslee, S. (1996, January 23). *Scientist at work: Vilayanur Ramachandran; Figuring out the brain from its acts of denial.* The New York Times. Retrieved February23, 2011 from http://www.nytimes.com/1996/01/23/science/scientist-work-vilayanur-ramachandran-figuring-brain-its-acts-denial.html?ref=sandrablakeslee&pagewanted=print

[126] Walsh, D. (2004). Risky business: Helping teens put on the brakes. In *Why do they act that way? A survival guide to the adolescent brain for you and your teen.* (pp. 55-73) New York, NY: Free Press.

> teen to keep talking. Keep an open posture and do not cross your arms. Ask clarifying questions, and check to make sure you understand correctly. Always remember, the first step in preventing out-of-control behavior in our teens is modeling. Never let your adolescent get what they want if they do not act civilly. Apologize if needed and be ready and be willing to accept an apology. Use time-out when things get off track and talk again later. Don't swear or use abusive language and don't accept it, either. Do not name call or put down. Never get in a yelling match. Don't leave conflict unresolved.[127]

These suggestions will not only allow for a respectful parent/child relationship, but they will also help you train your child's brain to mature faster rather than giving in to their primitive brain.

What teens do can affect them for the rest of their life. Experiences that have the greatest impact are the ones that occur in the brain's developmental stages during windows of opportunity and sensitivity. As parents, you are in the best possible position for positively impacting and supporting your child as they negotiate their way through these important formative years of adolescent brain development.

Practical Tips for On-going Communication with your Teen

The key to effective communication is the ability to focus on, and attach importance to, the thoughts and feelings of others and to be able to express yourself in a way that is understood. While this is important in relationships outside the family, it is vital within the family – and particularly in regard to having an on-going relationship with your child. Like most skills in life, people can practice and improve their communication ability.

First and foremost, listening carefully means putting one's own thoughts on hold, at least long enough to genuinely understand what another person is trying to get across. It's almost impossible to listen while you're talking, and while we want you to provide direction for your teen, we know they are much more likely to listen to you if you have truly heard them. Using simple phrases like "Tell me more!" sends a clear message that you are interested in what they are thinking and feeling.

When listening, it's crucial to notice not just the words, but the accompanying feelings by watching for facial and body expressions. If you then summarize what you heard and the feelings you think you are observing, others will generally help you along by either affirming your perceptions or correcting you until you do "get it." In Chapter Five, where we address emotional coaching, a list of emotions is provided that will help you better understand the nuances of what your

---

[127] Walsh, D. (2004). What we have here is a failure to communicate. In *Why do they act that way? A survival guide to the adolescent brain for you and your teen.* (pp. 74-91) New York, NY: Free Press.

teen is feeling. For example, he or she may feel overwhelmed and appear angry, when in fact they are actually feeling stressed. When you recognize that your teen's emotions are valid, and help him or her identify what he or she is feeling, you are laying a foundation not only for working through those feelings, but ultimately for connecting with your teen.

Remember that teens are not only dealing with the normal feelings everyone experiences day to day, but also the fluctuations in hormones and chemicals that accompany puberty. We often hear from teens that no one has ever talked with them about sexual activity, or their relationships. Practicing good communication skills, which involves learning how to be an active listener, is a first step toward enabling your child to open up to you and learn from you.

Once your teen knows you really are hearing him or her and know what he or she is feeling, it's your job to find a way to connect what he or she has expressed to what *you* are thinking and feeling. Connecting the thoughts and feelings of two people takes effort, but that's what relationship building is all about. Finding a way to say it, and conveying the appropriate feeling, takes repeated efforts – but that's what is needed for effective communication to take place! Making the effort to be reachable, and finding a way to get your own perceptions across, is key to making a genuine connection with another person and particularly with your teen. It's modeling how to build healthy relationships, which will help your teen learn the skills for developing relationships beyond the family.

Communication Do's and Don'ts (The following tips will be helpful as you try to communicate with your teen. These tips should also be shared with your teen so that he/she can also become a better communicator.)

When someone is speaking to you, DO:

- look directly into the person's eyes,
- be aware of facial expressions and body language,
- ask questions when you don't understand, and
- repeat what you think the person said to make sure you understood correctly.

When someone is speaking to you, DO NOT:

- do something else,
- look somewhere else,
- fidget or doodle, and
- think about something else/think about what you're going to say next.

When you are talking to someone, DO:

- think about the effect of what you're about to say before you speak,
- make sure you respond to the thoughts and feelings of the other person before you contribute your own thoughts and feelings,
- speak clearly so you can be heard accurately,
- take responsibility for your own thoughts and feelings by saying "I think," and "I feel," and
- be sure the person you are talking with heard not only what you said, but also what you meant.

When you are talking to someone, DO NOT:

- dominate the conversation (try to make sure each person gets equal talking time),
- interrupt the other person until he or she has finished his or her thoughts,
- mumble,
- just assume that the other person understood what you meant—ask to make sure, or
- attribute your own thoughts and feelings to others—don't say, "*People* think," or "*You* think," when you really mean "*I* think."

What parents can do to build abstinence skills in regards to the teenage brain

Adults, especially parents, must work with their teen to decide what is best and then guide them in that direction. This goes against everything our culture has taught, that teenagers should be given information so they can weigh the pros and cons and make wise decisions on their own. When this standard was being established in our culture, it was thought that teens are simply younger versions of adults. Now that research has revealed that the teen brain is not yet mature, it is becoming clear that the role of parents in the lives of their teens is crucial. The fact is that adolescents simply do not have the life experiences or the brain maturity to sort through all the nuances of sexual activity and its consequences.

Your teenager, no matter how smart, is not always capable of mulling over information, weighing risks and benefits, and then deciding what to do. Helping them develop the rational part of their brain as they are maturing is your job. Providing direction in those areas of life that they simply are not equipped to handle is an essential aspect of parenting teens that is often ignored to their peril. Your teen will eventually be capable of making wise decisions – if you provide the guidance and skill building they need during the maturation process.

In the next chapters we will talk about some skills your child will need in order to abstain from sexual activity.

For more information, view the video ***Brain Research.*** *(Go back to page 7 for information on how to access the video.)*

TEENAGE BRAINS AND BODIES

In a generalized way, describe some teenage attitudes and behaviors that sometimes make life challenging for you – and probably for them, as well!

What do you remember about being a teen? What were some of the challenges you, your friends, or even your siblings faced while growing up?

Were you surprised to learn during the "You are the Key" chapter that teens indicate parents and teachers are their most important role models? What does this information indicate to you about the importance of your parental role in shaping your child's future?

What are three things you learned about the teenage brain?

Now that you know that experiences create the soft-wiring of the brain, reflect on what kinds of situations your child is observing and experiencing. Who or what will your child be mirroring? How have you prepared your child(ren) for the "snap judgements" they will be making? Are you satisfied with the experiences that have wired – and are wiring – your child's brain?

What are some specific things you can do to make sure that you, as the parent, have the strongest influence?

Now that you know that the prefrontal cortex is responsible for planning ahead, considering consequences, and managing emotional impulses, and that this part of the teen brain is not fully developed, what are some specific things you can do to help train and guide your child during the maturation process?

How can you make sure that healthy experiences, rather than negative or unhealthy experiences, are wiring your child's brain? What are some specific changes you can make?

Draw a line from the parenting style on the left to its description on the right. Review the video again if you are unsure of your answers.

consists of few rules, few consequences, endless negotiation, limited leadership, and an emphasis on individuality	Structured/ Authoritative Style
consists of rigid rules, strict enforcement, no negotiation and an emphasis on conformity	Permissive Style
Consists of firm rules, firm enforcement, limited negotiation, stable leadership, balance and respect for the child	Authoritarian Style

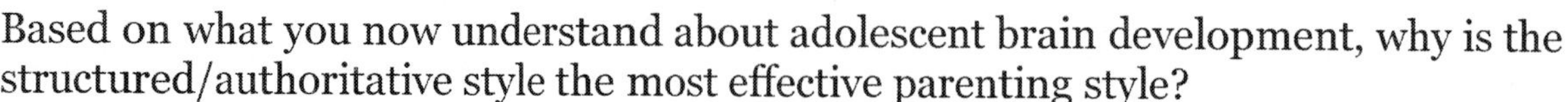

Based on what you now understand about adolescent brain development, why is the structured/authoritative style the most effective parenting style?

Reflect on your own parenting style. Do you tend to mostly use the structured/authoritative, permissive, or authoritarian approach to parenting? What are some specific things that you can do to practice a more structured parenting style?

What did you learn about teenage hormones?

How could these hormone fluctuations affect your daily interactions with your teen(s)? What are some things you can do to reduce the impact?

What are three things you could do to improve communication and listening skills with your teen(s)?

Chapter Five: Theories of Behavior Change and Influence

"My life has changed since this program because my boyfriend is always wanting to come over so we can have sex and I have to tell him "no" more than once. We have even had sex twice, and I think that it is time for me to wait until I am married. I am trying not to let anyone or anything fool my mind to have sex at any time at this point. I am only 15 years old! I am not ready for a baby."

Female *Heritage Keepers*® student

"My life has changed a lot because of this class. Now I'm focused on my life and career, and I want to be something."

Male *Heritage Keepers*® student

In this chapter we are going to be talking about how to establish protective boundaries with our teenagers and how to help them develop the skills to avoid risky behaviors and reach their full potential in life. Our approach is not "feel-good" or ideas that we simply hope will work or think teens need to hear, it is based upon sound scientific research. We will begin with some simplistic theory and move towards deeper intervention strategies.

The trans-theoretical model of behavior change[128]

The trans-theoretical model of behavioral change is built around an understanding that individuals making change progress over time through a series of stages.

This is in contrast to the standard approach, which views change as an action event rather than a process; many people believe change occurs one time. The premise of this theory is that change actually happens over time through five different stages:

- pre-contemplation,
- contemplation,
- preparation,
- action, and
- maintenance

The top of the list has to do with what is going on in the mind, the middle part has to do with how we feel about it and the bottom part of the list has to do more with actions, so we have to move ideas from the mind to the heart and then into action.

Pre-contemplation: At this stage people are not ready to change. They have no intention of changing their behavior in the foreseeable future. Oftentimes, they are unaware of the compelling reason for change.

Contemplation: People in this stage are aware of the negative impact of their unhealthy behavior and are seriously thinking about adopting new, healthy behavior, but have not yet made a commitment to take action.

Preparation: People in this stage intend to take action in the next month yet have unsuccessfully taken action in the past year.

Action: People at this stage modify their behavior in order to achieve positive change. They actually make a commitment and change their lives.

Maintenance: People in this stage work to prevent relapse and fortify gains. Recent brain research reveals that practicing a new desired behavior over a six-

---

[128] Prochaska, J.O., DiClemente, C.C. & Norcross, J.C. (1992). In search of how people change: Applications to addictive behaviors. *American Psychologist, 47,* 1102-1114.

month period actually wires the brain to integrate the new behavior throughout thoughts, feelings and actions.

What parents can do in regards to behavior change theory

Keep in mind that everywhere your child turns, they are being sold the perception that sexual activity as a teenager is expected. Changing their mind will most likely not happen with one talk. Keep talking to them about sexual issues.

Though the Behavior Change Model has been developed, in depth, as a clinical approach to smoking cessation, there are lessons that might be applied to other behavioral changes. The sequence of change, for example, is critical to behavior change.

Is your teen in a pre-contemplative stage about sex? Has he or she made a commitment, one way or the other? If your teen intends to abstain from sexual activity outside of a lifelong committed relationship such as marriage, he or she is more likely to do so than if he or she intends to have sex. Do you know your teen's intentions? If your teen perceives the benefits of abstaining from sex to be greater than the benefits of sexual activity, he or she is more likely to abstain.

Have you explored your teen's perceptions about the benefits of waiting versus the benefits of sexual activity? If your teen perceives a future that is bright, and that sexual activity could put that future in jeopardy, he or she is more likely to abstain. If your teen is equipped to make decisions about sexual activity independently from his or her peers, he or she is more likely to abstain. If your teen has a high level of self-worth and has a keen sense of his or her personal identity, it is less likely that he or she will feel the need to become sexually involved in order to win the approval of others.

Does your teen have the skills to negotiate situations that offer the opportunity for sexual activity? Is he or she able to verbalize his or her sexual values?

Answers to these questions have been found in research to help predict whether a teen will initiate sex, a topic covered more thoroughly in the next chapter. As you assess these questions and your child's answers, you can begin to judge whether your child is in the pre-contemplative stage, meaning they haven't given it much serious thought, or the contemplative stage, meaning they have given the subject a lot of careful thought. It is important that you know how they feel about it and whether they have a plan to abstain or to become sexually involved.

If your child is in the pre-contemplative stage, it will be necessary to help him or her get to a point where he or she is willing and able to consider these questions before he or she can absorb new information and contemplate your guidance. Heritage educators have found that it isn't unusual for teens to be skeptical about this topic. While they may be aware of sexual activity in the media, and perhaps among their peers (and some may already have experience), it is likely that they have not had a serious discussion on the topic with anyone. Particularly, it is likely that no one who loves them as much as you do has provided them with direction.

The key to getting the discussion started is opening it up in a manner that clearly indicates you care, deeply, about their well-being. While it is abundantly clear to you that you care about your child, probably more than anyone else, it is important to reassure your child that it is because you genuinely care about them and their well-being now and in the future, that you are opening up this subject. Remember, their amygdala, the seat of fear and the fight or flight, may trigger resistance if this is a topic you have not previously addressed. It is okay to work through those feelings with your teen; don't let their initial reactions scare you off.

Heritage instructors have found that with reassurance and patience, teens come around and are grateful that someone is addressing this issue with them in a thoughtful and genuine manner. Many teens say they wish their parents would talk with them about sex. Whether they act as though they welcome these discussions or not, it is likely that deep down they want and need your loving guidance. Remember this, if and when you meet with resistance.

Once your child is willing to contemplate the benefits of waiting, you will have at your disposal a wealth of information to offer from this series – from the benefits of marriage to information about sexually transmitted infections and their consequences, and from the emotional ramifications of early sexual activity to the challenges of early parenting.

The next stage of behavior change is preparation for action. If your teen has already made a commitment to abstain from sex outside of a lifelong committed relationship such as marriage, it may be that he or she is not able to rationally explain why. It is even less likely that they are able to verbalize their reasoning or to defend their intentions. Your preparation, by reading this book and answering the questions asked, will enable you to be ready to help them through the preparation stage. Remember, if your teen has already decided that he or she intends to be involved in sexual activity outside of marriage, or has already been sexually active, you will need to address the topic from a pre contemplative stage.

But once your child has contemplated the issue, and has decided to commit to abstaining – or if he or she has already committed to abstaining, preparation for abstaining is needed. This will involve not just convincing, but skill building. The Student Manual at the end of this book provides numerous skill building activities, particularly through role play, that will empower your teen to verbalize his or her commitment to abstinence and to defend that position should the opportunity or need present itself.

The importance of role playing with your child cannot be over emphasized. Consider what you learned about brain development, and in particular the way *wiring and firing* works. If your child has established neural pathways for verbalizing his or her position, it is much more likely that he or she will be prepared when the need arises than if he or she has not established neural pathways that have been reinforced through practice. Much like learning any new skill, preparation is key. The more one practices, the more likely he or she will be able to perform under pressure. Being able to verbalize a commitment to abstain, and having practiced the accompanying body language, will make all the difference if and when he or she is challenged.

The next stage, action, is the behavior itself. If your teen has already been sexually active, this will involve a behavior change. If he or she has not been sexually active, but has now made a commitment to abstain, this will involve behavior that requires the contemplation and preparation you are providing.

But this is not the final stage, because life is on-going. Getting through one challenge does not mean there will not be others. As adolescents mature, and relationships grow, the need for maintenance becomes increasingly important. High school years, college years, early career years – all come with opportunities for sexual involvement outside of a lifelong committed relationship such as marriage.

The seriousness of the potential consequences of sex outside of marriage – the emotional, physiological and financial problems they may face – don't go away with age. In fact, it can all become even more complex after they move further from their support system – you. Your commitment to continue to provide guidance and encouragement is crucial. Without maintenance from those who love your child most – his or her parents, it is not unlikely that someone will come along and try to convince him or her that the legal and ethical commitment of marriage is not necessary any more.

While it has become increasingly popular for young people to live together outside of marriage, or to hook up with someone for a night, the facts don't change. Sex outside of a lifelong committed relationship such as marriage often has serious consequences that can last a lifetime. Promises, and good intentions, are not marriage. Only marriage is a legal and ethical commitment for life, through all the challenges that come with each and every relationship – and particularly, those that come with having children and developing a family.

It's Never Too Late

A teenage girl came into the *Heritage Keepers® Abstinence Education* program on the first day, stating that the Heritage message was too late for most girls at that school. She included herself, saying there was no reason for the teacher to stay because no one would listen to what she had to say. Somewhere around day two at this school, the student started listening to the message. She started asking questions and encouraged others in the class to pay attention and listen to the message, too. By the last few days of the class, the student admitted that she wanted to stop the way she was living her life and to become focused on her future. She described her terrible living conditions and expressed that she wanted to succeed in life but she didn't know how. The teacher told her, along with the others in the class, the importance of being committed to something. She challenged them to start with a commitment to abstinence. The students thanked the teacher for coming and helping them make a commitment that will positively impact their bright future.

Social Learning Theory[129]

Social Learning Theory, first introduced by Albert Bandura, presents the concept that people learn from each other through observation, imitation, and repetition of the learned behavior.

People learn these ideas by observing the behavior of others and then practicing the skills required for the behavior. Much of that learning takes place as a result of cultural stimuli including the influence of parents, teachers, health experts, peers, media, and institutions in the community at large.

It is normal for teenagers to want to fit in. Even adults want to feel like they belong. It is not easy to go against the grain. In fact, sometimes it is down right painful and may seem easier to just blend in.

In the *You are the Key* chapter, the outside influences impacting your child were emphasized, such as TV, movies, games, song lyrics, magazines and the Internet. Social learning theory – the manner by which your child learns from what they are seeing and observing around them – is why it is so important to watch these media outlets carefully. Your children are absolutely learning from, and possibly replicating the behaviors shown in, the media that surrounds them daily. Your job is to negate those messages.

But why? Why do we learn from those around us? The answer is our social intelligence.

---

[129] Bandura, A. (1997). *Social Learning Theory.* Upper Saddle River, NJ: Prentice-Hall.

Heritage Program Isn't Just For Teens

While teaching the *Heritage Keepers® Abstinence Education* program, the classroom teacher told the Heritage educator "Man, I have to rethink my position on this whole abstinence idea." The teacher came from a community where it was considered a part of "growing up" to have sex during one's teenage years. He admitted that he was skeptical at first about our program but after listening and watching how the young males responded, he realized that it wasn't "unrealistic" to expect young men to actually wait until marriage before engaging in sexual activity. He acknowledged some of his own pitfalls because of poor choices that he had made. This teacher can now reinforce the idea that sex doesn't make a person a "man."

Social Intelligence[130]

The answer to the question that we asked earlier, "Why do we learn from those around us?" can be found in Dr. Daniel Goleman's book, *Social Intelligence.* The brain's very design makes us sociable. Humans are wired to connect to other people. Children learn from their environment and by observing others. Recent scientific findings reveal that observation of others registers in *mirror neurons* and *spindle cells.* As Goleman says, daily interactions have significant biological implications.

What children see, hear and otherwise experience becomes a part of their brains and ultimately who they are. If they are watching and hearing about sexual activity on TV, movies and the radio, it is almost certainly being presented as being outside of the legal and ethical protection of marriage. This perspective on sex becomes a part of their very being. But, the media doesn't teach the ramifications of such behavior, nor does it help them cope once the consequences hit. Teens are being persuaded that sex outside of a lifelong committed relationship such as marriage is fun, with only positive feelings. They are not being given the whole truth because that just wouldn't sell. So, they are not learning the skills they will need to cope with real life relationships. Life is not a movie or a song. Typically, movies and songs don't focus on the skill building needed to avoid risks. That's your job. Chances are, the very skills they need are being mocked by those pushing media onto teens. It is important that you and your teen fully realize that most media has one main purpose – getting money from your teen's pocket into their own.

The following section is indented because the concepts are from Dr. Goleman's book *Social Intelligence.*

> According to Dr. Goleman, mirror neurons sense both the move another person is about to make and their feelings, and instantaneously prepare us to imitate that movement and feel with

[130] Goleman, D. (2006). *Social intelligence: The new science of human relationships.* New York: Bantam Books.

> them. Mirror neurons make emotions contagious, letting the feelings we witness flow through us, helping us get in synch and follow what's going on. Mirror neurons explain how children can gain mastery simply from watching. As they watch, they are etching in their own brains a repertoire for emotion, for behavior, and for how the world works.[131]

The prefrontal cortex (PFC) is the "high road" of the brain – or the thinking brain. The limbic system is the low road of the brain, and is the primitive, emotional part of the brain system which contains the amygdala. Is there a place where the two connect? Yes, the OFC – or orbitofrontal cortex.

The OFC is located in the area of the brain behind and above the eyes. The OFC is the place in the brain where the brain stem (autonomic responses, like our heartbeat) the limbic system (emotions) and the PFC (the thinking brain) come together. Dr. Goleman says this is where we make sense of the social world around us. According to Goleman, when the OFC is handicapped, you will see inappropriate behavior.

He says that initial emotional responses happen quickly and spontaneously. We make instant judgments about situations and people, depending to a large extent on an unusual set of neurons called spindle cells. Dr. Goleman believes that spindle cells put the "snap" in snap judgment. These initial responses can happen, activating the amygdala - the more primitive part of the brain, before the cortical centers for higher thinking have even begun an intellectual analysis. Goleman explains that often, a situation has to be intentionally reappraised; first thoughts have to be replaced, initiating a cascade of mechanisms that quiet the amygdala and related circuits.

The more involved the prefrontal cortex is in this process, the more people can control their emotions. This is not easy to master, and children must be trained from a young age to do this successfully. Some adults continue to struggle later in life because they weren't taught how to negotiate this mental process. This will be discussed further in the next chapter.

What parents can do to build abstinence skills in regards to social learning theory and social intelligence

What does the OFC have to do with your child's feelings and actions as related to sexual activity? Everything! Unless he or she has established a sense of identity that incorporates how he or she *thinks and feels* about the benefits of waiting, it can be difficult - if not impossible - to process the moment rapidly enough to protect his or her boundaries when it really matters.

---

[131] Goleman, D. (2006). *Social intelligence: The new science of human relationships.* (p. 42). New York: Bantam Books.

The *Heritage Keepers®* program emphasizes that it is not only what young people *think* about themselves, their future and their worth, it's a lot about how they *feel.* In real life situations, it will matter whether they feel good about who they are, what they stand for, and how they perceive themselves. It will make a difference if they have adequately practiced skills needed to resist pressure to compromise.

Everyone struggles with emotional control - children, teens and adults. But, adults can process emotions faster and more accurately; they are more mature in all ways. For children and teens, the firing and wiring that takes place when you role play with them will make all the difference when their prefrontal cortex just isn't kicking in quickly enough.

These are not simplistic concepts. It is important that you recognize how uncomfortable it can feel to go against the culture unless one's sense of identity is so strong that risky situations provoke appropriate warning feelings of danger. Comments from students in our program confirm that it can be painful for adolescents to perceive themselves as different. They are relieved when they learn that the majority of teens are *not* having sex and that it is okay to wait, or to recommit, or to report abuse and make it stop. They appreciate knowing they are "normal."

People are, by nature, social. Offer your teenager an empathetic ear and your support during the difficult teen years. Again, be sure your teen knows that what the media presents is not reality; many teens abstain from risky behaviors, including sex outside of a lifelong committed relationship such as marriage. No matter what is perceived as the standard for your community, your teen has personal control over this aspect of his or her future. Unless there is sexual abuse, teens can determine whether they expose themselves to STIs; they can decide when and with whom they will start (or expand, if he or she already has a child) their family.

Help your teen understand, at a deep level, that adolescent sexual activity is an independent risk factor for developing low self-esteem, major depression, and attempting suicide.[132] These facts reinforce that everything is not always as it seems; those who engage in risky behavior are not necessarily as cool as they may try to appear.

Sexually active high school girls were found to be five times more likely to have been victimized by dating violence than girls who are abstinent.[133] Conversely, the longer young people wait to have sex, the happier they say they are within their marriage. Researchers surveyed 2,000 couples to determine relationship satisfaction based on timing of sexual activity. They controlled for religiosity, relationship length, the number of sexual partners, and education. The couples that

---

[132] Hallfors, D. D., Waller, M. W., Ford, C. A., Halpern, C. T., Brodish, P. H., & Iritani, B. (2004). Adolescent depression and suicide risk: association with sex and drug behavior. American *Journal of Preventive Medicine, 27,* 224-231.

[133] Silverman, J. G., Raj, A., & Clements, K. (2004). Dating violence and associated sexual risk and pregnancy among adolescent girls in the United States. *Pediatrics, 114,* e220-e225.

delayed sex until marriage were 20% more satisfied with their relationship than couples that had sex prior to marriage. Bottom line, developing the relationship with healthy communication and commitment prior to sexual involvement, ideally within marriage, was determined to be the best sequence for married couples.[134]

When your teen commits to abstain, recognize this as an important decision and accomplishment. Provide on-going praise for waiting. Not many people make a big deal about adolescents who have decided to wait, and some of their peers (and sadly some adults) may make fun of them. So, be sure you are rewarding that behavior and encouraging it.

Staying Committed

While teaching, a male student approached the Heritage teacher as they were leaving the campus of the school. The student thanked the teacher for coming to his school to teach the abstinence message. Before Heritage was a part of the school environment, he had been ridiculed and teased repeatedly by his peers for being a 'virgin.' However, since Heritage's abstinence education classes had begun, his friends were actually hearing and seeing someone else that lives the abstinence lifestyle . . . the Heritage teacher! Now his friends think he's a 'pretty smart' guy for remaining abstinent. With a smile, the student said his peers are now asking him questions as to how he has been able to stay committed to abstinence as a teenager. One of the key predictors that Heritage's curriculum addresses is *personal efficacy – the confidence that a student can abstain and has the skills to do so.*

Pay attention to the influences around your child. What are their friends doing? What is being taught at their school on sex? Here's a little hint: ask the school to see the program they are using and insist on talking to his or her sex education teacher to learn for yourself what he or she believes and teaches. Sex education teachers don't all necessarily follow a curriculum word for word.

Familiarize yourself with your local and state sex education standards and laws. What is the standard in your community and state regarding sex education for adolescents? How early is sex education taught? Can you opt your child out?

Make sure you know what media your child is listening to and watching. What is your child looking at on the computer?

In the next chapter, we will discuss the importance of role playing with your child, to form those firing and wiring pathways in the brain that will enable him or her to verbalize his or her boundaries.

---

[134] Busby, D. M., Carroll, J. S., & Willoughby, B. J. (2010). Compatibility or restraint? The effects of sexual timing on marriage relationships. *Journal of Family Psychology, 24,* 766-774.

Emotional Intelligence[135]

In summary, your child's brain is not fully formed, even into the late teens and early twenties. The brains of adolescents are very malleable, and they need clear direction from those who genuinely care about them. The smarter part of the brain, the prefrontal cortex or decision making part of the brain, is not fully wired. This means teens are often making decisions from their amygdala, or the emotional section of the brain, rather than the logical section of the brain. Much of what your child does on a day-to-day basis stems from an emotional reaction. Their amygdala will respond before their prefrontal cortex. In fact, this is true of adults, too. There are some adults who have never learned the ability to control their emotional reactions; therefore, they are never able to control themselves by using their prefrontal cortex and their reactions are typically based on emotion.

In his groundbreaking book, *Emotional Intelligence*, Dr. Goleman explains that successful people are not just intelligent – they also have the ability to control their emotions. They have learned the skills, and practiced them, that enable them to suppress their initial primal reactions and to use their higher thinking brain.

The ability to control emotions is not something people are just born with; people are trained to develop self-control – most likely by their parents. It is interesting to also know, however, that primal reactions never completely disappear. No matter how well-trained, facial expressions may show a more primal emotional reaction even as one is forming an intellectual response. Some are better at masking their initial reaction than others!

What parents can do in regards to emotional intelligence

As a parent you can help your child develop emotional intelligence. Be a surrogate executive thinking center for your child while their prefrontal cortex continues to develop – guiding them, directing them, helping them to think through situations. Train your child to use their prefrontal cortex and to control emotions.

Does this mean we encourage young people to be overly dependent on their parents? Or that mom and dad should be "hovering?" Not at all. What we do mean is that the decision to be involved in sexual activity outside of a lifelong committed relationship such as marriage can have ramifications emotionally and physically, even for adults. Assuming a teen can successfully negotiate all the associated risks can result in that person dealing with consequences they are not prepared to handle.

If you are interested in exploring Emotional Intelligence more, there are a lot of books that go into great detail on these subjects; we suggest *Raising an Emotionally Intelligent Child* by John Gottman, Ph.D.

As we discussed earlier in this book, both nature and nurture will determine who your child will become. According to Dr. Goleman, a child's brain is

---

[135] Goleman, D. (2006). *Emotional intelligence* (10th Anniversary Edition).New York: Bantam Dell.

programmed to grow, and all major influences in that child's life become active ingredients in neural development. The emotional climate fostered by the main people in a child's life is key. The way a child views himself or herself is determined almost entirely on how that child has been treated and almost not at all on genetics. When your child learns to control his or her emotions, he or she learns how to make better decisions. They can begin to recognize highly emotional situations and will be able to think rationally through them. For example, a teen will be able to recognize infatuation as an emotion rather than as a rational reason to have sex. We will discuss sexual emotions more in Chapter Seven.

Forming Neural Trails (or pathways)

In his book, *Social Intelligence*, Dr. Goleman explains that neural circuit connections become strengthened each time the same sequence gets followed until the pathways become so strong that they are the automatic route and a new circuit has been put in place. Over the course of childhood and the teen years, the brain will selectively lose half those overabundant neurons, keeping the ones that are used and dropping those that are neglected. The child's life experiences, therefore, sculpt his or her brain. The longest window for shaping occurs during the period of time when the prefrontal cortex is developing, which continues throughout early adulthood.

According to Dr. Goleman, the people in an adolescent's child's life have a decades-long opportunity to leave an imprint on that child's executive neural circuitry. The more a particular interaction occurs during childhood and adolescence, the more deeply it becomes imprinted in the brain's circuitry and the more *stickiness* it will have as he or she moves through life as an adult. These repeated moments from childhood, when reinforced during adolescence, become automatic paths in the brain for the young adult. This is crucial information for parents, who are pushed to *let go* of their maturing adolescents at the very moment in life when they are needed most for loving guidance – during their high school and college/military and early career days.

To learn how to emotionally coach your child for hardwiring their brain, we suggest reading *Raising an Emotionally Intelligent Child, The Heart of Parenting*[136] by John Gottman, Ph.D. Parents are often told to not be too authoritarian and to not be too permissive, but are seldom taught how to find a structured balance. This book helps parents learn how to work with their child's emotions – how to train their child in moving from primal reactions to effectively using their prefrontal cortex. Gottman focuses on the skills parents need to be their child's emotional coach rather than treating children's emotions in a dismissive, disapproving or laissez-faire manner. For those who have young children, a great resource is the *Positive Discipline* series by Jane Nelson, Ed.D.

---

[136] Gottman, J. (1997). *Raising an emotionally intelligent child, The heart of parenting*. New York: Simon & Schuster Paperbacks.

The following section is indented because the concepts are from Dr. Gottman's book *Raising an Emotionally Intelligent Child, The Heart of Parenting*.

According to Gottman, emotionally coached children have high "vagal tone." This is a term he coined to express the degree to which one is able to soothe one's self, focus, and inhibit action when appropriate. The term was derived from the vagus nerve – located in the brain, which supplies impulses for functions throughout the upper body, such as heart rate, respiration, and digestion. It is responsible for many functions of the parasympathetic branch of the autonomic nervous system. When a person is under stress, the sympathetic branch accelerates heart rate and breathing. Gottman explains that the parasympathetic system puts the brakes on, keeping the system under control, and that children with high vagal tone are able to recover better from excitement and stress. They are more aware of being under stress, able to identify their emotions, and subsequently handle situations more effectively. Gottman's research indicates that children who have parents that are emotional coaches:

- are able to regulate their own emotional state,
- are better at soothing themselves when upset,
- can calm their heart faster,
- have fewer infectious illnesses,
- are better at focusing attention,
- relate better to other people,
- are better at understanding people,
- have better friendships,
- scored higher academically,
- have fewer behavior problems,
- are less prone to acts of violence,
- experience fewer negative feelings and more positive feelings (are more emotionally healthy),
- are more resilient, and can bounce back from distress, and
- have less stress-related hormone in their urine within a 24-hour period.[137]

What is an emotional coach? Dr. Gottman explains,

When parents offer their children empathy and help them to cope with negative feelings like anger, sadness, and fear, parents build bridges of loyalty and affection. Within this context, although

[137] Gottman, J. (1997). *Raising an emotionally intelligent child, The heart of parenting.* (pp. 38-39) New York: Simon & Schuster Paperbacks.

Emotion-Coaching parents do effectively set limits, misbehavior is no longer the main concern. Compliance, obedience and responsibility come from a sense of love and connectedness the children feel within their families.[138]

Instead, they [emotional coaches] accept negative emotions as a fact of life and they use emotional moments as opportunities for teaching their kids important life lessons and building closer relationships with them.[139]

Dr. Gottman urges parents to practice positive forms of discipline as their children grow; to praise their kids more than they criticize them; to reward more, punish less; to encourage rather than discourage. He also explains that communication between parent and child must always preserve both parties' respect. While all behaviors are not acceptable, it is important to note that feelings are natural reactions to life. Put limits on actions, not emotions!

The communication skills you are practicing with your teen (see Chapter Four for reminder on communication tips) open the door for emotional coaching. If you tend to do most of the talking, it is less likely that your teen is saying what they need to say to initiate important conversations. Remember to listen carefully for emotions. Help your child identify those emotions; this will not only help him or her understand and cope with feelings, but it also lays a foundation for an open parent-child relationship. Teens often say they feel misunderstood, but parents often say they have a hard time getting their teen to open up. Remember, during maturation teens experience hormone and chemical surges. They struggle with emotions. When you help them differentiate between the various nuances of feelings, they begin to feel more in control. Following is a list of common emotions to get you thinking about the wide variety of feelings your teen might be experiencing.

---

[138] Gottman, J. (1997). *Raising an emotionally intelligent child, The heart of parenting.* (p. 17). New York: Simon & Schuster Paperbacks.

[139] Gottman, J. (1997). *Raising an emotionally intelligent child, The heart of parenting.* (p. 21). New York: Simon & Schuster Paperbacks.

Abandoned
Accepted
Adamant
Affectionate
Afraid
Aggressive
Ambivalent
Angry
Annoyed
Anxious
Apathetic
Appreciated
Argumentative
Ashamed
Awesome
Awful
Bad
Bashful
Beautiful
Belittled
Betrayed
Bitter
Blissful
Bold
Bored
Brave
Burdened
Calm
Capable
Caring
Catty
Cautious
Challenged
Charmed
Cheated
Cheerful
Childish
Clever
Combative
Comfortable
Competitive
Condemned
Concerned
Confident
Confused
Contented
Cruel
Crushed
Dangerous
Daring
Deceitful
Defeated
Defiant
Delighted
Desirous
Despairing
Destructive
Determined
Different
Diminished
Disappointed
Discouraged
Discontented
Disrespected
Distracted
Distraught
Disturbed
Divided
Dominated
Dominant
Down
Dumb
Eager
Ecstatic
Elated
Empty
Encouraged
Embarrassed
Energetic
Enraged
Envious
Evil
Exasperated
Excited
Exhausted
Fascinated
Fearful
Flirtatious
Flustered
Foolish
Frantic
Frightened
Frustrated
Funny
Furious
Good
Goofy
Grateful
Greedy
Guilty
Gullible
Gutsy
Happy
Hateful
Helpful
Helpless
Hesitant
Hopeful
Hopeless
Horrible
Hurried
Hurt
Hysterical
Ignored
Important
Impatient
Imposed upon
Impressed
Indifferent
Infatuated
Intimidated
Irritated
Isolated
Jealous
Joyous
Kind
Lazy
Left out
Let down
Lonely
Longing
Low
Lustful
Mad
Mean
Melancholy
Miserable
Moody
Naughty
Needy
Nervous

Neutral
Nice
Numb
Nutty
Obnoxious
Obstinate
Obsessed
Oppressed
Opposed
Outraged
Outnumbered
Overjoyed
Overwhelmed
Overworked
Pained
Panicky
Peaceful
Peeved
Peppy
Persecuted
Perturbed
Petrified
Pitiful
Playful
Pleasant
Pleased
Pompous
Possessive
Powerful
Pressured
Pretty
Proud
Provoked
Puny
Quarrelsome
Quiet
Raging
Ready
Reckless
Refreshed
Rejected
Relaxed
Relieved
Remorseful
Resentful
Respected
Restless
Reverent
Rewarded
Righteous
Sad
Satisfied
Scared
Screwed up
Secure
Settled
Sexy
Shocked
Shy
Silly
Skeptical
Snappy
Sneaky
Sorry
Spiteful
Startled
Stingy
Stunned
Stupid
Successful
Suffering
Surprised
Suspicious
Sure
Sympathetic
Talkative
Tempted
Tenacious
Tense
Terrible
Terrified
Threatened
Thwarted
Tired
Trapped
Troubled
Ugly
Uncomfortable
Understood
Uneasy
Unhappy
Unloved
Unsure
Used
Vindictive
Vehement
Victorious
Vindicated
Violated
Violent
Vivacious
Vulnerable
Weak
Weary
Weepy
Wonderful
Worried
Zealous

What parents can do to build abstinence skills in regards to emotional coaching

Sexual activity typically evolves out of a relationship that is packed with emotion, and adolescents are wired to make decisions based on their emotions. If they have not been taught how to handle relationships and if there are no neural pathways in place to help them defend their boundaries with clarity and conviction, they may find themselves in that category of young people who have serious regrets and face difficult consequences.

As such, it is important for you to help prepare your teen for such situations through role play. They must have already thought through, and practiced, what they will do and say if they find themselves in sexually tempting situations. Those neural pathways need to have been formed when they are not under pressure. Their boundaries must be heart felt – at a gut level. If their sense of identity is strong, they will not compromise who they are. When they understand that the benefits of waiting outweigh the fleeting benefits of sexual activity and when they have a strategy in place, there is a better chance that they will avoid risk than if they don't have a plan and haven't practiced for just such an occasion. And the more they overcome challenges, the better they will be at it.

Their reaction must be generated out of respect for themselves and others. When they are in the moment, their rational brain may not be working all that well, but when they have practiced for such a situation, they will be much more ready to handle it than if they haven't practiced. Role play is crucial, because that is how neural pathways (that will help them through challenging situations) are formed.

You Are Worth It

While teaching a *Heritage Keepers® Abstinence Education* class, I had the gift of being able to tell girls for the first time that they are "worth it." I had been an educator at Heritage for only a few months. However, one girl quickly reaffirmed my desire to teach abstinence to our local youth.

I will never forget the look on a seventh grade girl's face when I told her that she was worth reaching her goals of being a doctor, wife and mother. She was worth having a committed marriage with the man of her dreams. She was worth living her childhood free from fear of STIs and teen pregnancy. She was worth the wait, the wait of saving sex until marriage. She told me after that day that no one had ever told her that before I came along. No one had ever instilled in her the confidence that she was smart enough and strong enough to make good decisions that would allow her to live the life she was worthy of living. *Heritage Keepers®* provides the opportunity to tell kids everyday, "You are worth it," many for the first time.

According to Dr. Goleman, when one mentally rehearses an action – making a dry run of a speech or envisioning the fine points of, for example, one's golf swing – the same neurons activate in the pre-motor cortex as if one had uttered those words or made that swing. Simulating an act is, in the brain, the same as performing it, except the actual execution doesn't take place. Athletes know this concept, and there are coaches that help them go through such training. Role play forms neural pathways that will allow for a well thought-out response in an emotionally charged situation.

Here are some examples of some possible role play conversations that you can have with your teen. When you work with your teen on the Student Workbook, you will be asking him or her to think through similar situations as these, and asking him or her to rehearse both verbally and non-verbally (body language) how to respond. Actually saying the words until one is comfortable and acting out a reaction until it becomes natural forms neural pathways of protection from risk taking. We will provide more information on responses to common teenage sexual situations in Chapter Eight.

- You think you are in love with your boyfriend/girlfriend, and he or she wants to do something sexual with you. How do you tell him or her your boundaries without hurting his or her feelings?
- Your friends are pressuring you to have sex. You are committed to abstinence. How do you respond?
- The kids in your school are all having sex; you are not going to have sex, but they are making you feel different. Then a classmate asks you, "Hey, are you having sex?" What do you do? What do you say?
- Your friends tell you they all love having sex. They ask you if you love sex, too. You are committed to abstaining from sex until you are married. You want your friends to like you, so what do you say?
- Your boyfriend/girlfriend says you need to have sex with him/her because you are in love. You are not going to have sex with him or her. How do you respond?

When you work with your child on the Student Workbook, the following strategy is provided as a simple, easy-to-understand plan that your child can remember as a guideline for challenging situations.

SAFE Plan

State boundaries.

Establish boundaries. Everything covered by a modest bathing suit is off-limits.
Write boundaries. Fix boundaries clearly in the mind, which makes it easier to avoid compromise under pressure. Commit to maintaining boundaries.
Share boundaries. Verbalize your boundaries to friends and those you date, and accept help in maintaining those boundaries.

Avoid danger.

Stay away from dangerous situations that make it difficult to protect your boundaries, for sex and other risks, like drinking. Be firm, no compromise. Danger might be a friend who pressures you, a relationship that tempts you, or a time or place that offers opportunity (like a bedroom, an empty house, a party with drinking or drugs, etc.).

Firmly say, "No!"

Verbally
Use the word *no*; there is nothing clearer or more to the point.
Use strong words and a strong tone of voice; send your message loud and clear.
State what you are not going to do or what you want the other person not to do (i.e. "No. I'm not going upstairs with you," or "No. Do not put your hand on my butt.").
It's okay to state positive feelings about a person so they know it is the activity being rejected, not the person (i.e. "No. I think you are great, but I am NOT going to have sex with you.")
State reasons, but boundaries are not debatable. If someone pushes you to debate your boundaries, you must be ready to defend your position and not compromise.

Non-verbally
Say the same thing with your body that you are saying with your mouth.
Stiffen your body, sit up straight, fold your arms, hold up your palms to hold the other person away from you, or use other gestures to support what you are saying.
Use serious facial expressions and eye contact.

Exit
If all else fails, leave, which is the most definite, unmistakable non-verbal *no* you can give. This is your last line of defense; no matter how close you come to crossing your boundary, it is never too late to stop, get out of there, and keep safe. If a friend or boy/girlfriend continues to pressure you to have sex, you may need to "exit" that relationship in order to protect your boundaries and future.

Your History

For parents that were sexually active outside of marriage, it is crucial for you to feel comfortable when you are working on these exercises with your child. It will help to go through this exercise yourself. If you can't imagine someone resisting the opportunity to have sex, it may be that you will struggle with the idea that your child can. Work this out before you work with your child.

If you were sexually active outside of marriage and there were no negative consequences for you, it is important to realize that may not be the outcome for your child.

The prevalence of sexually transmitted diseases is ever rising, and for some there is no cure. The consequences are often not fully understood. For example, a very successful businessman contracted Herpes in college and unknowingly gave it to his wife while she was pregnant; his wife in turn gave it to their daughter during pregnancy/childbirth. After their daughter was born, she almost died from the infection, and she suffers to this day from periodic outbreaks through no fault of her own. No amount of money will fix this.

Others have cervical cancer and have no clue that it was caused by a sexually transmitted infection, HPV[140] (Human Papillomavirus). Though a vaccine is now available, it is not effective for all strains of HPV, and the vaccine cannot undo damage already done.

There are women who are infertile because of physiological damage from a sexually transmitted disease. Often, the harm is being done even when they are not aware that they have an infection, and the effect is not realized until they try to have a child.

For those who either fathered a child outside of marriage or who became pregnant outside of marriage, the ramifications are well documented for the young parents *and* their child(ren). Financial stress, familial complications, custodial battles, emotional turmoil – sadly, the list is long. It isn't that single parenting is impossible, it's just that it is, generally speaking, harder – on the parents and the child(ren).

If you did not experience any of these consequences, that doesn't mean your child won't. The risks are real, serious, and can be life long.

If you were sexually active outside of marriage and had to cope with challenges as a result, then you understand that your child should not have to learn the hard way. You can help him or her avoid risk and have the best possible chance

---

[140] Centers for Disease Control and Prevention. (2010, December). *Fact Sheet: Genital HPV*. Retrieved February 11, 2011 from http://www.cdc.gov/std/hpv/stdfact-hpv.htm

of reaching his or her potential without the added problems that can come out of early sexual activity.

If you did not have sex outside of marriage, you may already feel comfortable encouraging your child to wait. But that doesn't mean your child does not need the same level of coaching and encouragement as any other. Even single adults who have thought through their values and are committed to waiting until marriage can struggle with verbalizing their reasoning because role models are few and far between and support systems simply do not exist. This book is the beginning of common sense on this issue and a response to a growing sense that people want to push back against perceived politically correct norms, many of which ignore the facts.

Whether you are a parent that abstained until marriage or didn't, and whether your child has abstained or hasn't, there are no closed doors. Tomorrow is always a new day.

An Abstinence Educator's Story

I have always had a passion for high school and middle school kids. There is something about the opportunity to meet kids where they are at, encourage them, inspire them and simply tell them that they are capable. When I began looking for careers after my time with high school kids in upstate New York, I was amazed at the opportunity with *Heritage Keepers*®, the opportunity to do just the thing that I have become so passionate about.

Through my educator role with *Heritage Keepers*®, I have the opportunity to walk into a classroom and tell teens, some for the first time, that they are worth being waited for, worth a life of healthy relationships, worth more than the worries of STDs and untimely parenting. These are all truths that have been denied, twisted and warped by our culture. I have chosen to work with *Heritage Keepers*® and teach abstinence education because of its unique approach to loving the youth of our community and inspiring them to believe in themselves, as well as to take on the fight against the lies they are hearing through various cultural outlets.

Even in my short time with *Heritage Keepers*®, I have been so encouraged by the response from my students. They get excited about abstinence, about living a life free from the consequences of sex outside of marriage, and to be making decisions for themselves lives that will help them reach the goals they have set. The majority of teens I have spent time with through *Heritage Keepers*® have different expressions on their faces by the end of the program. We have built a relationship and they leave with a new hope and a new smile. It is amazing that I can stand in front of them and tell them, "I am doing this and you can too! We can do this together!"

Self-efficacy[141]

The concept of self-efficacy is foundational to equipping your child with the skills to actually practice abstinence until a lifelong committed relationship such as marriage. Role play is crucial to building your child's self-efficacy, that is, his or her belief that they can accomplish what they set out to do.

What is self-efficacy? It is important to note that self-efficacy and self-esteem are NOT the same. Bandura says perceived self-efficacy is concerned with judgments of personal capability, whereas self-esteem is concerned with judgments of self-worth. There is no fixed relationship between beliefs about one's capabilities and whether one likes or dislikes oneself.

All too often people, not just teenagers, surrender control to others, forming a dependence on others to show them what to do and even who to be. Why? Because it seems, at the time, to be the easier thing to do. Many times, people do not even realize they are copying someone else. Self-efficacy, however, is the belief that you are able to influence and control the direction your life will take.

The following section is indented because the concepts are from Bandura's book *Self–Efficacy: The Exercise of Control.*[142]

> Albert Bandura says that what people achieve depends on how deeply they believe they can do it and how much they are willing to work to sacrifice to be proficient in it.
>
> Unless someone really believes they can achieve a desired outcome, they will have little incentive to act. Bandura says people's self-efficacy influences
>
> - the courses of action they choose to pursue,
> - how much effort they put forth in given endeavors,
> - how long they will persevere in the face of obstacles and failures,
> - their resilience to adversity,
> - whether their thought patterns are self-hindering or self-aiding,
> - how much stress and depression they experience in coping with taxing environmental demands, and
> - the level of accomplishments they realize.

If people believe that they have no ability to reach a goal, they won't reach it. They probably won't even really try. This is true not just for your child, but for you as well.

---

141 Bandura, A. (1997). *Self-efficacy: The Exercise of Control.* New York: W.H. Freeman and Company.

142 Ibid.

If you do not believe you can influence your child, or that they can wait, the chances of achieving that goal is seriously reduced.

People must have confidence in their *abilities* in order to persevere and accomplish a given task. Though it's essential to know the importance of forming a healthy family, just knowing information is not sufficient to achieve a desired behavioral outcome. A deeper level of commitment must be reached that goes beyond even a set of values and beliefs. In order to actually behave consistently with one's values and beliefs, it is necessary to believe in one's ability to perform a given behavior. When that confidence is maintained, people will act habitually on that belief without having to keep reminding themselves of it. However, if they cease to believe in their ability, they would behave differently. In other words, they must have a *well-founded* deep belief that what they are doing is right for them *and* the skills and confidence that they can accomplish what they have set out to do.

What parents can do to build abstinence skills in regards to self-efficacy

Verbal Persuasion According to Bandura, verbal persuasion occurs when others express faith in what you are trying to achieve.

Constantly remind your teen that you believe he or she is capable of waiting to have sex until he or she is married. Help your child to have faith in what you are teaching through role play! Express confidence in their abilities and point out role models to them. Talk with your child about sex, always looking for teachable moments. You are building their confidence in you and in themselves! The greater your comfort level the more likely they will mirror your comfort with the subject!

If you are *not* personally comfortable with this subject, or with talking with your child about this subject, you may need to work on increasing your own self-efficacy in regard to verbal persuasion. You can practice talking about abstaining from sex until a lifelong committed relationship such as marriage with a supportive relative or friend, or in front of a mirror, or using a video or audio recorder – just as you might practice an important speech or business negotiation. *Heritage Keepers®* educators are required to not only be familiar with the theories and methodologies of our program, but they also must practice in front of their peers; they are not allowed to teach others until they have mastered the subject and their comfort level with the program. The outcome of their efforts on the students' sexual values, behavioral intention, future orientation and self-efficacy are scored, to provide them with feedback on whether they are achieving the goals of the program.

Parents may need similar time and practice before feeling completely comfortable and confident in presenting this message to their kids. Are you confident you will have a positive influence on your child's sexual values, behavioral intentions, future orientation and self-efficacy? If not, why not? Do you need more practice? That's what this book and the video series are for – practice until you are confident!

Just because someone believes in and/or practices abstinence outside of marriage, that does not necessarily mean they can convince others to do so. You may need to create some neural pathways of your own, as your generation has not had much coaching about setting sexual boundaries. Remember, one talk will probably not work. This is an issue they will be facing all through their teen and young adult years, so understand that you will want to make this something you and your teen talk about often.

Vicarious Experiences According to Bandura, observing successful role models allows for learning through vicarious experiences.

Encourage your child to hang around peers modeling the behaviors you want them to emulate. Seeking out other parents that have similar values provides a way for families to support one another in setting high standards for their children. Creating opportunities for pro-abstinence groups to provide speakers for parent meetings is way to build a coalition of like-minded adults and teens. The National Abstinence Education Association (www.abstinenceassociation.org), Abstinence Works (www.abstinenceworks.com), and the National Abstinence Clearinghouse (www.abstinence.net) provide information about effective abstinence education programs that provide speakers.

When you hear about celebrities endorsing abstinence until marriage, share that with your teen! For example, it was big news that Heisman Trophy winner and NFL quarterback Tim Tebow was willing for the world to know that he had made a commitment to waiting on sex until marriage. There are surveys that reveal the vast majority (70%) of teens 15-17 are not having sex,[143] and that most teens think being a virgin in high school is a good thing: in fact, close to six of ten teens surveyed (58%) said sexual activity for high school-age teens is not acceptable, even if precautions are taken against pregnancy and sexually transmitted diseases. Nearly 70% of younger teens (ages 12-14) said that high school-age teens should not engage in sexual activity. The vast majority of teens surveyed (87%) do not think it is embarrassing for teens to admit they are virgins. Contrary to conventional wisdom, eight of ten teen males surveyed (83%) do not think it is embarrassing for teens to admit they are virgins and most sexually experienced teens (60%) wish they had waited longer to have intercourse.[144,145] A majority of teens say that they want to get married and stay married during their lifetime.[146]

---

[143] Abma J. C., Martinez G. M., & Copen C.E. (2010, June) *Teenagers in the United States: Sexual activity, contraceptive use, and childbearing, National Survey of Family Growth 2006–2008.* National

[144] The National Campaign to Prevent Teen Pregnancy. (2000a, April 27) *The Cautious Generation? Teens tell us about sex, virginity, and "The Talk"* Retrieved February 11, 2011 from http://www.thenationalcampaign.org/resources/pdf/pubs/CautiousGen_FINAL.pdf

[145] Albert, B. (2007, February). *With One Voice 2007 America's Adults and Teens Sound Off About Teen Pregnancy.* Retrieved April 9, 2008 from http://www.thenationalcampaign.org/resources/pdf/pubs/WOV2007_fulltext.pdf

[146] Whitehead, B. D., & Pearson, M. (2006). *Making a Love Connection: Teen Relationships, Pregnancy, and Marriage.* Washington, DC: National Campaign to Prevent Teen and Unplanned Pregnancy. Retrieved April 9, 2008 from http://www.thenationalcampaign.org/resources/pdf/pubs/MALC_FINAL.pdf

Enactive Mastery Experiences According to Bandura, people need to be encouraged to master whatever it takes to succeed.

Remind your child to stick to his or her values and be sure to notice when he or she makes decisions consistent with waiting. These are mastery experiences that should be rewarded so they will continue. Discuss potential setbacks with him or her and be open about ways to overcome setbacks. Be real with them. Don't act as if this is the easiest decision they will ever make. It is not easy. Discuss obstacles and ways to get over or around them.

Encourage them constantly and provide positive feedback. Say things like, "I have noticed how careful you are with your boyfriend. You stay in the family room when you are together, and I appreciate that!" Or, "The respect you are showing for yourself, your girlfriend, and your future by waiting is awesome!"

Other tips Help your teen set sub goals. Each time they achieve a goal it increases their self-efficacy.

Some sub goals could be: I will abstain this week, this month, this year, until I am 18, until I am 21, until I am married – and, I will be faithful within marriage! Remind your teen that sub goals are markers along the way. Help your child stay motivated about abstaining until he or she is in a lifelong committed relationship such as marriage. Maybe offer a reward after each sub goal is reached. Celebrate that your teen, or young adult, is committed to his or her values and goals. Make sure he or she knows that you are proud of him or her. It means a great deal to children to know their parents are proud of them.

Help your child to have a future-oriented mindset rather than a present-oriented mindset. Have them visualize their future and how they will feel about reaching their goals. The Student Workbook has an exercise that helps teens visualize their wedding day and marriage and how it would feel to have been abstinent until that day – or to have recommitted to abstinence. Let them know that if and when they decide to marry, they will have plenty of time to practice having sex with their spouse!

Help them understand that if they choose to have sex, they may form a family, even if that is not what they intended. The child is here, the family is formed, ready or not. A lifetime commitment is essential, which will likely involve the other parent of your teen's child, even if the young parents "break up." And then there are all those other "relatives." These are important factors for your teen to have firmly in his or her mind to consider when someone is trying to convince them that it's *just sex*. Whether they are ready or not, if your teen has a child with someone, he or she will probably need to be involved with that person on some level for the rest of their lives, whether they want to or not. Having sex before marriage – that is, before two people actually make a thoughtful and legal decision to be committed to each other for the rest of their lives – involves responsibilities that are too often over-looked during the moment. Future orientation will be discussed more extensively in Chapter Six.

Heritage Program Shows Them They Have a Choice!

While teaching a *Heritage Keepers® Abstinence Education* class at a high school, I try my best to show the young men that they don't have to take the same road that their fathers, siblings, or close peers may have taken. I had a student who seemed not to care about anything that I was teaching about or discussing. When we would hold group discussions, he would keep eye contact with me, but wouldn't acknowledge any questions that were asked or even comment. Normally I can tell if something I have been saying has penetrated through the tough skin that some of the students try to portray. On the final day, as the class came to an end, I passed out the commitment cards, and the majority of the students were proud of themselves that they had taken the pledge to remain abstinent. I went back to the school about two weeks later to just check up on some of the students, and that same young man that had acted like I wasn't reaching him came up to me. He asked to speak to me outside of the cafeteria. When we went outside, he broke down and the tears started to run down his face. He said, "I felt like I was trapped and had no where to go because my father and brothers all had kids in high school and aren't doing anything positive with their lives." He said while in the class and listening to everything I was saying, he realized that he had a choice, and he didn't have to make the same decisions that they made. That really encouraged me to continuously put forth 100% because it was a reminder that what I am doing is truly a positive thing.

Levels of Intervention

Dr. Stan Weed, an evaluator of sex education programs for more than thirty years, has developed what he calls the *levels of intervention.*[147]

Knowledge alone does not translate into behavior. There must be something deep within the core of a person, their sense of identity, which motivates them to behave in a manner consistent with who they perceive themselves to be.

Someone who is at the bottom of the list of these levels of intervention has a deep understanding of what they believe in; someone at the top of the list of these levels of intervention has more superficial beliefs. Therefore, an effective program (or effective parent) must provide a deep enough influence to truly affect a teen's core, who they are deep within, for them to maintain behavior that protects them over time.

These levels of intervention are not necessarily sequential; someone can value abstinence without ever having been through the awareness process.

[147] Personal communication, 2004

Awareness - A person has been made aware of something, perhaps through an event such as a media spot, the news, a magazine article, an assembly or a pep rally. This is the point when the person says, "Oh, I have heard of that."
Knowledge - The person knows about something to the point that they can be tested on that information. They are not necessarily able to explain and defend what they have knowledge about, but they can regurgitate the information learned.
Understanding - The person knows about something to the point that they can describe and explain it rather than just regurgitating it on a test.
Attitude - The person has a feeling or a sentiment about something. The person has decided if they are for or against something. This can change day to day.
Belief - The person believes in something and has taken a firm position on it, but it still may not be a part of that person's value system.
Value - The person has made this a part of their value system. They more than just believe; they have made this a part of who they are.
Personal Efficacy - The person has made this a part of their life and believes he or she can do it.
Commitment - The person has made a conscious decision about this. They have committed to this either publicly or privately. Those people who commit publicly are more likely to carry through on their decision. It is important that they can voice their commitment to the world.
Practice and Reinforcement - Follow-up on the commitment. This person has personal accountability and/or friends and family that make sure they are following through on their commitment.

What parents can do to build abstinence skills in regards to levels of intervention

Cognitive (Awareness, Knowledge, Understanding) Cognitive goals, which are goals relative to the more intellectual aspects of your teen, can be set to increase his or her awareness of risks of sexual activity outside of marriage and the benefits of waiting. Provide information that expands his or her knowledge about, and understanding of, this subject. Your child should be able to describe what abstinence is and why sexual activity outside of a lifelong committed relationship such as marriage is considered a risky behavior. Can he or she articulate the possible consequences of sex outside of marriage and the benefits of abstaining? Working together on the Student Workbook provides a way to get information to your child, which will help him or her gain knowledge and increase in understanding regarding the ramifications of his or her decisions about sexual activity.

Affective (Attitude, Belief, Value) Affective goals, which are goals relative to your teen's emotions, can be developed to increase his or her positive feelings about gaining the control that abstaining provides. When one feels good about a decision, and incorporates those feelings into his or her belief system about who he or she is, what he or she stands for, and what he or she hopes to become, they are more likely to value a concept. When abstaining from risk is a part of one's sense of identity, he or she will be less likely to allow anyone to violate their boundaries. If one doubts the value of waiting, he or she is less likely to carry through with protecting those standards for their own behavior.

Behavioral (Efficacy, Commitment, Practice and Reinforcement) The deepest levels of intervention are related to personal efficacy, commitment, actual practice and reinforcement/maintenance. One can have information, knowledge, and understanding, and can feel that waiting is wise, and even value abstaining from risk, but not have the capacity to actually defend his or her values, or maintain them. This may be why many teens regret that they became sexually involved. There isn't much in our culture that teaches young people the skills associated with waiting. But, there is ample evidence that many do, and so it is possible. Working through pre contemplation, contemplation, planning, practice and maintenance empowers your teen to develop and maintain protective values. Going through the levels of intervention to the point of actually practicing resistance to risky behaviors provides them with the neural pathways they will need when they are in challenging situations. Helping your teen think through, and feel good about, establishing personal boundaries and goals, and a commitment to their own future establishes their sense of identity, which becomes the core of who they are and what they will or will not do.

Your child should have the skills needed to abstain from sexual activity and the belief that they *can* abstain from sexual activity and will. Consider holding a commitment ceremony of some type to provide your teen with an opportunity to publicly commit to abstinence and to garner the support he or she will likely need to keep that commitment (which will be described more in Chapter Six and Thirteen).

Predictors of Sexual Activity

Earlier in the book we mentioned Dr. Stan Weed and the studies he has conducted on teen sexual activity. Through research, he discovered that when survey questions are structured to reveal how adolescents are thinking regarding their behavioral intentions, sexual values, the influence of their peers, their future, and their self-confidence, their collective answers "predict" the likelihood of them initiating sex.

In the next chapter, we will explain the predictors in depth. If you are following along with the videos, you will get a brief explanation of each of the predictors in the video *How to Create a Behavior Change in Teens* and then more detail in the videos that correspond with the next chapter.

You cannot just work on one aspect of this subject. It is important to think through how to approach this important topic with your child on an ongoing basis. Making this a priority as a parent cannot be over-emphasized; you cannot expect your child to just pick up these concepts on his or her own. Parents are the key to influencing their children across all predictors.

Awareness about STDs and teen pregnancy is not the whole story. Young people are worthy of commitment and the kind of love that has their best interest at heart. This is why you as a parent cannot have just one conversation with your child. This important part of their lives must be incorporated into the relationship you are building together every day. Work at not just increasing levels of awareness, but make this a part of your value system. Make a commitment to establishing high standards at home, because your youngsters are watching you making decisions about their lives. As this becomes an important part of what you are thinking about and doing with your child, you are reinforcing protective values daily.

For more information view the video ***How to Create Behavior Change in Teenagers.*** *(Go back to page 7 for information on how to access the video.)*

THEORIES OF BEHAVIOR CHANGE AND INFLUENCE

What does it mean to have a goal of *changing the behavior causing the problem rather than only trying to minimize the outcomes of the behavior*? How does this concept apply to discussing sexual behavior with your child?

If you have had previous conversations with your child about sex, did you mostly focus on preventing the behavior (promoting abstinence) or preventing the outcomes of the behavior (promoting contraception)?

During this chapter you learned about social learning theory. This theory explains that people learn through observation, imitation and repetition. Keeping this in mind, what attitudes and values are you letting your child observe in regards to sexual activity?

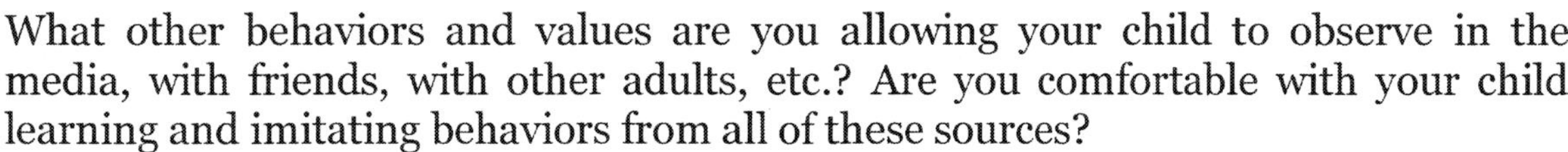

What other behaviors and values are you allowing your child to observe in the media, with friends, with other adults, etc.? Are you comfortable with your child learning and imitating behaviors from all of these sources?

What shows are your children watching on TV? If you don't know – find out and then come back – don't just skip this question.

What music/songs are your children listening to? If you don't know – find out and then come back – don't just skip this question.

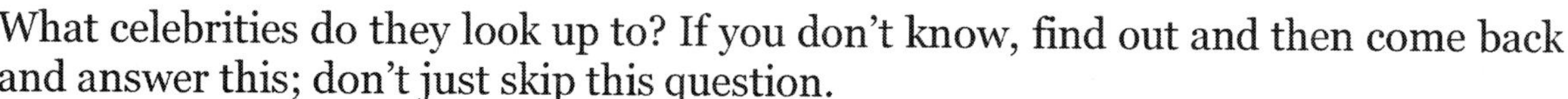

What celebrities do they look up to? If you don't know, find out and then come back and answer this; don't just skip this question.

Do any of these entertainment avenues model an abstinent lifestyle? If not, how can you make sure your child is getting the message to not imitate those people and actions?

In this chapter we pointed out something we naturally know, that people are by nature social and want to fit in. How are you making the decision to abstain from sex easier on your child? (Hint: Working with others in the community, like your friends parents, to make abstinence the norm for teens, is important! This question challenges you to think through what you could do to beyond working directly with you own child in order to raise the behavioral standards for your neighborhood, schools and community.)

How confident are you that you are being clear and repetitive in your message about abstinence? (with 1 being not at all confident and 10 being very confident)

1 2 3 4 5 6 7 8 9 10

What are some ways you can be more repetitive in the abstinence message? What are some other key words/phrases you can use to emphasize the message without always using the word "abstinence"?

How would you classify your child in terms of the different typologies of sexual experience? Circle One

Multiples	those who have had sex more than once and with two or more partners
Steadies	those people who have had sex more than once but with one partner
One-timers	those who have had sex one time
Anticipators	those who have not yet had sex but have high expectations that they will within the next year
Delayers	those who have not had sex and have low expectations that they will in the next year, but plan to some time before marriage
Abstainers	those who have not had sex and do not intend to do so anytime before marriage

How would you classify each of your child's friends in relation to the different typologies of sexual experience? Remember, teens often learn by observing what others are doing, or even their perception of what others or doing.

You also just learned about the transtheoretical model of behavior change that describes how individuals making a change tend to progress over time through a series of stages, rather than change being a one-time event (a model taken from successful smoking cessation programs). What stage do you believe your child is within when it comes to making a decision about abstinence until marriage? Circle one.

Pre-contemplation	At this stage people are not ready to change. They have no intention of changing their behavior in the foreseeable future. Oftentimes they are unaware of the compelling reason for change. They may not be aware of the reasons they should change their behavior.
Contemplation	People in this stage are aware of the negative impact of their unhealthy behavior and are seriously thinking about adopting new, healthy behavior, but have not yet made a commitment to take action. Not only do they know there is a problem, but they now have an idea of how it is negatively affecting their lives.
Preparation	People in this stage intend to take action in the next month yet have unsuccessfully taken action in the past year. Peer pressure continues to be a strong influencer. Often, people may be sure of their intentions but unsure of how to take action because no one has helped them develop the skills to follow through.
Action	People in this stage modify their behavior in order to achieve positive change. They actually make a commitment and change their lives. While they are less likely to give into peer pressure, the change is still short term, and they need to be held accountable to their decisions to change.
Maintenance	People in this stage work to prevent relapse and fortify gains. To help them maintain, they need encouragement to find a positive peer influence group where they are being held accountable and are not tempted to return to the behavior they left. Recent brain research reveals that practicing a new desired behavior over a six month period actually wires the brain to integrate the new behavior throughout the thoughts, feelings and actions.

If your child is not in the maintenance stage of abstaining, what are some specific things you could do to help your child move towards that stage?

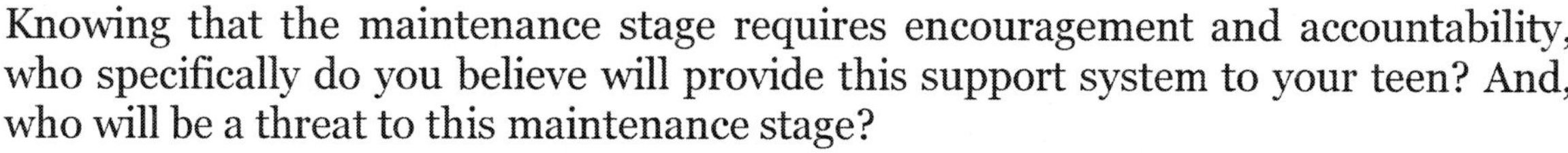

Knowing that the maintenance stage requires encouragement and accountability, who specifically do you believe will provide this support system to your teen? And, who will be a threat to this maintenance stage?

Why is role-play an important parenting tool? Why is role-play so important in helping teen(s) abstain from sexual activity?

How will you teach the SAFE plan to your child?

How will you express faith in your child's ability to abstain?

Which "level of intervention" do you believe your child is at in regards to sexual activity? How can you move him or her to the last stage, practicing abstinence and reinforcing the concept by maintaining abstinence?

Chapter Six: Influencing Predictors of Sexual Activity

"You guys showed me to reach for my goals and dreams and don't give up. You told me to be strong and work hard at what I do, or expect to do in my future. You helped me a lot. Thank you."

Male *Heritage Keepers*® student

"Before I took this class, I thought it was okay to have sex outside of marriage as long as you love the person. I also thought that condoms made sex totally 100% safe. During the program, I realized that you should wait till after marriage to have sex because if you have sex as a teenager, that could ruin some of your goals and stuff you want to do in life. Also, if you have sex outside of marriage, the man can leave you, and you could be raising a child by yourself. You want to wait till marriage because you want to make sure that person will commit themselves to you. I also learned that condoms don't make sex 100% safe. Girls can still get pregnant. I enjoyed the program and learned a lot."

Female *Heritage Keepers*® student

"I'll tell you no lie, this class has made a tremendous change in my life because if I had not taken this class, then my boyfriend could have had it easy, but now since I know and he does also, we both wanna really wait. And as for you, you've been so nice to us and all, and I think that I wanna do what you're doing. So, to tell the truth, you're a perfect role model for me and I'll try to keep in contact."

Female *Heritage Keepers*® student

Through more than twenty years of reviewing surveys of more than 500,000 students across the USA, Central America and Russia, Dr. Stan Weed of the Institute of Research and Evaluation identified concepts that are statistical predictors of whether a young person is likely to abstain or initiate sex.

It is important to understand these predictors and to address them with your child(ren) as you talk to them about sexual activity and their intentions to abstain.

The following predictors of sexual activity are subject to influence. If you are not doing the influencing, you may be assured that someone else – in school, through the media, in the neighborhood – is. The predictors are presented here as questions so that you can determine how your child may "score" on each predictor, revealing their sexual intent.

Abstinence Intentions – What does your child intend to do?

What is the likelihood your child will have sex in the next year? What is the likelihood that your child will have sex before he/she marries?

Behavioral Commitment

Has your child made a commitment to be abstinent outside of marriage?

Abstinence Values

What are your child's sexual values? To what degree do they value abstinence?

- **Affirmation of Abstinence** What is the extent to which your child defines sexual activity for unmarried adolescents as good or bad, right or wrong, important or not important?

- **Rejection of Permissiveness** Does your child reject a permissive attitude regarding sex outside of marriage? To what extent has your child rejected language and activities related to sexual permissiveness?

Justification of Sex

What is the degree to which your child may rationalize or justify their actual or expected behavior using such reasons as being in love, money spent, taking precautions (*safe sex*), etc.?

- **Contraception Justifies Sex** Does your child believe that using contraception justifies having sex with someone?

- **Depth of Relationship** Does your child believe that as a relationship progresses, sex becomes more justifiable?

- **Sex Proves** Does your child believe that having sex with someone proves love, popularity, desirability, maturity, etc.?

- **Love Justifies Sex** Does your child believe that he/she is justified in having sex because he/she loves the person?

Abstinence Efficacy

If your child values abstinence and wants to live accordingly, how confident is he or she in their ability to do what is necessary to successfully abstain? Can the child successfully engage in the instrumental behaviors that will lead to abstinent behavior?

Sexual Independence from Peers/Susceptibility to Peers

How likely is your child to resist pressure from their peers to go against their own standards and beliefs in order to be accepted by their peers? How susceptible is your child to their peers (negative peer pressure)?

Sexual Climate/Individual Opportunity

In your child's school or community, is it the standard to be abstinent or sexually active? Is sexual activity common in the school or community? How much opportunity is there for sexual activity?

Future Impacts of Sex

Does your child believe that he or she has viable and attractive options and opportunities in the future? Does your child believe that sexual activity and its consequences could be a barrier to those future opportunities?

Beliefs about Risks of Sex

Does your child value abstinence as a way to avoid risks?

Peer Group

Does your child hang around with peers who engage in risky behaviors?

My Worth

Does your child agree that he or she has value and worth as a unique person? Does your child believe that he or she should be treated with dignity and respect, rather than treated poorly or being pressured to jeopardize personal values and goals? Does your child demand recognition of his or her own value and worth, rather than allowing it to be compromised?

Love/Lust

Does your child know the differences between love, lust and infatuation – that love gives, lust takes, and infatuation is only temporary?

Sex as a Whole Person

Does your child see sex as more than just a physical experience, rather as a whole person?

Related Risk

Is your child involved in related risky activities (drinking, using drugs, or violence)? Does your child have low self-esteem; is he or she depressed?

Your daily conversations and interactions with your child can have an effect on each of these constructs. The following videos and text provide guidance for addressing each predictor. Dr. Weed's research has shown that adolescents that exhibit positive attributes across all predictors are more likely to abstain than those who do not.

What parents can do to build abstinence skills in regards to the predictors of sexual activity

Behavioral Commitment/Abstinence Intentions

Behavioral Intention is determined by asking individuals how they would behave in various scenarios. What is your child's attitudes and beliefs regarding sexual activity? Ask your child how they would behave in various scenarios like the ones we listed on page 134. This will help you gauge their behavioral intent in regards to sexual activity. Give them specific hypothetical situations that they can respond to.

Abstinence Values

Abstinence Values, which includes Affirmation of Abstinence, has to do with an adolescent's level of regard for the benefits of abstaining versus perceived benefits of having sex right now. Such values are often influenced by parent values and behaviors, as well as the cultural and social norms they experience. Children of parents who clearly value abstinence from sexual activity outside of marriage are more likely to abstain. Practicing the expression of these values with your child enhances their ability to verbalize and actualize their standard.

Teens who have a strong commitment to wait until marriage to initiate sexual activity, are able to state their values, and have practiced what they will say and do in a risky situation are more likely to abstain than those who are not prepared to handle pressure to initiate sex. Help your child move past the idea, "I think I want to be abstinent" to "I know I want to be abstinent."

Addressing Rejection of Permissiveness requires talking about what music they are listening to, what they see on TV, what they are doing on the computer, and what friends might be telling them in regards to sex. Ask your child to be aware of the media's use of sexual messages to sell their products and teach them the difference between the media's make-believe world and their own real lives.

Justification of Sex

Make it clear to your child that the only thing that justifies a sexual relationship is marriage. Love can fade. Contraception does not always work. Friends will likely come and go. A relationship is not solid until vows to be together until death are taken, and even then, the couple must remain committed. Be clear in the message that sex does not prove anything – certainly not love, popularity, or maturity.

Part of the predictor Justification of Sex is the belief that Love Justifies Sex. Does the teen believe they are justified in having sex because they love a person?

If teenagers believes they are in love and sexual intercourse just happens, they are more likely to initiate sex. They are in a much better position if they strongly disagree with this perception, and instead know that sex does not just happen – someone decides, step by step.

Teens who believe that having sex /sexual intercourse should be treated as a part of a dating relationship are more likely to initiate sex. Relationships are not just physical, but are also intellectual, emotional, social and familial. It's your job to make absolutely sure that your child understands this.

Loving someone does not mean you have to have sex with them. Your child should know that he or she does not have to give sex to prove love.

Talk with your son or daughter about what is and is not expected in relationships. Make sure they realize no one has the right to pressure them into sexual activity. Some teens believe that if someone buys them dinner or clothes, or pays for them to get their nails or hair done, they are obligated to have sex with them. Make sure your children understand that they should never allow themselves to be persuaded that they owe anyone sex. Help them understand that they must refuse to be used by another person only for their sexual pleasure.

Make sure your teen understands that while lust takes, love gives.

Abstinence Efficacy

It's imperative that teens have confidence in their ability to manage situations that could put them at risk. Helping them develop strategies and practice responses to use in difficult situations increases their ability to avoid risk through skill building for abstinent behavior. Role play is crucial to the firing and wiring process.

Unfortunately, the message our children often hear is that they aren't able to control their own sexual behavior. But, we know they can. Children tend to live up to the standards set by the adults around them and to the standards expected of them. These are called self-fulfilling prophecies. We want them to believe they can be abstinent. Parents who provide a clear and consistent standard are establishing protective boundaries for their adolescents and helping them know they can maintain abstinent behavior.

Ask teens how sure they are that they could explain their reasons to abstain if a girlfriend or boyfriend pushes them to have sex and how sure they are that they could stop seeing their girlfriend or boyfriend if pressured to have sex. We want them to get to a place where they are absolutely sure they could say no. We ask them questions about their peer environment. Do they hang around with peers that engage in risky behavior? If most of their close friends have had sex and think it is okay for unmarried people to have sexual intercourse, there is a chance they are convincing your child that it's okay as well. This is where you have to know your kids' friends and make sure you are intervening in any negative messages your son or daughter may be receiving. Make sure YOUR message about sex trumps all others and that you have equipped your child to act out the desired behavior through role play.

Sex in School is Not the Rule

A young man told his instructor that his ideas and views were already set and that, in his opinion, "High school is all about sex!" The instructor continued to teach and after completing the *Heritage Keepers*® program, the young man told his instructor, "You have taught me that I am somebody, and I can save sex until marriage. I now believe that the best sex is sex in a healthy marriage, and I plan to start practicing the values I have gained from this class. You have helped me to understand that instead of pre marital sex, my concerns need to be developing good character, respect, manners and self-control."

This young man, like so many of his peers, had the same risky mindset that sex in school is the rule. Often times, because this way of thinking is not challenged, it can lead to unwanted pregnancies, sexually transmitted diseases and emotional baggage that can last a lifetime.

Susceptibility to Peers

How susceptible is your child to his or her peers? If teens say that other kids talk them into doing things they know they shouldn't do, that's a clear indication that they need help with building skills for establishing and defending personal boundaries. Practice skill building by role playing situations with your child(ren) at home. If your child finds it difficult to make his or her own decisions in the face of pressure from close friends, your guidance and support is needed to help him or her stick with personal values. If they feel they may give in to things that they don't really want to do so their friends will think they are "cool," they may need help in finding supportive groups that value abstinence.

Sexual Independence from Peers

Find out whether your child feels pressured by his or her peers to initiate sexual activity. How sure are they that they can refute negative peer pressure? If you see that your child is constantly hanging out with a crowd involved in drugs, alcohol and sex, be especially attentive to this situation. Teach your child that it's important to do what is best for them, even if they lose some friends. It's not worth going against your own standards in order to be accepted. And certainly they should say "no" if they are being pressured to have sex. Let them know you are there to back them up and support them. As well, they must understand that they must refuse to be used by another person only for their sexual pleasure.

Neither parents nor teens are able to ensure a state of no influence. Human beings are social beings, and pressure is present wherever people are. One of the greatest decisions a teen can make is to choose to surround themselves with peers who uphold the same high standards you expect of your child. In fact, the positive pressure peers can put on each other to uphold high standards can be a significant support system for helping your child resist negative peer pressure!

There's an exercise that helps kids understand the power of peer pressure. One child stands on a chair trying to pull others up – and then the others try to pull the child down. You can imagine that it is much easier for the crowd to pull the child down than it is for him to pull the crowd up. What is it that determines whether the pressure your teen encounters is good or bad peer pressure? It's almost too simple – the peers! Parents can affect this by seeking out support systems that have similar values as your family's. This is critical for developing teen minds that are in need of sound guidance.

One of the most powerful things a parent can do for their child is to be aware of their social life. Be in the know. Knowing your child's friends and their values, knowing the parents and their values, having contact information at all times, and keeping the lines of communication flowing freely, is crucial to avoiding possible disasters in your child's life. Make an effort to know the people, places, and activities that happen within the group. The parent is responsible to speak and set boundaries for the teen if they fear that their teen's peer group is a source of negative influence.

Parents owe it to their children to help them avoid relationships that can be harmful to the child. Among all the challenges teens face in today's world, the importance of a strong support group can hardly be stressed enough. A parent's role in facilitating this is critical.

Helping your teen connect how their activities today will affect their tomorrows is one of the most important roles parents play. Teach them that instant gratification can get them into situations they may regret. This helps them develop the self-control necessary for reaching goals that they agree are important to their success. Having friends that support their values and holding them accountable for their actions will enable them to think and act independently from peers that may not practice the same values. When you take the time to search out and find supportive groups that have the same values you hold high can turn the potential for negative peer pressure into an opportunity for positive support.

Sexual Climate/Individual Opportunity

If the environment your child lives in is made up of young people who are sexually active, your child will be more likely to face pressure and opportunities to have sex. Recognize the difficulties related to the decision to be abstinent. Talk to your child about his or her struggles. Reward your child for good behavior. Your child does not live in a cultural bubble – remember that and help them through this!

Student Inspired to Persuade

Shortly after I taught *Heritage Keepers®*, the students had to write a persuasive essay for an English teacher who is also a friend of mine. A student whom I had taught wrote his essay on abstinence. In this paper, he attempted to persuade his peers to stay abstinent because, as he says, "it is wise and intelligent planning for one's future." I was not able to obtain a copy of the essay, but his teacher told me that he made a very good case. She mentioned a few parts of it that are in the Heritage curricula. She mentioned that he spoke about future orientation, saying that he would like to take control of his future and make a commitment to abstinence so that he is able to be more focused on where he is headed with his life. She also said that he talked about peer independence, when he said things like, "I am an individual and I am not worried about what my friends may or may not be doing with their girlfriends" (loosely quoted). It was a privilege to realize that the students I taught were integrating the lessons into their other subjects.

Future Impacts of Sex/Future Orientation

Does your child see a bright enough future ahead of them to not let anything get in the way? It's important for parents to talk with their children about their future goals and how the possible consequences of sexual activity could affect them. They need to know that the decisions they make today could affect their tomorrows. Make sure that you incorporate your child's values and goals. On page 94 we introduced you to the "values and goals" activity, which will require your child to truthfully examine who and what they value in their lives and to honestly consider the goals they set for their future.

A reflection on these things can be challenging, for teens and adults alike! If we were to stop and ask ourselves, "What do I value in my life" what would our answers be? As adults, another way of asking, "What do I value in my life?" is

"Where do I spend my time, energy, and money?" For some, this is a difficult question to face. While most adults would like to say, "I value my home and family," for many adults, the time and energy question reveals otherwise. Shopping. Possessions. Entertainment. Sometimes, these get in the way. The best thing a parent can do to help their teen realize their values is to honestly realize their own. First of all, your values are ones your teen is most likely to adopt. Second, the teen must hear by your words and see through your life that they themselves are highly valued by you, the parent. Actions, after all, speak louder than words.

Imagine that you are a teen. How would you answer "What do I value in life?" What do you think teens value the most? It might surprise you, but it's not music, celebrities, or their smart phones. Many of our teachers report, and research agrees, that *parents*, especially *Mom*, is the top answer.

When teens state their values, they are better equipped to make decisions according to those values. Helping them do this is relatively easy! If one says they value their Mom, what does it say if they treat her with disrespect? Does your teen like playing sports? How would getting pregnant effect that aspect of life? If something is of value to you, you cherish, protect, and even make sacrifices for it. Its worth is greater than the sacrifice. Put another way, you don't put at risk something you value. As you talk with your teen about what they value, help them to recognize the loss that could result from putting those things at risk.

When it comes to making sexual decisions, you as a parent can help your teen by encouraging them to value three key things. Number one is themselves. If they value themselves they will want the best for themselves. If a teen values him or herself, they know they deserve the best and will not allow themselves to be treated poorly in a relationship. They will not keep company with people who would encourage them to harm themselves. They will not tolerate negative pressure, sexual or otherwise. They will hold out for someone who wants the best for them. They will seek a relationship that recognizes their value and treats them accordingly.

Number two is their spouse. Teach them now to be thinking ahead about what their present behavior says about how they value that future relationship. How can they respect their future spouse now? Not by contracting an STD and passing it on in that future relationship. Not by accumulating emotional baggage. It is a statement of value to consider a person worthy of being the one and only. A person who values their future spouse recognizes that they are well worth the wait.

Last, you can teach your teen to value their future children in advance. How can a teen behave in a way that values the children they may have in the not-too-distant future? By keeping themselves healthy, not by becoming infertile from STD complications, and certainly not by passing an STD from mother to child. When young people fully understand the power of forming their families within the legal and ethical commitment of marriage, they give their future child a statistical advantage from the start. When a mother and father are committed to one another, and to raising their child together, the child is more likely to feel secure.

Not only is it important to help your teen state his or her values, it is equally important to help them state goals that align with their values. If values are your teen's compass, then goals are their destination. If a teen has never considered their goals, they are largely without direction. Helping your teen develop and reach their goals is the skill that lies at the heart of Future Orientation. Without a destination, a teen is ill-equipped to determine whether a given decision will take them in the right or wrong direction!

As a parent you can help them develop and navigate to their goals. A teen may decide, for instance, that they want to purchase a car. You might, in turn, offer to match the money your teen saves for the car. This makes saving money pay off, and makes failure to save even more costly. With that specific goal in mind, your teen is better equipped to decide whether it would be a good decision to buy that shirt he or she doesn't really need. It is crucial today that parents teach their children to "delay gratification."

In today's world this is more urgent than ever. To the corporate media your teen is primarily a consumer, and your teen is bombarded at every turn with slogans, music and images designed to erode their self-control. Those who live life controlled by their impulses buy a lot of stuff and build a lot of debt. It's difficult for them to reach their goals. When it comes to goal-setting, parents must take every opportunity to teach delayed gratification. The decisions they make today will either take them towards, or away from, their goals.

Delayed gratification is what makes abstinence possible, but may be less likely if no goals are in sight. Sexual decisions can profoundly affect the future of your teen. If your teen desires to go to college, help him or her consider how sexual activity and its consequences could effect this important goal.

Young people who have children while in middle or high school are statistically less likely to graduate. Would choosing to become sexually active take them towards or away from their goals? As a parent, you know better than anyone what your child's goals are, and you as a parent can help hold them accountable to a standard that will help them succeed. Be in constant communication with them about the future consequences of the present decisions they face.

Beliefs about Risks of Sex

Your child should understand and believe that abstinence from sexual activity is the only certain way to avoid STDs, premature parenthood, and emotional baggage. Again, knowledge will not change your child's behavior alone, but with all of the other predictors, it is an important part of the whole package.

Peer Group

Do you know your child's friends? Do you know if they are sexually active or participating in any other risky behaviors? Find out whether your child feels pressured by his or her peers to initiate sexual activity. How sure are they that they can refute negative peer pressure? If you see that your child is constantly hanging out with a crowd involved in drugs, alcohol and sex, be especially attentive to this situation. Teach your child(ren) that it's important to do what is best for them, even if they lose some friends. Help them understand that it's not worth going against their own standards in order to be accepted; they should certainly be ready to say "no" if they are being pressured to have sex. Let them know you are there to back them up and support them. As well, they must understand that they must refuse to be used by another person only for their sexual pleasure. Make sure they will call you, not someone else, if they are in a dangerous situation. They need to know that if they do have a problem that feels beyond their ability to cope with, you want to know and that they can trust you to come to the rescue.

My Worth

Does your child agree that he or she has value and worth? At home you are the major source for instilling self-worth. It is how you communicate with your child that solidifies this understanding. They must understand that they are worth your love. Don't shut them up by buying them things, thinking that this is a replacement for love and respect. This gives the wrong message because it shows them that their value is what they have and not who they are. Teach your child that they deserve the very best. They deserve someone who respects them; they are worth the wait. Do they believe they have a lot more to offer than just their body, that they are worth waiting for? Are they communicating their self-worth with their clothing, or are they communicating that they are only worth what you can see? Are they convinced that they have great value as an individual? Many young people settle for someone less than what they really want out of fear that no one will love them. Tell them that they deserve the best, not a girl or guy who treats them wrong.

As parents, it is critical that we, above all others, believe that our kids are worth the very best, and that they can achieve their goals in life no matter how challenging. If you believe it, they will, too. What is your child worth to you? If you say, "Everything," that means we can ask some challenging questions. What are you willing to do to promote their self-worth and what are you not willing to do? Are you willing to sacrifice for your child? Are you willing, for example, to turn off the television and interact with him or her? Or to stop reading magazines that you know do not model the kind of lifestyle you want for your child?

Could you come home from work earlier, maybe even work less hours, so you can monitor your teen's activities? We've spent a good deal of time in this series making the case that there is an enormous need for parental guidance during the adolescent years – as much or more than during their toddler years. What will you do to change your own behavior to meet that need?

Remember that the adolescent brain is undergoing major changes and that much of their mind is controlled by the emotional part of their brains. During this period there are windows of sensitivity – times when the hurts, fears, angers and confusions that accompany these years of rapid change can have a serious impact on their self-worth and self-efficacy for years to come.

When you are not around, someone or something will be providing direction for your child, which very well may not be in his or her best interest. Never forget that those who are eager to market their ideas and products to your child are almost always driven by a profit motive rather than what is best for him or her, and that they almost always use sexual images to get their attention. The norms they are selling hardly ever point out the emotional, physical, intellectual and familial risks of sexual activity outside of marriage.

The importance of one-on-one conversations and the building of family rapport in the maturation of our children, from the toddler years through adolescence, means our values and the way we spend our time and energy must be integrated.

It is essential to set up boundaries that communicate to your child that you consider them worthy of your protection, care and monitoring. Taking time to enforce these boundaries assures your child that he or she is genuinely loved. We're putting a lot on your shoulders because we want you to shape your teen into what they're becoming rather than someone else that doesn't truly value him or her. In order for them to believe they truly have great worth with others they must first know without doubt that they are of great worth to you. Your actions help convince them that they deserve the very best.

When low self-esteem begins to defeat a young person's confidence in who they are and what they might become, their ability to take on the world is diminished. But when Mom and Dad care enough to watch over them, putting aside those unhealthy habits that compromise the values we are trying to instill, the message that they have worth and can accomplish what they set out to do becomes a part of who they are as they enter into the opportunities and responsibilities of the adult world. It makes us – the adults, and them – the teens, better people!

When it comes to your child's education about sex, what do you believe he or she deserves to hear? Many reports on sex education have shown the content of well-known and widely used comprehensive sex education programs to be shocking. Find out exactly who is teaching your adolescent about sex, what they believe, and what they are saying. Insist on looking at everything they present, and hold them accountable for what they teach your child. You may want to consider taking them out of the program if the teacher's values are not consistent with the boundaries you have established for your family and your child, who is particularly vulnerable to direction as the brain undergoes tremendous change during those years of maturation.

If the message being pitched to your child offers *safe sex*, give careful thought to what that message is conveying to your son or daughter about their self-worth. If they are teaching your child that their worth is in stimulating their genitals, consider whether that is truly the value you place on your child. Do you truly want another adult teaching him or her a message that fails to help your son or daughter fully understand that they have great worth as a whole person? Help your child understand he or she is worthy of the lifetime commitment of marriage, not a temporary uncommitted relationship protected only by a condom.

Your child should understand worth is so much deeper than our bodies and what they can offer, worth comes from who we are deep inside. Be sure to praise your child when they exhibit character traits – this helps them recognize their internal worth. If he or she practices patience, understanding, faithfulness, cleanliness, respect, flexibility, self-control – or any of the many qualities you have hoped to develop in them, notice them and comment.

Don't reserve praise for only good grades or sports achievements. Instead, be quick to encourage those traits you want wired into their developing brains, reinforcing clearly the traits you expect in them. Praising for good character traits has a more lasting effect on confidence than praising for accomplishments. "Great job" is not the same as saying, for example, "Son, I noticed how you handled yourself when your coach criticized you in front of the other guys. I was really proud that you didn't get angry, and I want you to know that I see you using the self-control that will make you a good leader. I'm proud of you, and so is your Mom." Those thoughtful words go much deeper, and have more meaning, than "great job."

It isn't bad to praise for accomplishments, but add into it character traits, and you begin to help your son or daughter recognize what is important to you in life and the kind of person you expect them to become. You might tell your daughter, "You've shown amazing persistence in your practice every day. I'm so impressed that you've stuck with this. I've noticed that even when it isn't going exactly how you'd like it to go, you're resilient – you keep coming back. That's exactly what makes me proud; you're really the kind of daughter that I have always wanted, and I want you to know how much I value the strong character you've been displaying lately." Simple statements like these may last a lifetime, while harsh words of criticism can hurt in the exact same way a physical blow does to the body.

When you tell your son or daughter they "can do" and that you are there to support them, their self-efficacy begins to soar. When you emphasize that you see how their behavior today is building the character they will need to succeed in the future, they begin to understand that what they do today has a lot to do with who they will become tomorrow, that he or she is "going places."

Helping them realize that you value reliability prepares them to carry the opportunities and responsibilities of the adult world capably, with the kind of character you expect of them. Don't allow others to sell them short and tell them they are not capable of self-control; instead, help them stand strong and proud for who they are and to become the caring and responsible leaders you know they can be.

Try listing the characteristics you want your teen to demonstrate when he or she is 25 years old. If you have trouble thinking of descriptive words, consider buying materials that describe good character. A wealth of resources are available! Take the list you create and talk about it with the other parent and come into agreement – if possible, work on it together! It is crucial to understand that kids only develop those desirable traits by seeing them modeled, having them taught, and having the necessary structure, guidance, involvement, discipline, and love that makes them real. Remember how the brain works! The firing and wiring you want to take place will become hardwired into your child's mind only with daily practice.

Make a list for yourself as well, and challenge yourself to be accountable to your husband or wife, or a close caring friend, for working on the character traits you value. By writing these down, you are not only improving yourself, but you are providing a model for your child to follow. If you want your child to exhibit these traits, it must start with you so they can learn from you daily. No school or program can take the place of a child's parent. You have to help fill in for the adolescent's prefrontal cortex while their brain is maturing!

In the Heritage program, we do exercises called *A Real Man* and *A Real Woman*. What does it mean to be a real man or a real woman? Before you read any further, take a minute to think about what you believe makes a real man or woman.

Remember your children are watching and learning from your example. Adolescence is a social learning period and kids tend to mimic your example of what it means to be a woman or man. It's not so much what you say as what you do.

We say that manhood is not measured by what you have; having a girlfriend doesn't make you a man; having a car does not make you a man; having money doesn't make you a man. Being the best athlete doesn't make you a man.

A woman's worth is not how pretty she is or the shape of her body. Her worth is not based on her clothing or her jewelry, or her boyfriend or boyfriends. It's not based on her ability to cook or clean. It's not in how popular she is. Womanhood is not based upon popularity.

So, what is a real man and a real woman? From our perspective, they are strong and courageous. They have a clear understanding of who they are inside; and they master their minds, actions and emotions to reflect a consistent message. They know who they are and live accordingly. They have a strong sense of self.

A real man and a real woman are respectful; they treat all people with respect and treat those in authority with respect. Real men and women have a good work ethic; they give their best to whatever they are doing, whether it is on the sports field, at work, or in relationships. A real man or woman doesn't cheat to get ahead; they work with honesty and integrity.

Real men and women care about others; they do not hurt people or allow them to be hurt when it is within their power to help.

Love/Lust

Does your child know the difference between love, lust, and infatuation? Lust and infatuation are not the same as committed love. We will spend time in this series talking about commitment, so you'll know how to talk to your child at home about the critical differences between love, lust and infatuation.

Sex as a Whole Person

Much of the media leads to the conclusion that sex is simply a physical act. Much of the conversation centers on the physical repercussions - getting an STD or pregnancy. For too long, the concern has been that teens who are sexually active are only concerned about the physical pleasures of sex, but sex is about so much more than worrying about diseases, concern about untimely pregnancy, and sexual pleasure. Sex has emotional and intellectual implications because we are whole persons, not just sexual objects. Unless parents help young people understand these dimensions of sex, they have only the media to teach them these complex concepts.

Related Risk

Is your child involved in related risky activities (drinking, using drugs, or violence)? Does your child have low self-esteem, is he or she depressed?

If your child attends parties where there is drinking or drugs, they are at risk for losing control over their situation. It is crucial to help young people understand that drugs and alcohol actually decrease self-control and can lead to compromising personal values. Encourage your child to avoid situations which may make them vulnerable to having sex. Many young people initiate sex while under the influence of drugs or alcohol and then have serious regrets, sometimes lifelong. None of us want that for our children.

For more information, view the videos:
How to Create Behavior Change in Teenagers
My Worth and Personal Efficacy
Future Orientation and Peer Independence
(Go back to page 7 for information on how to access the video.)

A Young Girl's Plea

While teaching a *Heritage Keepers® Abstinence Education* class, the teacher noticed a young lady who was very quiet, and she seemed a little "distant." Periodically throughout the class, the teacher would call on her to see if she was paying attention. Surprisingly, she would have the right answer, but she was meek in her responses. By the third day of teaching, she seemed to be a little more receptive, and she was volunteering to answer questions on her own.

On the last day of teaching, that young lady pulled the teacher aside and told her, "Thank you for coming out here and talking to us. You helped me to realize that I am worth so much more than I thought I was." More importantly, she informed the teacher that she will now be held accountable for her actions, and she is going to make her boyfriend respect her wishes in wanting to recommit to abstinence.

Young Man Changes Mind

After teaching the first week of the *Heritage Keepers® Abstinence Education* program, a young man approached his teacher the next Monday morning and said, "I could have had sex this weekend, but I remembered what you said in class and I chose not to."

There is no doubt that the information that is being taught concerning sexual abstinence is making a positive impact on teenagers. Most of the students do not realize the consequences of sex outside of marriage until they attend the classes.

INFLUENCING PREDICTORS OF SEXUAL ACTIVITY

As you have just learned, there are predictors of sexual activity. What do you plan to do as a parent to influence these predictors? We will discuss these predictors in the next few pages.

> ***Behavioral Intention*** – *Those teens who intend to abstain are more likely to do so, especially if they have made a commitment to do so.*

Doesn't it make sense that teens that intend to abstain are more likely to do so than those that intend to initiate sex? What are some ways you will encourage your child to commit to abstinence (or recommit)?

How will you move your child(ren) from the mindset of "I think I want to be abstinent," to "I will be abstinent."?

How will you help your child maintain that commitment?

What are some role play situations you will do with your children to ensure they have the skills to keep that commitment?

***Sexual Values** – Those teenagers who value abstinence are more likely to abstain. Have you told your teen the benefits of abstaining?*

Do you know for certain what your teen's sexual values are? To what degree does your teen value abstinence?

One way to determine your teen's sexual values is to ask whether or not he/she is in agreement or disagreement with the following statements:

- It is important to me to wait until marriage before having sex.
- I think it would be wrong for me to have sex while I am unmarried.
- It is against my values to have sex while I am unmarried.
- I have a strong commitment to wait until marriage before having sex.

Write down what you believe your teen's sexual values are. Then, interview your teen to determine if your assumptions are correct.

Reflect on whether your family's values on sex encourage early sexual activity or abstinence. If you are unclear what your family has been communicating about sex, ask your teen to reflect and describe the family values that have been communicated.

How will you ensure that the healthiest sexual values are communicated to your child from this day forward?

Self-Worth – *Those teens who believe they are worth waiting for are more likely to abstain. How are you encouraging your teen to feel worthy?*

Reflect on the following questions about your teen:

- Does your teen believe that he or she has value and worth as a unique person?
- Does your teen believe that he or she should be treated with dignity and respect, rather than treated poorly or being pressured to jeopardize personal values and goals?
- Does your teen demand recognition of his or her own value and worth, rather than allowing it to be compromised?

If you answered "no" or "I don't know" to any of the above questions, what are some specific ways that you could increase your teen's self-worth?

Sex As a Whole Person *– Those teens who understand that sex is not just physical – that it also affects you mentally, emotionally and spiritually – are more likely to abstain.*

Does your teen believe that sex is more than just a physical experience? How can you negate the concept of the hook-up culture that believes sex is purely just a physical act with no emotional consequences?

Have you talked to your child about the physical, emotional, psychological and spiritual aspects and impacts of sex?

What are some things you could say to your teen to encourage their understanding of sex as a whole person (emphasizing the physical, emotional, psychological, and spiritual aspects)?

Self-Efficacy – *Those teens who are confident in their ability to abstain are more likely to do so.*

Reflect on your own attitudes about whether or not you believe your teen can actually abstain from sex until marriage. Have you always communicated a belief in your teen's self-efficacy or have you undermined it in any way? Then, interview your teen to determine if he/she has an opinion about whether or not you have always communicated a belief in his/her ability to abstain.

What are some specific things you could say and do to help your teen feel more confident in his/her ability to abstain?

Love Justifies Sex – *Those teens who believe that love is a valid reason for having sex are more likely to do so.*

Why is it dangerous for young people who think they are in love to act on that feeling? Have you talked to your teen about *feeling in love* not being a good enough reason to have sex outside of marriage? How can you portray to your teen that having sex will not give proof to a partner that love exists?

Teens may give other justifications for sex outside of marriage (such as "using contraception justifies sex," "relationship progression justifies sex," "love justifies sex," "sex proves worth," etc.). One way to determine if your teen has justifications for sex outside of marriage is to ask whether or not he/she is in agreement or disagreement with the following statements:

- I think it is ok for unmarried teens to have sex as long as they use condoms.
- I think it is ok for unmarried teens to have sex as long as they use some form of birth control.
- As a relationship progresses to be more serious, it is ok for unmarried teens to have sex.
- It is ok to have sex if two people just want to hook up.
- Having sex proves that I am mature. Having sex proves that I am desirable and wanted by others.
- It is alright for teenagers to have sex before marriage if they are in love.
- Having sex is the best way to show your partner that you really care about him/her.
- Having sex should be treated as a normal and expected part of teen dating relationships.
- If I am in love and sex "just happens," I don't see that as a problem.

If your teen agrees with any of the above statements/justifications how will you address and change those beliefs? Write rebuttals to each of the justifications mentioned above, plus any other rebuttals to any other additional justifications that you determine.

Peer Environment *– If a young person's friends are sexually involved, it is more likely that he or she will become so, too.*

Are you aware of what your teen's friends are doing? What are some ways you could increase your awareness?

Is sexual activity outside of marriage common among your teen's peers, family members, or in your community? Is your answer based on perception or actual knowledge?

If your teen's friends are sexually active, how likely is your teen to resist pressure from peers to go against personal standards in order to be accepted by the peers? What are some ways you could ensure your teen is independent from peers? How can you guide your teen's behavior to not give into negative peer pressure that compromises personal standards?

Does your teen have access to friends that can provide positive peer pressure and accountability? If yes, how are you encouraging your teen to build and maintain those healthy relationships with positive peers? If no, how will you help your teen reduce their negative peer influencers and build relationships with a positive peer group?

Future Orientation *– Those teens who believe they have a bright future are more likely to not have sex.*

Does your teen tend to be more present-oriented or future-oriented? Provide an example from your teen's life that led you to your conclusion.

Does your teen believe that he or she has viable and attractive options and opportunities in the future and that sexual activity and its consequences could be a barrier to those future opportunities? Reflect on how you as a parent have or have not encouraged your teen to consider a bright future full of endless opportunities.

What are some goals your teen has set for the future? How confident are you that your teen understands that sexual activity and its possible consequences could be a barrier to those goals for his or her future? If you are not positive that your teen can internalize and verbalize how decisions now could affect the future, describe practical ways to increase your teen's "future orientation."

What are the top five people you value? How would they be affected if your child gets a sexually transmitted disease, such as HIV? How would each be affected if your child begins his or her family outside of marriage, as a single parent? What are the top five things you value? How would these be affected if your child suffers emotional damage from a failed relationship that became too physical too early?

If you were to ask your kids who and what they think you value, what do you think their answers would reveal about where you spend the most time, energy, and money? Would their answers line up with the answers you gave in the previous question?

Knowing that teens typically tend to adopt the values that they see modeled to them, reflect on whether you have modeled the values that you want for them to have or whether you have modeled valuing something that you do not want them to value.

On page 95, we asked you to think about what you believe your teen values. What were some of the people and things you mentioned that you thought your teen values? Name at least five of each.

After your child fills out the values and goals section of the student manual, at the end of this book, review those answers with them. Are they different from what you answered above? In what way?

YES NO

What are three things you can do to help your teen live up to their values, or raise the standard of their values to meet a higher expectation?

When teens state their values, they are better equipped to make decisions according to those values. Once you know their values, you can help them realize that a person or thing of value is meant to be cherished and protected. How are you helping your teens realize that they should not jeopardize someone or something that is of high value to them?

Teens that value themselves will not allow themselves to be treated poorly in a relationship; will not keep company with people who would encourage them to harm themselves; will not tolerate negative pressure, sexual or otherwise; will hold out for someone who wants the best for them; and, will seek a relationship that recognizes their value and treats them accordingly. How can you make sure your teen values himself/herself and will not allow anyone to compromise or take advantage of them? What are three things you will do on a weekly basis to help him or her value himself or herself? To help them value their future spouse? To help them value their future family?

Teens should also be encouraged to value their future spouse. They can be thinking ahead about what their present behavior says about how they value that future relationship. How can you teach your child to value and respect a future spouse now?

Teens can also be encouraged to value any future children they may have. How can a teen behave in a way that values the children they may have in the not-too-distant future? How can you teach your child to value any future children now?

Not only is it important to help your teen state his or her values, it is equally important to help them state goals that align with their values. If values are your teen's compass, then goals are the destination. If a teen has never considered their goals, they are largely without direction. Helping your teen develop and reach their goals is the skill that lies at the heart of Future Orientation. Without a destination, a teen is not equipped to determine whether a given decision will take them in the right or wrong direction.

In Chapter Three we asked you what your child's goals are. What are four things you will do to help your teen achieve the goals that he or she has set?

What are three things you can do weekly to teach your child the important skill of delayed gratification?

After you have had conversations with your child about personal values and goals, you will need to discuss how sex now might negatively affect those values and goals. In order to be prepared for that discussion, write what you plan to say as it relates to the specific values and goals that your teen has set.

How confident are you that your child can reject negative peer pressure that could jeopardize the values and goals that he/she has set?

The positive pressure peers can put on each other to uphold high standards can be a significant support system for helping your child resist negative peer pressure. Who in your child's life is providing positive peer influence to your child? How can you encourage those friendships to grow and be maintained?

What do you know about the teens your child hangs out with? Do you know your child's friends and their values? Do you know their parents and their values? Do you have contact information for the friends and the parents? Do you know the people, places, and activities that happen within the group?

What does *self-worth* mean?

What does having *self-efficacy* mean? This is one of the most significant predictors of initiation of sex. If you have any doubts that you fully understand this concept, read about it again prior to answering. It has to do with confidence, mostly based upon a solid foundation of skills that enable one to accomplish what they set out to do. Expound upon that idea here, and include what it means in regards to your child and his or her ideas about initiating sex outside of a lifelong, legal and ethical commitment, such as marriage.

What are three things you can do to build your teen's confidence and personal efficacy? Think of three things that can help their belief that "I can" accomplish something that seems impossible.

What do you do, and what will you do, daily to show your teen that he or she is of great worth to you?

What other ways can you promote your teen's self-worth?

It is important for you to help your child set boundaries in regards to sexual activity and also important for you to explain to them **why** you are putting these boundaries in place – communicate to your child that you consider them to have great worth, worthy of your protection, care and monitoring and that you believe he or she is worth more than the consequences they might endure if they cross these boundaries. Talk to your teen about boundaries. A simple way to begin a conversation about boundaries is to start with the following questions:

> *What are boundaries on a map? What boundaries do states and countries need? Why? What boundaries do pets or farm animals need? Why? So, do people need boundaries? What would happen if they did not have boundaries? Why?*

We asked you to list some boundaries earlier for your teen in Chapter Three. Write those boundaries again here and explain why you have set those particular boundaries. Incorporate the predictors of sexual activity into your explanations. For example, you can integrate the predictor Peer Influence into this discussion. How able are they to stay within their boundaries is a peer is pressuring them to compromise their values? What will they say and do, exactly, to that peer? You can integrate the predictor Future Orientation. How will they actions now affect their future plans? What are their sexual values, what is important to them about relationships? Have they acted in a way that makes it clear they are Rejecting Permissiveness. Hope you are getting the idea of how to integrate predictors into your discussions. The more solid your teen is on these measurements of how your teen things and acts, the more likely he or she will abstain from risky behaviors.

Boundaries regarding **Alcohol**

Explanation for why you have set these boundaries for alcohol. Integrate predictors.

Boundaries regarding **Drugs**

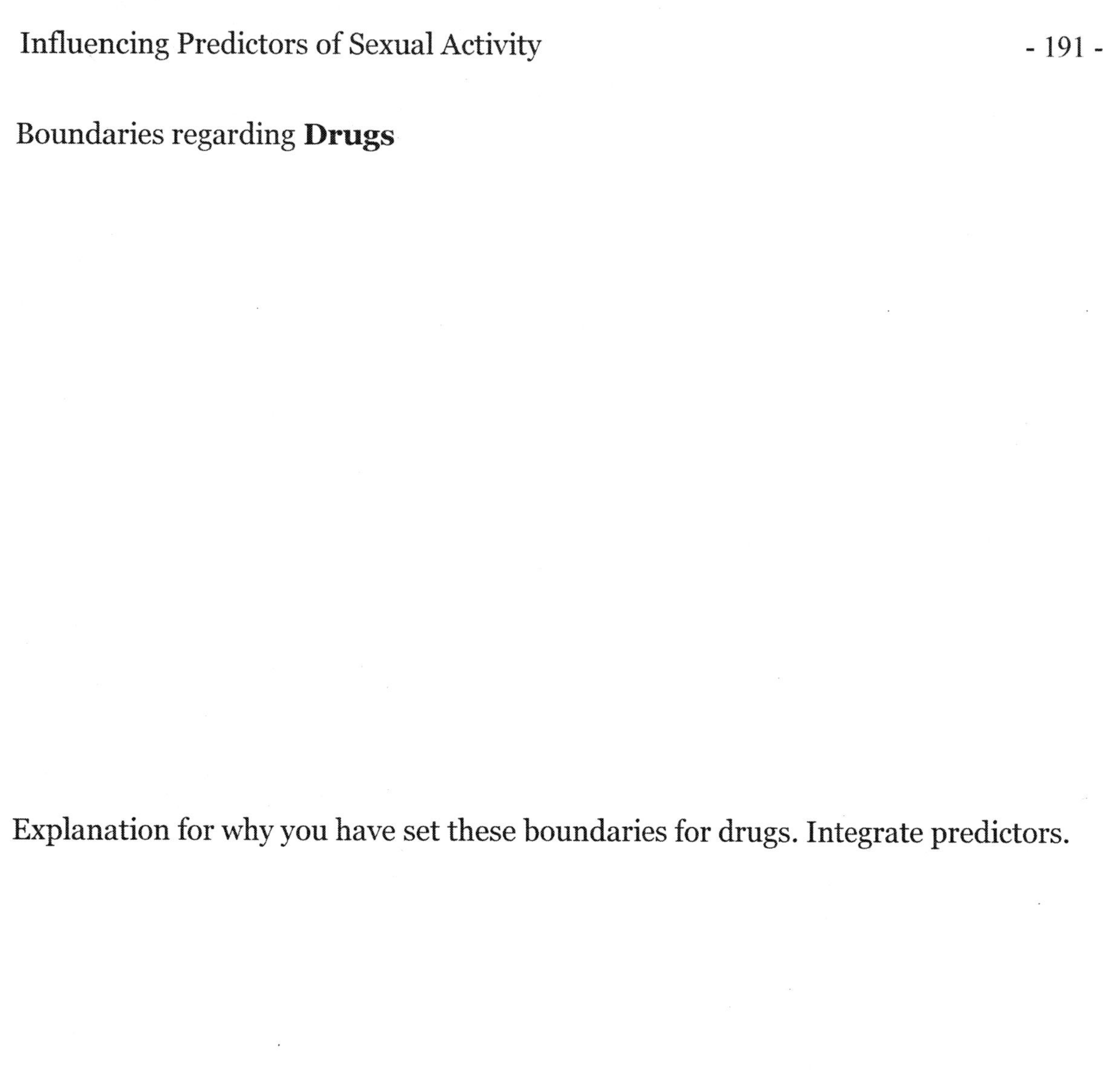

Explanation for why you have set these boundaries for drugs. Integrate predictors.

Boundaries regarding **Smoking**

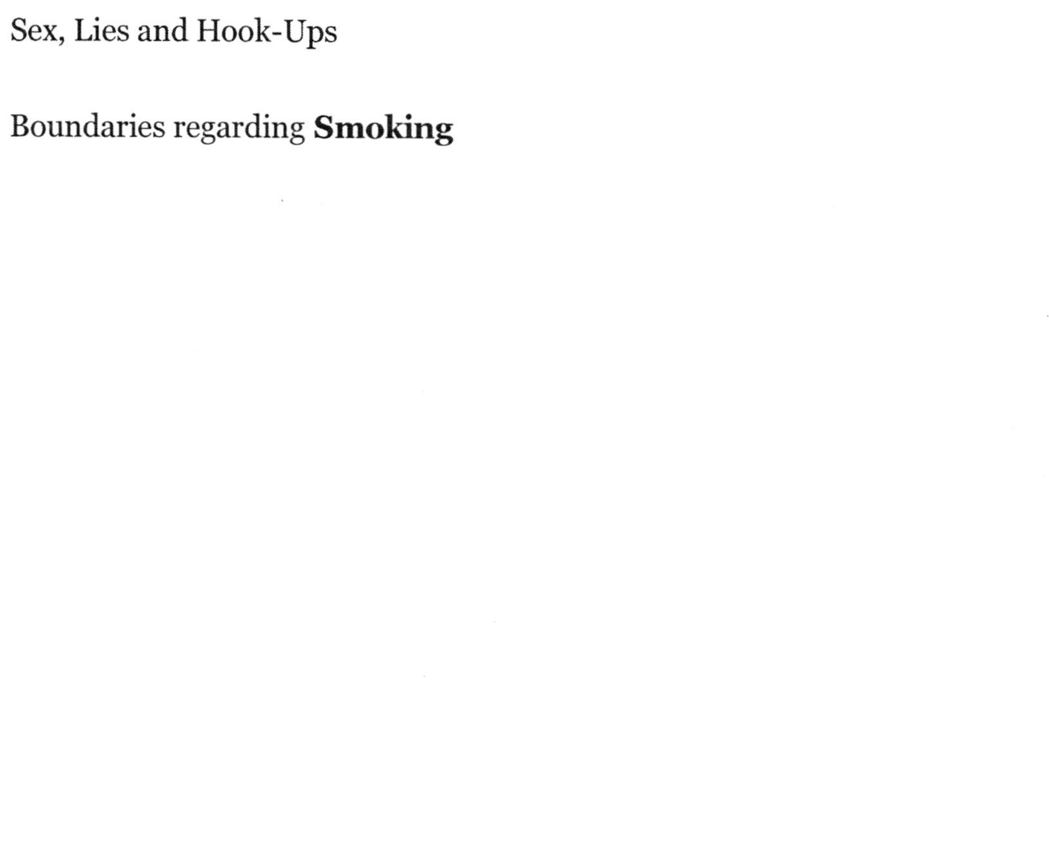

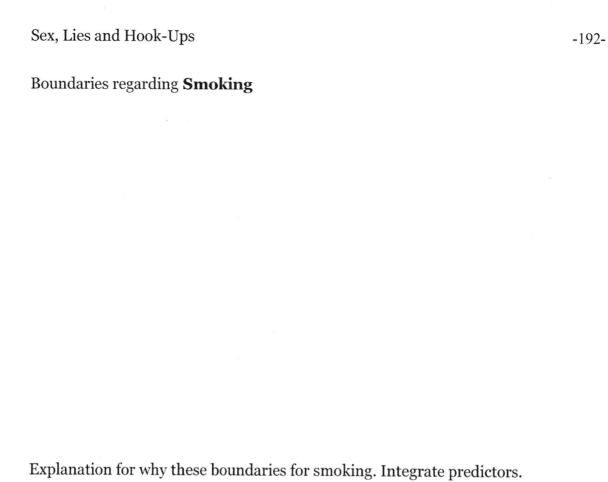

Explanation for why these boundaries for smoking. Integrate predictors.

Boundaries regarding **Dating**

Explanation for why you have set these boundaries for dating. Integrate predictors.

Boundaries regarding **Sex**

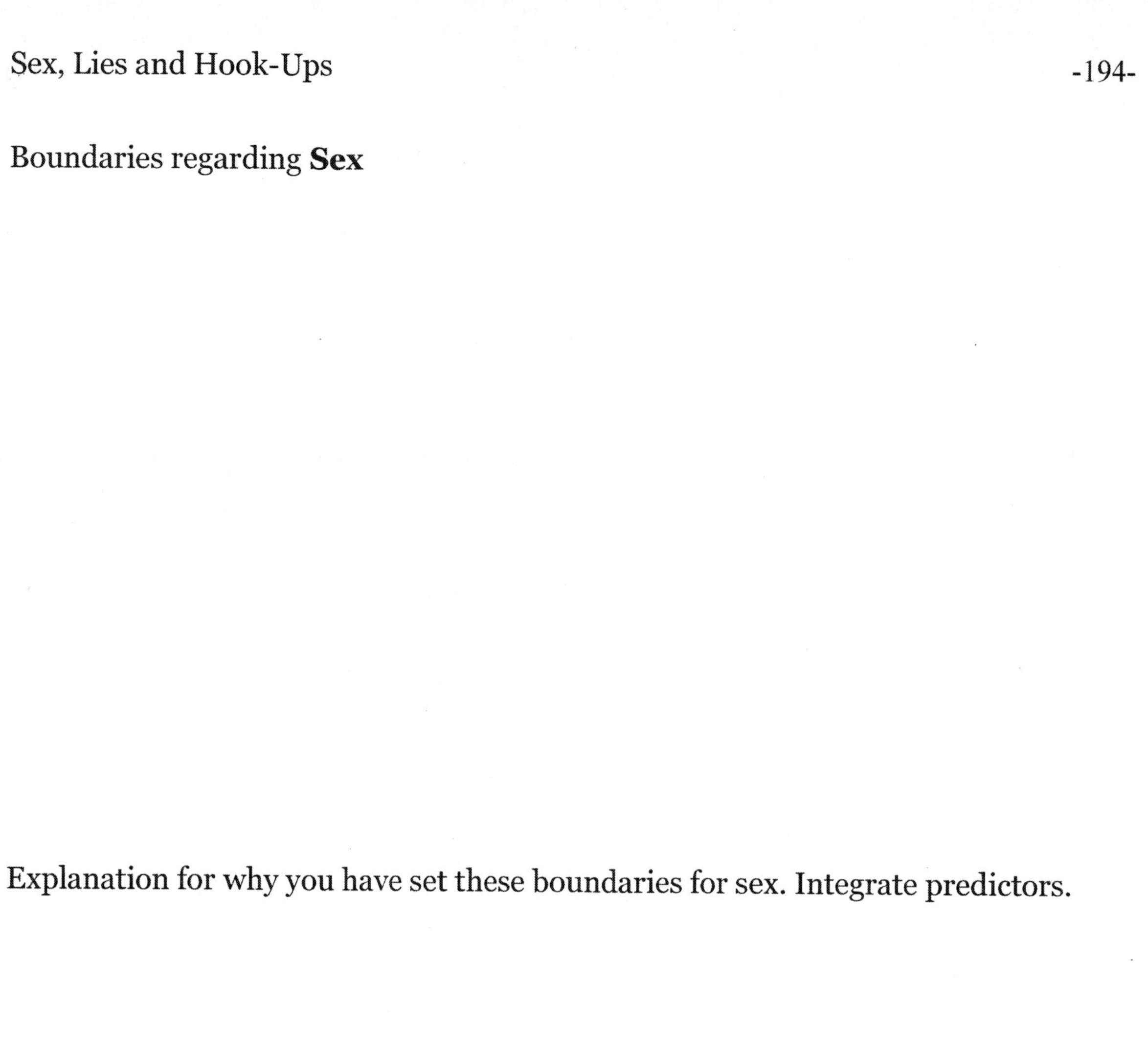

Explanation for why you have set these boundaries for sex. Integrate predictors.

Boundaries regarding **TV and Movies**

Explanation for why these boundaries for TV and movies. Integrate predictors.

Boundaries regarding **Internet** use

Explanation for why these boundaries for the Internet. Integrate predictors.

Boundaries regarding **Video Games**

Explanation for why these boundaries for video games. Integrate predictors.

Research what kind of sex education your teen's school provides. Read the entire curriculum, watch any videos, review any power points, and look at any handouts or other supplemental materials. Make sure that nothing is being taught that differs from your family's values. Take time to interview the person that will be presenting sex education to your child. Some teachers add their own perspective to programs. What is your strategy for handling any differences between what you value and what is being taught? Some *sex safe* curricula go way beyond what most parents imagine is covered, to the point of suggesting foreplay activities some advocates consider to be "safer" than those that can get someone pregnant. Some actually define *abstinence* as *sex with a condom*. It can confuse the most well-meaning parent.

Rather than only encouraging and emphasizing the performances your child is able to achieve, it is important to also notice the character traits they are exhibiting. Praising for good character traits has a more lasting effect on confidence than praising for accomplishments. If you are only striving towards performance, children are going to believe they have to perform to get your approval. They are going to believe that their self-worth is only in what they can do. It is vital instead for you to make it clear that their self-worth comes from who they are. That's where the character traits come in. What are five good character traits your child exhibits?

How have you praised your child for the character traits listed above, beyond simply saying “good job”, which is not specific enough to be effective? If you have not praised your child, what is your plan for encouraging character from now on?

What are some additional character traits you would like your teen to develop by the time he/she is an adult? Some people like to make a list of *family character traits* and post them somewhere in the house as reminders. Also, name one thing you could do to help build and encourage each trait in your child.

Analyze the list of character traits you created that you want your teen to exhibit by the time he/she is an adult. Reflect honestly on your own life and whether or not you exhibit the same traits that you want your teen to develop. Knowing that teens learn through observation of their parents, how can you make sure that you model each of the character traits that you want your teen to have?

What are you teaching your son/daughter about what it means to be a real man/woman?

By your example:

By your words:

The following are traits we suggest define real men and women. Copy it, discuss it with your child, and post it somewhere where the whole family can see it every day! You can add to the list according to your family's values!

Real men and women are measured by who they are, their character, and how they are, their actions, rather than by what they have.

- *They are strong and courageous.*
- *They have self-control over their mind, emotions, and behavior.*
- *They have a clear understanding of who they are inside, and they master their minds, actions and emotions to reflect a consistent message.*
- *They take time to figure out who they are, who they want to become, and what they want to accomplish.*
- *They do what is right even when they stand alone.*
- *They send a clear message about who they are without compromising it with negative impressions.*
- *They are confident and will not forget themselves to become a person that other negative influencers want them to become.*
- *They protect others and genuinely care for others' well-being.*
- *They are respectful; they treat all people with respect and treat those in authority with respect.*
- *They have a good work ethic; they give their best to whatever they are doing, whether it is on the sports field, at work, or in relationships.*
- *A real man or woman doesn't cheat to get ahead; they work with honesty and integrity.*

Chapter Seven: The Biology of Love

"I feel stronger about myself. I feel that I can say "NO" to a boy about sex and then feel good about it."

Female Heritage Keepers® student

"I know I won't have sex before marriage."

Male *Heritage Keepers®* student

"I'm going to be a secondary virgin because you showed me what can happen. Thank you."

Male *Heritage Keepers®* student

This chapter is going to discuss the changes going on within the body when someone is "in love." Before beginning, we want to briefly explain the differences between love, lust and infatuation. Our society tends to lump these three very different feelings together to describe "love," but they are actually all quite different.

Love

Love is a deep and lasting interest in the other person's happiness and well-being. Love is more than a feeling, not just wishing the best for the other person, but a commitment to pursue the best for the other person, helping them to become their best possible selves. *Love gives.*

Student Explains Real Love

We were talking about what real love is compared to what society says. I was going over the difference between love being just a feeling and what real love is, which is a commitment through the good and the bad times.

This quiet kid raises his hand and explains that he now understands what real love is by relating a story about his own family. He explained that his mom had gotten really sick a few years back and had to get her legs amputated and is now confined to a wheelchair the rest of her life. He then stated that his dad never left his mom's side from the moment she entered the hospital to today. He said his dad is more committed to her and her well-being than ever before. He then said in front of the class, "That is what real love is."

Lust

Lust is a selfish interest in your own happiness without regard for the other person's happiness and well-being. Lust is a feeling of wanting the other person or wanting something from them. Usually lust refers to sexual desire, but it could also mean a desire for status, money, affection or anything else you might get from a person or relationship. *Lust wants* and is never satisfied. Real *love gives* and is satisfying.

Infatuation

Infatuation is an often intense, but short-lived, interest in another person that does not necessarily consider the other person's happiness and well-being, or even one's own happiness and well-being. Infatuation is a feeling of excitement, fascination and, often, confusion; a person may not understand why he or she feels this way about this particular person. The *love* portrayed in movies, television, popular music, etc. is often, actually, infatuation. It's the happy, energetic restless phase of love as you will later see described by Dr. Helen Fisher in her book *Why We Love*. Infatuation may degenerate into lust, grow into love, or simply go away. Infatuation is not an inherently bad thing, but should not be mistaken for love.

Love, not infatuation, is the only sufficient foundation for a lasting, fulfilling relationship.

Love, A Biological Explanation

There are powerful changes going on in the body when someone is *in love*! And it's a short-lived experience, between twelve and eighteen months. What many think of as *being in love* is actually the short-lived excitement of *infatuation*. The characteristics of infatuation are consistent with the saying, "love is blind!"

As we all know and have probably personally experienced, there are emotional and physiological ramifications of infatuation, the initial feeling of being *in love*.

The following section is indented because the concepts are from Dr. Fisher's book, *Why We Love, The Nature and Chemistry of Romantic Love.*[148]

> Dr. Helen Fisher describes these emotional and physiological characteristics[149] in her book, as
>
> - believing the person you are in love with is somehow special and unique,
> - focusing your attention on the beloved,
> - aggrandizing the beloved,
> - intrusive thinking,
> - intense emotions,
> - intense energy,
> - mood swings,
> - yearning for emotional union,
> - looking for clues that your beloved loves you back,
> - changing priorities,
> - emotional dependence,
> - empathy,
> - passion from adversity,
> - a sexual connection/sexual exclusivity, and
> - jealousy.

Is infatuation beneficial to a relationship in the long run? These feelings are often what bring people together in the first place. But, is it the time to be making the decision to have sex with someone? No, it's not. It's a time when the mind and body are simply infatuated with another person; it could quickly wear off, build to something else, or lead to a sexual relationship, which could confuse things even more.

---

[148] Fisher, H. (2004). *Why we love: The nature and chemistry of romantic love.* New York: Henry Holt and Company

[149] Fisher, H. (2004). "What Wild Ecstasy": Being in Love In *Why we love: The nature and chemistry of romantic love.* (pp. 1-25). New York: Henry Holt and Company.

A Last Minute Choice of Character

An eighth grade girl revealed to her female *Heritage Keepers® Abstinence Education* teacher that she was considering sleeping with her boyfriend on his upcoming birthday. She had been abstinent since they began seeing one another a few weeks earlier, but was starting to give in to the pressure. She thought that giving herself to him on his birthday would show him how much she cared for him and that this act would make their relationship stronger. Her *Heritage Keepers®* teacher warned her against this and even volunteered to let the girl discuss the situation with a male *Heritage Keepers®* teacher in an effort to get a male's perspective. After talking with the male teacher, she came to the realization that sexual activity is not what makes a relationship stronger, especially in the early stages of the relationship. She also came to the realization that if he truly loved her and wanted to have a healthy relationship with her, he wouldn't demand sex from her. By talking with the male teacher, she was able to clear up her issues and prevent herself from making a potentially life-changing mistake.

As we discuss the biological implications of *being in love,* keep in mind that teens are, by the very nature of puberty, emotional. Because of their stage of brain development, they are not always known for using their prefrontal cortex to make rational decisions. In fact, in Dr. Walsh's book, he describes that in brain scans of teens that are in love, the prefrontal cortex (or the seat of reason) is actually *completely inactive.*[150] Revealing, isn't it?

So, what is going on biologically speaking when we are *infatuated* with someone? We discussed the chemicals that are related to puberty in Chapter Four. These same chemicals have a major effect on the brain and body when *in love*. After reading this chapter you will have a much better understanding of why telling teens to wait until they are *in love* or when they *feel ready* to have sex is bad advice.

Until a relationship gets beyond the effect of these chemicals, which typically settle down within a year or two of the relationship beginning, it can be difficult to assess how strong the relationship really is and whether it will last. Sex can confuse the issue and often becomes the focus. It's important for teens to realize that if they initiate sex while in the infatuation phase and the relationship ends, which will likely happen a few times before they are ready to marry, they may have to deal with the after-effects of their sexual involvement for a lifetime. For example, the strong feelings of attachment that are physiologically generated during sex are often felt years later, even though life has gone on and the relationship has ended.

When the feelings of *being in love* become the most important part of a relationship, people can become addicted to those feelings, going from person to

---

[150]Walsh, D. (2004). *Why do they act that way? A survival guide to the adolescent brain for you and your teen.* New York, NY: Free Press.

person when the chemicals that produce those feelings naturally diminish. When a young person does not understand the difference between a physiological high and real love, they may think it is time to have sex without realizing that decision could actually thwart the development of the relationship.

The following sections are indented because the concepts are from Dr. Fisher's book, *Why We Love, The Nature and Chemistry of Romantic Love.*

Dopamine

Elevated levels of dopamine in the brain produce extremely focused attention as well as unwavering motivation and goal-directed behaviors. As Dr. Fisher has discovered, people in love often intensely focus on the person they are in love with, often to the exclusion of those around them. Dr. Fisher believes that dopamine involvement may explain why love-stricken men and women become so dependent on their romantic relationship and why they crave emotional union with their beloved. As Dr. Fisher explains, dependency and craving are symptoms of addiction – and all major addictions are associated with elevated levels of dopamine. As dopamine increases in the brain, it often drives up levels of testosterone, the hormone of sexual desire. All of the basic needs, or human drives (like hunger and thirst), are associated with elevated levels of dopamine. So is romantic love![151]

Norepinephrine

Norepinephrine is a chemical derived from dopamine. Dr. Fisher explains that increasing levels of this stimulant generally produce exhilaration, excessive energy, sleeplessness, and loss of appetite, as well as increased memory for new stimuli.[152]

Serotonin

When we first fall *in love*, sometimes we simply cannot stop thinking about that person. Some may even say we are obsessed with the person with whom we are in love. As levels of dopamine and norepinephrine climb, they can cause serotonin levels to plummet. Dr. Fisher believes that low levels of this chemical compound may be to blame for couples' obsessive thinking about each other. It is interesting, Dr. Fisher points out, that treatment for

---

[151] Fisher, H. (2004). *Why we love: The nature and chemistry of romantic love.* (pp. 52-53). New York: Henry Holt and Company.

[152] Fisher, H. (2004). *Why we love: The nature and chemistry of romantic love.* (pp. 53-54). New York: Henry Holt and Company.

obsessive compulsive disorder involves taking medicines that elevate serotonin.[153]

The Caudate Nucleus

Dr. Fisher considers her most important finding to be that when scanning the brain in love, they found activity in the caudate nucleus. The caudate nucleus helps us detect and perceive a reward, discriminate between rewards, anticipate a reward and expect a reward. It produces motivation to acquire a reward and plans specific movements to obtain a reward.[154] This is why so many people search for love and when they get in a relationship are often quick to believe, "this is it, I have found the one!"

Lust and Love are not the same in the brain!

Dr. Fisher found that lust and romantic love are associated with different constellations of brain regions. She found through brain scans that lust and romantic love are not the same and actually light up very different sections of the brain. Love also changes over time; it becomes deeper and calmer. As Dr. Fisher explains, the mad passion, the ecstasy, the longing, the obsessive thinking and the heightened energy all dissolve. Those who are fortunate have this transform into feelings of security, comfort, calm and union with their partner.[155]

Fusion with Romantic Partner

There are brain chemicals that are produced that give us a feeling of fusion with a long-term mate. Dr. Fisher explains that vasopressin and oxytocin produce many of the behaviors associated with attachment. Oxytocin is secreted in women during nipple/genital stimulation and orgasm. Vasopressin is the chemical released by males during sexual intercourse that gives them their paternal instinct to lead them toward attachment. Called "cuddle chemicals," they contribute to the sense of fusion, closeness and attachment partners feel after sexual intercourse with their beloved.

According to Dr. Fisher, increasing levels of testosterone can drive down levels of vasopressin, and elevated levels of vasopressin can

---

[153] Fisher, H. (2004). *Why we love: The nature and chemistry of romantic love.* (pp. 54-55). New York: Henry Holt and Company.

[154] Fisher, H. (2004). *Why we love: The nature and chemistry of romantic love.* (p. 69). New York: Henry Holt and Company.

[155] Fisher, H. (2004). *Why we love: The nature and chemistry of romantic love.* (pp. 78-80). New York: Henry Holt and Company.

> decrease levels of testosterone. High levels of testosterone can reduce attachment. Men with high levels of testosterone are less likely to marry, but if married they have more adulterous affairs, commit more spousal abuse, and divorce more often.
>
> However, she states as a man becomes more and more attached to his family, levels of testosterone decline. In fact, at the birth of a child, expectant fathers experience a significant decline in testosterone. Increasing levels of oxytocin (found in men and women) interfere with dopamine and norepinephrine in the brain, decreasing the impact of these excitatory substances.

These chemicals are released regardless of relationship status when sex occurs – they will bond the hooking up, dating, engaged or married couple the same way. These chemicals do not discriminate between relationships. While it is a very positive bond for married couples, it can be detrimental to the two people hooking up or just dating. If and when they break up, the chemicals will often cause problems because the two, though apart, are physiologically bonded. This is why sex can cause so much drama and emotional consequences.

The following sections are indented because the concepts are from Dr. Fisher's book, *Why We Love, The Nature and Chemistry of Romantic Love.*

> People around the world complain that the exhilaration of romance wanes as their partnership becomes increasingly stable, comfortable and secure. Some even divorce. However, Dr. Fisher says people simply could not handle it if romantic love flourished endlessly in a relationship. Concentration would continue to be on "him" or "her" and not on other important things, like work and family.
>
> Dr. Fisher states, "The fire in the heart does tend to diminish as partners settle into the daily joys of togetherness, often replaced by another elegant circuit in the brain: attachment – or feelings of serenity and union with one's beloved."[156]
>
> Humans are designed to suffer when a relationship does not work out. Dr. Fisher describes that many people go through stages: Rejection, Protest, Abandonment, Rage, Protest, Resignation, and even Depression.[157]

---

[156] Fisher, H. (2004). Web of Love: Lust, Romance, and Attachment In *Why we love: The nature and chemistry of romantic love.* (pp. 77-98). New York: Henry Holt and Company.

[157] Fisher, H. (2004). Lost Love: Rejection, Despair, and Rage In *Why we love: The nature and chemistry of romantic love.* (pp. 153-180). New York: Henry Holt and Company.

These stages obviously intensify when two people have had sex and there are physiological changes in the body.

Emotional Consequences

After participating in a *Heritage Keepers® Abstinence Education* class, an eleventh grade student approached her teacher to thank her for how helpful the class had been. The student said she had never been aware of the emotional consequences of sex outside of marriage and how it could affect her relationships now and in the future. She said she had always been aware of the high risks of STDs and pregnancy, but she was not aware of how the emotional consequences could also last a lifetime. Later on that week, the student chose abstinence as her topic for an article she was writing for the school newspaper. The information shared with her by Heritage Community Services inspired her to spread the word to other teens about choosing to be abstinent. Too many teens today are unaware of the emotional consequences of sex outside of marriage and how one decision could alter their lives forever.

An attached love is better for individuals, their families, and their communities. A frenzied love – the infatuation stage, if acted upon sexually, can end up hurting the people involved as well as their loved ones. Couples often don't consider how the ramifications of their pregnancy, illness or emotional distress may affect those that care about them! Mature love, which involves deeper feelings of attachment and more long-term emotional satisfaction, provides substantial benefits.

A good example is the book and movie *The Notebook* (originally written by Nicholas Sparks), which so perfectly illustrates the feelings of being in love, the development of a mature relationship, and the lasting and satisfying nature of real love. The movie shows a young man passionately "in love" with a young woman (demonstrating all the typical signs of infatuation as he courts her) and also shows him in his old age reading to her. She has Alzheimer's and he reads their life story to her everyday hoping that she will remember her life for just a moment; this eloquently demonstrates a deep and lasting love. (We would not suggest this book/movie for your teens, because the characters do act on their feelings of infatuation and have sex before they marry. However, we believe this movie does beautifully illustrate the concept of satisfying life-long love, and so many movies do not.

In both Dr. Goleman's[158] and Dr. Fisher's[159] books, they make the case for the human need for strong, satisfying bonds in romantic relationships.

---

[158] Goleman, D. (2006). *Social intelligence: The new science of human relationships.* New York: Bantam Books.

[159] Fisher, H. (2004). Lost Love: Rejection, Despair, and Rage In *Why we love: The nature and chemistry of romantic love.* New York: Henry Holt and Company.

Here are a few hard questions we should be asking ourselves, culturally and personally, in light of theirs and others' research about relationships:

- What are we, as a society, setting our children up for if we teach them it is okay to start an intimate relationship based on sexual attraction alone? If an uncommitted couple has a baby, how will their relationship – or their lack of a relationship – affect their child's development?
- How do the powerful bonding hormones associated with sexual activity affect young relationships? Infatuation, the initial physiological phenomenon associated with initial attraction, lasts only 12 to 18 months. How might physiological sexual bonding effect a couple once infatuation wears off?
- How might sex without commitment contribute to chaotic, too often even violent, relationships and breakups? How can our culture address the fact that family structure, which is created by chaotic family formation, contributes to domestic violence?
- Much of our culture leads adolescents to believe they are supposed to have sex just for fun – or at least when they feel they are in love. But powerful attachment hormones and chemicals can make them think they are closer than they are. When this feeling wears off, they are too often left with serious consequences. What can adults do to provide them with clear direction regarding choices they make about sexual activity?
- *Falling in love* affects the same region of the brain as drugs and can mimic drug addiction. Going from partner to partner, looking for the next infatuation high, can lead to broken hearts, minds, bodies – and families. How can our society help young people understand the dynamics of sexual relationships and healthy family formation?
- Do we know enough about the effect on people that bond sexually with many partners over time? On any children they bear? If it affects family stability, is it something we need to address as a culture? How important is family stability for adults and children in general and in particular, how important is it to you as you help your child prepare for his/her future family life?

As we have shown in an earlier chapter, statistics clearly indicate that many teens have sex and then regret it. If someone had taught them how to set up boundaries and helped them practice stating and enforcing those boundaries, many of those situations might have been avoided.

Young people need a greater goal than being told to initiate sex "when you feel it is right," because (as brain research shows) they are not yet equipped to be able to discern the seriousness of the consequences. That is why they are deemed to be legal minors; they need their parents to help them establish protective boundaries. As we mentioned earlier, Dr. Walsh explains in his book that brain scans of young people who were *romantically in love* are revealing. The prefrontal cortex, the *seat of reason*, was found to be inactive! Teenagers simply cannot distinguish between a relationship that is *here and now* and a relationship that may be long term and beneficial.

This is why we teach that sex is best within a committed marriage. Biologically speaking, feelings of love can confuse someone into believing that they have a deep and lasting relationship, when they may not. Helping your child understand the difference between real love and infatuation is an important parenting responsibility. Even adults struggle with these concepts.

You can feel confident that you are teaching your child the right thing! Abstaining from sex is best for them on many levels.

What can you teach your child about *love* versus *infatuation*?

Remember,

Love is a deep and lasting interest in the other person's happiness and well-being. **Lust** is a selfish interest in your own happiness without regard for the other person's happiness and well-being. **Infatuation** is an often intense, but short-lived, interest in another person that does not necessarily consider the other person's happiness and well-being, or even one's own happiness and well-being.

As mentioned at the beginning of this chapter, love, not infatuation, is the only sufficient foundation for a lasting, fulfilling relationship.

On the following page is a chart that illustrates the differences between love, lust and infatuation in a relationship. Review this chart with your child. The chart is also located within the Student Manual.

Distinguishing Between Love and Infatuation		
QUESTION TO ASK	CLUES TO LOOK FOR: INFATUATION	CLUES TO LOOK FOR: LOVE:
What is my main interest? What attracts me the most?	The person's physical appearance; things that register with my five senses.	The total personality; what's inside.
How many things attract me?	Few--though some may be strong.	Many or most.
How did the romance start?	Fast (hours or days)	Slowly (months or years).
How consistent is my level of interest?	Interest varies, comes and goes; many peaks and valleys; not consistent over time.	Evens out; gets to be dependable and consistent; can predict it.
What effect does the romance have on my personality?	Disorganized, destructive; I'm acting strangely; I'm not myself.	Organized, constructive; I'm a better person.
How does the relationship end?	Quickly, unless there's been mutually satisfying sex, which can prolong, but not save the relationship.	Slowly, if at all. The relationship takes a long time to end; we'll never be quite the same.
How do I view my partner?	There's only one person in the world--my partner. My partner can do no wrong; I see my partner as faultless, idealizing him or her.	I'm realistic about my partner's strengths and weaknesses. I can admit my partner's faults, but I keep loving anyway.
How do others view our relationship? What's the attitude of friends and parents?	Few or none approve of the relationship.	Most or all approve. We get along well with each other's friends and parents.
What does distance (long separation) do to the relationship?	Withers away, dies; can't stand this added stress.	Survives; may even grow stronger.
How do quarrels affect the romance?	They get more frequent, more severe, and eventually kill the relationship.	They grow less frequent, less severe.
How do I feel about and refer to my relationship?	Much use of I/me/my; he/him/his; she/her/hers; little feeling of oneness.	Speak of we/us/our; feel and think as a unit, a pair; togetherness.
What's my ego response to the other?	Mainly selfish, conditional: "What does this do for me?"	Mainly unselfish, releasing; concerned equally for the other.
What's my overall attitude toward the other?	Attitude of taking; exploiting and using the other.	Attitude of giving, sharing; wanting to serve the other's needs and wants.
How much jealousy do I or my partner experience?	More frequent, more severe.	Less frequent, less severe.
REPRINTED WITH PERMISSION FROM THE FOUNDATION FOR THOUGHT AND ETHICS.[160]		

[160] Cole, D. D. & Duran, M. G. (1998). *Sex and Character.* (p. 148). Dallas, TX: Foundation for Thought and Ethics.

What do I teach my child about relationships?

Relationship Stages

It is always important to reiterate that real love grows over time and more often than not, it begins as infatuation. As many adults are aware, a healthy, enjoyable relationship is not a fixed state, and emotional bonds cannot be formed instantaneously. Instead, relationships grow through time and shared experience, progressing from *total separateness* through *attraction*, *closeness*, *bonding* and, ultimately, in marriage, to *union*. Look back at your own relationships and remember that most relationships will not progress through the final stage, but will end in one of the earlier stages. It is important that young people realize this so they don't take their young relationships too seriously. Share your own stories of past relationships – it helps re-enforce this concept.

Make it clear to your child that introducing physical intimacy (sexual activity) before a permanent union within a lifelong committed relationship such as marriage can confuse the development of genuine intimacy in the relationship because a sexual relationship often intensifies *feelings* of closeness without increasing *actual* closeness. *Actual* closeness (as opposed to just *feelings* of closeness) means sharing thoughts and feelings, getting to know one another's family and friends and sharing dreams and goals. Real love comes from give and take, sharing good and bad times, understanding and forgiveness, and mutual maturation and growth. Love develops with sacrifices for one another and emotional bonding to one another! Introducing physical intimacy before a lifelong committed relationship such as marriage too often leads to a relationship based on sexual lust, and it almost never turns out well.

Change of Perspective

On the first day of teaching *Heritage Keepers® Abstinence Education*, a group of 10th grade girls filed into the classroom. The Heritage educator noticed one young lady that had a "don't care" attitude enter the room. For the majority of the week, the young lady acted like she had "heard it all" and did not see abstinence as an attainable goal.

By the end of the week, the young lady began to identify with the emotional pain that comes with participating in sexual activity outside of marriage as well as the importance of a healthy marriage. She believed that it was a valid reason to choose abstinence or recommit to abstinence. She shared with the Heritage educator how she had a difficult home life growing up and does not want to follow in the same path as her mother. Finally, she thanked the educator for being honest about the effects of sexual activity outside of marriage and the benefits of abstinence. The educator was pleased to know that this young lady felt confident in recommitting to abstinence.

Remind your child that *lust wants* whereas *love gives*. Lustful relationships often focus on wanting sex from the other person instead of getting to know him or her, rather than forming a bond based upon intellectual, social, emotional and familial relationships. It can confuse or even stop the growth of genuine intimacy. A sexual relationship intensifies a feeling of closeness that may not be real – that could be based on taking, but not giving!

It might help to explain the following:

- Males and females are aroused at different levels of intimacy. Males are often more sight-oriented while females can be more aroused by emotional connections, touch, smells and the sense that a man can provide for her.[161]
- Physical intimacy often leads to sexual arousal. The further someone goes physically, the more they often want. Encourage your teen that a good minimum boundary is to not participate in touching anywhere that a modest bathing suit covers. Sexual intimacy outside of a lifelong committed relationship such as marriage can lead to relationships which progress too fast physically and too slow intellectually, emotionally and socially.

Seeing and touching are not equal to true intimacy. True intimacy, the kind that will last forever, comes from sharing thoughts and ideas, fears, goals, dreams and laughter together! That kind of intimacy lasts. When someone does get married, true intimacy will typically lead to a better sex life![162]

Teach your child to think of the opposite sex as people, not objects. It is important that your children learn the key to a good relationship is getting to know one another as a person rather than as a sexual object.

Familiarize your child with what stereotypes are and what it means to use someone as an object. Help him or her understand why objectifying someone is wrong. When you see things on TV or in a magazine that fit these descriptions, point them out to your child and tell them why you believe those are incorrect ways to view the opposite sex.

- Stereotypes – Stereotyping is thinking that all men are just alike and all women are just alike, and that they follow standard patterns of thought and behavior (for instance, all women are irrational and love shopping, or all men are stubborn and cannot match their clothes). Stereotypes are wrong and misleading; people must be considered as individuals with unique characteristics and personalities.
- Objects – Objectifying is thinking of young men and women primarily as bodies whose value lies in their ability to perform a desirable function; that

---

[161] Goleman, D. (2006). Desire: his and hers. In *Social intelligence: The new science of human relationships* (pp.198-210). New York: Bantam Books.

[162] Michael, R. T., Gagnon, J. H., Laumann, E. O., & Kolata, G. (1994). *Sex in America: A definitive survey.* Boston: Little, Brown, and Company.

function may be having sex, providing visual stimulation, cooking and cleaning, paying the bills, etc. Objects are to be used; people are to be related to. One uses an object, but has relationships with people.

It's important for teenagers to realize that all people, both male and female, have thoughts, feelings, dreams, goals, families and past histories, just like their own friends and family.[163] Teens should look for qualities in the person they wish to date that can develop into a truly intimate relationship. In order to attract a person of good character, on must be a person of good character. Spend time with your child(ren) helping him or her develop a list of character qualities they are looking for in the opposite sex. Make sure the emphasis is on character traits rather than physical attributes. Also, encourage your children to model all of the character traits that they are looking for in the opposite sex – "like" often attracts "like."

Suggestions of character qualities to look for and to model: intelligence, sense of humor, ambition, personal goals, similar likes and dislikes, family dynamics, similar life goals, and good personality.

Sex is Like Fire In Chapter Two, the marriage union was represented by a fireplace. The walls of the fireplace represent the intellectual, emotional, familial and social unions of a relationship. The cement that holds the fireplace together represents the lifetime commitment of marriage. A fire is safest within a well-built fireplace. If one were to build a fireplace without walls, or even with walls but without the cement that holds the walls together, there is no protection. Similarly, if one builds a sexual relationship with another outside of marriage, without developing the intellectual, emotional, social and familial aspects, or without the lifetime commitment, there is no protection.

Demonstration: Sex is Like Fire Following are exercises to help your child understand why sex is best within a lifelong committed relationship. This activity is in the Student Manual at the end of this book. Review this activity in preparation for the section of the Student Manual that corresponds and strategize how you want to go about doing this activity with your child.

Describe a scene in which fire is pleasant. Describe a fire in a fireplace. Paint an attractive mental picture. Narrate as if your child is presently in the scene – "You've just come in from the cold. You are sitting in front of a nice, warm fire." Describe in terms of the senses, mentioning the sights, sounds, smells and feeling of the scene. Use highly evocative words like *cozy*, *toasty*, *warm*, *nice* and *comfy*. Ask your child about the fire and write his or her responses on a piece of paper (or in the Student Manual). Include descriptions of the fire itself. Ask him or her to include descriptions of the fire, such as *enjoyable* and *nice feeling*. Finally, ask for words that describe how he or she feels about this scene, such as *safe* and *happy*.

---

[163] Tangney, J. P., Baumesiter, R. F., & Boone, A. L. (2004). High self-control predicts good adjustment, less pathology, better grades, and interpersonal success. *Journal of Personality, 72,* 271-322.

Describe a scene in which fire is dangerous and harmful. Ask your child, "What if you lived in a place where forest fires threaten homes?" Describe how forest fires can get out of control, and how fire can suddenly put people and their homes in serious danger. Even when they try to get control, by hosing down their roofs, for example, the fire can become consuming, and they may be helpless to stop it.

Describe the escape from the fire and paint a mental picture. Narrate as if your child is presently in the scene – "The wind is sweeping the fire into your yard. Cinders are falling on your roof. The grass has caught on fire, and your escape route is suddenly obscured by the smoke."

Describe the scene in terms of the senses, mentioning the sights, sounds, smells and feelings evoked by the oncoming flames. Use highly evocative words like *fiery, scorch, blistering* and *charred.* Ask questions about whom and what is being affected by the fire to personalize the emotional impact of the scene – perhaps family members, or a pet. Ask your child about the fire and to write his or her responses on a piece of paper (or in the Student Workbook). Include descriptions of the fire itself, perhaps *dangerous* or *frightening.* And finally, ask for words that describe how he or she feels about this scene, such as *scared* and *angry.*

Putting it all together Contrast their responses, from the fireplace scene and the forest fire scene. Conclude by explaining that, "Inside appropriate boundaries, fire is positive; but outside of appropriate boundaries, fire can be negative." In a similar way, sex is like fire. Tell your child that both sex and fire can be positive. Ask your child whether the list of positive words can apply to sex, putting some in the sentence, "Sex can be _______," to demonstrate your meaning. Tell your child that both sex and fire can be negative. Ask your child whether the list of negative words can apply to sex, putting some in the sentence, "Sex can be _______," to demonstrate your meaning. Remind your child that both sex and fire can be pleasurable, and that both sex and fire are powerful and important. Fire provides light, heat and energy. Sex is the primary means of human reproduction; it creates a bond between partners.[164] Sex is a vital part of life.[165,166,167] How else can sex be positive within the boundary of marriage? Inside appropriate boundaries, sex is positive; but outside of appropriate boundaries, sex can be negative.[168,169]

---

[164] Hsiu-Chen, Y., Lorenx, F. O., Wickrama, K. A. S., Conger, R. D., & Elder G. H. (2006). Relationships among sexual satisfaction [sic], marital quality, and marital instability at midlife. *Journal of Family Psychotherapy, 14,* 1-12.

[165] Brady, S. S., & Halperm-Flesher, B. L. (2007). Adolescents' reported consequences of having oral sex versus vaginal sex. *Pediatrics, 119,* 229-236.

[166] Kim, H. K., & McKenry, P. C. (2000). The relationship between marriage and psychological well-being: A Longitudinal analysis. *Journal of Family Issues, 23,* 607-911.

[167] Young, M., Denny, G., Luquis, R., & Young, T. (1998). Correlates of the sexual satisfaction in marriage. *The Canadian Journal of Human Sexuality, 7,* 115-127.

[168] Brady, S. S., & Halperm-Flesher, B. L. (2007). Adolescents' reported consequences of having oral sex versus vaginal sex. *Pediatrics, 119,* 229-236.

[169] Kim, H. K., & McKenry, P. C. (2000). The relationship between marriage and psychological well-being: A Longitudinal analysis. *Journal of Family Issues, 23,* 607-911.

Lifetime Commitment So, what makes marriage different? Think about the fireplace demonstration provided earlier in the book (page 74). If bricks or stones are put in place to form a fireplace, they could slip and slide or be knocked out of place easily unless there is *mortar*, or cement, to hold them together. It is the lifetime commitment that makes marriage different from all other relationships. Think about a lifetime commitment as the *mortar* that cements the building blocks of a marriage together. In marriage you promise that all of the unions will last for life.[170]

The fire in the fireplace represents the physical union, or the sexual bond. It is the commitment within the marriage union that makes sex safe and best. A partial boundary, made of only some of the unions but lacking the mortar of lifetime commitment, does not make sex safe. All the aspects of the union, bound together by faithfulness to one another, a lifelong commitment, creates a bond that provides benefits to the couple, society, and their family.[171,172,173]

Explain to your child that he or she might have one or more unions in their life like the unions above. You could have a familial union with your parents, an emotional union with your best friend, a social union with a teammate, and an intellectual union with a chess partner. But, in marriage, you share all of these unions and are bound to each other and the children you have together by a lifetime commitment.[174,175]

170 Nichols, W. C. (2005). The first years of marital commitment. In Harway, Michelle (Ed.) *Handbook of couples therapy.* Hoboken, New Jersey: John Willey & Sons, Inc.

171 Finger, R. Thelen, T., Vessey, J. T., Mohn, J. K., & Mann, J. R. (2003). Association of virginity at age 18 with educational, economic, social, and health outcomes in middle adulthood. *Adolescent & Family Health, 3,* 164-170.

172 Kline, G. H., Stanley, S. M., Markman, H. J., Olmos-Gallo, P. A., St. Peters, M., Whitton, S. W., & Prado, L. M. (2004). Timing is everything: Pre-engagement cohabitation and increased risk for poor marital outcomes. *Journal of Family Psychology,* 18, 311-318.

173 Whitehead, B. D., & Pearson, M. (2006). *Making a love connection: Teen relationships, pregnancy, and marriage.* Washington, DC: National Campaign to Prevent Teen Pregnancy. Retrieved February 10, 2011 from http://www.thenationalcampaign.org/resources/pdf/pubs/MALC_FINAL.pdf

174 Coley, R.L. (1998). Children's socialization experiences and functioning in single-mother households: The importance of fathers and other men. *Child Development, 69,* 219-230

175 Tamis-LeMonda, C. S., Shannon, J. D., Cabrear, N. J., & Lamb, M. E. (2004). Fathers and mothers at play with their 2- and 3- year-olds: Contributions to language and cognitive development. *Child Development, 75,* 1806-1820.

The Biology of Love

Have you ever been infatuated, as described by Dr. Fisher, with someone? It is likely that you have – many times. What can you tell your child about your own experiences with infatuation? What are some other examples you can give your child of infatuation – both positive and negative?

What are the three major chemicals involved when we think we are "in love," and what impact do they each have on the brain and body?

In this chapter, we posed some hard questions. What are your thoughts about the following:

What are we, as a society, setting our children up for if we teach them it is okay to start an intimate relationship based on sexual attraction alone? If an uncommitted couple has a baby, how will the relationship – or their lack of a relationship – affect their child's development?

How do the powerful bonding hormones associated with sexual activity affect young relationships? Infatuation, the initial physiological phenomenon associated with initial attraction, lasts only 12 to 18 months. How might sexual bonding effect a couple once infatuation wears off?

How might sex without commitment contribute to chaotic, too often even violent, relationships and breakups? How can our culture address the fact that family structure, which is created by chaotic family formation, contributes to domestic violence?

Much of our culture leads adolescents to believe they are supposed to have sex just for fun – or at least when they feel they are in love. But powerful attachment hormones and chemicals can make them think they are closer than they are. When this feeling wears off, they are too often left with serious consequences. What can adults do to provide them with clear direction regarding choices they make about sexual activity?

Falling in love affects the same region of the brain as drugs and can mimic drug addiction. Going from partner to partner, looking for the next infatuation high, can lead to broken hearts, minds, bodies – and families. How can parents help their children understand the dynamics of sexual relationships and healthy family formation?

Do we know enough about the effect on people that bond sexually with many partners over time? On any children they bear? If it affects family stability, is it something we need to address as a culture? How important is family stability for adults and children in general and in particular, how important is it to you as you help your child prepare for his/her future family life?

What will you teach your teen(s) about the difference between love, lust and infatuation? We suggest copying the chart in the book and posting it somewhere in your house as a reminder. What are some examples of love that you can give to your child?

How will you explain the "sex is like fire" analogy, in your own words, to your teen(s)?

Chapter Eight: Refuting Typical Reasons Teens Give For Having Sex

"I used to let people convince me to do things that were not right. My lifestyle has changed about peer pressure to have sex. Now I know that I can do what I think is right."

Male *Heritage Keepers*® student

"I think what this class has done for me is that it has taught me your body is a good thing and SO IS SEX. So, therefore you can wait until marriage to do those special things. Also that it's okay to say 'no!'"

Female *Heritage Keepers*® student

"I am more confident about sex and my self-esteem. I can easily say no. I know all the things about pregnancy and diseases."

Female *Heritage Keepers*® student

"This class helped me to learn how to state my boundaries."

Female *Heritage Keepers*® student

Guarding Your Boundaries

Upon completion of several weeks of *Heritage Keepers® Abstinence Education* and *Heritage Keepers® Life Skills*, a young male student approached the Heritage teacher to tell of a particular challenge/decision he had been forced to make recently. Apparently the male student was involved in a dating relationship with a young lady, and his feelings had grown strong toward her. The student then proceeded to tell the instructor how his girlfriend pressured him to have sex. He went on to explain that he found it necessary to use the communication skills he learned in Heritage's class to "defend" and "protect" his boundaries. The student found it essential to end the unhealthy relationship and felt good about standing up for his values. The student expressed just how much abstinence education had impacted his decision to end the relationship.

Over the 15 years that we have been teaching abstinence education in the classroom, we have heard many excuses given as to why teens choose to have sex. Some of the reasons we have heard include: pressure from boyfriend/girlfriend; pressure from friends; pressure to be liked/be popular/fit in; they were using alcohol or drugs; they were bored; they wanted some company; they thought they were in love; curiosity; thought they were ready because they had physically matured; they like it; it just happened; it's a normal part of dating; they thought sex proves you are a man/woman; it proves they are desirable; they were forced or coerced.

In the classroom, we lead young people through the process of seeing why these are not valid reasons to put themselves at risk. It is an eye opening process for the teens. It is important that your child know why rationalization is simply a way to justify excuses for putting themselves at risk. Read through this chapter–familiarizing yourself with this information. You will notice that under each excuse we listed, we suggest a predictor that addresses that issue. These predictors are important if you want to change your child's opinion on that excuse. Discuss these excuses with your teenager and in these discussions, focus on the protective predictor suggested. Remember, the predictors you want to focus on are affirmation of abstinence, rejection of permissiveness, sex is more than physical, future impacts of sex, peer independence, self-worth, self-efficacy, refuting justifications for sex, and related risks.

First, ask him or her to come up with some answers as to why the reasons presented above are not valid justifications for choosing to have sex outside of the legal and ethical commitment of marriage. Always connect the positive predictor you are working to improve. Remember, these are not theoretical predictors, they are actually proven predictors. They will, statistically, provide you with insight as to whether your adolescent is inclined to initiate sexual activity or not. If your teen is having a hard time, we have listed some responses you can suggest. Some of these exercises for your teen are also in the Student Workbook at the end of this book.

Excuses and Answers Exercises

Excuse: They were under pressure from their boyfriend/girlfriend. *(Address the Predictor: My Worth)* **Answer:** If your boyfriend or girlfriend is pressuring you to do anything, then they don't respect you or your values. You deserve to be treated as a whole person, not as a sex object. **Reminder:** Establish boundaries *before* getting in this situation. By establishing clear boundaries, you take the pressure off of yourself to give in to someone else's standards.

Excuse: They were under pressure from friends. *(Address the Predictor: Sexual Independence from Peers)* **Answer:** True friends respect your sexual values. They encourage you to be a better person rather than pressuring you to compromise your standards. **Reminder:** When you establish strong values and stand up for them, your friends and family are more likely to respect you.

Excuse: They were under pressure to be liked/to be popular/fit in. *(Address the Predictor: Sexual Independence from Peers)* **Answer:** Don't you want people to like you for who you really are rather than what someone else wants you to do sexually? Using your body sexually so that you feel that you are part of the crowd is superficial. If there are negative consequences, the people that you thought you were impressing may not be there to support you. **Reminder:** Waiting and recommitting to abstinence may make your relationships better because you'll spend more time getting to know each other.

Excuse: They were under the influence of alcohol or drugs. *(Address the Predictor: Related Risks)* **Answer:** Drugs and alcohol cause you to lose control of your thinking and your body. As a result, you may make decisions that you might later regret.[176] When you choose to be under the influence of alcohol or drugs, you may make decisions that put you at risk sexually.[177,178] Because you and your sexual health are worthy of a clear-headed decision, don't put yourself in situations where your loss of control may end up with you compromising your own or someone else's boundaries. **Reminder:** Waiting keeps you in control of your body, your emotions, and your sexual health, which helps you keep your self-respect.

---

[176] Alcohol Concern. (2002, March). *Alcohol & Teenage Pregnancy.* London: Alcohol Concern. Retrieved February 5, 2010 from http://www.slideshare.net/bpilmer/alcohol-and-teenage-pregnancy

[177] Kaiser Family Foundation. (2002). *Substance use & sexual health among teens and young adults in the U.S.* Retrieved August 21, 2007 from http://www.kff.org/youthhivstds/upload/KFF-CASAFactSheet.pdf

[178] Moore, N. B., & Davidson, J. K. (2006). College women and personal goals: Cognitive dimensions that differentiate risk-reduction sexual decisions. *Journal of Youth and Adolescence, 35,* 577-589.

Excuse: They were bored. *(Address the Predictor: Future Impacts of Sex)* **Answer:** There are various reasons people claim to be "bored." Some have never challenged themselves to use their talents to improve themselves or the world around them. Others may simply not know how to use their time creatively. That can change today, but you might need to change your thinking. Begin to notice resources around you like a school library, a club you could join, or school sports. Challenge yourself to excel. Don't use boredom as a reason for having sex. The possible consequences are just too serious for you and all of those who love you.
Reminder: Do something that helps you achieve your goals, which will better yourself and your life. Do something to improve the lives of others.

Excuse: They wanted some company, to feel better. *(Address the Predictor: My Worth)* **Answer:** You may not realize how valuable you are. Your mind, body and feelings are of great worth. Your hopes and dreams matter, and if you formulate your goals at an early age you will be more likely to reach the objectives that make them a real possibility. But, if you convince yourself that temporary – and uncommitted – company will really make you feel better, you may be fooling yourself. It's important to know that seeking immediate pleasure could result in unwanted worries and regrets. You are worth much more. **Reminder:** Waiting enables you to avoid possible negative consequences of sex and may give you peace of mind.

Excuse: They thought they were in love. *(Address the Predictors: Love/Lust, Love Justifies Sex, Sex Proves Love)* **Answer:** If you truly love someone, you will want what is best for that person's life rather than merely lusting after a temporary physical relationship. Feeling in love does not justify sex. Real love, within the commitments made in marriage, justifies sex. If someone pressures you to have sex on the basis that it will prove he or she loves you, they are more concerned about themselves than you – which is not love. Instead, they are willing to put you at risk for possible emotional, physical, mental and financial consequences. Love is much more than sex. If you love someone and someone really loves you, you both will be willing to wait until the true commitment of marriage has been made. **Reminder:** Real love requires character strengths, which are likely to attract someone who exhibits similar traits – the kind of person you may consider marrying and having as the father or mother of your children.

Excuse: They were curious. *(Address the Predictor: Future Impacts of Sex)* **Answer:** Curiosity about sex is completely natural. However, following through with that curiosity by having sex outside of marriage may have serious repercussions. As you mature, you will likely have thoughts about all kinds of potentially risky possibilities. It is important to understand the difference between having thoughts – or curiosities – and actually acting on those thoughts. Take time now to clarify your values and to develop the skills you will need to reach your goals. This will equip you to be more able to control both your thoughts and your actions. Your commitment to your values and boundaries must be stronger than your curiosity. **Reminder:** Waiting may make it easier to focus on your future, which helps you achieve your goals.

Excuse: They thought sex is a normal/expected part of dating. *(Address the Predictor: Abstinence Values, Depth of Relationship)* **Answer:** Less than half of teens are having sex.[179] Therefore, sex is not the standard for all teens. The media gives the impression that casual sex is the norm,[180] but the majority of high school teens say abstinence should be their standard. Remember that there are surveys that reveal the vast majority (70%) of teens 15-17 are not having sex[181] and that most teens think being a virgin in high school is a good thing; in fact - close to six of ten teens surveyed (58%) said sexual activity for high school-age teens is not acceptable, even if precautions are taken against pregnancy and sexually transmitted diseases. Nearly 70% of younger teens (ages 12-14) said that high school-age teens should not engage in sexual activity. The vast majority of teens surveyed (87%) do not think it is embarrassing for teens to admit they are virgins.[182] Why would so many teens report regretting their decision to have sex[183,184] if it is an expected part of dating? It may be because too often the physical act of sex becomes the focus. The drama associated with a sexual relationship and all of its ramifications may complicate dating and friendship relationships rather than make them better.[185] Choosing to wait shows your partner that you respect them and their sexual worth. Take the time to get to know them for who they really are, rather than focusing on a physical relationship. It is important to establish your own standards, expectations, and norms for dating. **Reminder:** Waiting means that you are not tempting others or pressuring others to have sex with you, which shows that you respect their sexual worth.

---

179 Centers for Disease Control and Prevention. (2009). *Trends in the prevalence of sexual behaviors: National YRBS 1991-2009.* Retrieved February 9, 2011 from http://www.cdc.gov/HealthyYouth/yrbs/pdf/us_sexual_trend_yrbs.pdf

180 Kunkel, D., Cope, K., & Biely, E. (1999). Sexual messages on television: Comparing findings from three studies. *The Journal of Sex Research, 36,* 230-236.

181 Abma J. C., Martinez G. M., & Copen C. E. (2010, June) *Teenagers in the United States: Sexual activity, contraceptive use, and childbearing, National Survey of Family Growth 2006–2008.* National

182 The National Campaign to Prevent Teen Pregnancy, (2000, April 27). *The cautious generation? Teens tell us about sex, virginity, and "the talk".* Retrieved February 11, 2011 from http://www.thenationalcampaign.org/resources/pdf/pubs/CautiousGen_FINAL.pdf

183 Albert, B. (2007). *With one voice 2007: America's adults and teens sound off about teen pregnancy.* Washington, DC: National Campaign to Prevent Teen Pregnancy. Retrieved November 28, 2007 from http://www.teenpregnancy.org/resources/data/pdf/WOV2007_fulltext.pdf

184 The National Campaign to Prevent Teen Pregnancy. (2000, June 30). *Not just another thing to do: Teens talk about sex, regret, and the influence of their parents.* Washington, DC: National Campaign to Prevent Teen Pregnancy. Retrieved February 8, 2011 from http://www.thenationalcampaign.org/resources/pdf/pubs/NotJust_FINAL.pdf

185 Kaestle, C . E. & Halpern, C. T. (2005). Sexual intercourse precedes partner violence in adolescent romantic relationships. *Journal of Adolescent Health, 36,* 386-392.

Excuse: They thought that their bodies were ready. *(Address the Predictor: Sex as a Whole Person)* [Note: Teenagers whose bodies mature early are statistically at greater risk of early sexual debut than their less physically mature peers.[186,187,188,189] Therefore, it is important to emphasize that physical qualities are not adequate indications of complete maturity.] **Answer:** Your body is becoming more physically mature, and you may have the physical capacity to have sex and conceive a child. But, there are serious considerations as to whether teens are ready for all of the possible consequences. For example, the surface of the adolescent female cervix is not fully mature and is much more susceptible to infections than that of a fully mature woman.[190,191] Also, the adolescent brain is not fully developed to process the possible repercussions that can be associated with sex.[192,193] What may seem okay at the time could become a life-changing experience. However, you may not realize how seriously your life has been changed until you are in the middle of living out those consequences. This is because sex is not just about a physical relationship. Sex involves your mind, your emotions, your future, your family – every aspect of your life. Waiting allows you to be in control rather than feeling pressured into risky behavior that you may not be ready to handle. **Reminder:** Committing to wait establishes clear boundaries, which takes pressure off of you.

Excuse: They've experienced it in the past and like it. *(Address the Predictor: Prior Experience)* **Answer:** Just because you have had sex in the past, does not mean you have to continue having sex. You might have enjoyed sex physically but are realizing there are consequences to sexual activity you do not enjoy, such as emotional pain or regret. Even if you have had sex one time or many times, you have the right to start over. Just because you like something does not mean you have to choose to do it continually. Instead, you can choose to start making decisions and acting in a way that will benefit your future and your relationships. When you find someone with whom you want to spend the rest of your life, in marriage, you will have every opportunity to develop a loving and satisfying sexual relationship that is unique to the two of you. **Reminder:** Practicing character traits that you admire can help

---

[186] Kim, K., & Smith, P. K. (1999). Family relations in early childhood and reproductive development. *Journal of Reproductive and Infant Psychology, 17,* 133-148.

[187] Miller, B. C., Norton, M. C., Curtis, T., Hill, E. J., Schvaneveldt, P., & Young, M. H. (1997). The timing of sexual intercourse among adolescents: Family, peer, and other antecedents. *Youth & Society, 29,* 54-83.

[188] Deardorff, J., Gonzales, N. A., Christopher, F. S., Roosa, M. W., & Millsap, R. E. (2005). Early puberty and adolescent pregnancy: The influence of alcohol use. *Pediatrics, 116,* 1451-1456.

[189] Billy, J. O. G., Brewster, K. L., and Grady, W. R. (1994). Contextual effects on the sexual behavior of adolescent women. *Journal of Marriage and the Family, 56,* 387-404.

[190] Moscicki, A. B., Burt, V. G., Darragh, T., & Shiboski, S. (1999). The significance of squamous metaplasia in the development of low grade squamous intraepithelial lesions in young women. *Cancer, 85,* 1139-1144.

[191] Centers for Disease Control and Prevention. (2007, December 19). *Pelvic inflammatory disease fact sheet.* Retrieved August 20, 2008 from http://www.cdc.gov/std/PID/STDFact-PID.htm

[192] McIlhaney, J. S. & Bush, F. M. (2008). *Hooked: New science on how casual sex is affecting our children.* Chicago: Northfield Publishing.

[193] Walsh, D. (2004). *Why do they act that way? A survival guide to the adolescent brain for you and your teen.* New York, NY: Free Press.

you to attract someone with similar character traits – the kind of person that you may like to marry and to have as the father or mother of your children.

Excuse: It just happened. *(Address the Predictor: Abstinence Efficacy, Sexual Climate/Individual Opportunity)* **Answer:** Unless someone is forced to have sex, it does not *just happen*. Decisions are made each step of the way – who you choose to be with, where you choose to go, and what you choose to do. You need to carefully think through the implications of your decision about whether to commit to abstinence outside of marriage, remembering your values, your aspirations for the future, and the possible consequences. For example, when you consider the kind of mother and father – the kind of family – you want for the children you may have, you don't want that decision to be made because it *just happened*. Building the skills to defend your boundaries is the first step to giving you the confidence you need to take control of your life and your future. It is your responsibility to apply those skills to avoid situations that may put you at risk for losing control – the kind of situations where others might use the excuse that sex *just happened*. **Reminder:** Practicing good judgment and self-control will benefit your life in all areas, which could ultimately make you more appealing for a lasting healthy relationship.

Excuse: They thought sex proves you're a real man or real woman. *(Address the Predictor: Abstinence Values, Sex Proves)* **Answer:** If you value the benefits of abstinence more than you value the benefits of sex outside of marriage, you will be more likely to abstain. Most teenagers have the physical capability to have sex, but the choice of whether to have sex or abstain depends on your values. Movies and songs might lead you to believe that the benefits of having sex right now are alluring, but reality is that the benefits of having sex as a teen are actually quite temporary. On the other hand, the benefits of abstaining can be life-long. When the measure of a man or woman is taken, those who demonstrate the strength to live out their values are often the ones who are most respected. That kind of person attracts others with similar character traits. **Reminder:** Waiting exhibits character strengths that may attract someone with similar character traits – the kind of person you would like to marry and have as the father or mother of your children.

Excuse: They thought sex proves that you're desirable. *(Address the Predictor: My Worth, Sex Proves)* **Answer:** Everyone has a strong need to feel valued, but that need is not going to be fulfilled by having sex outside of marriage. There is a difference between being temporarily desired for sex and being valued as a whole person. If someone asks you to have sex outside of the commitment of marriage, he or she is demonstrating some level of a physical desire without acknowledging the other vital aspects of human worth. Your mind, body and feelings are of great worth, and your self-worth is defined beyond what you can offer someone sexually. Genuine and lasting desirability, the kind that lets you know that you are truly valued as a person, comes from someone taking the time to get to know you and love you for who you really are. **Reminder:** Waiting may make your relationships better because rather than focusing on sex, you will spend more time getting to know each other and respecting each other's self-worth.

(Not an excuse, sometimes a fact): What if you are forced or coerced? (We will address prevention and recognition of sexual abuse in Chapter Twelve.) *(Address the Predictor: Prior Experience)* **Answer:** Your sexual being and the private parts of your body that are involved in sex are yours to control. If someone has taken control of you sexually, either by force or by talking you into it, you have a right to get that control back. Even if you have consented to have sex with someone because you were not aware of the benefits of waiting, you have the right to recommit to abstinence. You may not have been aware of your right to have control over your own sexual activity. Don't believe that your future choices are dictated by past circumstances. If you have been forced or coerced into sex, there are laws to protect you and people who want to help you. Understand that if someone has forced or coerced you into sex, something has been stolen from you without your permission. You have great worth. You can decide today to seek help from a trusted adult to stop an abuser, which can be the start of demanding respect. Anyone who has been abused should never accept the idea that they might as well continue having sex. People who have been abused in the past, once they have gained control over the situation, can choose to commit to abstaining until marriage. **Reminder:** Reporting abuse is the first step in taking control of your body, your emotions, and your sexual health, which can help you demand respect.

Tempter and Response Exercise

As we just covered, the first step to being ready to stand for personal boundaries in regards to sexual activity is to go through typical reasons teens might give for having sex, and then to think through why they are not good enough reasons to risk the consequences. Next, it is crucial to think through a nice, but firm, response to the arguments others might use to get young people off track.

Tempter: "Your body is ready, and you are free to have sex if you want to."
Response: READY = MARRIED

Parent to teen facing this pressure: The huge risk of STDs and untimely pregnancy means that no one in our society can have sex outside of the protection of marriage *freely*, with the guarantee of no harmful consequences to self or others.

A major part of your body is your brain, and recent research shows that your brain is *not* mature during the teen years – the decision-making capacity is still developing. Remember: Ready = Already Married. Give yourself time, and wait until you are *so ready* that you have *already gotten married*. Anything short of marriage can too easily be broken off, even promises and engagement.

Here are some responses your teen can use:

- "I've been studying STDs, and they are *not for me*. I'm not going to have sex until I'm married."
- "I'm not going to start my family until I am married. I'm not going to take any risks with something that important."
- "You might believe I'm ready, but I am not. I have a lot to do before I get married, and I'm not having sex until then."
- "Anyone that has functioning sexual organs can have sex. It means more to me than that."

Tempter: "If someone spends a lot of money on a person, she or he should be willing to have sex."
Response: THIS BODY IS NOT FOR SALE

Parent to teen facing this pressure: The day of people using their bodies sexually to get favors should be long past. Women can learn and earn as well as men. Men can prove themselves in much more meaningful ways than simply demonstrating that their genitals work. People who *demand* sex are looking for much more than just sex – it's about control. No one has the right to pressure anyone into having sex. People can work out their needs in a much more productive and less risky way than having sex.

Here are some responses your teen could use:

- "I would *never* expect a person to ask me to give them anything but the pleasure of my company and getting to know me. I'm not having sex until I'm married."
- "No one can buy me – I'm not for sale. I enjoy your company and would like to get to know you, but I'm not having sex until I'm married."
- "Thank you" should be said with your words and your smile, with kind and thoughtful actions, not with the intimacy of sexual activity, which should be saved for marriage and your spouse.

Tempter: "It is all right for people to have sex before marriage if they love each other and are really committed."
Response: MARRIAGE = COMMITMENT

Parent to teen facing this pressure: The wonderful feeling of being *in love* is actually called infatuation, and it generally doesn't last more than about a year and a half, at the most. Real love is much deeper and involves serious commitment. But even when people make promises to each other – even when they plan to marry, it is not the same as actually getting married. That is a true legal and moral commitment unlike any other.

People often feel in love with more than one person before they even meet the one they will love for a lifetime in marriage. Just because you love someone, or someone loves you, does not mean that he/ she is *the One* you will eventually marry. That feeling certainly is not enough to risk having a child before you and your partner (who could be the mother or father of your child) even decide you want to commit to each other. That is not fair to you or the child.

If you have already had a child, or more than one child, you can commit to abstain from this day forward, and wait for the person who will love you and form a family with you based on real and lasting love.

Here is a response your teen could use: "If we truly love one another, we will marry, and we can have sex with each other for the rest of our lives. Until then, we need to build our relationship in other ways, to see if we really want to make that commitment."

Tempter: "Practicing sex improves sexual satisfaction and technique."
Response: SAVE IT FOR THE PERSON I MARRY!

Parent to teen facing this pressure: Actually, practicing sex with a series of partners outside of marriage increases the chance of infidelity within marriage. Going from partner to partner not only increases the chance of disease and out-of-marriage pregnancy, it establishes a pattern. It also creates memories that too often do not go away after the wedding vows.

Married couples can not only practice with each other, but they can trust each other to learn what is most pleasing and what the other enjoys. In contrast, many couples involved in sexual activity outside of marriage often report feeling guilty, having regrets, and that sex becomes routine and sort of takes over the other aspects of the relationship. Instead of growing the couple, it can become the very thing that keeps them from really getting to know each other.

Here are some responses your teen could use:

- "I want to learn with my spouse. Right now, we are not married, and I'm waiting until I get married to have sex."
- "I'm not willing to be someone others practice with."

Tempter: "If I am in love and sexual intercourse just happens, I don't see that as a problem."
Response: UNLESS IT'S RAPE, SEX DOESN'T JUST HAPPEN. SOMEONE DECIDES.

Parent to teen facing this pressure: The idea that people meet, are overcome by sexual arousal, and somehow end up having sex when they didn't expect to is an idea that sells songs and movies, but is not based on real life. Under normal circumstances, someone decides. However, many teens report that they were not under control when they decided. They were either under the influence of drugs or alcohol, and they deeply regretted their decision afterward. But they couldn't turn back time. Don't allow drugs, alcohol, or emotions to inhibit your ability to make clear and wise decisions.

Here are some responses your teen could use:

- "Sex it too important to just let it happen. I don't want to feel out of control. This is something I want to do after I get married, not in the spur of the moment without much thought."
- "We're getting out of control. I'm ready to go home, now."

Tempter: "Having sex is a natural and expected part of a relationship."
Response: SEX IS FOR MARRIAGE, NOT DATING

Parent to teen facing this pressure: A lot of teens are choosing to not have sex. The possible consequences of sex outside of marriage are way beyond what two people who are just dating can handle. The emotional consequences of sexual bonding can be tremendously difficult for teen males and females. Even more important, the idea of having sex and taking the chance of creating a new person – a baby – before you have made a commitment to one another doesn't make sense. Neither does taking a chance on diseases that could cause infertility, sores, or even death. And the consequences for those who love you can be extremely serious, as well.

Here are some responses your teen could use:

- "Having sex outside of marriage is not for me. I'm waiting until I marry."
- "If you loved me, you'd wait."
- "There are a lot of things that come naturally to us that I don't choose to do, like craving sugar and chocolate or being jealous of those who have more than me. Many 'natural' things have consequences. I'm waiting for marriage."
- "If you are expecting sex in this relationship, then you and I have different expectations. I want to wait until I get married."

Tempter: "If you loved me, you'd do it."
Response: REAL LOVE REQUIRES REAL RESPECT FOR MY VALUES AND GOALS.

Parent to teen facing this pressure: True love is shown through devotion and understanding, caring and laughing, sharing and sacrificing for one another. It does not put the other person at risk. In contrast, it protects from risk. *Not* having sex – which is best for you, your boyfriend/girlfriend and your relationship – is the truly loving thing to do.

Here are some responses your teen could use:

- "Which is easier and shows more real love, having sex as soon as you want to or waiting? I'm waiting until I am married, and if you can't, then I'm not the right person for you."
- "If that is all love means to you, then you and I have different concepts of what real committed love means."

Tempter: "Having sex proves that you are desirable and wanted by others."
Response: SEX WITHOUT LOVE IS LONELY

Parent to teen facing this pressure: If someone truly wants *you* and not just your body, he or she will be willing to wait for the commitment of marriage. Some people might seem to want you when all they really want is what they can get from you, like the physical act of sex or the satisfaction of bragging to their friends about the experience.

Here are some responses your teen could use:
"Abstaining from sex outside of marriage requires self-control and discipline, which I have. I've thought this through, and I want more than just sex. And I don't want to start a family outside of marriage. I'm waiting for the real thing."

Tempter: "Sometimes you should do things so others will think you're cool."
Response: DON'T BECOME THEM

Parent to teen facing this pressure: The major struggle of teen years is figuring out who you are, what you stand for, your own value system and your future. Even though many teens are driven by popular culture – much of which is created by adults trying to make money off of the teen population, you can choose to be yourself. If you try to become like others, you lose yourself. It can take a while to figure out what is important for you. Take that time. Don't let the "buy and sell" culture define what you do with your body, your life, your future family. You will live with your decisions, they won't. Don't count on them when the child support check is due, or when you can't have children because you are infertile because of a STD.

Here are some responses your teen could use:

- "As much as I want you to like me, I can't compromise what I know is right for me and my future. I'm abstaining from sexual activity until I'm married."
- "I'm never going to have sex just because others may think it is cool."

Once teens make the decision to commit to abstinence and practice responses to familiar arguments, they will find that thinking of responses will become easier and more natural than imagined, and will quickly realize they are in control of themselves – their body and their destiny – and that is the beginning of the true maturity that makes a real man or real woman. Help your child to set their personal standards high and to use every opportunity to reach his or her potential. Tell him or her it's about avoiding the risks that could cause them pain. Remind your child that there are many good reasons to wait to have sex. Here are a few reasons:

- You are unique. There is no one on Earth like you, so don't just follow the crowd. You can think for yourself. Make decisions based on your goals.
- You have a great future ahead of you. Be wise about how you handle your life today so that you keep your options open tomorrow.
- You are smart. You can choose to weigh your options and possible consequences and make a wise decision on your own.
- You are worth loving. You are not disposable. Sex is more than physical, and you deserve genuine care and commitment.
- You deserve the best sex. People that report having the very best sex are not singles, but actually married people who were both virgins.[194,195]
- You have a right to sexual health. Waiting for sexual activity until marriage is healthy. Sex between two people who have not had any sexual activity with others and who are faithful to each other is obviously the best protection from sexually transmitted diseases.

---

[194] Stanton, G. T. (1997). *Why marriage matters: Reasons to believe in marriage in postmodern society.* Colorado Springs: Pinon Press.

[195] Michael, R. T., Gagnon, J. H., Laumann, E. O., & Kolata, G. (1994). *Sex in America: A definitive survey.* Boston: Little, Brown, and Company.

Refuting Typical Reasons Teens Give For Having Sex

How will you go about role-playing these situations with your teen(s) to ensure he or she is ready when these type of situations occur? Below, write at least three role play scenarios you will practice with you teen. Then, write your plan for when and how you will begin this exercise with your teen.

Chapter Nine: Setting Dating Standards

"Before I took sex ed, I thought it doesn't matter when you have sex. I thought you start whenever you feel ready, but I was wrong. When ya'll came, it changed me around. Thank you for teaching the right time to have sex, with the person I marry!"

Male *Heritage Keepers*® student

"My life is different now that I can see how precious sex is. Everyone talks about it like its nothing but, I think it is. After I came out of your class, I made a commitment to stay abstinent. I think it's very important. Thanks for teaching me!"

Female *Heritage Keepers*® student

The fact is, as described in the *Biology of Love* chapter, love can be a confusing time and sometimes it is downright hard to handle, even for adults. Young love can take an emotional toll on teens.

A study of 8,000 adolescents shows just how difficult young love can be. The study showed that romantic attachment as a teenager can result in an overwhelming amount of stress and often leads to depression or participation in risky behaviors. Kara Joyner, a sociologist at Cornell and co-author of the study, found that the age when young people begin dating is an important factor in affecting their stress level, depression, and participation in risky behaviors. Teens that begin seriously dating at an earlier age have a higher probability of being affected by these negative outcomes than teens who begin dating at a later age. The reason why teens tend to become damaged from a serious relationship that breaks up is what the study calls a *loss of self. Loss of self* can be defined as leaving behind the people and/or the things that you value to become the person that someone else is pressuring you to be.

When young people put all of their feelings and emotions into a relationship, there can be negative consequences. The *loss of self* is defined by the separation from their support network. If they separate themselves from family and friends, it can lead to increased levels of depression in girls and greater substance abuse or delinquent activities in boys.[196,197] These negative consequences worsen when sex enters the relationship prematurely.[198,199,200]

Also, adolescents that get involved in serious relationships have a higher correlation with a decline in school performance as compared with their peers that are not in serious romantic relationships. This decline in school performance may contribute to the increase in depression and stress.[201]

In fact, Dr. Miriam Kaufman says that 15 to 20 percent of teens will fall into a depression that is often triggered by a breakup.[202] She advises that young people not get involved in romantic relationships at a young age, but instead strengthen their friendships and find a strong sense of self so they can make it through the hard times.

---

196 Joyner, K., & Udry, J. R. (2000). You don't bring me anything but down: Adolescent romance and depression. *Journal of Health and Social Behavior, 41,* 369-391.

197 Horwitz, A. V., & White, H. R. (1987). Gender role orientations and styles of pathology among adolescents. *Journal of Health and Social Behavior, 28,* 158-170.

198 Coleman, J. (1996). Female status and premarital sexual codes [Letter to the editor]. *The American Journal of Sociology, 72,* 217

199 Hallfors, D. D., Waller, M. W., Bauer, D., Ford, C. A., & Halpern, C. T. (2005). Which comes first in adolescence-sex and drugs or depression? *American Journal of Preventative Medicine, 29,* 163-170.

200 Rector, R. E., Johnson, R. A., & Noyes, L. R. (2003, June 3). *Sexually active teenagers are more likely to be depressed and to attempt suicide.* Center for Data Analysis Report #30-04. Retrieved October 25, 2007 from http://www.heritage.org/Research/Abstinence/cda0304.cfm

201 Joyner, et al., 2000

202 Kaufman, M. (April 2001). *Puppy Love's Bite.* Time Magazine.

Based on the above study, warn your children to be especially careful about losing him or herself in a relationship. It is so important that teens continue to enjoy their friends and family, make time for exploring and excelling in activities they enjoy, and continue to work towards their personal goals. Make sure they do not become enmeshed with someone who may be obsessed with them today but gone tomorrow. Empower them to guard their heart, mind and body.

Personalizing the Possibilities

On the second day of teaching *Heritage Keepers® Abstinence Education*, the students seemed tired and somewhat disinterested. The class, comprised of mostly upper classmen, began by discussing values and goals the students had chosen to share with the rest of the class. One group of three students had mostly kept to themselves the first day and through the first part of day two of *Heritage Keepers® Abstinence Education.*

In noticing this isolation from the discussion and other students, the Heritage educator began engaging these students in conversation. The Heritage educator conversed mostly with the one young man who seemed to be the person whom the others followed. In doing so, the other two students in the group began to participate in discussion. The three young men had not said one word in class discussion until this point. As discussion led into an activity within the *Heritage Keepers® Abstinence Education* program, the three students seemed more interested, yet still closed to the idea that abstinence could be a realistic option for them.

The activity the class had started involved the risks that are taken when people choose to participate in sexual activity outside of marriage. This activity reveals how easy it would be for someone to contract an STD or cause an untimely pregnancy. When the Heritage educator used a hypothetical situation involving the three students, the other students quickly became interested and very assertive in the class discussion. At this point, the students began to realize that they are not immune to the consequences that may follow sex outside of marriage. As a result, the group of three students began to realize that abstinence was something that, although not an easy challenge for young men their age, needed to become a real goal in their lives. The remaining classes in the *Heritage Keepers® Abstinence Education* program at this rural high school were very involved, enthusiastic, and most definitely changed perspectives of young men who once had zero intentions of changing their lifestyles.

Our society places a lot of emphasis on education, career and financial success, yet very little emphasis is placed on forming and maintaining healthy families. Many teens have simply not been taught the skills that will enable them to have healthy friendships and healthy dating relationships that can lead into healthy marriages. When they lack these relationship skills, they are more likely to become confused by their emotions and make decisions that may not lead to a successful relationship and may cause physical and emotional pain as well as regret.

One trap that the teen culture seems to have fallen into is the concept of *hooking up* physically without the context of a committed relationship. Sometimes this phenomenon is known as *friends with benefits* or simply just as *hooking up*. Unfortunately, in today's culture many teenagers do not even date anymore. *Hooking up*, which can mean anything to a teen, from kissing to intercourse, has become acceptable to many. Some teens even choose to have *friends with benefits*, meaning there is no emotional attachment, just sex. *Hooking up* is meant to let two people participate in sexual activity almost anonymously, reaching for intimacy but denying the very dynamics that create closeness with another person. The term *hooking up* denotes sexual activity without genuine involvement in the life of another person. According to one researcher, *hooking up* can involve various levels of sexual involvement over a short or long period of time and "hooking up's *defining characteristic* is the ability to unhook from a partner at any time, just as they may delete an old song from their ipod." The researcher further explains, "Feelings are discouraged, and both partners share an understanding that either of them can walk away at any time.[203]"

Recommended Books

Unhooked: How Young Women Pursue Sex, Delay Love and Lose at Both
by Laura Sessions Stepp
Hooked: New Science on How Casual Sex is Affecting Our Children
by Joe S. McIlhaney, Jr, M.D. and Freda McKissic Bush, M.D.

What exactly is *hooking up*?

This is a great question that is difficult to answer since everyone seems to have a different opinion on what it means. Some teens will tell you that it simply involves kissing someone without any relational commitment. Other teens may tell you that it means that they have participated in some sort of physical touching (breasts and/or genitals) or oral sex without any relational commitment. Still, other teens may define *hooking up* as having intercourse without any commitment. Again, the key part of defining *hooking up* is that each partner can decide to *unhook* from the other at any point since there is no commitment involved – similar to merely deleting text messages after they have been read. However, this concept ignores the biological realty that humans bond, chemically and hormonally, during sexual activity. Our physiology is such that we are incapable of sexual intimacy without emotional attachment!

If your teens are talking about *hooking up*, ask them to define it for you since there are so many different interpretations—do not just assume that you know what they are talking about.

---

[203] Stepp, L. S. (2008). *Unhooked* (p. 27). New York: Riverhead Books.

Emotional Consequences of *Hooking Up*

Teens will most likely state that one of the benefits of *hooking up* is to avoid any unnecessary emotional expectations. They will state that both parties essentially agree that the hook-up is not supposed to involve feelings or any other expectation that the physical relationship will evolve into a dating relationship. If the above expectations are true, how can the emotional roller coaster often experienced after hook-ups be explained? Obviously there *are* often emotions generated from the casual hook-up. The physiological reactions are a natural part of being human, as are the emotions that follow.

Encouraging Healthy Relationships

Talk to your teens about how healthy relationships start. They typically need time to develop and should start as friendship before progressing into a dating relationship. When considering a potential dating partner, they should learn about the other person before jumping into a serious relationship.

Unfortunately, part of the appeal to teens of the hook-up culture is the fact that it takes much less time to hook up with someone than to get to know them. They think they are not tied down to any one person. Plus, many parents dissuade their teens from getting into serious relationships and to instead be involved in casual group hang-outs. When these casual group hang-outs become the standard, casual sexual encounters without commitment or love can become the expectation. They may not even know the person's name, much less like the person. A couple sexually intimate the night before may not publicly acknowledge recognition in the hall the next day and that usually hurts.

Therefore, there must be a balance between serious dating relationships at a young age (see *Dating Standards*, later in this chapter) and the hang-out culture that often times leads to hooking up.

There is no reason to rush into a relationship. Many teens find themselves in situations where they are dating one person but they like someone else. They were not ready for a commitment. Let them know that it can be more fun to just go out in large groups that practice avoiding risky behaviors. Then they can get to know numerous people of the opposite sex, instead of just one, and discover who shares their values.

Some fun group activities you can suggest to your teen: (These may sound cheesy, but many times teenagers don't know what to do with their time. When teens are bored, there are too many opportunities for them to get involved in activities that you would not approve.)

Have a scavenger hunt	Play soccer
Play ultimate Frisbee	Play softball
Play basketball	Play flag football
Start a band	Roller or ice skating
Make home movies/music videos	Go to a sporting event
Bowling	Play laser tag
Have a picnic in the park	Play volleyball at the beach/park
A movie	Hiking
Play board games	Play video games
The beach (make sand castles, play volleyball, surf, body board)	Work odd jobs, save money, buy an instrument and learn to play together
Go have dinner/make dinner for someone else	Study for tests together by quizzing each other
Train together for an upcoming community race or marathon	Join (or start) a theatrical group to make videos or to act out drama/plays
Ask a few friends to try recipes with you	Organize a talent contest for your school
Get involved in politics – help your favorite candidate	Make a giant sundae for all your friends to eat together
Volunteer	Play board games
Interview the mayor about a community project teens could work on	Learn about photography and take pictures of nature

Even for adults, dating can be downright confusing. People are just wired differently!

Here are a few things you can teach your child about dating. Remember, a great way for them to start learning, before they become emotionally tied to someone, is through group activities, as suggested above.

- Relationships are work! If you are not ready to commit to someone, then do not get involved in a relationship. Once you tell someone you are their girl/boyfriend, you have made a commitment. So, don't do it unless you are ready. It is not worth hurting yourself or the other person involved.
- Once you begin certain practices like holding hands or going on a few dates, the other person will probably think you are her or his boy/girlfriend. If you do not want that, don't lead that person on. If you would like to take them out – but don't want a relationship – be clear to that person about that!
- Too much flirting can confuse. Be careful — you might think you are innocently flirting, but it can be taken as a signal for something more.
- Being involved in someone else's life means that you have a responsibility in his or her life. If you do not want that responsibility, don't get involved.

Guidelines about dating have changed over the years, but one thing has never changed and that is the love and concern you, the parent, have for your child and his or her future. In days gone by, if a young man was interested in dating a young woman (some called it courting), the fellow would have to meet her parents. Only after her parents agreed that he would be suitable company for their daughter could the couple begin to see each other and always with a chaperone. Since this became out-dated, young people have had the responsibilities of controlling themselves while dating. With raging hormones, this is not an easy task – that is why you must set clear boundaries for your child and help them practice their verbal and non-verbal refusal skills.

As a parent you must determine when your child is ready to move away from being in groups with the opposite sex and into dating just one person. Make the decision early in your child's life and stick to it. Here are some things you may want to look for in determining when your child is ready to date one on one.

- ❑ Has your child established sexual boundaries? If not, help him/her do so.
- ❑ Are you confident your child can maintain those sexual boundaries? If not, role play potential scenarios with him/her.
- ❑ Is your child ready to accept responsibility for playing a part in someone else's life?
- ❑ Is your child financially able to pay for dating activities?
- ❑ Have you taught your child dating manners? If not, practice manners with your child such as table manners, engaging in conversations, offering to open doors, offering to pay, and any other social skills important to your family.
- ❑ Does your child have genuine respect for others or does he/she stereotype people? Have you set a good example for how to treat someone he/she is dating?
- ❑ Does your child have healthy relationships with members of the opposite sex?
- ❑ Does your child respect and honor himself or herself? Does your child know his or her personal worth?
- ❑ Is your child future orientated? Is he or she committed to his or her short-term and long-term goals and not willing to compromise those goals to please others?
- ❑ Does your child have a high standard for who he or she is willing to date and not date?
- ❑ Does your child value abstinence? Can he or she explain why he or she has chosen to abstain?
- ❑ Has your child made a commitment to abstain from sexual activity outside of a lifelong committed relationship such as marriage?
- ❑ Is abstaining until a lifelong committed relationship such as marriage a part of who he or she perceives himself or herself to be, and who he or she intends to become – his or her sense of identity?
- ❑ Does your child value his or her future family? Does he or she see clearly how decisions made today could impact that family?
- ❑ Does your child understand that there are physiological, emotional, familial, financial, and cultural ramifications of sex?
- ❑ Does your child have a plan in place in case he or she gets in an uncomfortable situation?

If you and your teen both feel that he or she is ready to date, great! Dating can be fun and exciting when there are appropriate boundaries in place and when those boundaries are respected and upheld.

A good idea before your child ever goes on a date with someone is to have the person come over to your house and have time with the family, or meet the family in a neutral place where interaction is possible. This way, you and your child can get to know and trust this person beforehand.

Here are some of the things that you can discuss to get to know who that person is. (Hint: Teach your child to ask the person they want to date these kinds of questions before going out on a date. They may come to a realization that they don't wish to date this person after all.)

Interests	Opinions
Plans	Ideas
Dreams/hopes for their future	Favorite subjects in school
Experiences	Personal goals
Values	Hobbies
Sports	Music
Politics	Tolerance
Clubs, after-school activities	Personal boundaries
Musical taste	Faith, religion
Respect for others	Childhood experiences

Remind your teen to keep dating casual and fun! Some of the things you can tell your child once they are dating:

- Just because you are dating someone does not mean you have to act as if you are married.
- Have fun while dating! Don't make a young relationship more than it is. You have a long way to go in life, so keep dating light and fun.
- Although some married couples begin dating in middle or high school, most do not!
- Dating is meant to be a learning process for people — you learn what you do and don't like about someone so that when you meet the right person, you will know!
- Somehow, dating and sex have been confused. Dating should be a time for getting to know each other without the added drama that sex can cause.
- Sex is way too heavy of an obligation for a young couple.[204] Sex is meant for marriage because that is where it is safest and best.[205]

---

[204] Kaestle, C. E. & Halpern, C. T. (2005). Sexual intercourse precedes partner violence in adolescent romantic relationships. *Journal of Adolescent Health, 36,* 386-392.

[205] Stanton, G. T. (1997). *Why marriage matters: Reasons to believe in marriage in postmodern society.* Colorado Springs: Pinon Press.

Also, remind your child of the *Sex is Like Fire* analogy mentioned in Chapter Seven.

Here are a few fun dates you can suggest to your child:

Cook or bake together	Go to the beach/lake/river/pool
Exercise	Do crafts
Go roller skating or ice skating	Visit a planetarium, aquarium, zoo or museum
Go bowling	Go to a park
Attend a sporting event	Attend a concert or play
See a movie	Go hiking
Go fishing or crabbing	Play a video game
Do homework	Paint pottery
Read to each other	Share favorite hobbies
Volunteer for charity	Visit a city park
Play a sport	Volunteer together
Train for a sport together, like tennis or track	Volunteer to help a political candidate together
Tutor younger students together	Compete to win video games/board games
Challenge other couples to a sports or gaming (board games, x-box, PlayStation, Wii, etc.) tournament	Learn something new together, like playing piano or guitar, building models, a new language
Train for a marathon together	Find a need and fill it

For Your Son

- Wear appropriate clothes; you should take care how you dress for a date.
- Always go to the door to pick up your date, as a common courtesy.
- Speak respectfully to your date's father and mother.
- Ask your date's mother and father about their rules and follow them. Talk about respect, and make a mutual agreement before the date.
- Open your date's car door (if they would like).
- Open all doors (if they would like).
- Walk on the side of your date that is exposed to traffic. It's an old school way of showing respect.
- Take your date to a public place; don't tempt yourselves by going somewhere secluded, dark or extremely private.
- Offer to pay for the entire date. Your date may or may not accept the offer.
- Don't touch, or allow your date to touch, any part of the body that would be covered by a modest bathing suit.
- Don't compromise your or your date's values, boundaries, and goals.
- Thank your date for going out with you.

For Your Daughter

- Take care how you dress; it's a time to get to know you, not your body.
- Speak respectfully to your date's father and mother if you meet them.
- Ask your date's mother and father about their rules and follow them. Talk about respect, and make a mutual agreement to respect each other.
- Know the plans for your time together – no surprises.
- Insist on public places only; no secluded or private areas.
- Tell your date *thank you* whenever they are especially attentive of your needs, such as if someone opens a door for you. If you would rather your date not open doors for you, thank them and ask them nicely not to.
- Respect yourself enough to not allow yourselves to get into a situation that is sexually compromising.
- Do not touch, or allow your date to touch, anything that would be covered by a modest bathing suit. Don't compromise your values, boundaries, and goals.
- Thank your date for going out with you.

Help your child to be aware when a relationship has moved into unhealthy or even dangerous territory.

Unhealthy Relationships

What can you tell your child about unhealthy relationships?

- Some relationships may put you at risk mentally and emotionally, and some relationships are physically dangerous.
- No relationship is worth the stress, and possible danger, of compromising your values.
- There are some people that will ask you to give endlessly. No matter what you do, it's not enough. They will never be satisfied and will always ask for more.
- Don't let your desire to please people allow you to stay in an unhealthy relationship.

If you think your child may be in a relationship that is putting pressure on him or her to do things he or she does not want to do, tell them this is an unhealthy relationship.[206] Explain to your child that if they ever need help getting out of such a relationship, never hesitate to ask you. Remind your child that no relationship is worth having to go through the stress, and possibly danger, of doing something you do not want to try in order to make the other person happy. Demanding people are seldom satisfied, no matter how much is given to them.

Teach your child that it is wrong for anyone to pressure him or her into smoking, violence, alcohol use, drugs, or sex. Make it clear to them that they should

---

[206] Albert, B., Brown, S., & Flanigan, C. M. (2003). *14 and younger: The sexual behavior of young adolescents: Summary.* Washington, DC: National Campaign to Prevent Teen Pregnancy. Retrieved February 8, 2011 from http://www.thenationalcampaign.org/resources/pdf/pubs/14summary.pdf

not allow anyone to make them feel that they should violate their own boundaries or put their own hopes and dreams at risk.

Practice with your child how to guard his or her boundaries if someone is putting negative peer pressure on them to compromise, and how to say "NO" in no uncertain terms (see the SAFE plan, in Chapter Four).

In addition, teach your child that there are many things that could be happening in a relationship that may signal that it is unhealthy.

POSSIBLE DANGERS Here are some warning indicators to share with your child that will help him or her become aware of danger in a relationship:

- Someone is making you feel bad about yourself or has shaken your confidence.
- Someone is acting jealous of your time with others.
- You feel you are not in control of your time because your partner wants you to always be with him or her.
- Someone is demanding you give up activities you enjoy to be with him or her.

Make it clear that in a healthy relationship, your partner will encourage you to spend time with your friends and your family rather than monopolizing all of your time. Jealousy and manipulation are not signs of extreme love; they are signs of an unhealthy tendency to control. In a healthy relationship you build each other up, not tear each other down. A healthy relationship should be based on respect and confidence rather than guilt or jealousy.

Again, role play with your child some things he/she can practice saying and doing to break off an unhealthy relationship.

Dangerous Relationships

Some relationships go beyond unhealthy; they are dangerous and can cause physical harm.[207] Always make it clear to your child that if the person he or she is dating has gone beyond pressuring them to do something they do not want to do and is forcing them to do things they do not want to do, like sexual activity outside of marriage, drugs, violent and even illegal activities, they must know how to ask for help. It's challenging for many adults to escape compromising or abusive relationships.

Some facts to share with your child: A dangerous relationships may be difficult or impossible for your teen to break off on his or her own, especially if there is physical, emotional, and/or sexual abuse involved in the situation. When someone forces them to do any risky behavior, it is wrong, and it can have serious consequences that could affect your teen's future and well-being. Research indicates

---

[207] Kaestle, C. E. & Halpern, C. T. (2005). Sexual intercourse precedes partner violence in adolescent romantic relationships. *Journal of Adolescent Health, 36,* 386-392.

that among the population studied, about 20 percent of the adolescent girls reported physical and/or sexual violence from dating partners. The rate of pregnancy among high school girls that reported violence from dating partners was 4 to 6 times the rate reported by their non-abused peers. Reports of smoking, binge drinking and cocaine use were higher among high school girls who reported abuse from dating partners.[208] Research has shown that "engaging in sexual intercourse [in adolescent romantic relationships] appears to dramatically increase the risk of partner violence, especially physical violence."[209]

Sex in a dating relationship might cause the relationship to become more violent. Research shows teens suggest that sex causes the relationship to become more intense emotionally which could cause "feelings of jealousy or a greater need for power" within the relationship, which in turn could cause violent reactions. Take the time to talk with your child about healthy ways to cope (rather than violence) with the strong emotions that teens may feel in romantic relationships.[210]

Always remind your child that America has set up laws to protect people from abuse, particularly minors, and that there are adults (such as yourself, a guidance counselor, their principal, etc.) who can get help to enforce these protective laws. Again, role play with your child ways to handle a relationship that is dangerous.

Older Partners

It can also be dangerous for your teen to date a much older partner. They are more mature physically and have more experience. They may want more from the relationship than a young person can or should give. They may be able to persuade a younger person to do things they are not ready for and do not wish to do because they've learned how to manipulate younger people.[211,212,213,214]

---

208 Silverman, J. G., Raj, A., Mucci, L. A., & Hathaway, J. E. (2001). Dating violence against adolescent girls and associated substance use, unhealthy weight control, sexual risk behavior, pregnancy, and suicidality. *Journal of American Medical Association, 286,* 572-579.

209 Keastle, et al., 2005

210 Ibid

211 Kilpatrick, D., Saunders, B., & Smith, D. (2003, April). *Youth victimization: Prevalence and implications.* U.S. Department of Justice, National Institute of Justice. Retrieved February 9, 2011 from http://www.ncjrs.gov/App/Publications/alphaList.aspx?alpha=Y

212 McCurley, C. & Snyder, H. (2004). *Victims of violent juvenile crime.* Juvenile Justice Bulletin, U.S. Department of Justice, Office of Juvenile Justice and Delinquency Prevention. Retrieved February 9, 2011 from http://www.ncjrs.gov/pdffiles1/ojjdp/201628.pdfhttp://ojjdp.ncjrs.org/publications/PubResults.asp#2004

213 Albert, B., Brown, S., & Flanigan, C. M. (2003). *14 and younger: The sexual behavior of young adolescents: Summary.* Washington, DC: National Campaign to Prevent Teen Pregnancy. Retrieved February 8, 2011 from http://www.thenationalcampaign.org/resources/pdf/pubs/14summary.pdf

214 Abel, G., Becker, J., Mittelman, M., Cunningham-Rathner, J., Rouleau, J., & Murphy, W. (1987). Self-reported sex crimes on non-incarcerated paraphiliacs. *Journal of Interpersonal Violence, 2,* 3-25.

Non-marital teenage pregnancies and births often result from relationships with males who are substantially older than the teen mother. In fact, the pregnancy rate in teens with older partners is almost four times the rate in girls whose partner is no more than two years older.

The following is indented because it is directly from the study cited below.

> Age of partner is associated with higher rates of pregnancy and birth. Approximately half of all pregnancies of adolescents under age 18 were fathered by males three or more years older. (In about 30% of the pregnancies, the male was three to five years older, and in the other 20%, the male was six or more years older.) Having an older partner also was associated with lower rates of contraceptive use and unintended pregnancy. Specifically, teens with a partner six or more years older were:
>
> - more likely to become pregnant and give birth;
> - less likely to report using contraception at last intercourse.
>
> Researchers also examined who was more likely to have an older partner. They found that women with older partners were more likely to have reported that they had been forced to have sex at some time in their lives and that they had first intercourse in more casual relationships rather than long-term relationships[215] (e.g., going steady or engaged.)

Explain to your teen that it may seem *cool* that someone older appears interested in him or her, but there are reasons why older people try to date or hang out with younger people. They know it is easier to impress and control a younger person than someone their own age. Tell them to not fall for it. It's a good idea for young people to date someone close to their own age and with similar values because they are going through similar experiences.

Dating can be one of the best or worst memories of one's life. The thrill of doing fun things with another person, whose company one enjoys, should not be complicated by risking serious adult-sized consequences – like having a child, getting a sexually transmitted disease, and becoming physiologically attached by complex chemical reactions.

---

[215] Darroch, J. E., Landry, D. J., & Oslak, S. (1999). Age differences between sexual partners in the U.S. *Family Planning Perspectives, 31,* 160-167.

SETTING DATING STANDARDS

Have you known anyone who was too intimate with someone at a young age? Do you know anyone who was psychologically harmed because of dating too seriously at a young age? Chances are you do. Describe how that person felt and acted.

Have you known anyone who has experienced a loss of self from becoming too enmeshed in a relationship? Describe that here. How will you caution your teen to recognize and resist loss of self?

On the opposite side of the scale, many of today's teens tend to simply hook up instead of date. What does hooking up mean to you?

Have you asked your teen what hooking up means to him or her?

Besides the activities we listed, think of additional safe activities teens could do together as they get to know additional friends they may potentially date.

What are your child's sexual boundaries? If you are not sure, how will you help him or her establish appropriate boundaries?

Why are you confident your child can maintain sexual boundaries? If you are not sure, how will you role play with them to help them develop the skills they need to maintain boundaries?

In what ways is your child ready to accept responsibility for playing a part in someone else's life? In what ways will you help him or her prepare for this aspect of his or her life?

Is your child financially able to pay for dating activities? How will you help him or her consider and plan for costs associated with dating?

What dating manners have you taught your child? How will you practice dating manners with your child, such as table manners, communication skills, offering to open doors, offering to pay, and other interactions important to your family?

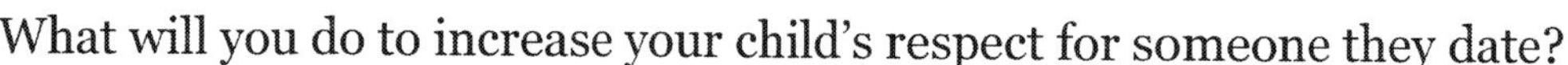
What will you do to increase your child's respect for someone they date?

Can you improve the examples you provide for your child in regards to your own relationships? What resources will you use to work on your own skills?

How does your child relate to friends of the opposite sex? If there are areas for improvement, what resources will you use to help you work with your child on healthy relationships?

How do you know whether your child respects and honors himself or herself? How will you begin a discussion with your child about his or her personal worth?

How do you daily build your child's future orientation? List the ways you will help him or her link daily behavior with his or her short-term and long-term goals.

What is your child's standard for who he or she is willing to date and not willing to date?

How do you know your child values abstinence? What is your plan for coaching your child on how to effectively verbalize why he or she has chosen to abstain?

Has your child made a commitment to abstain from sexual activity outside of a committed relationship such as marriage? If not, are you sure he or she values the benefits of waiting? What is your plan for improving his/her intentions to abstain?

How strongly does your child believe that "waiting for marriage" is an important part of who they are – their sense of identity?

How well does your child understand that decisions about sex made today could impact his or her family in the future? How will you help him or her connect today's actions with tomorrow's outcomes?

Describe how you will discuss the physiological, emotional, familial, financial, and cultural ramifications of sex with your child. How will you know he or she has incorporated these understandings into their value system?

What is your child's plan in case he or she gets in an uncomfortable situation? When will you teach him or her the SAFE plan? Have you reviewed the SAFE plan carefully, so you can explain it clearly with conviction?

What will you tell your child about unhealthy relationships?

What will you tell your child about older partners?

Chapter Ten: Anatomy - Be An Expert!

"This class has opened up my eyes to see the pleasure and benefits of having sex, but also to see the consequences that may occur. The class has helped me to make choices and maybe even wait until marriage to have sex."

Male *Heritage Keepers*® student

"My life has changed during this class a lot. I understand the importance of saving yourself until marriage. I am a virgin and proud of it, and I'm not giving it away easy! Thanks for giving me good ideas about a good sexual life!"

Female *Heritage Keepers*® student

"I liked that you all kept it real, didn't beat around the bush, did y'all's best to answer all questions, provided numbers to call for help, made yourself fit in with us so the girls would feel comfortable and open up."

Female *Heritage Keepers*® student

"Ever since the first day *Heritage Keepers*® has really got me into the facts about life. When I started I didn't even know what STDs were. Now, in the future when I hear a guy give me a lame excuse why he wants to have sex, I know to say 'no' because I care about myself, my future goals and plans."

Female *Heritage Keepers*® student

The following information was written for Heritage Community Services® by Joshua Mann, MD, MPH, University of South Carolina, Department of Family and Preventive Medicine.

You should understand male and female anatomy so that if your child comes to you with specific questions you can answer them appropriately. Giving your children and teens accurate answers about anatomy and reproduction will build their confidence in you and your knowledge in this subject. Obviously, you do not need to be an expert – and you may have to contact your doctor or look on the Internet to find the answers to some of your kids' questions. However, knowing the basics is a good place to start.

Male Reproductive System

Heritage Community Services ©

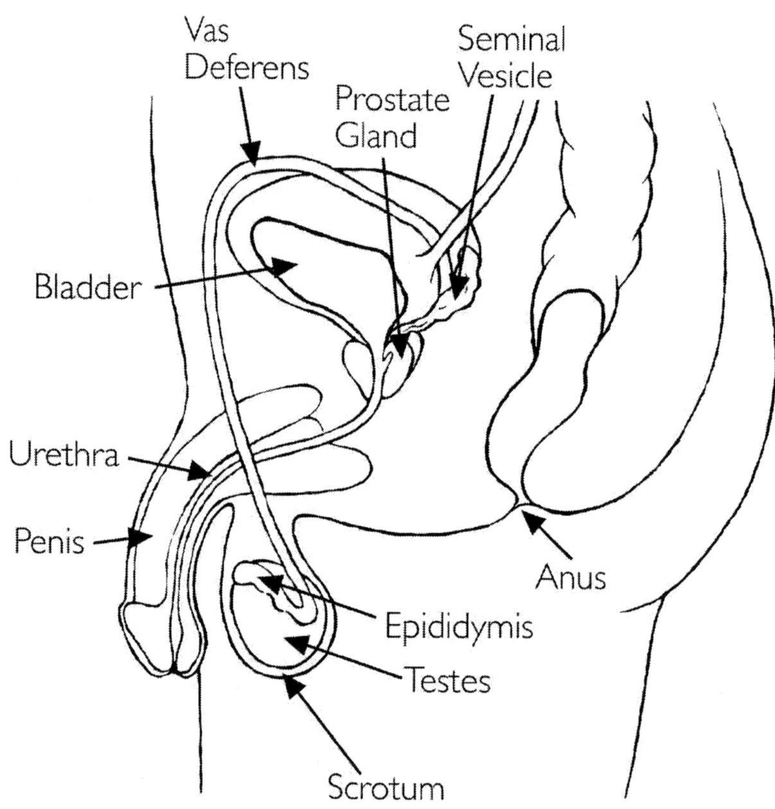

The male reproductive system is made up of the following:

- the penis, a tube-shaped organ that is covered in skin and emits fluids (urine and semen) from the body
- the urethra, a smaller tube inside the penis that carries urine from the bladder and sperm from the vas deferens to the outside of the body
- the scrotum, a pouch or sack of skin that hangs between the legs and holds the testes in place

- the two testes, which are located inside the scrotum and produce sperm and the hormone testosterone that causes the development of facial hair and other male physical features
- the epididymis, a tube attached to each testis, where sperm mature before passing to the vas deferens
- the vas deferens, long, thin tubes that transport sperm away from the epididymis
- the seminal vesicles and prostate, which produce the fluids that make up semen, which nourishes sperm and provides a vehicle for sperm to get to a female's egg.

Sperm are cells produced by the testes that contain genetic information (genes) from a male. These cells can join with (fertilize) a female's egg, which has the female's genetic information, to bring about a pregnancy. Sperm have a tail that allows them to "swim" in fluid, so that they can get to a woman's egg and fertilize it.

Immediately after they are produced, sperm are not capable of movement. They pass from the testes to the epididymis where they mature and acquire the ability to move. Once mature, the sperm then enter the vas deferens. These tubes pass through the seminal vesicles and the prostate gland, which secrete fluids that mix with the sperm to provide nourishment and effectively carry the sperm. This fluid is called semen.

During sexual activity, blood flow into the penis increases, and blood flow out of the penis decreases, causing the penis to become stiff; this is called an erection. If sexual stimulation is continued, ejaculation occurs. During ejaculation, muscles in the penis contract, pushing the semen (containing millions of sperm) through the urethra and out the tip of the penis, into the female's reproductive tract. A valve in the urethra prevents the emission of both semen and urine at the same time.

Some possible concerns males may have:

Erections. As described above, erections occur when blood fills the penis, causing it to become stiff. Erections most often occur because of sexual stimulation such as sexual thoughts, erotic touching, or other sexual situations. However, during puberty, "spontaneous erections" – erections that occur in the absence of sexual stimulation – sometimes occur. This is a common part of puberty and should not cause a person to worry unless the erection causes pain or does not go away within an hour or so.

Nocturnal emissions. Sometimes a male may ejaculate during his sleep, often as a result of a sexually stimulating dream. This is also a normal occurrence during puberty that usually occurs less frequently with age.

Penis and testicular size. The size of a boy's or man's penis and testes varies from one person to another. This is usually nothing to worry about. However, if someone is worried about the size of his reproductive organs, he should discuss those concerns with his doctor.

Testicular lumps. A man can develop a lump in one or both of his testes. If this occurs, he should see his doctor right away, since it is possible to develop cancer of the testes. Testicular cancer can usually be treated effectively if it is detected early, but treatment is less effective if it is delayed.

Circumcision. Circumcision is a minor surgical procedure usually performed soon after birth, which removes all or part of the foreskin of the penis. Not all parents choose to circumcise their male children; the decision is most often based on religious or cultural traditions rather than medical benefits. However, circumcision probably is helpful in maintaining good hygiene. Uncircumcised men and boys should pull back their foreskin and wash underneath it every day. It is also important to make sure the foreskin can be pulled back. Occasionally a man's foreskin can cause problems by becoming too firmly attached to the penis or by covering up the tip of the penis. Pulling the foreskin back and washing underneath it can also help prevent this problem.

Impotence. Young men rarely have problems getting an erection and ejaculating. However, older men sometimes have problems with these necessary aspects of sexual activity. Men who do have these problems can discuss them with their doctor, as there are effective treatments available. However, the best approach is to prevent these problems by avoiding behaviors that can cause impotence. Two of the most common causes of impotence are tobacco use and diabetes. Avoiding tobacco use and diabetes substantially reduces the likelihood that a man will have problems with sexual function. The best way to avoid diabetes is to get plenty of exercise and avoid overeating. Men who are already diabetic can reduce the likelihood of impotence by sticking very closely to the treatments prescribed by their doctor.

The Female Reproductive System

Unlike the male reproductive system where the reproductive organs are visible outside the body, the female reproductive system has elements that can be seen from the outside, but also a number of important parts that are internal (not visible). Therefore, discussions of female reproduction usually distinguish between the external and internal reproductive organs.

Female External Reproductive Organs (side view, shows internal as well)

Heritage Community Services ©

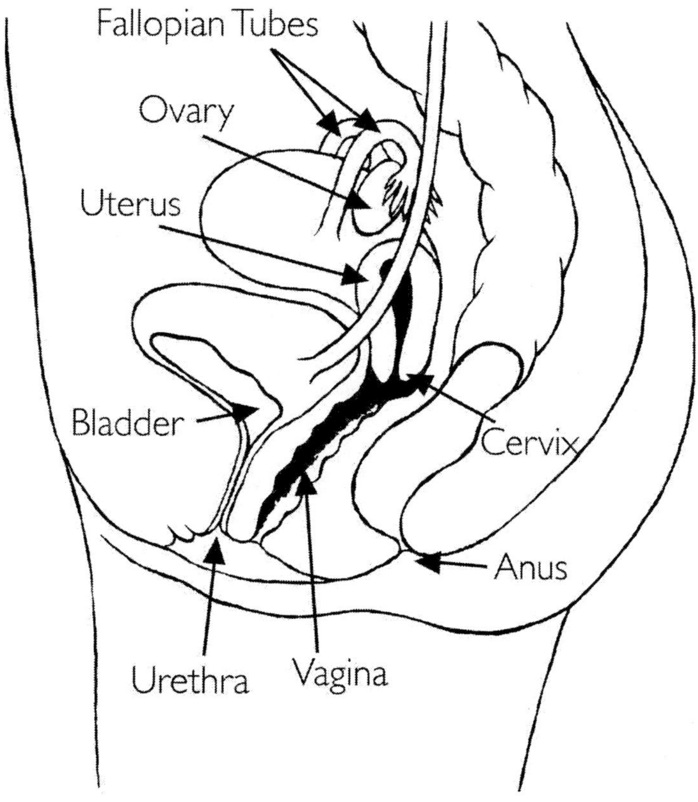

The female external reproductive organs are also called the vulva. They include:

- the labia majora (external fatty folds surrounding the urinary and vaginal openings)
- the labia minora (two thinner folds of skin located within the outer lips)
- the clitoris, a structure containing sensitive nerve endings
- the hymen, a flexible membrane which covers the opening to the vagina.

Interestingly, during a baby's development inside the mother's womb, the labia majora and labia minora develop from the same tissues that form a boy's scrotum, while the clitoris develops from the same tissues that form a boy's penis.

Female Internal Reproductive Organs

Heritage Community Services ©

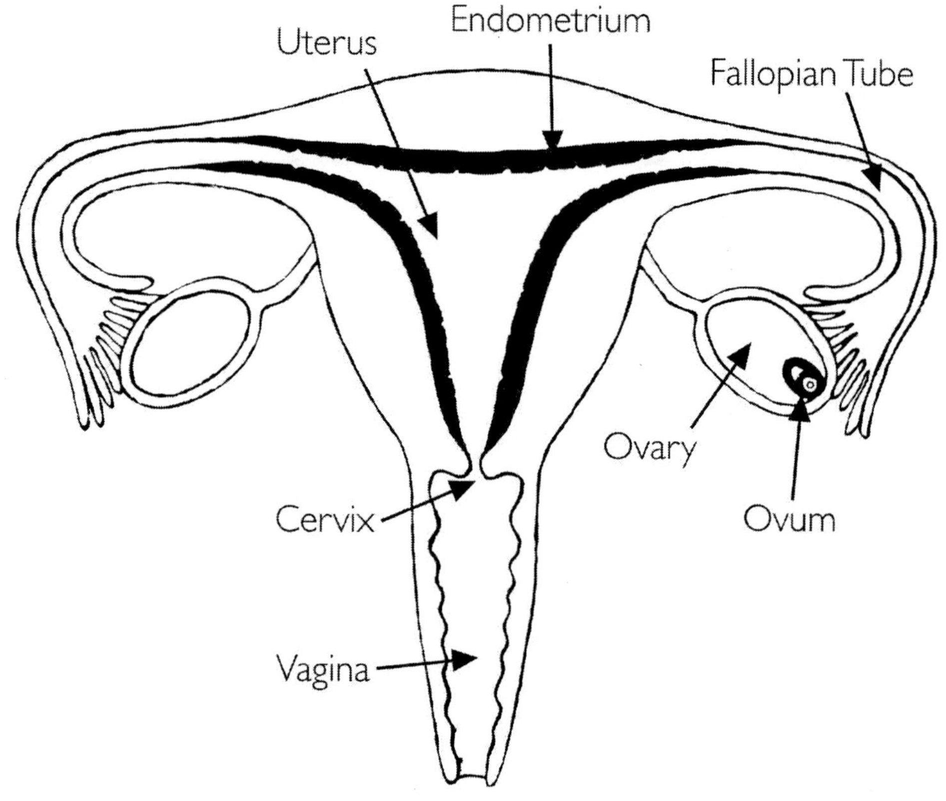

The female internal reproductive system is made up of:

- the vagina, which is a pouch between the woman's legs (just inside the vulva)
- the ovaries, two glands each containing thousands of eggs located in the woman's abdomen – the ovaries also produce estrogen, a hormone responsible for female features such as enlarging breasts
- the fallopian tubes, that connect each ovary to the uterus
- the uterus, also called the womb, which is where a fertilized egg implants and a baby develops prior to birth. The bottom of the uterus is connected to the top of the vagina.

About once a month, an egg is released from one of the ovaries into one of the fallopian tubes. This is called ovulation. At about the same time, the lining of the uterus builds up with blood vessels, providing a place for a fertilized egg to implant; the blood vessels provide a supply of the mother's blood to provide nourishment and sustain the new life. The implanted egg develops into a fetus, which is a developing baby inside the mother's womb. If no egg is fertilized (because there is no sexual activity around the time of ovulation, effective contraception is used, or there are simply no sperm that make it to the egg to bring about fertilization), the egg remains in the uterus a few days and then is released into the vagina where it essentially dies. Similarly, sometimes an egg will become fertilized but will fail to implant in the uterus. In this case, the fertilized egg also dies and is eliminated through the vagina.

If a fertilized egg implants in the lining of the uterus, hormones are produced that maintain the lining so that normal development can occur, leading to the birth of a baby.

If no egg is fertilized or a fertilized egg fails to implant, the uterine lining dies and sloughs off, passing out of the body through the vagina. Tissue and blood will pass through the vagina – this is called a woman's menstrual flow.

Normally, about 14 days pass between the time ovulation occurs and the beginning of menstrual flow. The first day of menstrual flow is usually counted as the first day of the menstrual cycle. This usually lasts for four or five days, with the first day or two being the heaviest. There is usually a 7- to 21-day span of time between the first day of menstrual flow and ovulation. Therefore, the "normal" time span between menstrual periods is between 21 and 35 days, with an average of about 28 days. Menstrual cycles in this range are considered normal. If a woman's cycles occur more frequently than every 21 days or less frequently than every 35 days, she should tell her doctor about her cycles to make sure there is no medical problem that needs to be treated.

Similarly, the amount of blood loss during a period should be fairly small – about four to six tablespoons during the course of the menstrual period. If there is substantially more blood loss than this, or if menstrual flow continues longer than about seven days, a woman should talk to her doctor to make sure everything is normal.

The onset of menstrual periods is fairly unpredictable; some girls start menstruating as early as 9 years of age. Others start significantly later. If menstruation starts before age 9 or after age 16, a doctor should be consulted to make sure nothing is wrong.

Some possible concerns females may have:

Pre-Menstrual Syndrome. Levels of certain hormones change just before menstruation. Sometimes these hormones can cause symptoms such as mood swings, bloating and breast tenderness in the days leading up to menstrual flow. Usually these symptoms can be handled fairly easily with over-the-counter medications and behavioral changes such as getting regular exercise and cutting down on salt and caffeine (coffee, tea, many sodas, etc.).

Dysmenorrhea. Many women also experience symptoms of abdominal and back discomfort and possibly nausea or other symptoms shortly before and during menstrual flow. This occurs because of uterine contractions pushing out the menstrual flow that cause a cramping sensation. Again, over-the-counter medications can often help with these symptoms. If they are severe, talk with your doctor to get additional input on how to decrease symptoms of dysmenorrhea.

Irregular periods. Adolescents often experience irregular menstrual cycles – sometimes occurring more frequently and other times occurring less frequently. This is normal, and should resolve within a year or so as the reproductive system fully "gets going."

Feminine hygiene products. During menstruation, a woman should use a sanitary product to soak up menstrual flow to prevent staining of clothes and furniture. Most women use either sanitary napkins (pads) or tampons. Pads work by providing an absorbent layer over the underwear that soaks up the menstrual flow. Tampons are finger-shaped and are inserted into the vagina; like sanitary napkins, they soak up menstrual flow. Both pads and tampons should be changed frequently (several times a day) to maintain good hygiene.

Toxic shock syndrome. In the late 1970s, a number of women became seriously ill during their menstrual cycle while using tampons. Symptoms included fatigue, fever, chills, nausea, and confusion, and the condition sometimes progressed to organ failure and death. It was determined that the illness was due to improper tampon use. The women were not changing their tampons frequently enough, allowing an overgrowth of bacteria in the tampon. These bacteria produced toxic chemicals that caused the serious illnesses. Modern tampons are less likely to foster toxic shock syndrome (TSS); however, women using tampons are still at risk. The surest way to avoid TSS is to use pads rather than tampons. The best way for tampon users to avoid TSS is to change their tampons frequently – at least every few hours. Women who have had TSS in the past should not use tampons. TSS can also happen as a result of other conditions, such as infected skin wounds, or after certain medical or surgical procedures. If symptoms of TSS occur, it is important to contact a physician sooner rather than later.

Twins. Women may have twins for one of two reasons: either more than one egg was produced by the ovaries and fertilized by sperm or one egg was fertilized then divided in two after fertilization. In the first case, the twins are called fraternal twins and are NOT identical. In the second case, the twins are identical.

"What Do Students Think?"

On the last day of the *Heritage Keepers® Abstinence Education* class, the school nurse wanted feedback from the boy's seventh grade class about the program. The three questions she asked, and some of their answers, were:

1) **What do you think about this class?** *I think it is a very important class. It is very informative. It was fun. I learned a lot of stuff. I liked this class. This class was a great educational class.*

2) **What is the main thing you learned?** *I learned about the reproductive tract. I learned how the sperm fertilizes the egg. I learned about all kinds of STDs. I learned that abstaining from sex is important to my future. I learned about the consequences of having sex outside of marriage.*

3) **What would you change about the class and would you recommend it to others?** *They do not have to change. I would definitely recommend this class. It was a great class. I wish this class was longer. Keep doing what you are doing. This was the best abstinence class I've ever taken. It was a good class to have in middle school. I would like to say that this class was educational and proper for the school and thank you. I think a lot of people (especially high school) should take this class.*

There is no doubt that the information that is being taught concerning sexual abstinence is making a positive impact on teenagers.

ANATOMY – BE AN EXPERT

What other questions about anatomy and reproduction do you think your child may ask? Write them here and then find the answers!

Ask your child to write any questions about anatomy and reproduction that he or she may have. Find the answers together.

Chapter Eleven: Other Risky Behaviors

"My life has been changed by you opening my eyes and letting me see, instead of experiencing the things that can happen if you aren't careful. I only wish that you could have taught me more of the things that can happen in the world around me."

Male *Heritage Keepers*® student

"You have helped me in a tremendous way. I have learned some things that I have always questioned in my mind but didn't really know who to ask. You have done a very nice job because some girls in our class really needed to hear some of the things you said. My opinion about the Heritage services is they should try to go national. Thank you."

Female *Heritage Keepers*® student

"To tell ya'll the truth, I had a personal experience this weekend, and I have decided to make a safe decision with my sex life b/c ya'll got me thinking, and now that ya'll got me to thinking, I realize how dangerous I'm being, and I never thought I was doing anything wrong but I am doing everything wrong. Thank you!"

Female *Heritage Keepers*® student

Most of us can agree that teenagers want to be popular; they want to be liked, to fit in. Even adults want to feel loved and appreciated. It hurts when people are mean, call us names, or ignore us. But, like with everything, a line must be drawn that determines just how much someone should give up of themselves in order to be accepted.

Your child will have to deal with an amazing amount of peer pressure to do things that you most likely will not want them to do during their young life. Popularity can come at great cost, and often that cost means being everything to everyone, which can mean involvement in sex, drugs, alcohol, and even violence.

Many people regret that they completely lost themselves during their teenage and young adult years. In an almost desperate attempt to please people, they may have given up their personality, jeopardized their goals, compromised their values and crossed their personal boundaries just hoping someone would like them.

Losing one's identity can hurt as much as not fitting in. Watching one's hopes and dreams dissipate, negotiating risky situations – it's too much for a young mind and heart to handle. When others push an adolescent into behaviors that compromise their well-being, it can be devastating – for them and for you.

As a parent, it is important to teach your child to balance popularity with honoring their own values and goals. Help them to set boundaries for themselves when it comes to drugs, alcohol, violence and sex. And help them to have an exit plan when things are spinning out of control. Be open with your child so that when they come to you, there will be no fear of shame and punishment – but rather a sense that they know their parents will love them and help them through all of life's ups and downs. That does not mean there will not be consequences, but there is a sense of trust your child should have with you.

Many teens can feel misunderstood and lonely in the midst of partying. That is because they may feel the kids they want as friends don't really even know them. They only know one side of that person— the party side. But each person is worth so much more than what they might be like when they are using drugs or alcohol, or because they have had sex. Do not allow your child to be defined by drugs, alcohol or sex – that is an empty definition. People have hopes, dreams, values, families, ideas, opinions, intelligence, and many more qualities that cannot be shared properly while drunk or high.

Attitude Adjustment

Heritage Community Services reaches some of the most at risk youth. In a school for juvenile males, one particular student did not like the *Heritage Keepers® Abstinence Education* class. Initially his belief was that everyone is having sex and so the class is a waste of time. However, as the days went by, his attitude about the class changed. He became the most vocal supporter in the class. The program provided him with an opportunity to reflect on the choices he has made and the consequences he now faces because of those choices. On the last day at the school, this young man wrote a letter to the *Heritage Keepers®* instructor, sharing with him how much he had changed and thanking the teacher for challenging him to take responsibility for his actions. He informed the instructor that he had made the decision to recommit to abstinence.

Help your child let other people know who they really are by teaching them to stand up for the qualities that make him or her unique! Your child will be confronted with these issues at some point in his or her life; no one lives in a bubble. They will most likely want and need a social life. Therefore, there needs to a balance between you protecting your teen from dangerous situations and equipping your teen to handle such situations when they arise. Have a game plan ready to help your child deal with negative peer pressure; help them by role playing so that they can communicate their personal values, boundaries and goals.

We have compiled some helpful information for you regarding several risky behaviors that your teens may be pressured into trying in order to fit in or feel popular. Use the information on the following pages to help your teen set boundaries regarding alcohol, drugs, and Internet safety.

Alcohol Getting drunk has become a common activity among high school and college students. Alcohol is illegal for anyone under the age of 21, and if teens choose to drink before that, they may get a record they don't want.

Drinking is not a low risk activity. It can lead to many potentially harmful consequences. Drinking takes away self-control. It actually slows down your brain. This leaves you with slurred speech, confused thinking, and uncontrolled and uncoordinated movements.[216,217] Therefore, people under the influence of alcohol typically have lower inhibitions, a reduced sense of self-control, a lessened sense of judgment, and a reduced capability to accurately assess risks.[218,219] People under the

---

[216] Schulenberg, J., O'Malley, P. M., Bachman, J. G., Wadsworth, K. N., & Johnston, L. D. (1996). Getting drunk and growing up: Trajectories of frequent binge drinking during the transition to young adulthood. *Journal of Studies on Alcohol, 57,* 289-304.

[217] Tangney, J. P., Baumesiter, R. F., & Boone, A. L. (2004). High self-control predicts good adjustment, less pathology, better grades, and interpersonal success. *Journal of Personality, 72,* 271-322.

[218] Alcohol Concern. (2002, March). *Alcohol & Teenage Pregnancy.* London: Alcohol Concern. Retrieved February 5, 2010 from http://www.slideshare.net/bpilmer/alcohol-and-teenage-pregnancy

influence of alcohol often make decisions they regret, such as getting involved in aggression, violence, and sex. When someone chooses to be under the influence of alcohol or drugs, he or she may make decisions that put him or her at risk sexually.[220,221,222] Many young people wake up the next morning after drinking with deep regrets about their behavior from the night before.[223]

Alcohol and Sex Teens who drink alcohol are seven times more likely to have intercourse than those who do not drink, and those who use drugs are five times more likely to have sex.[224] Teens who use drugs and alcohol are likely to have more sexual partners[225] which puts them at greater risk for sexually transmitted infections.[226] Studies show that most rapes or acts of sexual aggression involved drinking or drug use by the attacker or the victim.[227,228,229] It's not just the victim that loses control. The person using drugs and alcohol can become more abusive while under the influence of alcohol or drugs.[230] Many teens report losing their virginity while they were drunk.[231,232,233] and most of those teens woke up regretting that decision the next morning.[234] Many teens also report "doing more sexually than they had planned" because they were under the influence of drugs or alcohol.[235]

---

219 Hennessy, M., Manteuffel, B., Dilorio, C., & Adame D. (1997). Identifying the social contexts of effective sex refusal. *Journal of American College Health, 46,* 27-34.

220 Kaiser Family Foundation. (2002, February). *Substance use & sexual health among teens and young adults in the U.S.* Retrieved August 21, 2007 from http://www.kff.org/youthhivstds/upload/KFF-CASAFactSheet.pdf

221 Moore, N. B., & Davidson, J. K. (2006). College women and personal goals: Cognitive dimensions that differentiate risk-reduction sexual decisions. *Journal of Youth and Adolescence, 35,* 577-589.

222 Epstein, J. A., Griffin, K. W., & Botvin, G. J. (2001). Risk taking and refusal assertiveness in a longitudinal model of alcohol use among inner-city adolescents. *Prevention Science, 2,* 193-200.

223 Alcohol Concern, et al., 2002

224 The National Center on Addiction and Substance Abuse at Columbia University. (1999, December). *Dangerous Liasons: Substance Abuse and Sex* (p. 2). Retrieved March 16, 2011 from http://www.casacolumbia.org/articlefiles/379-Dangerous Liaisons.pdf

225 Santelli, J. S., Robin, L., Brener, N. D., & Lowry, R. (2000). Timing of alcohol and other drug use and sexual risk behaviors among unmarried adolescents and young adults. *Family Planning Perspectives, 33,* 200-205.

226 Moore, et al., 2006

227 The National Center on Addiction and Substance Abuse at Columbia University, et al., 1999.

228 Johnson, T. J., & Stahl, C. (2004). Sexual experiences associated with participation in drinking games. *The Journal of General Psychology, 131,* 304-320.

229 Champion, H. L. O., Foley, K. L., DuRant, R. H., Hensberry, R., Altman, D., & Wofson, M. (2004). Adolescent sexual victimization, use of alcohol and other substances, and other health risk behaviors. *Journal of Adolescent Health, 35,* 321-328.

230 Johnson, et al., 2004

231 Alcohol Concern, et al., 2002

232 Bingham, C. R., & Crockett, L. J. (1996). Longitudinal adjustment patterns of boys and girls experiencing early, middle, and late sexual intercourse. *Developmental Psychology, 32,* 647-658.

233 Blinn-Pike, L., Beger, T. J., Hewett, J., & Olsen, J. (2004). Sexually abstinent adolescents: An 18-month follow-up. *Journal of Adolescent Research, 19,* 495-511.

234 Alcohol Concern, et al., 2002

235 Kaiser Family Foundation. (2002, February). *Substance use and risky sexual behavior: Attitudes and practices among adolescents and young adults.* Retrieved July 20, 2008 from http://www.kff.org/youthhivstds/20020207a-index.cfm

Many high school and college students binge drink. This is defined as "the consumption of five or more drinks in a row on at least one occasion." Binge drinking is often associated with partying and is extremely serious. In fact, alcohol is often a factor in the four leading injury-related deaths among teens: vehicle crashes, homicides, suicides and drowning.[236]

Teens report using alcohol for many different reasons: to fit in, curiosity, to forget their problems, or even just to feel grown up. These reasons to drink indicate immaturity.

According to Alcoholics Anonymous, your child may have a problem with alcohol if they drink:

- because they have a problem, or to relax,
- because they get mad at other people,
- when they are alone,
- so much their grades are starting to slip,
- so much they have tried to stop and can't,
- in the morning before school,
- in gulps,
- so much they lose their memory,
- so much they lie about their drinking,
- so much they are getting into trouble because of it,
- so much that they get drunk when they don't mean to, and/or
- so much they think it is cool that they can "handle their liquor."

Health Risks Associated with Alcohol Chronic alcohol abuse promotes the occurrence of gastro-esophageal reflux and increases the risk of cancer of the esophagus.[237] Liver disease can be caused by alcohol. The longer the duration of alcohol use and the larger the consumption, the greater the probability of developing liver disease.[238]

- Intoxication is involved in an average of 41 percent of traffic accident deaths,[239] 40-65 percent of fatal injuries in the home, almost 40 percent of drowning accidents, and up to 80 percent of fatal fire accidents.[240]
- Alcohol-related psychosis (causing hallucinations) occurs in many alcohol-related conditions, including intoxication, [alcohol] withdrawal after a major

---

[236] Dowshen, S. (2009, April) *Binge Drinking.* Jacksonville, Florida: The Nemours Foundation. Retrieved February 7, 2011 from http://kidshealth.org/teen/drug_alcohol/#cat20139

[237] Souza, R. & Spechler, S. (2005). Concepts in the prevention of adenocarcinoma of the distal esophagus and proximal stomach. *CA: A Cancer Journal for Clinicians, 55,* 334-351.

[238] Lieber, C. S. (2005). Relationships between nutrition, alcohol use, and liver disease. *Alcohol Research & Health, 27,* 220-231.

[239] National Highway Traffic Safety Administration. (2011). *Persons Killed, by Highest Driver Blood Alcohol Concentration (BAC) in the Crash, 1994 - 2009 - State : USA* Retrieved February 8, 2011 from http://www-fars.nhtsa.dot.gov/Trends/TrendsAlcohol.aspx

[240] Brismar, B & Bergman, B. (1998). The significance of alcohol for violence and accidents. *Alcoholism: Clinical & Experimental Research, 22,* 299s-306s.

decrease in alcohol consumption, etc.[241] Psychosis can prevent people from functioning normally and caring for themselves. If untreated, people can harm themselves and others.[242]

- Researchers are now finding that women who drink too much alcohol are at a higher risk of breast cancer.[243]
- Alcohol, when used by pregnant women, can cause spontaneous abortion, premature labor, stillbirths, and fetal alcohol syndrome, which causes malformations and retarded physical and mental development.[244]
- Studies show that alcoholics have more decayed and missing teeth than non-alcoholics.[245]

Health Risks Specifically Regarding Teens Who Use Alcohol

- Teens who drink are more likely to be sexually active and to have unsafe, unprotected sex.
- One-half of all drowning deaths among teen guys are related to alcohol use.
- Teen drinkers are more likely to [become overweight].
- Teens who continue drinking into adulthood risk damaging their liver, heart and brain.
- Use of alcohol slightly increases the chance that a teen will be involved in a car crash, homicide or suicide.[246]

Most teens are not aware of the risks associated with alcohol. Your child might be surprised to learn that many of the teens that initiated sex outside of a lifelong committed relationship such as marriage were under the influence of alcohol or drugs. If they did not have clear boundaries before they were under the influence, the risk is multiplied when they are drinking or doing drugs. Thus the regrets. Helping your teen understand the nature of alcohol is a first step to resisting opportunities to drink. Is your teen aware that alcohol is a depressant? Does he or she know that one loses control while under the influence and that others can take advantage of him or her more easily? Ask your child to tell you the effect of alcohol on the body and mind. If they are not aware of alcohol's effect on the body and mind, you can teach them to remember the following: The brain? It slows it down. Speech? Becomes slurred. Thinking? Becomes confused. Movements? Become uncontrolled. Appearance? Uncoordinated. Inhibitions? Lowered. Self-control? Reduced. Sense of judgment? Decreased. Risk assessment capacity? Reduced.

---

[241] Larson, M. (2006). *Alcohol-related psychosis* (from WebMD). Retrieved August 5, 2008 from http://www.emedicine.com/MED/topic3113.htm

[242] Ballas, C. (2008). P*sychosis.* Washington, DC: U.S. Department of Health and Human Services, Retrieved August 5, 2008 from The National Institutes of Health Web site: http://www.nlm.nih.gov/medlineplus/ency/article/001553.htm

[243] Standridge, J. B., Zylstra, R. G., & Adams, S. M. (2004). Alcohol consumption: An overview of benefits and risks. *Southern Medical Journal, 97*, 664-672.

[244] March of Dimes. (2005). *Drinking alcohol during pregnancy*. Retrieved June 16, 2008 from http://www.marchofdimes.com/professionals/14332_1170.asp

[245] Robb, N. (1990). Alcoholism and the dentist. *British Journal of Addiction, 85,* 437-439.

[246] Dowshen, S. (2009). *Alcohol.* Then Nemours Foundation. Retrieved February 23, 2011 from http://kidshealth.org/PageManager.jsp?dn=KidsHealth&lic=1&ps=207&cat_id=20139&article_set=20368

There is a perception among some that teens are going to drink, have sex, or try drugs, no matter what adults do or say. This is a false belief. Instead, statistics indicate that these behaviors cluster. Young people participating in one risky behavior are more likely to be participating in others. And one can lead to the other. As we mentioned earlier in this chapter, many teens initiated sex for the first time under the influence of alcohol or drugs, and regretted it later, when they were back in their right mind.

Even adults struggle with the effects of drugs, alcohol and sexual relationships outside of marriage. Teens, who are still under the effects of puberty and whose brains are still developing, often handle these risky behaviors poorly, with outcomes that they – and their families – wish could be undone. Helping your teens understand that they have a bright future and empowering them to have a sense of identity that is built upon self-worth, high expectations, the self-efficacy to succeed, as well as the skills to avoid risks, will put them in a category of youth that are more likely to do well – educationally, in their career, and with their family life.

Cigarettes Many teens think smoking is a cool, easy thing to do because it is more accessible than drugs and alcohol. But smoking is a serious addiction and can cause serious health risks, including death.

According to the Centers for Disease Control, smoking is the single most preventable cause of premature death in the United States. Since 1964, ten million people in America have died from smoking-related illnesses, such as heart disease, emphysema, lung cancer, and other respiratory diseases.[247] About 40,000 Americans on average die each year from health problems due to smoking.[248] On average, smokers die 13 to 14 years earlier than nonsmokers.[249]

Smoking is often considered the first step to other risky behaviors. The National Household Survey on Drug Abuse found that adolescents who smoked cigarettes were eight times more likely to use other drugs and 11 times more likely to use alcohol than their nonsmoking counterparts.[250] Many people underestimate the addictiveness of nicotine and believe they will be able to quit within a few years. But studies show that about 75 percent of these people are still smoking five or six years later. Seventy percent of adolescent smokers say they wish they had never started.[251]

---

[247] Center for the Advancement of Health. (2001, March/April). Reducing tobacco use: The quest to quit. *Facts of Life (online journal), 6 (3).* Retrieved June 3, 2008 from http://www.cfah.org/factsoflife/vol6no3.cfm

[248] Centers for Disease Control and Prevention. (2006). *Cigarette smoking-related mortality.* Retrieved June 3, 2008 from http://www.cdc.gov/tobacco/data_statistics/factsheet/cig_smoking_mort.htm

[249] Centers for Disease Control and Prevention. (2008). *Smoking & tobacco use.* Retrieved June 10, 2008 from http://www.cdc.gov/tobacco/basic_information/FastFacts.htm#toll

[250] Substance Abuse & Mental Health Services Administration. (1996). *Preliminary estimates from the 1995 national household survey on drug abuse. Office of Applied Studies Advance Report Number 18.* Washington, DC: SAMHSA. Retrieved on February 8, 2011 from http://oas.samhsa.gov/nhsda/ar18ttoc.htm

[251] Childrens Hospital Boston. (2007). *Smoking.* Retrieved on June 3, 2008 from http://www.childrenshospital.org/az/Site1618/mainpageS1618PO.html

Nicotine is the main addictive drug in cigarettes. There are 4,000 harmful chemicals in a cigarette, including:[252]

- Carbon monoxide, the dangerous gas that comes out of our cars,
- Formaldehyde, the chemical used to preserve dead bodies,
- Ammonia, a kitchen and bathroom cleaner,
- Cyanide, the gas used to exterminate pests,
- Benzene, made mostly of petroleum, and
- Acetylene, a compressed gas used in the welding and cutting of metals.

The following effects of these chemicals should cause anyone, teen or adult, to reconsider whether smoking is worth these serious risks.

Carbon Monoxide Exposure can cause changes in body temperature, irregularities in blood pressure, nausea, vomiting, chest pain, difficulty breathing, irregular heartbeat, headache, drowsiness, dizziness, hallucinations, pain in extremities, tremors, loss of coordination, hearing loss, visual disturbances, eye damage, suffocation, blood disorders, convulsion, and coma. It may cause visual disturbances, heart disorders, heart damage, nerve damage, birth defects and reproductive effects or brain damage in long term exposure.[253]
Formaldehyde Symptoms to exposure include irritation and burns of the eyes, nose, and throat. Long term exposure may cause cancer.[254]
Ammonia Exposure can cause irritation and burns to the eyes, skin, throat, and lungs.[255]
Cyanide It can cause irritation, rash, nausea, chest pain, irregular heartbeat, headache, blindness, bluish skin color, suffocation, lung congestion, paralysis, convulsions, coma and death.[256]
Benzene Inhaling benzene can cause drowsiness, dizziness, rapid heart rate, headaches, tremors, confusion and unconsciousness. Breathing high levels can result in death. Long-term exposure can lead to anemia, excessive bleeding, and can affect the immune system.[257]
Acetylene Symptoms of exposure include headache, dizziness and suffocation by causing central nervous system depression.[258]

---

[252] QuitSmokingStop, (2010). *Chemicals in cigarettes.* Retrieved February 15, 2011 from http://www.quit-smoking-stop.com/harmful-chemicals-in-cigarettes.html

[253] Centers for Disease Control and Prevention. (2006, July). *Carbon monoxide poisoning.* Retrieved February 15, 2011 from http://www.cdc.gov/co/faqs.htm

[254] Centers for Disease Control and Prevention. (2010, September 1). Public Health Statement for Formaldehyde. Retrieved February 15, 2011 from http://www.atsdr.cdc.gov/ToxProfiles/tp111-c1-b.pdf

[255] Centers for Disease Control and Prevention. (2010, September 1). *Medical management guidelines for ammonia.* Retrieved February 15, 2011 from http://www.atsdr.cdc.gov/mmg/mmg.asp?id=7&tid=2

[256] Centers for Disease Control and Prevention. (2004, January 27). *Facts about cyanide.* Retrieved February 15, 2011 from http://www.bt.cdc.gov/agent/cyanide/basics/facts.asp

[257] Centers for Disease Control and Prevention. (2005, August 29). *Facts about benzene.* Retrieved February 15, 2011 from http://www.bt.cdc.gov/agent/benzene/basics/facts.asp

[258] Centers for Disease Control and Prevention. (2010, November 18). *Acetylene.* Retrieved February 15, 2011 from http://www.cdc.gov/niosh/npg/npgd0008.html

Smoking leads to

- 90 percent of lung cancer deaths in men
- 80 percent (almost) of lung cancer deaths in women
- Cancers of the bladder, oral cavity, pharynx, voice box, esophagus, cervix, kidney, lung, pancreas and stomach[259]

Test your child on his or her knowledge of the harmful ingredients in cigarettes. Simply ask him or her to tell you the quickest and easiest way to get the above mentioned poisons into their body. It is highly likely that they have no idea that these poisons are inhaled into the lungs by smokers and by those who are around others that smoke. Have your child practice (role play with you) resisting the invitation to try smoking until you are satisfied he or she has the skills needed to resist peer pressure. Smoking can be addictive and once it is started they may end up smoking until it kills them. Many experts also consider smoking the gateway to other risky behaviors.

Drugs Illegal drug use among teens is on the rise, but drugs are a dangerous substance. As with any illegal substance, there are no warning labels that describe or regulate dosage. Your child won't know what he or she is taking or what effects it will have. Illegal drugs can cause a violent, painful death almost instantly. Teach your child it is simply not worth taking the chance.

Drugs are addictive and deadly. Drugs impair judgment and can lead to a loss of self-control. When the user sobers up, there are often consequences from decisions made while under the influence. Tell your child simply not to risk it. Advise him or her to stay in control!

Make sure your teen is aware that it is not just the physical harm done by drugs that they should avoid, but the associated behaviors they might engage in while under the influence. They may have regrets, but the damage they may do to themselves or others may be impossible to undo.

---

[259] Center for Disease Control and Prevention. (2010, September 15). *Tobacco-related mortality*. Retrieved February 9, 2011 from http://www.cdc.gov/tobacco/data_statistics/fact_sheets/health_effects/tobacco_related_mortality/

Drug Information[260] *(Information provided by The National Institute on Drug Abuse [drugabuse.gov], which supports research on and provides current information on drug abuse and addiction)*

MDMA (Methylenedioxymethamphetamine) One of many "Club Drugs", it is a drug often used at bars, nightclubs, concerts or parties

Street Names: Ecstasy, XTC, Adam, Clarity, Lovers' Speed, X, hug, beans, love drug

Effects while on drug: dehydration, hypertension, heart, kidney or cardiovascular failure, increase in body temperature, muscle breakdown
Effects of drug after it is taken: confusion, depression, sleeping problems, anxiety, paranoia
Long-term effects: damage to neurons, which can lead to severe depression

Steroids

Possible long term effects: liver tumors, cancer, jaundice, fluid retention, high blood pressure, increase in bad cholesterol and decrease in good cholesterol, kidney tumors, severe acne, trembling, shrinking testicles, reduced sperm count, infertility, baldness, development of breasts in men, increased risk of prostate cancer
Women: growth of facial hair, baldness, changes in menstrual cycle, deepened voice
Adolescents: could experience premature halting of growth

LSD (Lysergic Acid Diethylamide) One of many "Club Drugs", it is a drug often used at bars, nightclubs, concerts or parties

Street Names: Acid, Boomers, Yellow Sunshines, Blotter, Dots

Effects: unpredictable behavior, hallucinations, increased blood pressure, increased heart rate and temperature, activates sweat glands, loss of appetite, dry mouth, body tremors, numbness, weakness, nausea
Long Term Effects: persistent psychosis, flashbacks

Ketamine One of many "Club Drugs", it is a drug often used at bars, nightclubs, concerts or parties

Street Names: Special K, K, Vitamin K, Cat Valiums

Effects: hallucinations, delirium, amnesia, impaired motor function, high blood pressure, depression, potentially fatal respiratory problems

---

[260] National Institute on Drug Abuse. (2011). Retrieved March 30, 2011 from http://www.drugabuse.gov

Rohypnol One of many "Club Drugs", it is a drug often used at bars, nightclubs, concerts or parties

Street Names: Roofies, Rophies, Roche, Forget-me Pill

This is a tasteless, odorless drug that dissolves in carbonated beverages. Its sedative effects are aggravated by alcohol. Even without alcohol, a small dosage can impair a victim for eight to twelve hours.

This drug causes amnesia, which means forgetting events that took place while under its control. It is commonly used in sexual assaults.

Other side effects: decreased blood pressure, drowsiness, visual disturbances, dizziness, confusion, gastrointestinal disturbances, and urinary retention.

Remind your child to never accept drinks from strangers or anyone they do not know well. Tell your child, "If you are accepting a drink, even from someone you know, make sure it's from an unopened container and that you open it yourself. Don't put your drink down or leave it unattended even to go to the restroom. If you accidentally put your drink down, don't drink it and get a new unopened drink."

Methamphetamine One of many "Club Drugs", it is a drug often used at bars, nightclubs, concerts or parties

Street Names: Speed, Ice, Chalk, Meth, Crystal, Fire, Glass

Effects: memory loss, aggression, violence, psychotic behavior, potential cardiac and neurological damage

GHB (Gamma-hydroxybutyrate) One of many "Club Drugs", it is a drug often used at bars, nightclubs, concerts or parties

Street Names: Grievous Body Harm, G, Liquid Ecstasy, Georgia Home Boy

GHB is increasingly used in: poisonings, overdoses, date rapes (it is increasingly causing fatalities). Overdoses occur quickly and, by the time people realize they are in danger, it is too late.

Effects: central nervous system depression, slow breathing, heart rate goes up to dangerous levels, coma

PCP (Phencyclidine)

Street Names: Angel dust, Ozone, Whack, Rocket fuel

Effects: leads to psychological dependence, cravings and compulsive PCP-seeking behavior; it makes people delusional, agitated and irrational; it is known as the drug with bad reactions and not worth the risk; hospitals find PCP users to be violent and suicidal.

Cocaine

Street Names: Crack, Coke, C, Snow, Flake, Blow

Effects of small amounts: blood vessels constrict, temperature, heart rate and blood pressure increase *Effects of large amounts:* bizarre, erratic, violent behavior, toxic reactions resulting in tremors, vertigo, twitching muscles, paranoia, and reactions similar to poisonings.

It can cause disturbances in heart rhythm and heart attacks, chest pain, respiratory failure, strokes, seizures, headaches, abdominal pain, fever, muscle spasms, convulsions, coma and nausea.

Cocaine has been linked to: heart disease, chaotic heart rhythms, ventricular fibrillation *Regular use can cause:* loss of sense of smell, nosebleeds, problems with swallowing, hoarseness, chronic runny nose, bowel gangrene, "tracks" in the forearms, allergic reactions resulting in death, malnutrition

A person who uses cocaine needs higher and higher doses every time they use it. Cocaine is extremely addictive. This is the hardest drug to get off of, if addicted a person may actually get sick when not continuing use (making withdrawal symptoms seem worse than the addiction, which in turn typically forces the user to remain stuck in the addiction).

Heroin

Street Names: Smack, H, Ska, Junk

Heroin causes physical dependence, which means that any abstinence from the drug causes the body to experience withdrawal symptoms. This can include drug cravings, restlessness, muscle and bone pain, insomnia, diarrhea, vomiting, cold flashes, goose bumps, and kicking movements. *Heroine is associated with major health problems:* fatal overdoses, collapsed veins, HIV/AIDS, hepatitis

Chronic Users Experience: infection of the heart lining and valves, collapsed veins, abscesses, cellulites, liver diseases, pulmonary complication (including various types of pneumonia) and depressing effects on respiration

Marijuana

Street Names: Pot, Herb, Weed, Boom, Mary Jane, Gangster, Grass, Ganga, 420

Short term effects: problems with learning, distorted perception, difficulty thinking and solving problems, loss of coordination, increased heart rate, anxiety and panic attacks

Long Term Effects: coughing up phlegm, chronic bronchitis, frequent chest colds, lung tissue can be injured or destroyed

Marijuana changes the way sensory information gets into and is processed by the brain. Research shows marijuana users, when given tests, make more errors, have difficulty paying attention and have problems registering, processing and using information.

Inhalants

Street Names: Whippets, Poppers, Snappers

Inhalants include a large group of chemicals that are found in such household products as aerosol sprays, cleaning fluids, glue, paint, paint thinner, gasoline, propane, nail polish remover, correction fluid, and marker pens. One use of an inhalant can disrupt the heartbeat and cause instant death from cardiac arrest or low oxygen levels that cause suffocation and death.

Summary Drugs, alcohol and sex are a dangerous combination.

- More than five million (almost one quarter) of sexually active teens and young adults report having unprotected sex because of substance abuse.
- Of the 15 to 24 year olds surveyed, 50 percent said people their age mix alcohol or drugs and sex often.
- Current data suggests that those who engage in any "risk behaviors" tend to take part in more than one, and that many health risk behaviors occur in combination with other risky activities.
- Prior substance use increases the probability that an adolescent will initiate sexual activity. One-quarter of sexually active 9th-12th graders report using alcohol or drugs during their last sexual encounter.
- Fifty-five percent of teenagers say having sex while drinking or on drugs is often a reason for unplanned pregnancies.[261]

Don't just close your eyes to the dangers your child faces. Get involved with him or her. Make sure he or she knows what you know, that you have set clear boundaries for him or her, and that you have helped him or her practice saying his or her boundaries out loud, as well as defending them when challenged.

---

[261] Kaiser Family Foundation. (2002, February). *Substance use and risky sexual behavior: Attitudes and practices among adolescents and young adults.* Retrieved July 20, 2008 from http://www.kff.org/youthhivstds/20020207a-index.cfm

OTHER RISKY BEHAVIORS

There is a clear connection between alcohol, drug use and sexual activity. Earlier in the book you wrote what you want your child's boundaries to be in regards to these risky behaviors. What will you tell them in regards to the following behaviors to show their connection to sex?

Alcohol –

Drugs –

What will you tell your child about the health risks associated with the following:

Alcohol –

Drugs –

Smoking –

Chapter Twelve: Recognizing and Preventing Child Sexual Abuse

Because of the sensitive nature of this topic, Heritage educators are trained in mandated reporting of suspected abuse. Because of the topics we cover, we have had many young people come forward with their personal stories of abuse. We take this seriously and report all disclosures to the appropriate authorities. We do not gather or share stories of abuse. For that reason, we have not included student stories in this chapter.

Unfortunately, in today's society, sexual abuse is not something that can be ignored. There are people all around us who have experienced or are experiencing sexual abuse, but it is almost always kept secret and hardly ever revealed.

Whenever our educators talk to their students about sex, they are sensitive to the fact that some type of abuse may have happened or may be taking place currently with one or more children in the classroom.

Every parent has a responsibility to protect children from sexual predators. Often, predators are people a child would ordinarily trust. *In more than 90% of sexual abuse cases, the child and the child's family know and trust the abuser.*[262] When they know what behaviors are inappropriate, and specifically which parts of their bodies may not be touched, they are more likely to recognize the abuse and to tell you if someone is attempting to abuse them. However, the burden of responsibility falls on adults to provide protection against sexual abuse rather than expecting children to protect themselves.

Abusers may threaten a child into submitting and promising to not tell. Help your child know what to do if someone tries to touch them inappropriately or tries to get them to touch someone else inappropriately. This training will provide vital protection if your child is targeted. Adults appear all powerful to children, even to older teens. But, when kids are confident that the adults in their lives are taking active precautions to protect children from abuse, the kids feel safer and more comfortable alerting those adults.

Studies indicate one in four girls and one in five boys will be sexually abused prior to age 18.[263,264,265,266,267] In about 80 percent of cases the offender is someone close to the child.[268] Because evidence of sexual abuse is only present in about 10 percent of cases, do not assume there will be visible physical symptoms of sexual abuse.[269]

---

262 Darkness to Light (n.d.). *The issue of child abuse.* Retrieved February 9, 2011 from http://www.d2l.org/site/c.4dICIJOkGcISE/b.6069255/k.F1A5/The_Issue.htm

263 Dube, S. R., Anda, R. F., Whitfield, C. L., Brown, D. W., Felitti, V. J., Doug, M., & Giles, W. H. (2005). Long-term consequences of childhood sexual abuse by gender of victim. *American Journal of Preventive Medicine, 28*, 430-438.

264 Finkelhor, D., Hotaling, G., Lewis, I. A., & Smith, C. (1990). Sexual abuse in a national survey of adult men and women: Prevalence, characteristics, and risk factors. *Child Abuse & Neglect, 14,* 19-28.

265 Simpson, C., Odor, R., & Masho, S. (2004 August). Childhood sexual assault victimization in Virginia. Center for Injury & Violence Prevention. Virginia Department of Health.

266 Bolen, R. M. & Scannapieco, M. (1999). Prevalence of child sexual abuse: A corrective meta-analysis. *Social Service Review, 73*, 281-313.

267 Doll, L. S., Koenig, L. J., & Purcell, D. W. (2004). Child *sexual abuse and adult sexual risk: Where are we now?* In L.S. Doll, S.O. O'Leary, L.J. Koenig, & W. Pequegnat (Eds.) From *child sexual abuse to adult risk* (pp.3-10). Washington, DC: American Psychological Association.

268 Snyder, H. N. (2000). *Sexual assault of young children as reported to law enforcement: Victim, incident, and offender characteristics.* Washington, DC: National Center for Juvenile Justice, U.S Department of Justice. Retrieved May 5, 2008 from http://www.ncjrs.gov/App/Publications/alphaList.aspx?alpha=S

269 Beitchman, J. H., Zucker, K. J., Hood, J. E., daCosta, G. A., Alman, D., & Cassavia, E. (1992). A review of the long term effects of child sexual abuse. *Child Abuse & Neglect, 16,* 101-118.

What exactly is sexual abuse? Sexual abuse involves a continuum of behaviors from inappropriate sexual talk through touch to penetration involving force. Not all offenses involve contact (e.g., exposing a child to pornography). Behavior is designed/motivated by the gratification of the abuser. Some things you can do to open up communication with your child in terms of sexual abuse:

- Give them appropriate words for their body parts so they can discuss sexual questions and observations with you. (see Chapter Ten)
- Tell them to not keep secrets from you; make sure they feel comfortable telling you anything and everything.
- Tell them adults, or older children, should never do anything sexual with them, including using sexual words or showing them sexual material.
- Sexual abuse can have a devastating long-term effect on your child. If your child discloses sexual abuse to you, believe him or her them and seek help immediately. Be calm if your child tells you he or she has experienced inappropriate sexual contact. You don't want them to feel any blame. Assure them it is not their fault and they did the right thing in telling you. A good resource for further instruction is darknesstolight.org.
- If you suspect your child has been abused, contact your local child advocacy center to set up an appointment for your child. (More information to follow.)

The prevention of the sexual abuse of children It is the job of adults to protect children from sex abuse. Children, even teens, are not capable of recognizing that someone is grooming them for their sexual enjoyment. The percentage of young people who report having been sexually abused is shockingly high. According to darknesstolight.org,[270] an internationally recognized non-profit whose mission is to empower adults to prevent child sexual abuse:

- One in five children are sexually solicited while on the Internet.
- Nearly 70% of all reported sexual assaults (including assaults on adults) occur to children ages 17 and under.
- The median age for reported sexual abuse is nine years old.
- Approximately 20% of the victims of sexual abuse are under age eight.
- 50% of all victims of forcible sodomy, sexual assault with an object, and forcible fondling are under age twelve.
- 30-40% of [abused] children are abused by family members.
- As many as 60% are abused by people the family trusts; abusers frequently try to form a trusting relationship with parents.
- Nearly 40% are abused by older or larger children.
- Those who sexually abuse children are drawn to settings where they can gain easy access to children, such as sports leagues, faith centers, clubs, and schools.

---

[270] Darkness to Light. (2010) Retrieved June 3, 2011 from http://www.d2l.org

Children who have been abused often suffer other consequences later in life. The website darknesstolight.org provides the following data:

- 70-80% of sexual abuse survivors report excessive drug and alcohol use.
- One study showed that among male survivors, 50% have suicidal thoughts and more than 20% attempt suicide.
- Young girls who are sexually abused are more likely to develop eating disorders as adolescents.
- More than 60% of teen first pregnancies are preceded by experiences of molestation, rape or attempted rape. The average age of the offenders is 27 years old.
- Approximately 40% of sex offenders report sexual abuse as children.
- Both males and females who have been sexually abused are more likely to engage in prostitution.
- Approximately 70% of sexual offenders of children have between one and nine victims; 20-25% have 10 to 40 victims.
- Serial child molesters may have as many as 400 victims in their lifetimes.

Don't expect that your child will know how to protect him or herself from a predator. As his or her parent, it is your responsibility to be sure you do not allow your child to be in a one-on-one situation with someone that could hurt him or her. Group situations are safer, but are not a guarantee of safety. Sexual abuse is not limited only to younger children. Teens are susceptible to adults that find ways to befriend them, or even the entire family, in order to gain access. If an older person takes an exceptional interest in your child, ask yourself why that person needs to associate with someone younger. Be sure that if your child is in a class or sport, there is some way to monitor that participation and there is a system of accountability in place. Remember that older children sometimes abuse younger children – abuse does not always come from an adult.

The website darknesstolight.org provides sound and protective advice to parents:

- Talk with program administrators about the supervision of older youth who have responsibility for the care of children.
- Insist on screenings that include criminal background checks, personal interviews, and professional recommendations for all adults who serve children. Avoid programs that do not use all of these methods.
- Insist that youth-serving organizations train their staff and volunteers to prevent, recognize, and react responsibly to child sexual abuse.
- Ensure that youth-serving organizations have policies for dealing with suspicious situations and reports of abuse.

Behavioral and Physical Indicators of Child Sexual Abuse[271,272]

Unwilling to change for gym	Excessive risk taking
Withdrawal, fantasy, infantile behavior	Unusual sexual behavior or knowledge
Fearful of adults, closeness	Difficulty walking or sitting
Overly compliant	Torn, stained or bloody underclothing
Poor peer relationships	Pain or itching in the genital areas
Delinquent behavior	Injury or bleeding in the genital areas
Depressed, suicidal thoughts or actions	Venereal diseases, especially in pre-teen

Experts warn that if a child reports sexual abuse and is not believed they may shut down; very few reports, they say, are false. The website darknesstolight.org provides the following advice:

- Offer support. Think through your response before you suspect abuse. You'll be able to respond in a more supportive manner. Believe the child and make sure the child knows it.
- Thank the child for telling you and praise the child's courage.
- Encourage the child to talk but don't ask leading questions about details. Asking about details can alter the child's memory of events. If you must ask questions to keep the child talking, ask open-ended ones like "what happened next?"
- Seek the help of a professional who is trained to interview the child about sexual abuse. Professional guidance could be critical to the child's healing and to any criminal prosecution.
- Assure the child that it's your responsibility to protect him or her and that you'll do all you can.
- Report or take action in all cases of suspected abuse, both inside and outside the immediate family.
- Don't panic. Sexually abused children who receive support and psychological help can and do heal.
- Child sexual abuse is a crime. Know the legal requirements for reporting, which can be found at www.childwelfare.gov.

Know the agencies that handle reports of abuse. To find an advocacy center near you, contact the National Children's Alliance at www.nca-online.org or call 1-800-239-9950. The opportunity to convict a child molester may depend on evidence from an examination. If you suspect abuse and are not sure what to do, you may contact the Darkness to Lights helpline, 1-866-FOR-LIGHT, to be routed to resources in your community, or call the Childhelp USA National Child Abuse Hotline, 1-800-4-A-CHILD.

---

[271] Finkelhor, D., & Browne, A. (1985). The traumatic impact of child sexual abuse: A conceptualization. *American Journal of Orthopsychiatry, 55*, 530-539.

[272] Browne, A., & Finkelhor, D. (1986). Impact of child sexual abuse: a review of the research. *Psychological Bulletin, 99*, 66-77.

Recognizing and Preventing Child Sexual Abuse

What did you learn about child sexual abuse that you didn't know before?

If child sexual abuse is ever reported to you, how will you handle it? Write your plan of action, including local services and phone numbers, so you are prepared.

What can you could do in your community to help prevent child sexual abuse?

Chapter Thirteen: Parent as Partner

"The teacher didn't say 'Sex is wrong for teenagers!' Instead, he encouraged us towards abstinence and told us that eliminating the negative things [risks] helps to ensure a great life!"

Male *Heritage Keepers®* student

"When I first came in this class, I really didn't want to be here, and I thought I would not learn anything that I didn't know already, but you changed that. I had already made a commitment to myself after the first day in here. Before this class I did not think I could wait until marriage to have sex, but after hearing you talk about it, I realized I could do it if I really put my heart to it and if I was really committed. Since this class, I have changed my total outlook on sex. Mostly, this is because of you. Thank you so much for actually taking the time to come and talk to us. No one else did. I can tell you that I really benefited from it. Thanks! We hope you'll come back soon!"

Female *Heritage Keepers®* student

"This class really hasn't changed anything. I am totally stuck on abstinence. There are opinions and decisions. Sex outside of marriage is not ok. That is my wall! There's no way. Now I have the facts to support my decision. Thanks!!"

Female *Heritage Keepers®* student

"My life has changed in this class because I don't want a disease or any thing that makes me sick. Sex before marriage can make life difficult so that's why I decided not to have sex before marriage."

Male *Heritage Keepers®* student

As your child is developing, you are his or her most significant life partner. Your children are learning by what they see you and others doing. You are the most influential model of relationships that your child has. They will likely do as you do – your behavior, rather than as you say – your words. It is your responsibility to set an example of what being in a healthy relationship means.

If you have never married

- Don't let people you are dating stay over. Your kids are watching.
- Don't stay in a relationship that may be violent.
- Consider practicing abstinence outside of marriage yourself and talk to your child about that decision.
- One of the major causes of sexual abuse in girls comes from a stepfather or other man living in the home. A study of 156 victims of child sexual abuse found that the majority of the [abused] children came from disrupted or single-parent homes; only 31 percent of the abused children lived with both biological parents. Although stepfamilies make up only about 10 percent of all families, 27 percent of the abused children lived with either a stepfather or the mother's boyfriend.[273] Mothers who are not married, that are allowing men into the home, have a responsibility to be cautious about who is allowed access to their children.

We recognize that some couples are able to work out meaningful long-lasting relationships outside a formal marriage. We are aware of all those possible outcomes. However, the probability – statistical odds – of emotional scars, children being raised by a single struggling parent, the spread of sexually transmitted diseases and financial difficulty are dramatically reduced when young people 1) chose to reserve sexual activity for the person they marry, and 2) remain faithful to that person for a lifetime.

Remember, a high standard must be put in place for our children if we want them to strive for excellence. Even if they don't reach the exact standard, they will be better off if they come close than if no standard had been established at all. And for those who do reach that standard, the consequences of sexual activity outside of marriage are completely eliminated.

If you are divorced

- You and your ex need to remember that it is not about you – it is about what you model to your children.
- Do not put your ex down in front of your child(ren). This person is their mother or father – they look up to that person. Don't put your child(ren) in that position.
- Do not involve your child(ren) in your fights. Your children probably love you both, they are not mediators; don't treat them like they are.

There will always be marriages that can not survive and therefore are better off ending in divorce. However, it is important to be aware that research has shown that children of divorce do not fare well if their parents are not able to settle their differences

---

[273] Horowitz, J., Gomez-Schwartz, B., & Cardarelli, A. J. (1988, July). *Child sexual assault victims and their treatment.* Washington, DC: U. S. Department of Justice.

maturely.[274] However, if parents can uphold a healthy relationship, the negative effects can be minimized. The most important factor for children's well-being seems to be limiting the amount and intensity of conflict between parents. Minimizing the conflict and hostility between parents following the divorce can contribute to the child's growth. Agreement between the parents on discipline and child rearing, as well as love and approval from both parents, contributes to the child's sense of well-being and self-worth.[275,276]

If you are married

- Model a healthy marriage to your children. Make marriage something your children desire by making your marriage a priority. Always work on making your marriage better.
- If you feel as if your marriage is not where it should be – fix it. Show your children that your marriage is worth it! Seek counseling, or read one of the many marriage help books that are readily available.

A book we highly recommend for improving marital relationships is *The Seven Principles for Making Marriage Work* by Dr. John Gottman.[277] Through studying couples he found that there were trends in what made a marriage happy or not. Some of the things he found:

- Happy marriages are not perfect or without conflict, but happy couples get over conflict quickly (whether it was resolved or not).
- Happy marriages are based on friendship and optimism about the marriage.
- Happy couples support each other's dreams and build a sense of purpose together.

In his book he does not just hypothesize about what might make a marriage work; he actually provides research on the seven proven principles he lists for successful marriages, such as:

- Enhancing your love map,
- Nurturing your fondness and admiration for each other,
- Choosing to turn toward each other instead of away,
- Letting your partner influence you,
- Solving solvable problems and compromising on unsolvable ones,
- Being tolerant of each other's faults,
- Overcoming gridlock, and
- Creating a shared meaning of life.

---

[274] Institute for American Values. (2005). *Why marriage matters: Twenty-six conclusions from the social sciences.* (2nd ed.). NY: Institute for American Values.

[275] DeBord, K. (1997, June). Focus on kids: The effects of divorce on children. Raleigh, NC: North Carolina State University, North Carolina Cooperative Extension Service.

[276] Hughes, R., & Scherer, J. (1986, February). *Parenting on Your Own: How Divorce Affects Kids.* Urnana, IL: University of Illinois Cooperative Extension Project.

[277] Gottman, J. M. (1999). The seven principles for making marriage work. New York: Three Rivers Press.

The commitment of marriage is not kept by hoping for magical moments. Forming and maintaining a healthy and happy marriage is a lifelong endeavor. Working to improve your relationship skills is worth the effort.

Couples often spend months planning for a "perfect" wedding and no time at all preparing for the rest of their lives together. The important part of a wedding is the vows and having friends and family come together in support of the marriage. This may seem obvious, but some people believe that until they can afford a big fancy wedding, they will live together. They have missed the point. Where a wedding is held and the money spent on flowers and food is not what is important. By making vows in front of friends and family – and for many, within a religious context – a marriage has taken place, with all the rights and benefits and recognition the relationships deserves.

A wedding brings two families together in celebration as a new family is formed. It is a time when the community recognizes you are a legally united couple. That day will come and go; the marriage is meant to be forever. The challenges and rewards of getting along, and of making it through the good and the bad times, is what creates a family.

Encourage your child(ren) to not get married just to have a dream wedding. It is important that they understand that they are worth more than just passing sexual relationships. Couples that live together before they marry are more likely to divorce than couples who do not.[278] It only makes sense that when a person wants to be able to walk away when things get tough, going from one person to the next, they may carry that attitude into a marriage.

We hope you realize that you have the power to influence your child's intentions and decisions, and that this series has helped prepare you to provide appropriate parental guidance for him or her in regard to making decisions about sexual activity. You are their partner when it comes to abstaining. They need your guidance and your love through this important transition in their life.

Ask your child(ren) to make a commitment to abstain from sexual activity outside of marriage with your help. You can commit to them as well – by helping them, guiding them, and loving them through this important aspect of maturation. Remember the SAFE plan on page 137! When teens don't have clear boundaries, incremental sexual activity can quickly move beyond their ability to be in control of a situation. Have them commit to abstaining from all sexual activity outside of marriage. Also, encourage them to set sub-goals to help them keep their commitment.

---

[278] Institute for American Values (2005). *Why marriage matters: Twenty-six conclusions from the social sciences.* (2nd ed.). NY: Institute for American Values.

Still Committed

On the last day of teaching the abstinence education class at a school, the educator passes out our commitment cards. The commitment card states: *From this day forward, I will abstain from sexual activity outside of marriage.* The student can sign and date the card if they want to make the commitment. While teaching, the teacher was approached by a young lady who had participated in the abstinence program years ago. She commented to the teacher, "I still have my card from several years ago, and I am still committed to abstinence."

This is just one story that proves that abstinence education has a lasting effect on young people today. There is no doubt that the information that is being taught concerning sexual abstinence is making a positive impact on teenagers.

The conversation with your child might sound something like this:

"I am asking you to make a commitment to abstain from sexual activity outside of marriage. I want to spend time talking with you about why this is important!

I want you, not someone else, to have the power over your body, your mind, your heart and your future. You are worthy of the best. Waiting for someone that respects you and your values enough to make a serious commitment to you protects you from the consequences of sexual activity outside of marriage, some of which can last your whole life. I want you to be free to reach for all you hope for, to reach your full potential.

Making a commitment to wait is a serious sommitment – for yourself, for your relationships now and in the future, for those of us that love you, and for the family you may have in the future. As your parent, I am here for you. I will support and guide you. I will love you through these coming years, some of the most important years of your life. You can talk with me and I will not judge or condemn you. I love you and I know we can do this together."

You can probably create a much better on-going conversation! If your child accepts, have him or her sign a pledge. Write the pledge out yourself and make it something personal between you, the parents, and him or her. Think about getting your child something to celebrate – like some jewelry, a ring, or a pendant.

Congratulations! You are now equipped to build sexual values in your teen!

PARENT AS PARTNER

If you have never been married, what are some of the things you can do to be an example to your child in regards to abstinence from sexual activity outside of marriage, in addition to what was listed within the chapter?

If you are divorced, what are some of the things you can do to be an example to your child in regards to abstinence from sexual activity outside of marriage, in addition to what was listed within the chapter?

If you are married, what are some of the things you can do to be an example to your child in regards to abstinence from sexual activity outside of marriage, in addition to what was listed within the chapter?

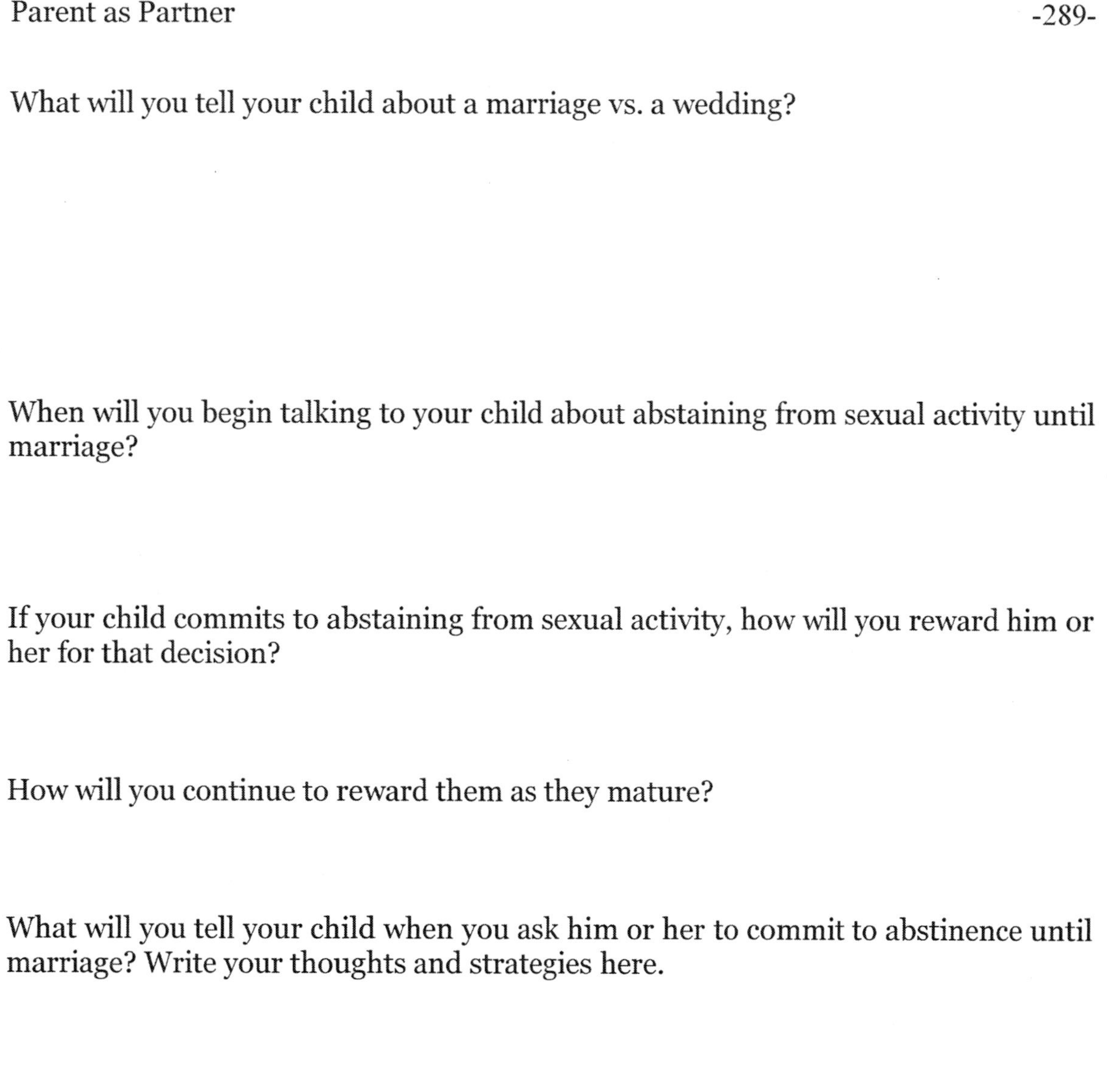

What will you tell your child about a marriage vs. a wedding?

When will you begin talking to your child about abstaining from sexual activity until marriage?

If your child commits to abstaining from sexual activity, how will you reward him or her for that decision?

How will you continue to reward them as they mature?

What will you tell your child when you ask him or her to commit to abstinence until marriage? Write your thoughts and strategies here.

Bibliography
Alphabetized by chapter, p239 APA 5th edition

Foreword

Abma J. C., Martinez G. M., & Copen C. E. (2010, June) *Teenagers in the United States: Sexual activity, contraceptive use, and childbearing, National Survey of Family Growth 2006–2008.* National Center for Health Statistics. Vital Health Stat 23(30). Retrieved February 11, 2011 from http://www.cdc.gov/nchs/data/series/sr_23/sr23_030.pdf

American College of Pediatricians. (2010, October 26). *Abstinence Education*. Retrieved February 14 2011 from http://www.acpeds.org/Download-document/129-Abst-Ed-Oct26.2010.html

Centers for Disease Control and Prevention. (2009). *Trends in the prevalence of sexual behaviors: National YRBS 1991-2009.* Retrieved February 9, 2011 from http://www.cdc.gov/HealthyYouth/yrbs/pdf/us_sexual_trend_yrbs.pdf

Gallagher, M. (2003, July 14). The stakes: Why we need marriage. *National Review Online*. Retrieved March 28, 2011 from http://www.nationalreview.com/articles/207483/stakes/maggie-gallagher

Hallfors, D. D., Waller, M. W., Ford, C. A., Halpern, C. T., Brodish, P. H., & Iritani, B. (2004). Adolescent depression and suicide risk: association with sex and drug behavior. *American Journal of Preventive Medicine, 27,* 224-231.

Kaiser Family Foundation (2003, October). *Virginity and the first time: A series of national surveys of teens about sex* (Publication No. 3368). Retrieved February 14, 2011 from http://www.kff.org/entpartnerships/upload/Virginity-and-the-First-Time-Summary-of-Findings.pdf

McIlhaney, J. S. & Bush, F. M. (2008). *Hooked: New science on how casual sex is affecting our children* (pp.77-78). Chicago: Northfield Publishing.

Weed, S. E., Birch, P. J., Erickson, I. H., & Olsen, J. A. (2011). *Testing a predictive model of youth sexual intercourse initiation.* Unpublished manuscript. Retrieved March 30, 2011 from http://instituteresearch.com/docs/IREPredictors_(1-17-2011).pdf (manuscript in preparation)

Weed, S. E., Erickson, I. H., & Birch, P. J. (2005, November). An evaluation of the Heritage Keepers Abstinence Education program. In A. Golden (ed.) Evaluating Abstinence Education Programs: Improving Implementation and Assessing Impact (pp. 88-103). Washington DC: U.S. Department of Health and Human Services, Office of Population Affairs and the Administration for Children and Families.

Chapter 1: YOU are the key

Abma J. C., Martinez G. M., & Copen C.E. (2010, June) *Teenagers in the United States: Sexual activity, contraceptive use, and childbearing, National Survey of Family Growth 2006–2008.* National Center for Health Statistics. Vital Health Stat 23(30). Retrieved February 11, 2011 from http://www.cdc.gov/nchs/data/series/sr_23/sr23_030.pdf

Albert, B. (2003, December). *America's adults and teens sound off about teen pregnancy. An annual national survey.* Retrieved January 28, 2009 from http://www.thenationalcampaign.org/resources/pdf/pubs/WOV_2003.pdf

Albert, B. (2004, December). *With one voice 2004: America's adults and teens sound off about teen pregnancy. An annual national survey.* Retrieved February 14, 2011 from www.thenationalcampaign.org/national-data/pdf/WOV2004.pdf

Albert, B. (2007, February). *With one voice 2007: America's adults and teens sound off about teen pregnancy. A periodic national survey.* Retrieved November 28, 2007 from http://www.thenationalcampaign.org/resources/pdf/pubs/WOV2007_fulltext.pdf

Centers for Disease Control and Prevention. (2009). *Trends in the prevalence of sexual behaviors: National YRBS 1991-2009.* Retrieved February 9, 2011 from http://www.cdc.gov/HealthyYouth/yrbs/pdf/us_sexual_trend_yrbs.pdf

Committee on Public Education, American Academy of Pediatrics (2001). Children, adolescents, and television. *Pediatrics, 107,* 423-426.

Darkness to Light (n.d.a). *Realities, Not Trust, Should Influence Your Decisions Regarding Children.* Retrieved February 22, 2011 from http://www.d2l.org/site/c.4dICIJOkGcISE/b.6069317/apps/s/content.asp?ct=8575945

Escobar-Chaves, S. L., Tortolero, S. R., Markham, C. M., & Low B. J. (2004, January 30). *Impact of the media on adolescent sexual attitudes and behaviors.* (p. 25). Austin, TX: The Medical Institute for Sexual Health.

Escobar-Chaves, S. L., Tortolero, S. R., Markham, C. M., & Low B. J. (2004, January 30). *Impact of the media on adolescent sexual attitudes and behaviors.* (p. 27). Austin, TX: The Medical Institute for Sexual Health.

Goleman, D. (2005). *Vital lies, simple truths The psychology of self-deception.* New York: Simon & Schuster Paperbacks.

Goleman, D. (2005). *Vital lies, simple truths The psychology of self-deception* (p. 227). New York: Simon & Schuster Paperbacks.

Goodman, B. & Dretzin, R. (Producers). (2001, February 27). The merchants of cool. [1911]. In Sullivan, M. (Executive producer), *Frontline*, Boston, Public Broadcasting Service.

Goodman, R. D. & Goodman, B. (Producers). (1999, October 19). The lost children of rockingham county [1804]. In Fanning, D. (Executive Producer). *Frontline.* Boston, Public Broadcasting Service.

Hagelin, R. (2005, August 5). *It's a Mad, Mad, Mad, Mad World: Home Invasion.* Paper presented at the meeting of the 9th Annual Abstinence Clearinghouse Conference, Hollywood, CA.

Laippley, J. (2005, August 3). *Do the Right Thing: Educational Best Practices.* Paper presented at the meeting of the 9th Annual Abstinence Clearinghouse Conference, Hollywood, CA.

Martino, S. C., Collins, R. L., Elliott, M. N., Strachman, A., Kanouse, D. E., & Berry, S. H. (2006). Exposure to degrading versus nondegrading music lyrics and sexual behavior among youth. *Pediatrics, 118,* e430-e441

Meeker, M. (2006). *Strong Fathers, Strong Daughters* (pp. 23-24). Washington: Regenery Publishing, Inc.

Ozretich, R. (2000). *TV and video games affect children, culture.* Parentingresearch.Org Retrieved June 2, 2011 from http://www.parentingresearch.org/papers/WalshTV1.pdf

Rideout, V. J., Foehr, U. G.,Roberts, D. F. (2010, January) *Generation M2: Media in the lives of 8- to 18-year-olds. Kaiser family Foundation.* Retrieved February 24, 2011 from http://www.kff.org/entmedia/upload/8010.pdf

Roberts, D. F., Foehr, U. G., Rideout, V. J., & Brodie, M. (1999, November). *Kids & media @ the new millennium.* Kaiser Family Foundation. Retrieved February 16, 2011 from http://www.kff.org/entmedia/upload/Kids-Media-The-New-Millennium-Report.pdf

Roberts, D. F., Foehr, U. G., & Rideout, V. J., (2005, March). *Generation M2: Media in the lives of 8- to 18-year-olds.* Kaiser family Foundation. Retrieved February 24, 2011 from http://www.kff.org/entmedia/upload/Generation-M-Media-in-the-Lives-of-8-18-Year-olds-Report.pdf

Slane, C. (n.d.) US News and World Report compiled in *Why are kids so angry.*

The National Campaign to Prevent Teen Pregnancy, (n. d.). *Parent Power: What Parents Need to Know and Do to Help Prevent Teen Pregnancy.* Retrieved February 14, 2011 from http://www.thenationalcampaign.org/resources/pdf/pubs/ParentPwr.pdf

Walsh, D. (2004). *Why do they act that way? A survival guide to the adolescent brain for you and your teen.* (p. 162) New York, NY: Free Press.

United States House of Representatives, Committee on Government Reform. (2006, October) *Abstinence and it's critics.* Retrieved February 14, 2011 from www.acpeds.org/Download-document/105-Abstinence-and-Its-Criticx.html

Walsh, D. (2004). *Why do they act that way? A survival guide to the adolescent brain for you and your teen.* (p. 161). New York, NY: Free Press.

Walsh, D. (2004). *Why do they act that way? A survival guide to the adolescent brain for you and your teen.* (p. 164). New York, NY: Free Press.

Walsh, D. (2004). *Why do they act that way? A survival guide to the adolescent brain for you and your teen.* (p. 165). New York, NY: Free Press.

Weed, S. E., Erickson, I. H., & Birch, P. J. (2005, November). An evaluation of the Heritage Keepers Abstinence Education program. In A. Golden (ed.) Evaluating Abstinence Education Programs: Improving Implementation and Assessing Impact (pp. 88-103). Washington DC: U.S. Department of Health and Human Services, Office of Population Affairs and the Administration for Children and Families.

Chapter 2: Avoiding Risk Healthy Family Formation

4Parents.gov. (2009, July 24). *Common sexually transmitted diseases (STDs).* Retrieved February 15, 2011 from http://www.4parents.gov/sexrisky/stds/common_std/common_std.html

Abma J. C., Martinez G. M., & Copen C.E. (2010, June) *Teenagers in the United States: Sexual activity, contraceptive use, and childbearing, National Survey of Family Growth 2006–2008.* National Center for Health Statistics. Vital Health Stat 23(30). Retrieved February 11, 2011 from http://www.cdc.gov/nchs/data/series/sr_23/sr23_030.pdf

Abma J. C., Martinez G. M., & Copen C.E. (2010, June) *Teenagers in the United States: Sexual activity, contraceptive use, and childbearing, National Survey of Family Growth 2006–2008.* National Center for Health Statistics. Vital Health Stat 23(30) (p. 23). Retrieved February 11, 2011 from http://www.cdc.gov/nchs/data/series/sr_23/sr23_030.pdf

Albert, B. (2007, February). *With one voice 2007: America's adults and teens sound off about teen pregnancy. A periodic national survey.* Retrieved November 28, 2007 from http://www.thenationalcampaign.org/resources/pdf/pubs/WOV2007_fulltext.pdf

Albert, B., Brown, S., & Flanigan, C. M. (2003). 14 and younger: *The sexual behavior of young adolescents*: Summary. Washington, DC: National Campaign to Prevent Teen Pregnancy. Retrieved September 5, 2007 from http://www.thenationalcampaign.org/resources/pdf/pubs/14summary.pdf

Alexander, L. L., Cates, J. R., Herndon, N, Ratcliffe, J. F., American Social Health Association, & Kaiser Family Foundation. (1998,December). *Sexually transmitted diseases in America: How many cases and at what cost?* Rerieved October 12, 2010 from http://www.kff.org/womenshealth/1445-std_rep.cfm

Axinn, W., & Thornton, A. (2000). The transformation in the meaning of marriage. In L. Waite, C. Bachrach, M. Hindin, E. Thompson, & A. Thornton (Eds.), *Ties That Bind: Perspectives on Marriage and Cohabitation* (pp. 147-165). New York: Aldine de Gruyter.

Bearman, P. S., & Bruckner, H. (2001). Promising the future: Virginity pledges and first intercourse. *The American Journal of Sociology, 106*, 859-911.

Begley, E., Crosby, R. A., DiClemente, R. J. Wingood, G. M., & Rose, E. (2003). Older partners and STD prevalence among pregnant African American teens. *Sexually Transmitted Diseases, 30,* 211-213.

Bennett, N. G., Blanc, A. K., & Bloom, D. E. (1988). Commitment and the modern union: Assessing the link between premarital cohabitation and subsequent marital stability. *American Sociological Review, 53,* 127–138.

Brady, S. S., & Halperm-Flesher, B. L. (2007). Adolescents' reported consequences of having oral sex versus vaginal sex. *Pediatrics, 119,* 229-236.

Centers for Disease Control and Prevention. (2010c, December). *Fact Sheet: Genital HPV*. Retrieved February 11, 2011 from http://www.cdc.gov/std/hpv/stdfact-hpv.htm

Centers for Disease Control and Prevention. (2000) *Tracking The Hidden Epidemics: Trends In STDs in the United States 2000.* Retrieved February 11, 2011 from www.cdc.gov/std/trends2000/Trends2000.pdf

Child Trends (2010). *Percentage of Births to Unmarried Women.* Retrieved February 23, 2011 from http://www.childtrendsdatabank.org/sites/default/files/75_Births_to_Unmarried_Women.pdf

Clinton, B. (1995, December 6). *The White House Conference on HIV and AIDS, Washington.* [Keynote address] Retrieved February 11, 2011 from http://clinton4.nara.gov/ONAP/youth/youth4.html

Cooper, L. M., Shapiro, C. M., & Powers, A. M. (1998). Motivations for sex and risky sexual behavior among adolescents and young adults: A functional perspective. *Journal of Personality and Social Psychology, 75,* 1528-1558.

Forehand, R., & Long, N. (n. d.). *How parents can enhance their child's adjustment during and after parental divorce.* Retrieved February 22, 2011 from http://www.aboutourkids.org/articles/how_parents_can_enhance_their_child039s_adjustment_during_after_parental_divorce

Gallagher, M. (2003, July 14). The stakes: Why marriage matters. *National Review Online*. Retrieved March 28, 2011 from http://www.nationalreview.com/articles/207483/stakes/maggie-gallagher

Gottman, J. M. (1999). *The seven principles for making marriage work.* New York: Three Rivers Press.

Hallfors, D. D., Waller, M. W., Bauer, D., Ford, C. A., & Halpern, C. T. (2005). Which comes first in adolescence-sex and drugs or depression? *American Journal of Preventative Medicine, 29,* 163-170.

Institute for American Values (2005). *Why marriage matters: Twenty-six conclusions from the social sciences.* (2nd ed.). NY: Institute for American Values.

Kalmuss, D. S., & Namerow, P. B. (1994). Subsequent childbearing among teenage mothers: The determinants of a closely spaced second birth. *Family Planning Perspectives, 26*, 149-153.

Lickona, T. (1991). *Educating for character: How our schools can teach respect and responsibility.* New York: Bantam Books

Liu, L. (1999, September). Do you have HPV? *Mademoiselle,* 112.

Martin, S., Rector, R., & Pardue, M. G. (2004). *Comprehensive sex education vs authentic abstinence: A study of competing curricula.* The Heritage Foundation. Retrieved June 8, 2011 from http://thf_media.s3.amazonaws.com/2004/pdf/67539_1.pdf

McLanahan, S., & Sandefur, G. 1994. *Growing Up with a Single Parent: What Hurts, What Helps.* Cambridge: Harvard University Press.

Meeker, M. (2006). *Strong Fathers, Strong Daughters.* Washington: Regenery Publishing, Inc.

Miller, H. G., Cain, V. S., Rogers, S. M., Gribble, J. N., & Tuner, C. F. (1999). Correlates of sexually transmitted bacterial infections among U.S. women in1995. *Family Planning Perspectives, 31,* 4-23.

Mirowsky, J., & Ross, C. E. (2002). Depression, parenthood, and age at first birth. *Social Science and Medicine, 54,* 1281-1298.

National Fatherhood Initiative, (n.d.). *The father factor.* Retrieved February 24, 2011 from http://www.fatherhood.org/Page.aspx?pid=403

Newcomb, M. D., & Bentler, P. M. (1980). Assessment of personality and demographic aspects of cohabitation and marital success. *Journal of Personality Assessment, 44,* 11–24.

O'Donnell, L., O'Donnell, C. R., & Stueve, A. (2001). Early sexual initiation and subsequent sex-related risks among urban minority youth: The reach for health study. *Family Planning Perspectives, 33,* 268-275.

Pergamit, M. R., Huang, L., & Lane, J. (2001). *The long term impact of adolescent risky behaviors and family environment.* Chicago: National Opinion Research Center, University of Chicago. Retrieved September 6, 2007 from http://aspe.hhs.gov/hsp/riskybehav01

Popenoe, D., & Whitehead, B. D. (2002). *Should we live together? What young adults need to know about cohabitation before marriage.* Retrieved February 22, 2011 from http://www.virginia.edu/marriageproject/nextgenerationseries.html

Rector, R. E., Johnson, K. A., & Marshall, J. A. (2004, September 21). *Teens who make virginity pledges have substantially improved life outcomes.* The Heritage Foundation Center for Data Analysis Report #04-07. Retrieved October 25, 2007 from http://www.heritage.org/Research/Reports/2004/09/Teens-Who-Make-Virginity-Pledges-Have-Substantially-Improved-Life-Outcomes

Rector, R. E., Johnson, R. A., & Noyes, L. R. (2003). *Sexually active teenagers are more likely to be depressed and to attempt suicide.* The Heritage Foundation Center for Data Analysis Report #30-04. Retrieved October 25, 2007 from http://www.heritage.org/Research/Reports/2003/06/Sexually-Active-Teenagers-Are-More-Likely-to-Be-Depressed

Shuford, J. A. (2008a October). *What is the impact of nonmarital teenage pregnancy?* Retrieved February 14, 2011 from http://www.medinstitute.org/public/118.cfm

Shuford, J. A. (2008b October). *How effective are condoms in preventing sti's?* Retrieved February 14, 2011 from http://www.medinstitute.org/public/126.cfm

Shuford, J. A. (2008c October). *I heard that there are 6 steps to correct condom use. What are they?* Retrieved February 14, 2011 from http://www.medinstitute.org/public/124.cfm

The Commission on Children at Risk, (2003). *Hardwired to connect, The new scientific case for authoritative communities.* New York, Institute for American Values.

The Institute for Research and Evaluation (2010a, December 31). *Federally funded teen pregnancy prevention programs: Not what they claim to be* Retrieved March 28, 2011 from http://instituteresearch.com/docs/IRE_Critique_of_28TPP_Programs_(12-3110).pdf

The Institute for Research and Evaluation (2010b, December 3). *Misconceptions about sex education effectiveness.* Retrieved March 28, 2011 from http://instituteresearch.com/docs/Misconceptions_About_Sex_Education_Effectiveness_(IRE,_12-3-10).pdf

The National Campaign to Prevent Teen Pregnancy. (July 2014). *Virgin Territory: What Young Adults Say About Sex, Love, Relationships and the First Time*. Washington, DC: National Campaign to Prevent Teen Pregnancy.

The National Campaign to Prevent Teen Pregnancy. (2000b, June 30). *Not just another thing to do: Teens talk about sex, regret, and the influence of their parents.* Washington, DC: National Campaign to Prevent Teen Pregnancy. Retrieved February 8, 2011 from http://www.thenationalcampaign.org/resources/pdf/pubs/NotJust_FINAL.pdf

Thomson, E., Hanson, T. L., & McLanahan, S. S. (1994). Family Structure and Child Well-Being: Economic Resources vs. Parental Behaviors. *Social Forces, 73,* p221-242.

Tiller, C. M. (2002). Chlamydia during pregnancy: Implications and impact on prenatal and neonatal outcomes. *Journal of Obstetric and Gynecologic, and Neonatal Nursing, 31,* 93-98.

Tucker, M. B., & Mitchell-Kernan, C. (1998). Psychological well-being and perceived marital opportunity among single african american, latina and white women. *Journal of Comparative Family Studies, 29,* 57-72.

U.S. Department of Health and Human Services. (2000, November). Sexually transmitted diseases. In *Healthy People 2010: Vol 2.* (2nd ed.). Retrieved February 13, 2011 from http://www.healthypeople.gov/2010/Document/pdf/Volume2/25STDs.pdf

Waite, L. J. & Gallagher, M. (2000). *The case for marriage.* New York: Broadway books.

Weed, S. E., Birch, P. J., Erickson, I. H., & Olsen, J. A. (2011). *Testing a predictive model of youth sexual intercourse initiation.* Manuscript in preparation. Retrieved March 30, 2011 from http://instituteresearch.com/docs/IREPredictors_(1-17-2011).pdf

Weinstock, H., Berman S., & Cates, W. (2004). Sexually transmitted diseases among American youth: Incidence and prevalence estimates, 2000. *Perspectives on Sexual and Reproductive Health, 36,* 6-10.

Chapter 3: Life Goals and Healthy Family Formation

Begley, E., Crosby, R. A., DiClemEnte, R. J. Wingood, G. M., & Rose, E. (2003). Older partners and STD prevalence among pregnant African American teens. *Sexually Transmitted Disease, 30,* 211-213.

Finkelhor, D., & Browne, A. (1985). The traumatic impact of child sexual abuse: A conceptualization. *American Journal of Orthopsychiatry, 55,* 530-539.

Miller, K. S., Clark, L. F., Wendell, D. A., Levin, M. L., Gray-Ray, P., Velez, C. N., & Webber, M. P. (1997). Adolescent heterosexual experience: A new typology. *Journal of Adolescent Health, 20,* 179-186.

Sorensen, T. & Snow, B. (1991). How children tell: The process of disclosure in child sexual abuse. *Child Welfare, 70,* 3-15.

Summit, R. C. (1983). The child sexual abuse accommodation syndrome. *Child Abuse & Neglect, 7,* 177-193.

Van Bruggen, L. K., Runtz, M. G., & Kadlec, H. (2006). Sexual revictimization: The role of sexual self-esteem and dysfunctional sexual behaviors. *Child Maltreatment, 11,* 131-145.

Whitehead, B. D., Pearson, M. (2006). *Making a Love Connection: Teen Relationships, Pregnancy, and Marriage.* Washington, DC: National Campaign to Prevent Teen and Unplanned Pregnancy. Retrieved April 9, 2008 from http://www.thenationalcampaign.org/resources/pdf/pubs/MALC_FINAL.pdf

Chapter 4: Teenage Brains and Their Bodies

Blakeslee, S. (1996, January 23). *Scientist at work: Vilayanur Ramachandran; Figuring out the brain from its acts of denial.* The New York Times. Retrieved February23, 2011 from http://www.nytimes.com/1996/01/23/science/scientist-work-vilayanur-ramachandran-figuring-brain-its-acts-denial.html?ref=sandrablakeslee&pagewanted=print

Goleman, D. (2006). *Social intelligence: The new science of human relationships*. New York: Bantam Books.

Walsh, D. (2004). *Why do they act that way? A survival guide to the adolescent brain for you and your teen.* New York, NY: Free Press.

Walsh, D. (2004). In *Why do they act that way? A survival guide to the adolescent brain for you and your teen.* (pp. 6-7). New York, NY: Free Press.

Walsh, D. (2004). In *Why do they act that way? A survival guide to the adolescent brain for you and your teen.* (p. 28). New York, NY: Free Press.

Walsh, D. (2004). In *Why do they act that way? A survival guide to the adolescent brain for you and your teen.* (p. 32). New York, NY: Free Press.
Walsh, D. (2004). A guided tour of their brains. In *Why do they act that way? A survival guide to the adolescent brain for you and your teen.* (pp. 26-38). New York, NY: Free Press.

Walsh, D. (2004). In *Why do they act that way? A survival guide to the adolescent brain for you and your teen.* (pp. 61-62). New York, NY: Free Press.

Walsh, D. (2004). In *Why do they act that way? A survival guide to the adolescent brain for you and your teen.* (p. 62). New York, NY: Free Press.

Walsh, D. (2004). In *Why do they act that way? A survival guide to the adolescent brain for you and your teen.* (pp. 63-64). New York, NY: Free Press.

Walsh, D. (2004). Risky business: Helping teens put on the brakes. In *Why do they act that way? A survival guide to the adolescent brain for you and your teen.* (pp. 55-73) New York, NY: Free Press.

Walsh, D. (2004). What we have here is a failure to communicate. In *Why do they act that way? A survival guide to the adolescent brain for you and your teen.* (pp. 74-91) New York, NY: Free Press.

Chapter 5: Theories of Change and Influence

Abma J. C., Martinez G. M., & Copen C.E. (2010, June) *Teenagers in the United States: Sexual activity, contraceptive use, and childbearing, National Survey of Family Growth 2006–2008.* National

Albert, B. (2007, February). *With One Voice 2007 America's Adults and Teens Sound Off About Teen Pregnancy*. Retrieved April 9, 2008 from http://www.thenationalcampaign.org/resources/pdf/pubs/WOV2007_fulltext.pdf

Bandura, A. (1997a). *Social Learning Theory.* Upper Saddle River, NJ: Prentice-Hall.

Bandura, A. (1997b). *Self-efficacy: The Exercise of Control.* New York: W.H. Freeman and Company.

Busby, D. M., Carroll, J. S., & Willoughby, B. J. (2010). Compatibility or restraint? The effects of sexual timing on marriage relationships. *Journal of Family Psychology, 24,* 766-774.

Centers for Disease Control and Prevention. (2010c, December). *Fact Sheet: Genital HPV.* Retrieved February 11, 2011 from http://www.cdc.gov/std/hpv/stdfact-hpv.htm

Goleman, D. (2006). *Social intelligence: The new science of human relationships*. New York: Bantam Books.

Goleman, D. (2006). *Social intelligence: The new science of human relationships.* (p. 42). New York: Bantam Books.

Goleman, D. (2006a). *Emotional intelligence* (10th Anniversary Edition).New York: Bantam Dell.

Gottman, J. (1997). *Raising an emotionally intelligent child, The heart of parenting*. New York: Simon & Schuster Paperbacks.

Gottman, J. (1997). *Raising an emotionally intelligent child, The heart of parenting*. (p. 17). New York: Simon & Schuster Paperbacks.

Gottman, J. (1997). *Raising an emotionally intelligent child, The heart of parenting*. (p. 21). New York: Simon & Schuster Paperbacks.

Gottman, J. (1997). *Raising an emotionally intelligent child, The heart of parenting*. (pp. 38-39). New York: Simon & Schuster Paperbacks.

Hallfors, D. D., Waller, M. W., Ford, C. A., Halpern, C. T., Brodish, P. H., & Iritani, B. (2004). Adolescent depression and suicide risk: association with sex and drug behavior. American *Journal of Preventive Medicine, 27,* 224-231.

Prochaska, J.O., DiClemente, C.C. & Norcross, J.C. (1992). In search of how people change: Applications to addictive behaviors. *American Psychologist, 47,* 1102-1114.

Silverman, J. G., Raj, A., & Clements, K. (2004). Dating violence and associated sexual risk and pregnancy among adolescent girls in the United States. *Pediatrics, 114,* e220-e225.

The National Campaign to Prevent Teen Pregnancy. (2000a, April 27) *The Cautious Generation? Teens tell us about sex, virginity, and "The Talk"* Retrieved February 11, 2011 from http://www.thenationalcampaign.org/resources/pdf/pubs/CautiousGen_FINAL.pdf

Whitehead, B. D., & Pearson, M. (2006). *Making a Love Connection: Teen Relationships, Pregnancy, and Marriage.* Washington, DC: National Campaign to Prevent Teen and Unplanned Pregnancy. Retrieved April 9, 2008 from http://www.thenationalcampaign.org/resources/pdf/pubs/MALC_FINAL.pdf

Chapter 6: Influencing Predictors of Sexual Activity

No References

Chapter 7: The Biology of Love

Brady, S. S., & Halperm-Flesher, B. L. (2007). Adolescents' reported consequences of having oral sex versus vaginal sex. *Pediatrics, 119,* 229-236.

Cole, D. D. & Duran, M. G. (1998). *Sex and Character.* (p. 148). Dallas, TX: Foundation for Thought and Ethics.

Coley, R. L. (1998). Children's socialization experiences and functioning in single-mother households: The importance of fathers and other men. *Child Development, 69,* 219-230.

Finger, R. Thelen, T., Vessey, J. T., Mohn, J. K., & Mann, J. R. (2003). Association of virginity at age 18 with educational, economic, social, and health outcomes in middle adulthood. *Adolescent & Family Health, 3,* 164-170.

Fisher, H. (2004). *Why we love: The nature and chemistry of romantic love.* New York: Henry Holt and Company

Fisher, H. (2004). "What Wild Ecstasy": Being in Love In *Why we love: The nature and chemistry of romantic love.* (pp. 1-25). New York: Henry Holt and Company.

Fisher, H. (2004). *Why we love: The nature and chemistry of romantic love.* (pp. 52-53). New York: Henry Holt and Company.

Fisher, H. (2004). *Why we love: The nature and chemistry of romantic love.* (pp. 53-54). New York: Henry Holt and Company.

Fisher, H. (2004). *Why we love: The nature and chemistry of romantic love.* (pp. 54-55). New York: Henry Holt and Company.

Fisher, H. (2004). *Why we love: The nature and chemistry of romantic love.* (p. 69). New York: Henry Holt and Company.

Fisher, H. (2004). Wh*y we love: The nature and chemistry of romantic love.* (pp. 78-80). New York: Henry Holt and Company.

Fisher, H. (2004). Web of Love: Lust, Romance, and Attachment In *Why we love: The nature and chemistry of romantic love.* (pp. 77-98). New York: Henry Holt and Company.

Fisher, H. (2004). Lost Love: Rejection, Despair, and Rage In *Why we love: The nature and chemistry of romantic love.* (pp. 153-180). New York: Henry Holt and Company.

Goleman, D. (2006). *Social intelligence: The new science of human relationships.* New York: Bantam Books.

Goleman, D. (2006). Desire: his and hers. In *Social intelligence: The new science of human relationships* (pp.198-210). New York: Bantam Books.

Hsiu-Chen, Y., Lorenx, F. O., Wickrama, K. A. S., Conger, R. D., & Elder G. H. (2006). Relationships among sexual satisfactin [sic], marital quality, and marital instability at midlife. *Journal of Family Psychotherapy, 14,* 1-12.

Kim, H. K., & McKenry, P. C. (2000). The relationship between marriage and psychological well-being: A Longitudinal analysis. *Journal of Family Issues, 23,* 607-911.

Kline, G. H., Stanley, S. M., Markman, H. J., Olmos-Gallo, P. A., St. Peters, M., Whitton, S. W., & Prado, L. M. (2004). Timing is everything: Pre-engagement cohabitation and increased risk for poor marital outcomes. *Journal of Family Psychology,* 18, 311-318.

Michael, R. T., Gagnon, J. H., Laumann, E. O., & Kolata, G. (1994). *Sex in America: A definitive survey.* Boston: Little, Brown, and Company.

Nichols, W. C. (2005). The first years of marital commitment. In Harway, Michelle (Ed.) *Handbook of couples therapy*. Hoboken, New Jersey: John Willey & Sons, Inc.

Tamis-LeMonda, C. S., Shannon, J. D., Cabrear, N. J., & Lamb, M. E. (2004). Fathers and mothers at play with their 2- and 3- year-olds: Contributions to language and cognitive development. *Child Development, 75,* 1806-1820.

Tangney, J. P., Baumesiter, R. F., & Boone, A. L. (2004). High self-control predicts good adjustment, less pathology, better grades, and interpersonal success. *Journal of Personality, 72,* 271-322.

Walsh, D. (2004). *Why do they act that way? A survival guide to the adolescent brain for you and your teen.* New York, NY: Free Press.

Whitehead, B. D., & Pearson, M. (2006). *Making a love connection: Teen relationships, pregnancy, and marriage.* Washington, DC: National Campaign to Prevent Teen Pregnancy. Retrieved February 10, 2011 from http://www.thenationalcampaign.org/resources/pdf/pubs/MALC_FINAL.pdf

Young, M., Denny, G., Luquis, R., & Young, T. (1998). Correlates of the sexual satisfaction in marriage. *The Canadian Journal of Human Sexuality, 7,* 115-127.

Chapter 8: Refuting Typical Reasons Teens Give For Having Sex

Abma J. C., Martinez G. M., & Copen C. E. (2010, June) *Teenagers in the United States: Sexual activity, contraceptive use, and childbearing, National Survey of Family Growth 2006–2008.* National

Center for Health Statistics. Vital Health Stat 23(30). Retrieved February 11, 2011 from http://www.cdc.gov/nchs/data/series/sr_23/sr23_030.pdf

Albert, B. (2007). *With one voice 2007: America's adults and teens sound off about teen pregnancy.* Washington, DC: National Campaign to Prevent Teen Pregnancy. Retrieved November 28, 2007 from http://www.teenpregnancy.org/resources/data/pdf/WOV2007_fulltext.pdf

Alcohol Concern. (2002, March). *Alcohol & Teenage Pregnancy.* London: Alcohol Concern. Retrieved February 5, 2010 from http://www.slideshare.net/bpilmer/alcohol-and-teenage-pregnancy

Billy, J. O. G., Brewster, K. L., and Grady, W. R. (1994). Contextual effects on the sexual behavior of adolescent women. *Journal of Marriage and the Family, 56*, 387-404.

Centers for Disease Control and Prevention. (2009). *Trends in the prevalence of sexual behaviors: National YRBS 1991-2009.* Retrieved February 9, 2011 from http://www.cdc.gov/HealthyYouth/yrbs/pdf/us_sexual_trend_yrbs.pdf

Centers for Disease Control and Prevention. (2007, December 19). *Pelvic inflammatory disease fact sheet.* Retrieved August 20, 2008 from http://www.cdc.gov/std/PID/STDFact-PID.htm

Deardorff, J., Gonzales, N. A., Christopher, F. S., Roosa, M. W., & Millsap, R. E. (2005). Early puberty and adolescent pregnancy: The influence of alcohol use. *Pediatrics, 116,* 1451-1456.

Kaestle, C . E. & Halpern, C. T. (2005). Sexual intercourse precedes partner violence in adolescent romantic relationships. *Journal of Adolescent Health, 36*, 386-392.

Kaiser Family Foundation. (2002). *Substance use & sexual health among teens and young adults in the U.S.* Retrieved August 21, 2007 from http://www.kff.org/youthhivstds/upload/KFF-CASAFactSheet.pdf

Kim, K., & Smith, P. K. (1999). Family relations in early childhood and reproductive development. *Journal of Reproductive and Infant Psychology, 17,* 133-148.

Kunkel, D., Cope, K., & Biely, E. (1999). Sexual messages on television: Comparing findings from three studies. *The Journal of Sex Research, 36,* 230-236.

McIlhaney, J. S. & Bush, F. M. (2008). *Hooked: New science on how casual sex is affecting our children.* Chicago: Northfield Publishing.

Michael, R. T., Gagnon, J. H., Laumann, E. O., & Kolata, G. (1994). *Sex in America: A definitive survey.* Boston: Little, Brown, and Company.

Miller, B. C., Norton, M. C., Curtis, T., Hill, E. J., Schvaneveldt, P., & Young, M. H. (1997). The timing of sexual intercourse among adolescents: Family, peer, and other antecedents. *Youth & Society, 29,* 54-83.

Moore, N. B., & Davidson, J. K. (2006). College women and personal goals: Cognitive dimensions that differentiate risk-reduction sexual decisions. *Journal of Youth and Adolescence, 35,* 577-589.

Moscicki, A. B., Burt, V. G., Darragh, T., & Shiboski, S. (1999). The significance of squamous metaplasia in the development of low grade squamous intraepithelial lesions in young women. *Cancer, 85,* 1139-1144.

Stanton, G. T. (1997). *Why marriage matters: Reasons to believe in marriage in postmodern society.* Colorado Springs: Pinon Press.

The National Campaign to Prevent Teen Pregnancy. (2000b, June 30). *Not just another thing to do: Teens talk about sex, regret, and the influence of their parents.* Washington, DC: National Campaign to Prevent Teen Pregnancy. Retrieved February 8, 2011 from http://www.thenationalcampaign.org/resources/pdf/pubs/NotJust_FINAL.pdf

The National Campaign to Prevent Teen Pregnancy, (2000a, April 27). *The cautious generation? Teens tell us about sex, virginity, and "the talk".* Retrieved February 11, 2011 from http://www.thenationalcampaign.org/resources/pdf/pubs/CautiousGen_FINAL.pdf

Walsh, D. (2004). *Why do they act that way? A survival guide to the adolescent brain for you and your teen.* New York, NY: Free Press.

Chapter 9: Setting Dating Standards

Abel, G., Becker, J., Mittelman, M., Cunningham-Rathner, J., Rouleau, J., & Murphy, W. (1987). Self-reported sex crimes on non-incarcerated paraphiliacs. *Journal of Interpersonal Violence, 2,* 3-25.

Albert, B., Brown, S., & Flanigan, C. M. (2003). *14 and younger: The sexual behavior of young adolescents: Summary.* Washington, DC: National Campaign to Prevent Teen Pregnancy. Retrieved February 8, 2011 from http://www.thenationalcampaign.org/resources/pdf/pubs/14summary.pdf

Coleman, J. (1996). Female status and premarital sexual codes [Letter to the editor]. *The American Journal of Sociology, 72,* 217

Darroch, J. E., Landry, D. J., & Oslak, S. (1999). Age differences between sexual partners in the U.S. *Family Planning Perspectives, 31,* 160-167.

Hallfors, D. D., Waller, M. W., Bauer, D., Ford, C. A., & Halpern, C. T. (2005). Which comes first in adolescence-sex and drugs or depression? *American Journal of Preventative Medicine, 29,* 163-170.

Horwitz, A. V., & White, H. R. (1987). Gender role orientations and styles of pathology among adolescents. *Journal of Health and Social Behavior, 28,* 158-170.

Joyner, K., & Udry, J. R. (2000). You don't bring me anything but down: Adolescent romance and depression. *Journal of Health and Social Behavior, 41,* 369-391.

Kaestle, C. E. & Halpern, C. T. (2005). Sexual intercourse precedes partner violence in adolescent romantic relationships. *Journal of Adolescent Health, 36,* 386-392.

Kaufman, M. (April 2001). *Puppy Love's Bite.* Time Magazine.

Kilpatrick, D., Saunders, B., & Smith, D. (2003, April). *Youth victimization: Prevalence and implications.* U.S. Department of Justice, National Institute of Justice. Retrieved February 9, 2011 from http://www.ncjrs.gov/App/Publications/alphaList.aspx?alpha=Y

McCurley, C. & Snyder, H. (2004). *Victims of violent juvenile crime.* Juvenile Justice Bulletin, U.S. Department of Justice, Office of Juvenile Justice and Delinquency Prevention. Retrieved February 9, 2011 from
http://www.ncjrs.gov/pdffiles1/ojjdp/201628.pdfhttp://ojjdp.ncjrs.org/publications/PubResults.asp#2004

Rector, R. E., Johnson, R. A., & Noyes, L. R. (2003, June 3). *Sexually active teenagers are more likely to be depressed and to attempt suicide.* Center for Data Analysis Report #30-04. Retrieved October 25, 2007 from http://www.heritage.org/Research/Abstinence/cda0304.cfm

Silverman, J. G., Raj, A., Mucci, L. A., & Hathaway, J. E. (2001). Dating violence against adolescent girls and associated substance use, unhealthy weight control, sexual risk behavior, pregnancy, and suicidality. *Journal of American Medical Association, 286,* 572-579.

Stanton, G. T. (1997). *Why marriage matters: Reasons to believe in marriage in postmodern society.* Colorado Springs: Pinon Press.

Stepp, L. S. (2008). *Unhooked* (p. 27). New York: Riverhead Books.

Chapter 10: Anatomy – Be An Expert

No references

Chapter 11: Other Risky Behaviors

Alcohol Concern. (2002b, March). *Alcohol & Teenage Pregnancy.* London: Alcohol Concern. Retrieved February 5, 2010 from http://www.slideshare.net/bpilmer/alcohol-and-teenage-pregnancy

Ballas, C. (2008). P*sychosis*. Washington, DC: U.S. Department of Health and Human Services, Retrieved August 5, 2008 from The National Institutes of Health Web site: http://www.nlm.nih.gov/medlineplus/ency/article/001553.htm

Bingham, C. R., & Crockett, L. J. (1996). Longitudinal adjustment patterns of boys and girls experiencing early, middle, and late sexual intercourse. *Developmental Psychology, 32,* 647-658.

Blinn-Pike, L., Beger, T. J., Hewett, J., & Olsen, J. (2004). Sexually abstinent adolescents: An 18-month follow-up. *Journal of Adolescent Research, 19,* 495-511.

Brismar, B & Bergman, B. (1998). The significance of alcohol for violence and accidents. *Alcoholism: Clinical & Experimental Research, 22*, 299s-306s.

Centers for Disease Control and Prevention. (2004, January 27). *Facts about cyanide.* Retrieved February 15, 2011 from http://www.bt.cdc.gov/agent/cyanide/basics/facts.asp

Centers for Disease Control and Prevention. (2005, August 29). *Facts about benzene.* Retrieved February 15, 2011 from http://www.bt.cdc.gov/agent/benzene/basics/facts.asp

Centers for Disease Control and Prevention. (2006a). *Cigarette smoking-related mortality.* Retrieved June 3, 2008 from http://www.cdc.gov/tobacco/data_statistics/factsheet/cig_smoking_mort.htm

Centers for Disease Control and Prevention. (2006b, July). *Carbon monoxide poisoning.* Retrieved February 15, 2011 from http://www.cdc.gov/co/faqs.htm

Centers for Disease Control and Prevention. (2008). *Smoking & tobacco use*. Retrieved June 10, 2008 from http://www.cdc.gov/tobacco/basic_information/FastFacts.htm#toll

Centers for Disease Control and Prevention. (2010a, September 1). *Medical management guidelines for ammonia.* Retrieved February 15, 2011 from http://www.atsdr.cdc.gov/mmg/mmg.asp?id=7&tid=2

Centers for Disease Control and Prevention. (2010b, November 18). *Acetylene.* Retrieved February 15, 2011 from http://www.cdc.gov/niosh/npg/npgd0008.html

Center for Disease Control and Prevention. (2010c, September 15). *Tobacco-related mortality*. Retrieved February 9, 2011 from http://www.cdc.gov/tobacco/data_statistics/fact_sheets/health_effects/tobacco_related_mortality/

Centers for Disease Control and Prevention. (2010d, September 1). Public Health Statement for Formaldehyde. Retrieved February 15, 2011 from http://www.atsdr.cdc.gov/ToxProfiles/tp111-c1-b.pdf

Center for the Advancement of Health. (2001, March/April). Reducing tobacco use: The quest to quit. *Facts of Life (online journal), 6 (3)*. Retrieved June 3, 2008 from http://www.cfah.org/factsoflife/vol6no3.cfm

Champion, H. L. O., Foley, K. L., DuRant, R. H., Hensberry, R., Altman, D., & Wofson, M. (2004). Adolescent sexual victimization, use of alcohol and other substances, and other health risk behaviors. *Journal of Adolescent Health, 35,* 321-328.

Childrens Hospital Boston. (2007). *Smoking*. Retrieved on June 3, 2008 from http://www.childrenshospital.org/az/Site1618/mainpageS1618PO.html

Dowshen, S. (2009a, April) *Binge Drinking*. Jacksonville, Florida: The Nemours Foundation. Retrieved February 7, 2011 from http://kidshealth.org/teen/drug_alcohol/#cat20139

Dowshen, S. (2009b). *Alcohol*. Then Nemours Foundation. Retrieved February 23, 2011 from http://kidshealth.org/PageManager.jsp?dn=KidsHealth&lic=1&ps=207&cat_id=20139&article_set=203 68

Epstein, J. A., Griffin, K. W., & Botvin, G. J. (2001). Risk taking and refusal assertiveness in a longitudinal model of alcohol use among inner-city adolescents. *Prevention Science, 2,* 193-200.

Hennessy, M., Manteuffel, B., Dilorio, C., & Adame D. (1997). Identifying the social contexts of effective sex refusal. *Journal of American College Health, 46,* 27-34.

Johnson, T. J., & Stahl, C. (2004). Sexual experiences associated with participation in drinking games. *The Journal of General Psychology, 131,* 304-320.

Kaiser Family Foundation. (2002, February). *Substance use and risky sexual behavior: Attitudes and practices among adolescents and young adults.* Retrieved July 20, 2008 from http://www.kff.org/youthhivstds/20020207a-index.cfm

Kaiser Family Foundation. (2002b, February). *Substance use & sexual health among teens and young adults in the U.S.* Retrieved August 21, 2007 from http://www.kff.org/youthhivstds/upload/KFF-CASAFactSheet.pdf

Larson, M. (2006). *Alcohol-related psychosis* (from WebMD). Retrieved August 5, 2008 from http://www.emedicine.com/MED/topic3113.htm

Lieber, C. S. (2005). Relationships between nutrition, alcohol use, and liver disease. *Alcohol Research & Health, 27,* 220-231.

March of Dimes. (2005). *Drinking alcohol during pregnancy.* Retrieved June 16, 2008 from http://www.marchofdimes.com/professionals/14332_1170.asp

Moore, N. B., & Davidson, J. K. (2006). College women and personal goals: Cognitive dimensions that differentiate risk-reduction sexual decisions. *Journal of Youth and Adolescence, 35,* 577-589.

National Highway Traffic Safety Administration. (2011). *Persons Killed, by Highest Driver Blood Alcohol Concentration (BAC) in the Crash, 1994 - 2009 - State : USA* Retrieved February 8, 2011 from http://www-fars.nhtsa.dot.gov/Trends/TrendsAlcohol.aspx

National Institute on Drug Abuse. (2011). Retrieved March 30, 2011 from http://www.drugabuse.gov

QuitSmokingStop, (2010). *Chemicals in cigarettes.* Retrieved February 15, 2011 from http://www.quit-smoking-stop.com/harmful-chemicals-in-cigarettes.html

Robb, N. (1990). Alcoholism and the dentist. *British Journal of Addiction, 85,* 437-439.

Santelli, J. S., Robin, L., Brener, N. D., & Lowry, R. (2000). Timing of alcohol and other drug use and sexual risk behaviors among unmarried adolescents and young adults. *Family Planning Perspectives, 33,* 200-205.

Schulenberg, J., O'Malley, P. M., Bachman, J. G., Wadsworth, K. N., & Johnston, L. D. (1996). Getting drunk and growing up: Trajectories of frequent binge drinking during the transition to young adulthood. *Journal of Studies on Alcohol, 57,* 289-304.

Souza, R. & Spechler, S. (2005). Concepts in the prevention of adenocarcinoma of the distal esophagus and proximal stomach. *CA: A Cancer Journal for Clinicians, 55*, 334-351.

Standridge, J. B., Zylstra, R. G., & Adams, S. M. (2004). Alcohol consumption: An overview of benefits and risks. *Southern Medical Journal, 97*, 664-672.

Substance Abuse & Mental Health Services Administration. (1996). *Preliminary estimates from the 1995 national household survey on drug abuse. Office of Applied Studies Advance Report Number 18.* Washington, DC: SAMHSA. Retrieved on February 8, 2011 from http://oas.samhsa.gov/nhsda/ar18ttoc.htm

Tangney, J. P., Baumesiter, R. F., & Boone, A. L. (2004). High self-control predicts good adjustment, less pathology, better grades, and interpersonal success. *Journal of Personality, 72,* 271-322.

The National Center on Addiction and Substance Abuse at Columbia University. (1999, December). *Dangerous Liasons: Substance Abuse and Sex* (p. 2). Retrieved March 16, 2011 from http://www.casacolumbia.org/articlefiles/379-Dangerous Liaisons.pdf

The National Center on Addiction and Substance Abuse at Columbia University. (1999, December). *Dangerous Liasons: Substance Abuse and Sex* (p. 42). Retrieved March 16, 2011 from http://www.casacolumbia.org/articlefiles/379-Dangerous Liaisons.pdf

Chapter 12: Recognizing and Preventing Child Sexual Abuse
Beitchman, J. H., Zucker, K. J., Hood, J. E., daCosta, G. A., Alman, D., & Cassavia, E. (1992). A review of the long term effects of child sexual abuse. *Child Abuse & Neglect, 16,* 101-118.

Bolen, R. M. & Scannapieco, M. (1999). Prevalence of child sexual abuse: A corrective meta-analysis. *Social Service Review, 73,* 281-313.

Browne, A., & Finkelhor, D. (1986). Impact of child sexual abuse: a review of the research. *Psychological Bulletin, 99,* 66-77.

Darkness to Light. (2010) Retrieved June 3, 2011 from http://www.d2l.org

Darkness to Light (n.d.). *The issue of child abuse*. Retrieved February 9, 2011 from http://www.d2l.org/site/c.4dICIJOkGcISE/b.6069255/k.F1A5/The_Issue.htm

Doll, L. S., Koenig, L. J., & Purcell, D. W. (2004). Child *sexual abuse and adult sexual risk: Where are we now?* In L.S. Doll, S.O. O'Leary, L.J. Koenig, & W. Pequegnat (Eds.) From *child sexual abuse to adult risk* (pp.3-10). Washington, DC: American Psychological Association.

Dube, S. R., Anda, R. F., Whitfield, C. L., Brown, D. W., Felitti, V. J., Doug, M., & Giles, W. H. (2005). Long-term consequences of childhood sexual abuse by gender of victim. *American Journal of Preventive Medicine, 28,* 430-438.

Finkelhor, D., Hotaling, G., Lewis, I. A., & Smith, C. (1990). Sexual abuse in a national survey of adult men and women: Prevalence, characteristics, and risk factors. *Child Abuse & Neglect, 14,* 19-28.

Finkelhor, D., & Browne, A. (1985). The traumatic impact of child sexual abuse: A conceptualization. *American Journal of Orthopsychiatry, 55,* 530-539.

Simpson, C., Odor, R., & Masho, S. (2004 August). Childhood sexual assault victimization in Virginia. Center for Injury & Violence Prevention. Virginia Department of Health.

Snyder, H. N. (2000). *Sexual assault of young children as reported to law enforcement: Victim, incident, and offender characteristics.* Washington, DC: National Center for Juvenile Justice, U.S Department of Justice. Retrieved May 5, 2008 from http://www.ncjrs.gov/App/Publications/alphaList.aspx?alpha=S

Chapter 13: Parent as Partner

DeBord, K. (1997, June). Focus on kids: The effects of divorce on children. Raleigh, NC: North Carolina State University, North Carolina Cooperative Extension Service.

Gottman, J. M. (1999). The seven principles for making marriage work. New York: Three Rivers Press.

Horowitz, J., Gomez-Schwartz, B., & Cardarelli, A. J. (1988, July). *Child sexual assault victims and their treatment.* Washington, DC: U. S. Department of Justice.

Hughes, R., & Scherer, J. (1986, February). *Parenting on Your Own: How Divorce Affects Kids.* Urnana, IL: University of Illinois Cooperative Extension Project.

Institute for American Values. (2005). *Why marriage matters: Twenty-six conclusions from the social sciences.* (2nd ed.). NY: Institute for American Values.

HERITAGE KEEPERS®

Abstinence Education

Student Manual I

"The publication revisions in this curriculum were made possible by Grant Number APH PA 006012-05 from the U.S. Department of Health and Human Services. The statements and opinions expressed are solely the responsibility of the authors and do not necessarily represent the official views of the Department."

Contents

Sexual Abstinence: The New Revolution:

Why abstain from SEX until you're married? First and foremost, you are worthy of real love and commitment. And...you have phenomenal potential to make something out of your life. But, did you know that sexual activity outside of the commitment of marriage could put YOUR FUTURE at risk?[279] WAIT – for the real thing, the commitment of marriage, if you want to have *REALLY GREAT SEX*...and if you want to provide the very best chance for success for your family in the future.

Statistics show that the people who report having the very best sex are not singles, as in many songs and movies, but actually married people who were both virgins![280] What do you think about this statement, and what it might mean for you personally?

WAIT for the best sex; the kind of sex that is in marriage. There are many reasons why sex within marriage is best, but first, do you know what abstinence is? Sexual Abstinence is "not participating in any sexual activity outside of marriage." Abstinence means not just abstaining for the moment, or until you find someone you really like, but actually saving all sexual activity for marriage. In a healthy marriage, spouses have a lifelong commitment to each other and to any children or extended family involved, and they actively support the physical health, moral development, and emotional growth and maintenance of all parties without fear of violence or infidelity.

YOU, and the people you know, may have had different levels of sexual experience. Some people abstain and intend to wait for marriage – others think they should wait for the right person at the right moment – whatever that is. Some have experimented with sexual activity and regretted it. Sadly, some have been sexually abused. Some are very sexually active with a lot of people, but don't yet realize the extremely serious personal consequences – for their health, financial well-being and emotional happiness.[281][282][283][284]

---

[279] Whitehead, B. D., & Pearson, M. (2006). *Making a love connection: Teen relationships, pregnancy, and marriage.* Washington, DC: National Campaign to Prevent Teen Pregnancy. Retrieved February 10, 2011 from http://www.thenationalcampaign.org/resources/pdf/pubs/MALC_FINAL.pdf

[280] Michael, R.T., Gagnon, J.H., Laumann, E.O., & Kolata, G. (1994). *Sex in America: A definitive survey* (p.1, p.131, p.225) Boston: Little, Brown and Company.

[281] Brady, S. S., & Halpern-Felsher, B. L. (2007). Adolescents' reported consequences of having oral sex versus vaginal sex. *Pediatrics, 119*, 229-236.

[282] Hallfors, D. D., Waller, M. W., Bauer, D., Ford, C. A., & Halpern, C. T. (2005). Which comes first in adolescence-sex and drugs or depression*? American Journal of Preventive Medicine, 29*, 163-170.

[283] Leitenberg, H., & Saltzman, H. (2003). College women who had sexual intercourse when they were underage minors (13-15). Age of male partners, relation to current adjustment, and statutory rape implications. *Sexual Abuse: A Journal of Research and Treatment, 15*, 135-147.

[284] Rector, R. E., Johnson, R. A., & Noyes, L. R. (2003). Sexually active teenagers are more likely to be depressed and to attempt suicide. Center for Data Analysis Report #30-04. Retrieved June 11, 2011 from www.heritage.org/research/reports/2003/06/sexually_active_teeangers_are_more_likely_to_be_depressed.html

This valuable information is for ALL those people – every single person has a right to know! What you are about to learn could change your expectations of yourself, your friends, and your future family. No one should feel badly about his or her past, but it is essential for every person to think of his or her FUTURE. You should do everything possible TODAY to empower yourself to REACH YOUR POTENTIAL!

Research indicates that there are different levels of sexual experience.[285]

1. Those who are committed to abstaining from all sexual activity outside of marriage.*
2. Those who are delaying sex and do not currently intend to initiate sex.
3. Those who anticipate initiating sex.
4. Those who have had sex one time.
5. Those who have had sex with one partner more than one time.
6. Those who have had sex with more then one partner.
7. Those who have been forced or pressured to have sex.[286][287]* If you were forced to have sex, or are being abused now, GET HELP. Your parents or a trusted adult can help you.[288][289]

* These categories (1, 7) have been added by Heritage Community Services®

What many people may not realize is that those who abstain from sexual activity outside of marriage are protecting themselves physically, financially, and emotionally, by waiting until someone loves them enough to make a real commitment to them and to their future children.[290][291][292][293]

And, those who are sexually experienced can do the exact same thing, starting right now! The past does not necessarily govern your future; you can abstain from sexual activity until you are protected by the love and commitment of marriage. You can begin NOW to take control of your destiny. A person who has

---

[285] Miller, K. S., Clark, L. F., Wendell, D. A., Levin, M. L., Gray-Ray, P., Velez, C. N., & Webber, M. P. (1997). Adolescent heterosexual experience: A new typology. *Journal of Adolescent Health, 20*, 179-186.

[286] Finkelhor, D., & Browne, A. (1985). The traumatic impact of child sexual abuse: A conceptualization. *American Journal of Orthopsychiatry*.

[287] Van Bruggen, L. K., Runtz, M. G., Kadlec, H. (2006). Sexual revictimization: The role of sexual self-esteem and dysfunctional sexual behaviors. *Child Maltreatment, 11*, 131-145.

[288] Sorensen, T. & Snow, B. (1991). How children tell: The process of disclosure in child sexual abuse. *Child Welfare, 70*, 3-15.

[289] Summit, R. C. (1983). The child sexual abuse accommodation syndrome. *Child Abuse & Neglect, 7*, 177-193.

[290] Bearman, P. S., & Bruckner, H. (2001). Promising the future: Virginity pledges and first intercourse. *The American Journal of Sociology*, 106, 859-911.

[291] Bingham, C. R., & Crockett, L. J. (1996). Longitudinal adjustment patterns of boys and girls experiencing early, middle, and late sexual intercourse. *Developmental Psychology, 32*, 647-658.

[292] Brady, S. S., & Halpern-Felsher, B. L. (2007). Adolescents' reported consequences of having oral sex versus vaginal sex. *Pediatrics, 119*, 229-236.

[293] Rector, R. E., Johnson, R. A., & Noyes, L. R. (2003). Sexually active teenagers are more likely to be depressed and to attempt suicide. Center for Data Analysis Report #30-04. Retrieved June 11, 2011 from www.heritage.org/research/reports/2003/06/sexually_active_teeangers_are_more_likely_to_be_depressed.html

been sexually active, but who makes the commitment to protect his or her heart, body and future by abstaining from future sexual activity until marriage, is recommitting to abstinence. Anyone who has had sex in the past can start over! You can still choose to be abstinent! This means you can physically, mentally, and emotionally recommit to saving sex for marriage. Abstinence is always an option no matter what your past has been.[294][295] Remember, you can never get your physical virginity back, but you can start over emotionally!

Recommitting to abstinence is "Physically, mentally and emotionally recommitting to saving sex for marriage." Right now, think of three reasons some choose abstinence or a recommitment to abstinence, until marriage.

1.

2.

3.

Did you consider 1) prevent STDS, 2) prevent pregnancy outside of marriage, and 3) prevent emotional pain? All three are good reasons as to why many choose to commit to abstinence, or to recommit to abstinence after they have already had sex.[296]

Remember, sexual abstinence is "Not participating in any sexual activity outside of marriage." Recommitting to sexual abstinence is "Physically, mentally and emotionally recommitting to saving sex for marriage."

All forms of sexual activity can have serious health risks, including those that are not actually intercourse.[297] This will be covered later in more detail.

This manual is called "*Heritage Keepers® Abstinence Education*" for good reason. Many people have made tremendous sacrifices in order to make possible the opportunities you have today and in your future. Whatever your family history, you have a heritage to keep and a future to create. You can make your life whatever you choose, starting today. But if you don't understand the risks of sexual activity outside of marriage, and the possible consequences, you may get involved in risky situations that could make life much more difficult than you ever imagined. You have a right to know. You have a right to keep the heritage that has been given to you by those before you, and to make a wonderful life for you and your future family. This could be one of the most important workbooks you have ever done; make the most of it, and become ALL you are meant to be!!!

---

[294] Borawski, E. A., Trapl, E. S., Lovegreen, L. D., Colabiachi, N., & Block, T. (2005). Effectiveness of abstinence-only intervention for middle school teens. *American Journal of Health Behavior*, 29, 423-434.

[295] Loewenson, P. R., Ireland, M., & Resnick, M. D. (2004). Primary and secondary sexual abstinence in high school students. *Journal of Adolescent Health, 34*, 209-215.

[296] Loewenson, et al., 2004

[297] Begley, E., Crosby, R. A., Di Clemente, R. J. Wingood, G. M., & Rose, E. (2003). Older partners and STD prevalence among pregnant African American teens. *Sexually Transmitted Diseases*, 30, 211-213.

I am a significant person.
I want others to know what interests me!

Right now, you may not realize how important this information is - for today and for tomorrow. But, by the end of this workbook and after your parents talk to you about sex, you will know! For now, think about your interests. Write the answer to these questions on a separate piece of paper and share them with your parent(s) to help them learn about you.

What is your favorite kind of music?

What is your favorite television show?

What do you like to do when you are not in school?

Who are your role models?

What question(s) about sex would you like your parent(s) to answer?

My Values

Who do I really value? Who makes a difference in my life?

Circle the people you really value and write their names on the lines below. Write any others not included in the list below.

Mother	Sisters	Friends
Father	Brothers	Religious Leaders
Grandmother	Aunts	Coaches
Grandfather	Uncles	Teachers

Who do I value (names)

Anyone else?

What do I really value? What really matters in my life?

Circle the things you really value and write anything not in the list, on the lines below.

Family	Respect	Religion
Education	Helping my community	Truth
Success	Justice	Fitness
Friendship	Fun	Love

What else do I value?

What are my goals? What do I want to do and become with my life?[298]

Circle your goals in each section and write any others that are not included on the lines below. Over the next few years I want to . . .

Play sports	Make my family proud
Enjoy being a teenager	Get to know my parents/learn from them
Make good grades	Earn a high school diploma
Develop deep, lasting friendships	Earn a college diploma

---

[298] Duckworth, A. L., & Seligman, M. E. P. (2005). Self-discipline outdoes IQ in predicting academic performance of adolescents. *Psychological Science, 16*, 939-944.

These are other goals that are important to me (be very specific):

Over my lifetime I want to . . .

Succeed in a career I enjoy and am proud of
Marry a great person
Achieve a lifelong, fulfilling marriage
Raise good kids
Develop deep, lasting friendships
Make my family proud
Be a good, loving spouse

These are other goals that are important to me (be very specific):

What character traits do I value? What kind of person do I want to be?
I want to be . . .

Circle the character traits important to you and write any traits that are not included on the list below.

Respectful
Loving
Helpful
Trustworthy
Fair
Committed
Fun
Responsible
Truthful
Respected
Honest
Faithful

These are other character traits that are important to me:

Rolling the Dice

Get some of your friends together and ask your parent(s) to play the *Rolling the Dice* game mentioned in *the Sex, Lies and Hook-Ups* book with you!

Roll the dice and remember the number you got. After your parent(s) have shared with you what your number means, answer the following questions:

What was your number?

As your parent called out negative consequences, was there one you were hoping to get?

Why wouldn't you want ANY of the negative consequences?

What consequence was associated with your number?

How would it make you feel if you really were experiencing these negative consequences?

Consider the people you value. How would each one take the news if these consequences actually happened to you?

Consider the things you value – especially your family now, as well as the family you may have in the future. Write a few ways that the consequences mentioned could affect the people and things you value, today and in the future.

Consider your immediate goals one by one. Write how each goal could be affected by the consequences of sexual activity outside of marriage.

Consider your long-term goals. Describe how a few of the consequences discussed could effect you and your goals.

Having sex outside of marriage is gambling with your future. Don't take the risk! You could have avoided the consequences if you had abstained, if you had refused to roll the dice. Don't play games with your life, even if your friends do.[299][300][301] Resist the temptation to go along with risky behaviors, even if others try to get you to give in. It's *YOUR VALUES THAT MATTER*. Your goals, health, feelings and future are important. Don't give in – go for the best. You are worth it.[302][303][304][305][306][307][308]

---

[299] Begley, E., Crosby, R. A., Di Clemente, R. J. Wingood, G. M., & Rose, E. (2003). Older partners and STD prevalence among pregnant African American teens. *Sexually Transmitted Diseases*, 30, 211-213.

[300] Miller, H. G., Cain, V. S., Rogers, S. M., Gribble, J. N., & Tuner, C. F. (1999). Correlates of sexually transmitted bacterial infections among U.S. women in1995. *Family Planning Perspectives, 31*, 4-23.

[301] Tiller, C. M. (2002). Chlamydia during pregnancy: Implications and impact on prenatal and neonatal outcomes. *Journal of Obstetric and Gynecologic, and Neonatal Nursing, 31*, 93-98.

[302] Bearman, P. S., & Bruckner, H. (2001). Promising the future: Virginity pledges and first intercourse. *The American Journal of Sociology*, 106, 859-911.

[303] Brady, S. S., & Halpern-Felsher, B. L. (2007). Adolescents' reported consequences of having oral sex versus vaginal sex. *Pediatrics, 119*, 229-236.

[304] Cooper, L. M., Shapiro, C. M., & Powers, A. M. (1998). Motivations for sex and risky sexual behavior among adolescents and young adults: A functional perspective. *Journal of Personality and Social Psychology, 75*, 1528-1558.

[305] Mirowsky, J., & Ross, C. E. (2002). Depression, parenthood, and age at first birth. *Social Science and Medicine, 54*, 1281-1298.

[306] O'Donnell, L., O'Donnell, C. R., & Stueve, A. (2001). Early sexual initiation and subsequent sex-related risks among urban minority youth: the reach for health study. *Family Planning Perspectives, 33*, i268-275.

[307] Rector, R. E., Johnson, K. A., & Marshall, J. A. (2004). *Teens who make virginity pledges have substantially improved life outcomes.* Center for Data Analysis Report #04-07. Retrieved June 11, 2011 from www.heritage.org.

[308] Rector, R. E., Johnson, R. A., & Noyes, L. R. (2003). Sexually active teenagers are more likely to be depressed and to attempt suicide. Center for Data Analysis Report #30-04. Retrieved June 11, 2011 from www.heritage.org/research/reports/2003/06/sexually_active_teeangers_are_more_likely_to_be_depressed.html

Family Formation

The following information was written for Heritage Community Services® by Joshua Mann, MD, MPH, University of South Carolina, Department of Family and Preventive Medicine.

Male Reproductive System

Heritage Community Services ©

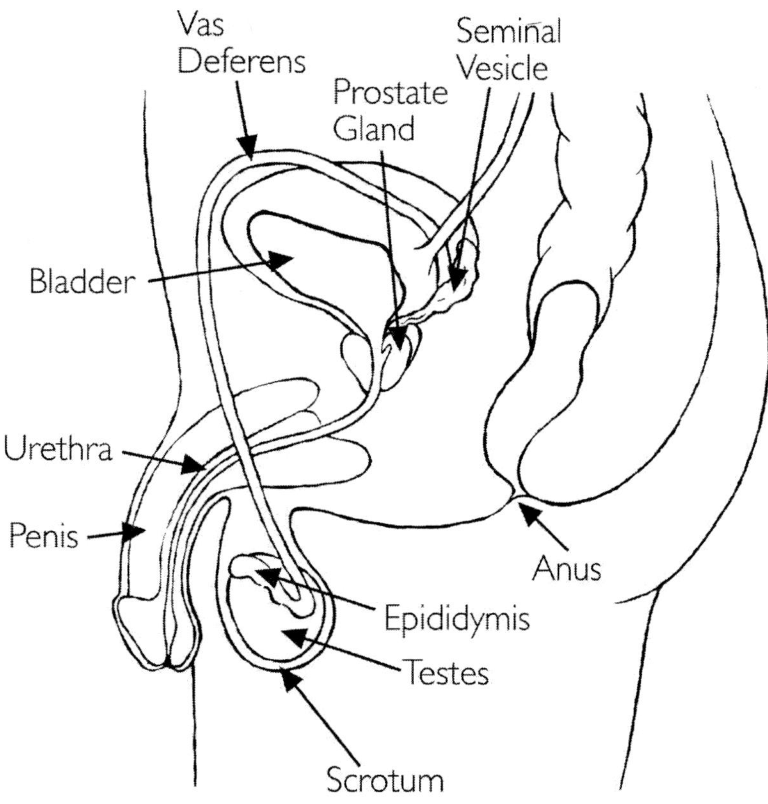

The male reproductive system is made up of the following:

- the penis, a tube-shaped organ that is covered in skin and emits fluids (urine and semen) from the body
- the urethra, a smaller tube inside the penis that carries urine from the bladder and sperm from the vas deferens to the outside of the body
- the scrotum, a pouch or sack of skin that hangs between the legs and holds the testes in place
- the two testes, which are located inside the scrotum and produce sperm and the hormone testosterone that causes the development of facial hair and other male physical features
- the epididymis, a tube attached to each testis, where sperm mature before passing to the vas deferens
- the vas deferens, long, thin tubes that transport sperm away from the epididymis
- the seminal vesicles and prostate, which produce the fluids that make up semen, which nourishes sperm and provides a vehicle for sperm to get to a female's egg.

Sperm are cells produced by the testes that contain genetic information (genes) from a male. These cells can join with (fertilize) a female's egg, which has the female's genetic information, to bring about a pregnancy. Sperm have a tail that allows them to "swim" in fluid, so that they can get to a woman's egg and fertilize it.

Immediately after they are produced, sperm are not capable of movement. They pass from the testes to the epididymis where they mature and acquire the ability to move. Once mature, the sperm then enter the vas deferens. These tubes pass through the seminal vesicles and the prostate gland, which secrete fluids that mix with the sperm to provide nourishment and effectively carry the sperm. This fluid is called semen.

During sexual activity, blood flow into the penis increases and blood flow out of the penis decreases, causing the penis to become stiff; this is called an erection. If sexual stimulation is continued, ejaculation occurs. During ejaculation, muscles in the penis contract, pushing the semen (containing millions of sperm) through the urethra and out the tip of the penis, into the female's reproductive tract. A valve in the urethra prevents the emission of both semen and urine at the same time.

Some possible concerns males may have:

Erections. As described above, erections occur when blood fills the penis, causing it to become stiff. Erections most often occur because of sexual stimulation such as sexual thoughts, erotic touching, or other sexual situations. However, during puberty, "spontaneous erections" – erections that occur in the absence of sexual stimulation – sometimes occur. This is a common part of puberty and should not cause a person to worry unless the erection causes pain or does not go away within an hour or so.

Nocturnal emissions. Sometimes a male may ejaculate during his sleep, often as a result of a sexually stimulating dream. This is also a normal occurrence during puberty that usually occurs less frequently with age.

Penis and testicular size. The size of a boy's or man's penis and testes varies from one person to another. This is usually nothing to worry about. However, if someone is worried about the size of his reproductive organs, he should discuss those concerns with his doctor.

Testicular lumps. A man can develop a lump in one or both of his testes. If this occurs, he should see his doctor right away, since it is possible to develop cancer of the testes. Testicular cancer can usually be treated effectively if it is detected early, but treatment is less effective if it is delayed.

Circumcision. Circumcision is a minor surgical procedure usually performed soon after birth, which removes all or part of the foreskin of the penis. Not all parents choose to circumcise their male children; the decision is most often based on religious or cultural traditions rather than medical benefits. However, circumcision probably is helpful in maintaining good hygiene. Uncircumcised men and boys should pull back their foreskin and wash underneath it every day. It is also important to make sure the foreskin can be pulled back. Occasionally a man's foreskin can cause problems by becoming too firmly attached to the penis or by covering up the tip of the penis. Pulling the foreskin back and washing underneath it can also help prevent this problem.

Impotence. Young men rarely have problems getting an erection and ejaculating. However, older men sometimes have problems with these necessary aspects of sexual activity. Men who do have these problems can discuss them with their doctor, as there are effective treatments available. However, the best approach is to prevent these problems by avoiding behaviors that can cause impotence. Two of the most common causes of impotence are tobacco use and diabetes. Avoiding tobacco use and diabetes substantially reduces the likelihood that a man will have problems with sexual function. The best way to avoid diabetes is to get plenty of exercise and avoid overeating. Men who are already diabetic can reduce the likelihood of impotence by sticking very closely to the treatments prescribed by their doctor.

The Female Reproductive System

Unlike the male reproductive system where the reproductive organs are visible outside the body, the female reproductive system has elements that can be seen from the outside, but also a number of important parts that are internal (not visible). Therefore, discussions of female reproduction usually distinguish between the external and internal reproductive organs.

Female External Reproductive Organs

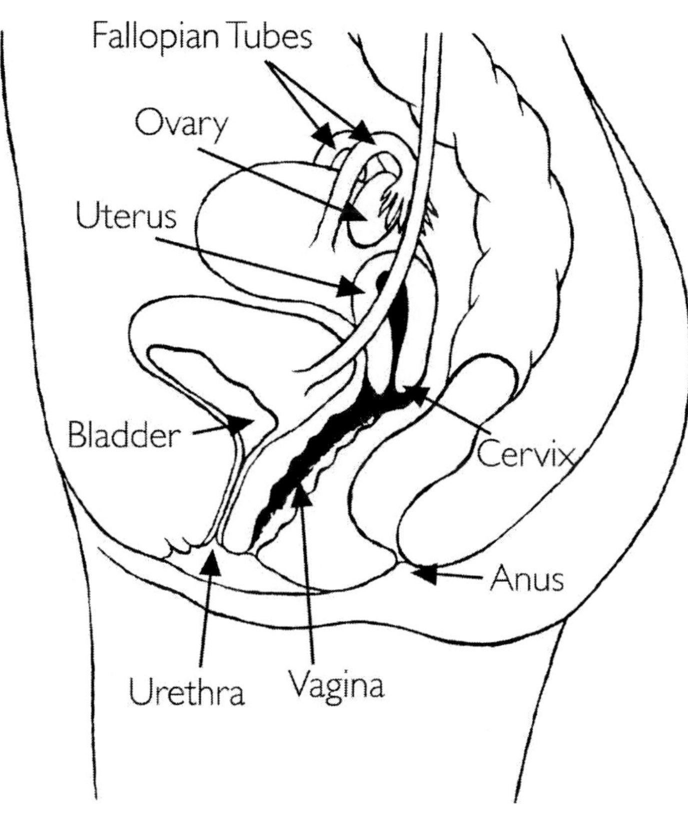

The female external reproductive organs are also called the vulva. They include:

- the labia majora (external fatty folds surrounding the urinary and vaginal openings)
- the labia minora (two thinner folds of skin located within the outer lips)
- the clitoris, a structure containing sensitive nerve endings
- the hymen, a flexible membrane which covers the opening to the vagina.

Interestingly, during a baby's development inside the mother's womb, the labia majora and labia minora develop from the same tissues that form a boy's scrotum, while the clitoris develops from the same tissues that form a boy's penis.

Female Internal Reproductive Organs

Heritage Community Services ©

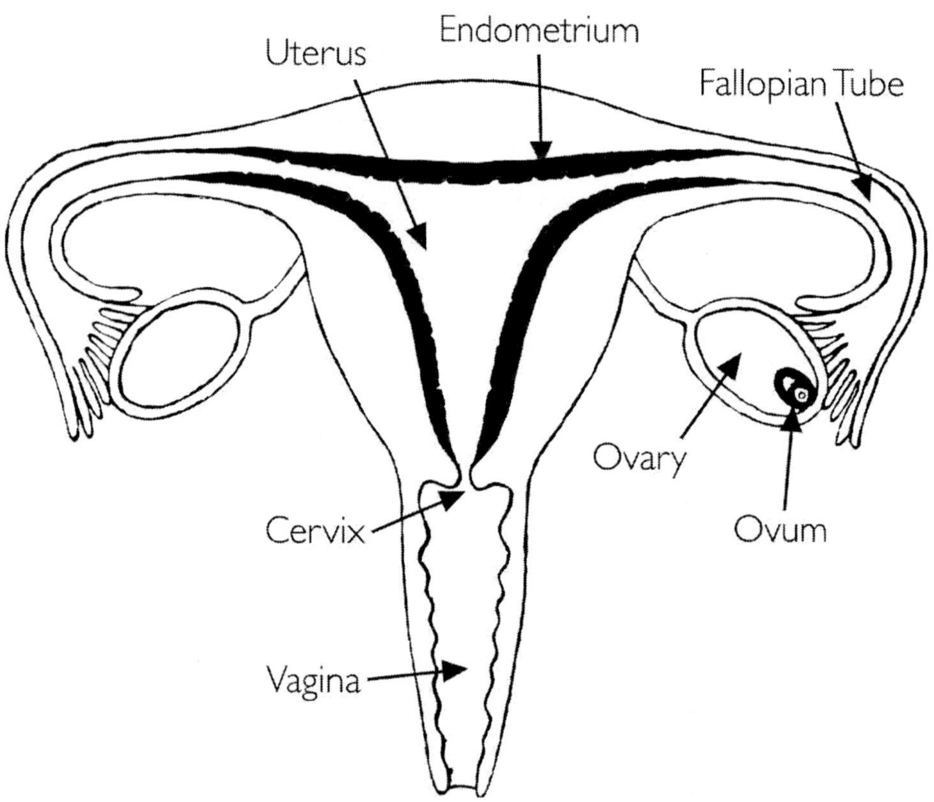

The female internal reproductive system is made up of:

- the vagina, which is a pouch between the woman's legs (just inside the vulva)
- the ovaries, two glands each containing thousands of eggs located in the woman's abdomen – the ovaries also produce estrogen, a hormone responsible for female features such as enlarging breasts
- the fallopian tubes, that connect each ovary to the uterus
- the uterus, also called the womb, which is where a fertilized egg implants and a baby develops prior to birth. The bottom of the uterus is connected to the top of the vagina.

About once a month, an egg is released from one of the ovaries into one of the fallopian tubes. This is called ovulation. At about the same time, the lining of the uterus builds up with blood vessels, providing a place for a fertilized egg to implant; the blood vessels provide a supply of the mother's blood to provide nourishment and sustain the new life. The implanted egg develops into a fetus, which is a developing baby inside the mother's womb. If no egg is fertilized (because there is no sexual activity around the time of ovulation, effective contraception is used, or there are simply no sperm that make it to the egg to bring about fertilization), the egg remains in the uterus a few days and then is released into the vagina where it essentially dies. Similarly, sometimes an egg will become fertilized but will fail to implant in the uterus. In this case, the fertilized egg also dies and is eliminated through the vagina.

If a fertilized egg implants in the lining of the uterus, hormones are produced that maintain the lining so that normal development can occur, leading to the birth of a baby.

If no egg is fertilized or a fertilized egg fails to implant, the uterine lining dies and sloughs off, passing out of the body through the vagina. Tissue and blood will pass through the vagina – this is called a woman's menstrual flow.

Normally, about 14 days pass between the time ovulation occurs and the beginning of menstrual flow. The first day of menstrual flow is usually counted as the first day of the menstrual cycle. This usually lasts for four or five days, with the first day or two being the heaviest. There is usually a 7- to 21-day span of time between the first day of menstrual flow and ovulation. Therefore, the "normal" time span between menstrual periods is between 21 and 35 days, with an average of about 28 days. Menstrual cycles in this range are considered normal. If a woman's cycles occur more frequently than every 21 days or less frequently than every 35 days, she should tell her doctor about her cycles to make sure there is no medical problem that needs to be treated.

Similarly, the amount of blood loss during a period should be fairly small – about four to six tablespoons during the course of the menstrual period. If there is substantially more blood loss than this, or if menstrual flow continues longer than about seven days, a woman should talk to her doctor to make sure everything is normal.

The onset of menstrual periods is fairly unpredictable; some girls start menstruating as early as 9 years of age. Others start significantly later. If menstruation starts before age 9 or after age 16, a doctor should be consulted to make sure nothing is wrong.

Some possible concerns females may have:

Pre-Menstrual Syndrome. Levels of certain hormones change just before menstruation. Sometimes these hormones can cause symptoms such as mood swings, bloating and breast tenderness in the days leading up to menstrual flow. Usually these symptoms can be handled fairly easily with over-the-counter medications and behavioral changes such as getting regular exercise and cutting down on salt and caffeine (coffee, tea, many sodas, etc.).

Dysmenorrhea. Many women also experience symptoms of abdominal and back discomfort and possibly nausea or other symptoms shortly before and during menstrual flow. This occurs because of uterine contractions pushing out the menstrual flow that cause a cramping sensation. Again, over-the-counter medications can often help with these symptoms. If they are severe, talk with your doctor to get additional input on how to decrease symptoms of dysmenorrhea.

Irregular periods. Adolescents often experience irregular menstrual cycles – sometimes occurring more frequently and other times occurring less frequently. This is normal, and should resolve within a year or so as the reproductive system fully "gets going."

Feminine hygiene products. During menstruation, a woman should use a sanitary product to soak up menstrual flow to prevent staining of clothes and furniture. Most women use either sanitary napkins (pads) or tampons. Pads work by providing an absorbent layer over the underwear that soaks up the menstrual flow. Tampons are finger-shaped and are inserted into the vagina; like sanitary napkins, they soak up menstrual flow. Both pads and tampons should be changed frequently (several times a day) to maintain good hygiene.

Toxic shock syndrome. In the late 1970s, a number of women became seriously ill during their menstrual cycle while using tampons. Symptoms included fatigue, fever, chills, nausea, and confusion, and the condition sometimes progressed to organ failure and death. It was determined that the illness was due to improper tampon use. The women were not changing their tampons frequently enough, allowing an overgrowth of bacteria in the tampon. These bacteria produced toxic chemicals that caused the serious illnesses. Modern tampons are less likely to foster toxic shock syndrome (TSS); however, women using tampons are still at risk. The surest way to avoid TSS is to use pads rather than tampons. The best way for tampon users to avoid TSS is to change their tampons frequently – at least every few hours. Women who have had TSS in the past should not use tampons. TSS can also happen as a result of other conditions, such as infected skin wounds, or after certain medical or surgical procedures. If symptoms of TSS occur, it is important to contact a physician sooner rather than later.

Twins. Women may have twins for one of two reasons: either more than one egg was produced by the ovaries and fertilized by sperm or one egg was fertilized then divided in two after fertilization. In the first case, the twins are called fraternal twins and are NOT identical. In the second case, the twins are identical.

A Birth Video

Ask your parents to show you a video of how new life develops. We suggest the National Geographic documentary, *In the Womb* (it can be ordered off of Amazon.com). After you have watched a video about development in the womb, continue with this section.

This is how every human begins – it is how you started in your mother's womb. You are a truly wonderful combination of your mother and father, genetically unique and special in every way. Think carefully about what this might mean in your life and the lives of your friends. Consider the implications for those you love and those who love you. When you have sexual intercourse with someone there is a good chance that you could create an entirely new person – a living human being, a son or daughter. It is important to that person that his or her parents are committed to one another, within a loving and faithful marriage, and committed to giving him, or her, the very best opportunities possible. And it is important to be the kind of mother or father that you dream of being.[309][310][311][312][313] Allow yourself to really ponder what you really want in life – what is important to YOU.

If you already have a child, perhaps outside of marriage, you understand the importance of commitment and love in a child's life. You can decide today that you will not put yourself in the position of having sex until you are married to someone who will love you and commit to you in every way- legally, emotionally, financially and physically. That is best for you and best for your future family. You and any children you may have in the future are worthy of such love and commitment. Do not allow yourself to be swayed by anyone who thinks you deserve less than the very best.[314][315][316][317][318][319]

---

[309] Cabrera, N. J., Tamis-LeMonda, C. S., Bradley, R. H., Hofferth, S., & Lamb, M. E. (2000). Fatherhood in the twenty-first century. *Child Development, 71,* 127-136.

[310] Coley, R. L. (1998). Children's socialization experiences and functioning in single-mother households: The importance of fathers and other men. *Child Development,* 69, 219-230.

[311] Jaffee, S., Caspi, A., Moffitt, T. E., Belsky, J., & Silva, P. (2001). Why are children born to teen mothers at risk for adverse outcomes in young adulthood? Results from a 20-year longitudinal study. *Development and Psychopathology, 13,* 377-397.

[312] Mirowsky, J., & Ross, C. E. (2002). Depression, parenthood, and age at first birth. *Social Science and Medicine, 54,* 1281-1298.

[313] Tamis-LeMonda, C. S., Shannon, J. D., Cabrera, N. J., & Lamb, M. E. (2004). Fathers and mothers at play with their 2- and 3- year-olds: contributions to language and cognitive development. *Child Development, 75,* 1806-1820.

[314] Brady, S. S., & Halpern-Felsher, B. L. (2007). Adolescents' reported consequences of having oral sex versus vaginal sex. *Pediatrics, 119,* 229-236.

[315] Coley, et al, 1998

[316] Huang, C. C. (2005). Pregnancy intention from men's perspectives: Does child support enforcement matter? *Perspectives on Sexual and Reproductive Health, 37,* 119-124.

[317] Jaffee, et al., 2001

[318] Kim, H. K., & McKenry, P. C. (2000). The relationship between marriage and psychological well-being: A Longitudinal analysis. *Journal of Family Issues, 23,* 885-911.

[319] Tamis-LeMonda, et al., 2004

The space below is for you to write your thoughts and observations about what you just viewed – things you might want to remember later.

How did the birth video make you feel about the wonder of new human life forming?

Did you learn anything new, or did anything surprise you? If so, what was it?

Key points about life in the womb:

- ❑ conception is when the sperm fertilizes the egg
- ❑ a baby's heart begins beating just three weeks after conception
- ❑ a baby's brain waves begin at about forty days after conception
- ❑ every human being went through this development process before being born

LIFE is amazing! Remember just how precious a gift you are giving someone when you choose to have sex. You could create a child, who deserves the love and protection of parents who are committed to each other in every way. This should not be taken lightly!

Every sports hero, president, civil rights leader, physician, lawyer, coal miner, nurse, congressman, senator, judge, policeman, musician, actor, producer, advertising executive, car salesman, teacher... every person who ever lived began this way. You were a very small fertilized egg when you first started your life, and you have grown and matured ever since.

Give yourself and your future family the best chance of all.

Humans are incredible, all with different genetic make ups! And most of all, you are incredible! You can pursue your dreams and work hard to make the most of your life, and you can give your children the very best chance of success.

You are too special to waste on risky behaviors. And your future children will be precious to you. Give yourself and them the best chance in life by waiting on sex until you are married to the person you care enough about to make a life-long commitment. Life is too wonderful to gamble with – make the most of it.

If you have already had sexual intercourse and think you, or your girlfriend, might be pregnant, get help. A mother and developing baby need prenatal care! Also, remember that everything the mother eats, drinks and breaths ends up in her blood stream and the baby's. Alcohol, drugs, and tobacco are especially harmful and could cause the baby to be born before it is fully developed, to have physical and/or emotional problems, or even to be stillborn (meaning dead when born).

A little human being growing in the womb is vulnerable and what the mother does during the nine months the baby is developing can affect that tiny person's life forever. The womb should be a safe place for growth.

Abstinence gives you and your future family the best chance of success.[320][321] If you have not had sexual intercourse, the very best thing you can do is to remain abstinent until you are married, so you do not have a baby out of wedlock. If you have had sexual intercourse, and are pregnant or already have a child, you can make the commitment to abstain until marriage from this day forward.

Remember, sexual abstinence is "Not participating in any sexual activity outside of marriage." Recommitting to sexual abstinence is "Physically, mentally and emotionally recommitting to saving sex for marriage."

Sex is Like Fire

Fire can be positive or negative:

Ask your parents to share the "sex is like fire" demonstration they learned about in the *Sex, Lies and Hook-Ups* book. Once they have done so, proceed with this section.

What makes fire a positive thing? It can provide....

When fire is in a safe place such as a fireplace, it is wonderful. It makes you feel warm, cozy, and happy. You can cook things, like marshmallows on it. It can create a very happy experience.

When is fire a negative or even scary thing?

---

[320] Bearman, P. S., & Bruckner, H. (2001). Promising the future: Virginity pledges and first intercourse. *The American Journal of Sociology*, 106, 859-911.

[321] Kim, H. K., & McKenry, P. C. (2000). The relationship between marriage and psychological well-being: A Longitudinal analysis. *Journal of Family Issues, 23*, 885-911.

When a fire is outside of a fireplace or other safe place, it is dangerous. It can burn down trees, houses and buildings. It can burn you and hurt you. It is very scary! Even when you try to build a fire in a safe place such as a trash can, sometimes it can get out of control.

If you built a fire and then suddenly it was out of control, hot, and dangerous, consuming everything around you – flaming enough to seriously harm you and those around you, how would you feel?

Would you feel in danger, scared, worried or angry? Probably. Inside appropriate boundaries like a well-built fireplace, a fire is a great thing. But outside of that fireplace, fire can get dangerous.

Sex is like fire. Inside the appropriate boundary of a faithful marriage, sex is a great thing! Outside of marriage, sex can be dangerous.[322][323]

Remember, sexual abstinence is "Not participating in any sexual activity outside of marriage." Recommitting to sexual abstinence is "Physically, mentally and emotionally recommitting to saving sex for marriage."

What do SEX and FIRE have in common?

Think of some of the reasons that you gave for why fire can be positive. Could those same reasons apply to why sex can be positive? Think about it. Sex can also make you feel warm, cozy and happy! Think of some of the reasons that you gave for why fire can be negative. Could those same reasons fit with why sex can be negative? Think about it. Sex can also make you feel danger, scared, worried and angry when it is outside of a faithful marriage.

STDs, pregnancy and emotional pain can all make you feel worried and scared, just like uncontrolled fire.[324][325][326] Do you know, or have you ever seen, anyone who has been hurt by fire? How did he or she feel, or appear?

---

[322] Brady, S. S., & Halpern-Felsher, B. L. (2007). Adolescents' reported consequences of having oral sex versus vaginal sex. *Pediatrics, 119*, 229-236

[323] Kim, H. K., & McKenry, P. C. (2000). The relationship between marriage and psychological well-being: A Longitudinal analysis. *Journal of Family Issues, 23*, 885-911.

[324] Brady, S. S., & Halpern-Felsher, B. L. (2007). Adolescents' reported consequences of having oral sex versus vaginal sex. *Pediatrics, 119*, 229-236

[325] Kim, H. K., & McKenry, P. C. (2000). The relationship between marriage and psychological well-being: A Longitudinal analysis. *Journal of Family Issues, 23*, 885-911.

[326] Bearman, P. S., & Bruckner, H. (2001). Promising the future: Virginity pledges and first intercourse. *The American Journal of Sociology*, 106, 859-911.

You might have mentioned that he or she was scarred, hurt, or burned.

Do you know anyone who has been hurt by sex? How did he or she feel?

Sometimes people are hurt by fire even when they chose to start the fire. It might have gotten out of control, even though they didn't mean for it to – like when someone builds a fire in the woods for fun, but it gets outside the boundaries and becomes a forest fire, burning everything in its path. Sometimes people are hurt by sex even when they chose to become sexually involved. Unexpected consequences, like emotional pain, sexually transmitted diseases, having a child outside of marriage and financial problems can hurt deeply and for a long time.[327][328][329]

Too often, people make sexual choices without enough information about the consequences, or just because they want to feel loved. Sadly, the love they needed was a deeper love. The momentary sexual activity didn't provide that kind of love, and ended up hurting instead.[330][331][332]

To protect young people, most states have laws to define the "age of consent" for sexual activity. Having sex with someone who has not reached the "age of consent" is called statutory rape, which is a crime (see http://www.4parents.gov/sexrisky/teen_sex/statelaws_chart/statelaws_chart.html for a chart of state laws of consent[333]). All persons are protected by the law from unwanted sexual advances. Just as people can be victims of a fire they didn't start, people can also be hurt by unwanted sex, such as when they are raped or sexually molested.[334] If this has happened to you, get help. This kind of hurt is not your fault and it is illegal. Your physical virginity should be yours to be given away and that was stolen from you. But you can physically, mentally and emotionally choose to be abstinent until you are married, even after a horrible experience such as this.[335] You have the right to decide with whom you will share sexual intimacy.

---

[327] Brady, et al., 2007

[328] Rector, R. E., Johnson, R. A., & Noyes, L. R. (2003). Sexually active teenagers are more likely to be depressed and to attempt suicide. Center for Data Analysis Report #30-04. Retrieved June 11, 2011 from www.heritage.org/research/reports/2003/06/sexually_active_teeangers_are_more_likely_to_be_depressed.html

[330] Bingham, C. R., & Crockett, L. J. (1996). Longitudinal adjustment patterns of boys and girls experiencing early, middle, and late sexual intercourse. *Developmental Psychology*, *32*, 647-658.

[331] Rostosky, S. S., Regnerus, M. D., & Wright, M. L. C. (2003). Coital debut: the role of religiosity and sex attitudes in the Add Health Survey. *Journal of Sex Research, 40*, 358-367.

[332] Hallfors, D. D., Waller, M. W., Bauer, D., Ford, C. A., & Halpern, C. T. (2005). Which comes first in adolescence-sex and drugs or depression*? American Journal of Preventive Medicine, 29*, 163-170.

[333] 4parents.gov (2007). *State laws on age requirements and sex*. RetrievedJune 14, 2011, from http://www.4parents.gov/sexrisky/teen_sex/statelaws_chart/statelaws_chart.html

[334] Finkelhor, D., & Browne, A. (1985). The traumatic impact of child sexual abuse: A conceptualization. *American Journal of Orthopsychiatry*.

[335] Finkelhor, et al., 1985.

If you are being (or have been) sexually abused, it is crucial that you get help immediately. Your school guidance counselor, a teacher, your parents, or a trusted adult can help you if you do not know where to turn.[336][337] You have the right to your own sexual boundaries. NO ONE has the right to abuse you, under any circumstances.

If you knew some one who was hurt by fire, you would want to treat that person with loving kindness, and help in every way possible. If you know of someone who has been hurt by sex, whether by choice or through abuse, it is extremely important to help in every way possible. And if you know of someone who is pregnant, or who has one or more children outside of marriage, do everything you can to help him or her, and the child or children. Those who suffer from the unexpected consequences of sex outside of marriage, whether it is having AIDS, having trouble with infertility, cancer from HPV, or the challenges of raising kids as a single mother or father, deserve the loving support of friends and family.[338][339][340]

Both SEX and FIRE are important. Why is fire important?

You might have said that fire provides heat, light and energy! It is very important!

Why is sex important?

One reason why sex is so important is that sex is how humans reproduce. It's how families are formed. Sex can be enjoyable, a source of deep happiness that bonds a couple together within a marriage where they are joined physically, emotionally, legally and financially[341][342]! Sex is a vital part of life.[343][344][345]

---

[336] Sorensen, T. & Snow, B. (1991). How children tell: The process of disclosure in child sexual abuse. *Child Welfare, 70,* 3-15.

[337] Summit, R. C. (1983). The child sexual abuse accommodation syndrome. *Child Abuse & Neglect, 7,* 177-193.

[338] Bearman, P. S., & Bruckner, H. (2001). Promising the future: Virginity pledges and first intercourse. *The American Journal of Sociology,* 106, 859-911.

[339] Brady, S. S., & Halpern-Felsher, B. L. (2007). Adolescents' reported consequences of having oral sex versus vaginal sex. *Pediatrics, 119,* 229-236

[340] Young, M., Denny, G., & Luquis, R. (1998). Correlates of the sexual satisfaction in marriage. *The Canadian Journal of Human Sexuality, 7,* 115-127.

[341] Hsiu-Chen, Y., Lorenx, F. O., Wickrama, K. A. S., Conger, R. D., & Elder, G. H. (2006). Relationships among sexual satisfaction [sic], marital quality, and marital instability at midlife. *Journal of Family Psychology, 20,* 339-343.

[342] Young, et al., 1998

[343] Brady, et al., 2007

[344] Kim, H. K., & McKenry, P. C. (2000). The relationship between marriage and psychological well-being: A Longitudinal analysis. *Journal of Family Issues, 23,* 885-911.

[345] Young, et al., 1998

Can you tell the difference between situations when sex can be harmful and dangerous and when sex is safe? Explain below.

Remember, sex within the boundaries and protection of marriage is the safest sex. Sexual activity outside the boundaries and protection of marriage can have negative consequences for you and your children. If you haven't lived through those consequences, it may be difficult to imagine how seriously they can change your life. Don't experiment and find out the hard way; you are much too valuable to risk the negative physical, emotional, and financial risks that too often are associated with sexual activity outside of marriage.[346][347][348] It is not that you can't survive—it's just that the consequences can make life much more difficult in many ways for you and those you love.[349]

Having a baby alone—or paying for a baby when you don't really love his or her mother or father, is a difficult way to live. And getting an STD can result in early death, the inability to have your own baby, or uncomfortable symptoms that keep coming back.

Marriage is the boundary that makes sex safe!

Marriage

Remember: In a healthy marriage, spouses have a lifelong commitment to each other and to any children or extended family involved, and they actively support the physical health, moral development, and emotional growth and maintenance of all parties without fear of violence or infidelity.

From what you have observed from TV, movies and the radio, who would you think is having the most satisfying sex? Research shows that sex can be most pleasurable and satisfying when you wait for that person who loves you enough to get married.

---

[346] Brady, S. S., & Halpern-Felsher, B. L. (2007). Adolescents' reported consequences of having oral sex versus vaginal sex. *Pediatrics, 119*, 229-236

[347] Kim, H. K., & McKenry, P. C. (2000). The relationship between marriage and psychological well-being: A Longitudinal analysis. *Journal of Family Issues, 23*, 885-911.

[348] Young, M., Denny, G., & Luquis, R. (1998). Correlates of the sexual satisfaction in marriage. *The Canadian Journal of Human Sexuality, 7*, 115-127.

[349] Loewenson, P. R., Ireland, M., & Resnick, M. D. (2004). Primary and secondary sexual abstinence in high school students. *Journal of Adolescent Health, 34*, 209-215.

And when you decide together that you will protect and care for any children that you have, together, your future family has the best chance for success. Don't buy into the media's portrayal of sex. TV, movies and the radio exist to entertain. They seldom tell the whole story.[350][351][352][353][354][355][356]

According to "the first truly scientific study[357][358] on sexuality in America, conducted at the University of Chicago, researchers found some very interesting things about sex. These scholars learned, "The public image of sex in America bears virtually no relationship to the truth.[359]"

So, what is the truth?

The team of leading sociologists explain, "in real life, the unheralded, seldom discussed world of married sex is actually the one that satisfies people the most.[360]"

Of all sexually active people, the group reporting the highest levels of being "extremely" satisfied with the amount of physical pleasure and emotional satisfaction they received from their partner are not the "hip" singles on television's sitcoms or Hollywood's movies.[361]

This and other research tells us it is the faithfully married. And the most sexually satisfied married couples are those that enter marriage as virgins. In fact, sexual satisfaction tended to decline as the level of past sexual experience increased. Think about that! Practice makes perfect, but not when it comes to sex with different people. Just the opposite is true.[362]

---

[350] Bearman, P. S., & Bruckner, H. (2001). Promising the future: Virginity pledges and first intercourse. *The American Journal of Sociology*, 106, 859-911.

[351] Finger, R. Thelen, T., Vessey, J. T., Mohn, J. K., & Mann, J. R. (2003). Association of virginity at age 18 with educational, economic, social, and health outcomes in middle adulthood. *Adolescent & Family Health, 3*, 164-170.

[352] Jaffee, S., Caspi, A., Moffitt, T. E., Belsky, J., & Silva, P. (2001). Why are children born to teen mothers at risk for adverse outcomes in young adulthood? Results from a 20-year longitudinal study. *Development and Psychopathology, 13*, 377-397.

[353] Kim, H. K., & McKenry, P. C. (2000). The relationship between marriage and psychological well-being: A Longitudinal analysis. *Journal of Family Issues, 23*, 885-911.

[354] Tamis-LeMonda, C. S., Shannon, J. D., Cabrera, N. J., & Lamb, M. E. (2004). Fathers and mothers at play with their 2- and 3- year-olds: contributions to language and cognitive development. *Child Development, 75*, 1806-1820.

[355] Whitehead, B. D., & Pearson, M. (2006). *Making a love connection: Teen relationships, pregnancy, and marriage.* Washington, DC: National Campaign to Prevent Teen Pregnancy. Retrieved February 10, 2011 from http://www.thenationalcampaign.org/resources/pdf/pubs/MALC_FINAL.pdf

[356] Young, M., Denny, G., & Luquis, R. (1998). Correlates of the sexual satisfaction in marriage. *The Canadian Journal of Human Sexuality, 7*, 115-127.

[357] Elmer-Dewitt, P. (1994, October 17). *Now for the truth about Americans and sex*. Time, p. 64-71.

[358] Schrof, J. M., & Wagner, B. (1994, October 17). *Sex in America.* U.S. News & World Report, pp. 74–81.

[359] Michael, R.T., Gagnon, J.H., Laumann, E.O., & Kolata, G. (1994). *Sex in America: A definitive survey* (p.1, p.131, p.225) Boston: Little, Brown and Company.

[360] Michael, et al., 1994

[361] Michael, et al., 1994

[362] Michael, et al., 1994

The numbers are as follows for those reporting being "extremely" and "very" sexually satisfied.

Partner	Physical Pleasure	Emotional Satisfaction
Only one:		
Spouse	87.4%	84.8%
Cohabitant	84.4%	75.6%
Neither	78.2%	71.0%
More than one: (in a lifetime)		
Spouse	61.2%	56.7%
Cohabitant	74.5%	57.9%
Neither	77.9%	61.7%

The distinction between physical pleasure and emotional satisfaction is important. People can have a physically pleasurable experience, in fact many do, but finding emotional satisfaction is even more important...and difficult. It is the emotional satisfaction that leaves you truly fulfilled, satisfied, and feeling loved. Without this emotional satisfaction, people often feel used. And it is in marriage where we are most likely to find both of these.

"Married people are significantly more likely to say their sex life makes them feel 'satisfied,' 'loved,' 'thrilled,' 'wanted' and 'taken care of.[363]'"

Those who have sex outside of marriage are more likely "to report sex making them feel 'sad,' 'anxious or worried,' 'scared or afraid' or guilty.[364]'"

Additionally, married women are significantly less likely to be forced to do something sexually against their will than women in any other relationship. "Nine percent of married women are forced by their spouse to perform a sexual act, while forty-six percent of women report being forced by someone they were 'in love with', nineteen percent of women report being forced by an 'acquaintance' and twenty-two percent report being forced by someone they 'knew well.[365]'"

Relationship	Suffered from forced sex
Spouse	9%
Acquaintance	19%
Someone she knew well	22%
Someone she loved	46%

[363] Michael, R.T., Gagnon, J.H., Laumann, E.O., & Kolata, G. (1994). *Sex in America: A definitive survey* (p.1, p.131, p.225) Boston: Little, Brown and Company.
[364] Michael, et al., 1994
[365] Michael, et al., 1994

This seems to indicate that women who are married are women who are least likely to be treated as sexual objects. This is good for women.

This is no doubt why the faithfully married are *least* likely to report having no interest in sex.[366]

Consider what Andrew Greeley of the University of Chicago, another sociologist who examined how marriage affects sexual satisfaction, discovered. Based on his research, Greeley explains, "premarital sex with someone other than the intended spouse correlates with marital infidelity.[367]"

Specifically, only 3 percent of spouses who did not engage in premarital sex with someone other than their present spouse were unfaithful in marriage. For those who engaged in premarital sex with someone other than their spouse "fairly often," 18 percent were unfaithful in marriage.[368]

A question for young people to consider is can you really be sure that this boyfriend or girlfriend will be your spouse one day, regardless of "how in love" you feel today? Only a wedding can really provide that answer.

Additionally, a joint study conducted at the University of Maryland and the National Center for Health Statistics found that "women who were sexually active prior to marriage faced a considerably higher risk of marital disruption than women who were virgin brides.[369][370]"

One reason may be that when people bond closely through sexual activity, then break up and bond with someone else, and then someone else, it may become increasingly difficult to maintain a lasting bond.[371]

---

366 Laumann, E. O., Gagnon, J. H., Michael, R. T., & Michaels, S. (1994). *The social organization of sexuality: Sexual practices in the United States* (p. 370, table 10.8). Chicago: University of Chicago Press.

367 Greeley, A. M. (1991). *Faithful attraction: Discovering intimacy, love, and fidelity in American marriage* (p. 244). New York: Tom Doherty Associates.

368 Greeley, A. M. (1991). *Faithful attraction: Discovering intimacy, love, and fidelity in American marriage*. New York: Tom Doherty Associates.

369 Kahn, J. R., & London, K. A. (1991). Premarital sex and the risk of divorce. *Journal of Marriage and the Family, 53*, 845–855.

370 Teachman, J. (2003). Premarital sex, premarital cohabitation, and the risk of subsequent marital dissolution among women. *Journal of Marriage and Family, 65*, 444-455.

371 McIlhaney, J. S. & Bush, F. M. (2008). *Hook*

ed: New science on how casual sex is affecting our children. Chicago: Northfield Publishing.

Cohabitation (when two people live together before marriage) is not like marriage!

Many people assume that living together without marriage is exactly like living together in marriage as long as two people love each other. This is a myth that needs busting. Consider...

1. The nation's leading academic institution which studies domestic violence finds, "Cohabitors are much more violent than marrieds." The overall rates of general violence for cohabiting couples was twice as high, and the overall rate for "severe" violence was nearly five times as high for cohabiting couples when compared with married couples.[372]
2. The divorce rates of women who cohabit before marriage with their future spouse are, on average, nearly 80 percent higher than the rates of those who do not.[373]
3. Research conducted at UCLA found that, "cohabitors experienced significantly more difficulty in their marriages with adultery, alcohol, drugs, and independence (not wanting to depend on each other for help and support) than couples who had not cohabited.[374]"
4. Numerous studies have consistently shown that cohabitors have much higher levels of infidelity than married couples.[375] Specifically, "the odds of a recent infidelity were more than twice as high for cohabitors than for married person.[376]"
5. Sociologist Linda Waite finds "during their twenties, young men and women who lived together showed very high and increasing rates of health-destroying and dangerous behaviors." These include heavy smoking, drinking, infidelity, carousing and illegal drug use.[377]

Given the findings of the scientific literature, sociologists conclude, "It is difficult to argue that cohabiters resemble married people.[378]" Premarital sex and cohabitation are not the ways to find happy, fulfilling relationships in adulthood. Making wise choices today will pay-off in greater health and happiness later.

The Marriage Union

---

[372] Yllo, K., & Straus, M. A. (1981). Interpersonal violence among married and cohabiting couples. *Family Relations, 30*, 339–347.

[373] Bennett, N. G., Blanc, A. K., & Bloom, D. E. (1988). Commitment and the modern union: assessing the link between premarital cohabitation and subsequent marital stability. *American Sociological Review*, *53*, 127–138.

[374] Newcomb, M. D., & Bentler, P. M. (1980). Assessment of personality and demographic aspects of cohabitation and marital success. *Journal of Personality Assessment, 44*, 11–24.

[375] Treas, J., & Giesen, D. (2000). Sexual Infidelity among married and cohabiting Americans. *Journal of Marriage and the Family, 62*, 48-60.

[376] Cunningham, J. D., & Antill, J. K. (1994). Cohabitation and marriage: Retrospective and predictive comparisons. *Journal of Social and Personal Relationships, 11*, 77–93.

[377] Waite, L. J., & Gallagher, M. (2000*). In sickness and in health. The case for marriage: Why married people are happier, healthier, and better off financially,* (pp. 63-64). New York: Doubleday.

[378] Goldscheider, F., Thornton, A., & Young-DeMarco, L. (1993). A portrait of the nest leaving process in early adulthood. *Demography, 30*, 683-699.

What does the word "union" mean to you? It is actually the joining of separate things to make one whole. What separate entities are joined in the marriage union? Of course the answer is two individuals!

How are two individuals joined in the marriage union?

The answer is by marriage vows, the vows they make to each other to remain together through thick and thin, until death do they part! A vow is a serious promise.

What is created through the marriage "union?"

Through marriage a new ***family*** is created, making a "whole" (complete) family!

In the marriage union, the lives of a man and a woman are joined together by their vows to make one whole; ***a new family***.

The marriage union is different from all other relationships in that it involves an intellectual, emotional, social and familial union. You might never have seen a marriage like the one we will be discussing in the next few pages. But you will learn that marriage relationships can be deep, full and rewarding. You can prepare to have a healthy relationship like this![379]

The Building Blocks of Marriage What are the building blocks of a good marriage? A strong union between a man and a woman is not achieved all at once. As relationships grow and two people share interests and life experiences, they will move from complete separateness into union. The fullest relationships have many building blocks in each aspect of union. What are the different aspects of a relationship between two people that build protection for a physical union?

Intellectual Union involves knowing one another. "Intellectual" means having to do with the mind. In an intellectual union, you know how a person thinks, what makes him or her laugh, what interests him or her, what makes him or her cry, how he or she is likely to respond in a given situation, his or her favorite movies, books, music, etc.

Emotional Union involves the commitment to love, honor, cherish and comfort each other. In an emotional union, you share feelings for one another, take care of one another, help and respect one another, shield one another from the difficulties of life, etc.

---

[379] Kim, H. K., & McKenry, P. C. (2000). The relationship between marriage and psychological well-being: A Longitudinal analysis. *Journal of Family Issues, 23*, 885-911.

Social Union involves letting the people around you know that you are together. In a social union, everyone associates you and this person as being together; your relationship is not a secret or something you never mention. It is common knowledge. The wedding ceremony, announcements in the newspaper and wedding rings are all part of the social union, as are the legal and financial bonds and responsibilities.

Familial Union involves living together as a new family unit. In a familial union, you live in one household and typically share the same name. Children born to the two of you will be part of your new family.

Lifetime Commitment These aspects of a relationship between two people build protection for a physical relationship, but by themselves, they are not enough to make the relationship stable and lasting – the kind you can depend on through the good and bad days. These are not sufficient to hold a relationship together through the extremely important days of having and raising children together. So, what makes marriage different? To help you understand the missing element, first think about a fireplace. If bricks or stones are put in place to form a fireplace, they could slip and slide, or be knocked out of place easily unless there is "mortar," or cement, to hold them together. It is the lifetime commitment that makes marriage different from all other relationships. Think about lifetime commitment as the "mortar" that holds the building blocks of a marriage together. In marriage you promise that all of the unions will last for life.[380]

[380] Nichols, W. C. (2004) The first years of marital commitment (pp. 28-43). In Harway, M (Ed.) *Handbook of couples therapy.* Hoboken, New Jersey: John Wiley & Sons, Inc.

The fire in the fireplace represents the physical union of the couple, or their sexual bond. It is the commitment within the marriage union that makes sex safe and best. A partial boundary, made of only some of the unions but lacking the mortar of lifetime commitment, does not make sex safe. All the aspect of the union, bound together by faithfulness to one another – a lifelong commitment, creates a bond that provides benefits to the couple, society, and their family.[381][382][383]

What thoughts have crossed your mind while thinking about the fireplace and marriage? Have you ever seen a healthy marriage such as the one described? Do you think it is possible? Most important, do you realize it is possible for you? You can have a healthy relationship, and form the family of your dreams, if you are willing to wait for someone who is also eager to work on having this kind of love and commitment. Would a partial boundary, made up of only some of the unions lacking the mortar of a lifetime commitment make sex safe? The answer is no. The fireplace could fall apart when the union of mortar is not there. Just like a marriage could fall apart if there is not a commitment to all of the unions.[384]

Remember abstinence is…"Not participating in any sexual activity outside of marriage."

Remember recommitting to abstinence is…"Physically, mentally and emotionally recommitting to saving sex for marriage."

[381] Finger, R. Thelen, T., Vessey, J. T., Mohn, J. K., & Mann, J. R. (2003). Association of virginity at age 18 with educational, economic, social, and health outcomes in middle adulthood. *Adolescent & Family Health, 3*, 164-170.
[382] Kline, G. H., Stanley, S. M., Markman, H. J., Olmos-Gallo, P. A., St. Peters, M., Whitton, S. W., et al., (2004). Timing is everything: Pre-engagement cohabitation and increased risk for poor marital outcomes. *Journal of Family Psychology, 18*, 311-318
[383] Whitehead, B. D., & Pearson, M. (2006). *Making a love connection: Teen relationships, pregnancy, and marriage.* Washington, DC: National Campaign to Prevent Teen Pregnancy. Retrieved February 10, 2011 from http://www.thenationalcampaign.org/resources/pdf/pubs/MALC_FINAL.pdf
[384] Whitehead, et al., 2006

STD Facts

George Washington was America's first president.	**FACT**
Both US World Trade towers were hit by planes on September 11, 2001	**FACT**
The USA experienced a great financial depression during the 1930's	**FACT**

What are some facts (not opinions to be debated) that you know to be true?

Facts are not created, invented, or thought up; they are discovered. Regardless of anyone's opinions a fact remains the same. Statistics are facts that indicate what is true about groups of people or things. Statistics come from observing lots of situations and determining how often something happens. Statistics cannot predict whether a certain thing will happen in any one person's case, but are good guidelines for what is likely to happen.

In the *Sex, Lies and Hook-Ups* book your parent(s) learned about resources for STD information. Ask your parents to take you to those resources so you can talk with them about STD information. Also ask them to discuss what they learned in the book about STDs and condom effectiveness. It's important for you to understand and take seriously your sexual health. A failure to do so could lead to many complications (such as death, infertility, cancer, etc). There is also information on all the major STDs in the back of this Student Manual. Review that information with your parent (s).

Once you have completed this, answer the following questions.

How many diseases shown in the STD presentation did you already know about?

1-5 6-10 11-15 16-20 21-25

How does the information about STDs make you feel?

Get a group of friends together (preferably at least 10) and ask your parent (s) to do the Pink Water game they learned about in the *Sex, Lies and Hook-Ups* book.

After you have done the Pink Water game, describe your reaction to the Pink Water game. What did you learn from this exercise?

The fact is, sexually transmitted diseases are spreading at an alarming rate among young people. All forms of sexual activity can spread sexually transmitted infections (STIs). Statistically, half of all new STIs occur in 15-24 year old.[385][386][387][388]

Even if you have only one sexual partner, and he or she had only one sexual partner before you, you could still get a sexually transmitted infection that can become a disease with lifelong implications.[389]

But, if you decide you are not willing to subject yourself to this risk, you are truly taking control over your own body and your own future. With that control comes the power over when and how you will form your family. That means you can work on reaching your potential in life so that your future is full of hope and possibilities.

Remember abstinence is…"Not participating in any sexual activity outside of marriage."

Remember recommitting to abstinence is…"Physically, mentally and emotionally recommitting to saving sex for marriage."

---

[385] American Social Health Association Panel (1998). *Sexually transmitted diseases in America: How many cases and at what cost?* American Social Health Association, Research Triangle Park, NC: Kaiser Family Foundation. Retrieved June 6, 2011 from http://www.kff.org/womenshealth/1447-std_rep.cfm

[386] Begley, E., Crosby, R. A., Di Clemente, R. J. Wingood, G. M., & Rose, E. (2003). Older partners and STD prevalence among pregnant African American teens. *Sexually Transmitted Diseases*, 30, 211-213.

[387] Miller, H. G., Cain, V. S., Rogers, S. M., Gribble, J. N., & Tuner, C. F. (1999). Correlates of sexually transmitted bacterial infections among U.S. women in1995. *Family Planning Perspectives, 31*, 4-23.

[388] Tiller, C. M. (2002). Chlamydia during pregnancy: Implications and impact on prenatal and neonatal outcomes. *Journal of Obstetric and Gynecologic, and Neonatal Nursing, 31*, 93-98.

[389] Mademoiselle (1999). *Do you have HPV?* Mademoiselle, September, 112.

How to Abstain from Sexual Activity

What are some reasons that teenagers choose to have sex?

You've studied some of the possible consequences.

Circle the consequences that you DO NOT want in your life.

Sexually Transmitted Infections	Increased chance of abuse from a partner
Hurting people you value	Raising a child alone
HIV/AIDS	Emotional hurt and regret
Missing out on an education	Legal and financial responsibility for a child until he or she is at least 18

Are there others that you want to avoid?

Considering the possible consequences, the reasons are not good enough. A new generation of teens are saying "no" to sexual activity outside of marriage because of the many negative consequences. They also realize it does not provide the deeply satisfying experience they are really looking for in a relationship. More than half of teens are abstaining from sex.[390]

But how do they keep that commitment?[391][392] The first step is to go through the reasons and think through why they are not good enough to risk the consequences. Next, it is crucial to think through a nice, but firm response, to the arguments others might use to get you off track. Here are some common reasons teens give for choosing to have sex and some possible responses. Think through what some of your own responses to these situations might be. You can even ask your parent(s) to role play these situations with you.

---

[390] Centers for Disease Control and Prevention, (2005). *Trends in the prevalence of sexual behaviors.* National Youth Risk Behavior Survey. Washington, DC: Centers for Disease Control and Prevention. Retrieved June 6, 2011 from www.cdc.gov/HealthyYouth/yrbs/pdf/us_sexual_trend_yrbs.pdf

[391] Bearman, P. S., & Bruckner, H. (2001). Promising the future: Virginity pledges and first intercourse. *The American Journal of Sociology*, 106, 859-911.

[392] Rector, R. E., Johnson, K. A., & Marshall, J. A. (2004). *Teens who make virginity pledges have substantially improved life outcomes.* Center for Data Analysis Report #04-07. Retrieved June 11, 2011 from www.heritage.org.

Tempter: "Your body is ready and you are free to have sex if you want to."
Response: READY = MARRIED

The huge risk of STDs and untimely pregnancy means that no one in our society can have sex outside of the protection of marriage *freely*, with the guarantee of no harmful consequences to self or others.

A major part of your body is your brain, and recent research shows that your brain is *not* mature during the teen years – the decision making capacity is still developing.[393] Remember: Ready = Already Married. Give yourself time, and wait until you are *so ready* that you have *already gotten married*. Anything short of marriage can too easily be broken off, even promises and engagement.

Some responses you could use:

- "I've been studying STDs, and they are *not for me*. I'm not going to have sex until I'm married."
- "I'm not going to start my family until I am married. I'm not going to take any risks with something that important."
- "You might believe I'm ready, but I am not. I have a lot to do before I get married, and I'm not having sex until then."
- "Anyone that has functioning sexual organs can have sex. It means more to me than that."

Tempter: "If someone spends a lot of money on a person, she or he should be willing to have sex."
Response: THIS BODY IS NOT FOR SALE

The day of people using their bodies sexually to get favors should be long past. Women can learn and earn as well as men. Men can prove themselves in much more meaningful ways than simply demonstrating that their genitals work. People who *demand* sex are looking for much more than just sex – it's about control. No boy has the right to pressure a girl into having sex, and no girl has the right to pressure a guy into the risks involved in sex outside of marriage. People can work out their needs in a much more productive and less risky way than having sex.

Some responses you could use:

- "I would *never* expect a person to give me anything but the pleasure of her/his company and the privilege of getting to know her/him. I'm not having sex until I'm married."
- "No one can buy me – I'm not for sale. I enjoy your company and would like to get to know you, but I'm not having sex until I'm married."
- "Thank you" should be said with your words and your smile, with kind and thoughtful actions, not with the intimacy of sexual activity, which should be saved for marriage and your spouse.

---

393 Walsh, D. (2004). *Why do they act that way?* New York, NY: Free Press.

Tempter: "It is all right for people to have sex before marriage if they love each other and are really committed."

Response: MARRIAGE = COMMITMENT

The wonderful feeling of being *in love* is actually called infatuation, and it generally doesn't last more than about a year and a half, at the most. Real love is much deeper and involves serious commitment. But even when people make promises to each other – even when they plan to marry, it is not the same as actually getting married. That is a true legal and moral commitment unlike any other.

People often feel in love with more than one person before they even meet the one they will love for a lifetime in marriage. Just because you love someone, or someone loves you, does not mean that he/ she is *the One* you will eventually marry. That feeling certainly is not enough to risk having a child before you and your partner (who will be the mother or father of your child) even decide you want to commit to each other. That is not fair to you or the child. If you have already had a child, or more than one child, you can commit to abstain from this day forward, and wait for the person who will love you and form a family with you based on real and lasting love.

A response you could use: "If we truly love one another, we will marry, and we can have sex with each other for the rest of our lives. Until then, we need to build our relationship in other ways, to see if we really want to make that commitment."

Tempter: "Practicing sex improves sexual satisfaction and technique."

Response: SAVE IT FOR THE PERSON I MARRY!

Actually, practicing sex outside of marriage with a series of partners increases the chance of infidelity within marriage.[394] Going from partner to partner not only increases the chance of disease and out-of-marriage pregnancy, it establishes a pattern. It also creates memories that often do not go away after the wedding vows.

Married couples can not only practice with each other, but they can trust each other to learn what is most pleasing and what the other enjoys.[395] In contrast, many couples involved in sexual activity outside of marriage often report feeling guilty, having regrets,[396] and that sex becomes routine and sort of takes over the other aspects of the relationship. Instead of growing the couple, it can become the very thing that keeps them from really getting to know each other.

Some responses you could use:

- "I want to learn with my wife/husband. If we marry, that will be you. But right now, we are not married, and I'm waiting until I get married to have sex."
- "I'm not willing to be someone others practice with. I'm waiting."

---

[394] Finger, R. Thelen, T., Vessey, J. T., Mohn, J. K., & Mann, J. R. (2003). Association of virginity at age 18 with educational, economic, social, and health outcomes in middle adulthood. *Adolescent & Family Health, 3*, 164-170.

[395] Hsiu-Chen, Y., Lorenx, F. O., Wickrama, K. A. S., Conger, R. D., & Elder, G. H. (2006). Relationships among sexual satisfaction [sic], marital quality, and marital instability at midlife. *Journal of Family Psychology, 20*, 339-343.

[396] Sprecher, S., Barbee, A., & Schwartz, P. (1995). "Was it good for you, too?" Gender differences in the first sexual intercourse experiences. *Journal of Sex Research, 32*, 3-15.

Tempter: "If I am in love and sexual intercourse just happens, I don't see that as a problem."

Response: UNLESS IT'S RAPE, SEX DOESN'T JUST HAPPEN. SOMEONE DECIDES.

The idea that people meet, are overcome by sexual arousal, and somehow end up having sex when they didn't expect to is an idea that sells songs and movies, but is not based on real life. Under normal circumstances, someone decides. However, many teens report that they were not under control when they decided. They were either under the influence of drugs or alcohol, and they deeply regretted their decision afterward.[397] But they couldn't turn back time.

Some responses you could use:

- "Sex it too important to just let it happen. I don't want to feel out of control. This is something I want to do after I get married, not on the spur of the moment without much thought."
- "We're getting out of control. I'm ready to go home, now."

Tempter: "Having sex is a normal and expected part of a relationship."

Response: SEX IS FOR MARRIAGE, NOT DATING

A lot of teens are choosing to not have sex. The possible consequences of sex outside of marriage are way beyond what two people who are just dating can handle. The emotional consequences of sexual bonding can be tremendously difficult for teen males and females. Even more important, the idea of having sex and taking the chance of creating a new person – a baby – before you have made a commitment to one another doesn't make sense. Neither does taking a chance on diseases that could cause infertility, sores, or even death. And the consequences for those who love you can be extremely serious, as well. What are some possible responses to this argument?

Some responses you could use:

- "Having sex outside of marriage is not for me. I'm waiting until I marry."
- "If you loved me, you'd do it."
- "There are lots of things that come naturally to us that I don't choose to do-like craving sugar and chocolate or being jealous of those who have more then me. Many 'natural' things have consequences. I am waiting for marriage."

---

[397] Johnson, T. J., & Stahl, C. (2004). Sexual experiences associated with participation in drinking games. *The Journal of General Psychology, 131*, 304-320.

Tempter: "If you loved me, you'd do it."
Response: REAL LOVE REQUIRES REAL RESPECT FOR MY VALUES AND GOALS.

True love is shown through devotion and understanding, caring and laughing, sharing and sacrificing for one another. It does not put the other person at risk. In contrast, it protects from risk. *Not* having sex – which is best for you, your boyfriend/ girlfriend and your relationship – is the truly loving thing to do.

Some responses you could use:

- "Which is easier and shows more real love, having sex as soon as you want to or waiting? I'm waiting until I am married, and if you can't, then I'm not the right person for you."
- "If that is all love means to you, then you and I have different concepts of what real committed love means."

Tempter: "Having sex proves that you are desirable and wanted by others."
Response: SEX WITHOUT LOVE IS LONELY

If someone truly wants *you* and not just your body, he or she will be willing to wait for the commitment of marriage. Some people might seem to want you when all they really want is what they can get from you, like the physical act of sex or the satisfaction of bragging to their friends about the experience.

Some responses you could use:

- "Abstaining from sex outside of marriage requires self-control and discipline, which I have.[398][399]"
- " I've thought this through, and I want more than just sex."
- "I don't want to start a family outside of marriage. I'm waiting for the real thing."

---

[398] Bearman, P. S., & Bruckner, H. (2001). Promising the future: Virginity pledges and first intercourse. *The American Journal of Sociology*, 106, 859-911.

[399] Sprecher, S., Barbee, A., & Schwartz, P. (1995). "Was it good for you, too?" Gender differences in the first sexual intercourse experiences. *Journal of Sex Research, 32*, 3-15.

Tempter: "Sometimes you should do things so others will think you're cool."
Response: DON'T BECOME THEM

THE major struggle of teen years is figuring out who you are, what you stand for, your own value system and your future. Even though many teens are driven by popular culture – much of which is created by adults trying to make money off of the teen population, you can choose to be yourself.[400] If you try to become like others, you lose yourself. It can take a while to figure out what is important for you. Take that time. Don't let the "buy and sell" culture define what you do with your body, your life, your future family. You will live with your decisions, they won't. Don't count on them when the child support check is due, or when you can't have children because you are infertile because of a STD.

Some responses you could use:

- "As much as I want you to like me, I can't compromise what I know is right for me and my future. I'm abstaining from sexual activity until I'm married."
- "I'm never going to have sex just because others may think it is the cool thing to do. I'm waiting for marriage."

Once you make the decision to commit to abstinence, and practice responses to familiar arguments, you will find that thinking of responses will become easier and more natural than imagined, and you will quickly realize YOU are in control of yourself; your body and your destiny – and that is the beginning of the true maturity that makes a real man or real woman. Set your personal standards high and to use every opportunity to reach your potential. Avoid those risks that could cause you pain and hardship. Good reasons to wait to have sex until marriage:

- You are unique. There is no one on Earth like you, so don't just follow the crowd. You can think for yourself and make decisions that help you reach your potential.
- You have a great future ahead of you. Be wise about how you handle your life today so that you keep your options open tomorrow.
- You are smart. You can choose to weigh the options and possible consequences and make a wise decision on your own.
- You are worth loving. You are not disposable. Sex is more than physical, and you deserve genuine care and commitment.
- You deserve the best sex. Statistics show that the people who report having the very best sex are not singles, but actually married people who were both virgins.[401][402]
- You have a right to sexual health. Waiting for sexual activity until marriage is healthy. Sex between two people who have not had any sexual activity with others and who are faithful to each other is obviously the best protection from sexually transmitted diseases.

---

[400] Goodman, B. (Director/Producer), & Dretzin, R. (Writer/Producer). (2001). *The merchants of cool* [Motion Picture]. United States: PBS Home Video.

[401] Stanton, G. T. (1997). *Why marriage matters: Reasons to believe in marriage in postmodern society.* Colorado Springs: Pinon Press

[402] Michael, R.T., Gagnon, J.H., Laumann, E.O., & Kolata, G. (1994). *Sex in America: A definitive survey* (p.1, p.131, p.225) Boston: Little, Brown and Company.

Love, Infatuation.....or Just Plain Lust

Remember abstinence is..."Not participating in any sexual activity outside of marriage."

Remember recommitting to abstinence is..."Physically, mentally and emotionally recommitting to saving sex for marriage."

Have you ever heard of infatuation? What do you think infatuation means? Infatuation is an intense, but short-lived interest in another person that does not consider anyone else's happiness or well-being. It is a feeling of excitement, fascination and often confusion. People who are infatuated often don't understand why they feel the way they do, nor can they explain it. "Being in love," as it is described in movies, music and television is more often than not, infatuation. Infatuation may degrade to lust, or it could grow into love. It might also go away. Some people are addicted to these feelings, and go from relationship to relationship to relationship, never really learning how to truly love another person. Infatuation is not love.

Have you ever heard of lusting after someone or something? What do you think lust means? Lust is a selfish interest in one's own happiness without regard for the other person's happiness and well-being. Lust is a feeling of wanting someone or something. Lust often refers to sexual desire, but people can also lust for money, status, affection, pretty things and fame all for selfish reasons that can disregard right and wrong. It is prone to using people—it wants and wants and is seldom satisfied. Lust is not love.

If infatuation and lust are not love, then what is love?

What do you think love is? Love is a deep and lasting interest in the other person's happiness and well-being. Love is more than a feeling. It is not just wishing the best for others, but a commitment to pursue the best for them, helping them become the best they can be. Love gives. Love does not take away.

Distinguishing Between Love and Infatuation		
QUESTION TO ASK	CLUES TO LOOK FOR: INFATUATION	CLUES TO LOOK FOR: LOVE:
What is my main interest? What attracts me the most?	The person's physical appearance; things that register with my five senses.	The total personality; what's inside.
How many things attract me?	Few--though some may be strong.	Many or most.
How did the romance start?	Fast (hours or days)	Slowly (months or years)
How consistent is my level of interest?	Interest varies, comes and goes; many peaks and valleys; not consistent over time.	Evens out; gets to be dependable and consistent; can predict it.
What effect does the romance have on my personality?	Disorganized, destructive; I'm acting strangely; I'm not myself.	Organized, constructive; I'm a better person.
How does the relationship end?	Quickly, unless there's been mutually satisfying sex, which can prolong, but not save the relationship	Slowly, if at all. The relationship takes a long time to end; we'll never be quite the same.
How do I view my partner?	There's only one person in the world--my partner. My partner can do no wrong; I see my partner as faultless, idealizing him or her.	I'm realistic about my partner's strengths and weaknesses. I can admit my partner's faults, but I keep loving anyway
How do others view our relationship? What's the attitude of friends and parents?	Few or none approves of the relationship.	Most or all approve. We get along well with each other's friends and parents.
What does distance (long separation) do to the relationship?	Withers away, dies; can't stand this added stress.	Survives; may even grow stronger.
How do quarrels affect the romance?	They get more frequent, more severe, and eventually kill the relationship.	They grow less frequent, less severe.
How do I feel about and refer to my relationship?	Much use of I/me/my; he/him/his; she/her/hers; little feeling of oneness.	Speak of we/us/our; feel and think as a unit, a pair; togetherness.
What's my ego response to the other?	Mainly selfish, conditional: "What does this do for me?"	Mainly unselfish, releasing; concerned equally for the other.
What's my overall attitude toward the other?	Attitude of taking; exploiting and using the other.	Attitude of giving, sharing; wanting to serve the other's needs and wants.
How much jealousy do I or my partner experience?	More frequent, more severe.	Less frequent, less severe.
REPRINTED WITH PERMISSION FROM THE FOUNDATION FOR THOUGHT AND ETHICS[403].		

[403] Cole, D. D., & Duran, M. G. (1998). *Sex and Character.* (p. 148) Dallas, TX: Foundation for Thoughts and Ethics

Infatuation is not always a bad thing, but it SHOULD NOT be mistaken for love. Lust is never a good thing as it can destroy both the person and the object of the lust. The only sufficient foundation for a lasting, fulfilling relationship is genuine love.

Don't rush into love! It will happen naturally as you get to know the RIGHT person! You will not love everyone you date; you are not supposed to! There is a difference between dating and actually marrying someone!

Review the differences between infatuation, lust and true love in the chart on the previous page.

Heritage Community Services has taught over 250,000 young people abstinence until marriage. In the classroom we split female and male students. An activity we do asks both groups to list the qualities they would like to see in the person they date vs. their future spouse. Try this activity with some of your own friends to see what you can learn about how guys and girls think!

After talking with each other about what each group thinks is important, discuss what most surprises you about what they say they want in the person they wish to date. Now compare that with what they want in a spouse. See any differences or similarities? Are there any qualities that were mentioned that sound more like lust? You are worthy of genuine love. Those who would use another to satisfy their own lusts will not only destroy themselves, but the object(s) of their lust as well. And those who lust are never truly satisfied—they want more and more. What are the lessons to be learned from this exercise?

It is important to think through what you really want in a boyfriend or girlfriend and to compare those qualities with those you want in a spouse.[404]

It may surprise you to figure out what you really think is important. Always remember, the person you are with now will most likely be someone's husband or wife eventually. Treat him or her the way you would want your future husband or wife treated. Everything you do now will impact your future.

Remember abstinence is..."Not participating in any sexual activity outside of marriage."

Remember recommitting to abstinence is..."Physically, mentally and emotionally recommitting to saving sex for marriage."

---

[404] Cooper, L. M., Shapiro, C. M., & Powers, A. M. (1998). Motivations for sex and risky sexual behavior among adolescents and young adults: A functional perspective. *Journal of Personality and Social Psychology, 75*, 1528-1558.

Building Relationships Without Having Sex

Have you ever heard of "love at first sight"? It should be "infatuation at first sight"! It takes time for genuine love to grow. Real love comes from give and take, sharing good and bad times, understanding and forgiveness, and mutual maturation and growth. Love develops with sacrifices for one another and bonding to one another!

Introducing physical intimacy before marriage too often leads to a relationship formed based on sexual lust. How could this hurt a relationship? Remember, lust takes whereas love gives. You begin to want sex from the other person instead of getting to know him or her and forming a bond based upon intellectual, social, emotional and familial relationships. It confuses the growth of genuine intimacy. A sexual relationship intensifies a feeling of closeness that may not be real – that may be based on taking rather than giving!

People are aroused at different levels of intimacy. Be careful what you wear because others are looking! You might be thinking fashion, while someone else is thinking sex. For this reason, wear modest clothing that doesn't invite lustful thoughts. And be careful about touching, because physical curiosity may be mistaken for actual love.

Physical intimacy can lead to sexual arousal. The further you go, the more you may want. Don't touch each other anywhere that a modest bathing suit covers. Sexual intimacy outside of marriage can lead to relationships which progress too fast physically and too slow intellectually, emotionally and socially.

Seeing and touching are not true intimacy. True intimacy, the kind that will last forever, comes from sharing thoughts and ideas, fears, goals and dreams, and laughter together! That kind of intimacy lasts. When you do get married true intimacy will lead to a better sex life![405]

Thinking of the opposite sex as people, not objects:

The key to a good relationship is getting to know one another as a person, rather than as a sexual object. If you cannot think of those you wish to date as people, this will be a huge problem in forming a truly intimate relationship.

Consider the way you think of and look at people you wish to date. What are your immediate thoughts?

[405] Michael, R.T., Gagnon, J.H., Laumann, E.O., & Kolata, G. (1994). *Sex in America: A definitive survey* (p.1, p.131, p.225) Boston: Little, Brown and Company.

Look at your answers. Do you look at these people lustful qualities? Are your answers based on what you can get from the person or how that person looks? This will not develop an intimate relationship. Think again of qualities you look for. This time include in your thoughts your loved ones. What is important to you and your immediate and long term goals? Which character traits do you admire? What kind of man or woman do you hope to be? Now, think again of the qualities that will develop intimate relationships. Write a few down.

Suggestions:

intelligence	sense of humor	ambition
goals	their likes	their dislikes
honesty	similar goals	personality

Remember...

Don't believe in stereotypes! Thinking and believing that all men and women are alike can lead to conclusions that are not based on who the person really is, deep inside where it really counts. People have different gifts, talents, thoughts, experiences, work ethics, and goals...all of which make them unique. They are worthy of getting to know beyond first impressions, and certainly deserve respect and admiration for who they are and all they will become.[406]

People are not sexual objects for others to simply look at. The most attractive people on earth, who end up as famous actors or models, have challenges in relationships just like everyone else. Every person has value, and that value has nothing to do with a perfect body, or how well it performs a sexual function. Judging anyone based on their physical appearance IS WRONG. Looking for a boyfriend or girlfriend based on outward appearance doesn't work very well since very few people are nearly perfect in their physical appearance. It's a set-up for disappointment and low self-esteem if the only way you can be a success is to be the boyfriend or girlfriend of the best looking person in school. Don't fall for that. The issues that really matter go much deeper than physical appearance. Someone may look great, but if you can't have a conversation with your partner, you will not be happy.

---

[406] Tangney, J. P., Baumesiter, R. F., & Boone, A. L.(2004). High self-control predicts good adjustment, less pathology, better grades, and interpersonal success. *Journal of Personality, 72*, 271-322.

Where did these stereotypes that many people apply in judging both guys and girls come from? Often, it's the media that sets the standard. In the last century, following the recession, money and food were hard to come by. Subsequently, full figured women were admired. In the later part of the same century, when there was plenty of food and many were overweight, it was the skin and bones women that appeared on magazine covers.

The media tells us that the value of a person comes from their sex appeal. This sends the message that sexy people are valuable and those who are not should be left alone. This has created a whole culture of people trying to buy 'sexiness,' from plastic surgery that takes away fat to plastic surgery that adds inches in other areas. This is wrong for many reasons. First of all, who is making those decisions in the media and why? Could they be feeding into the lust factor, trying to get your money by appealing to the elements of lust that may be in you? Don't allow sales gimmicks to tell you the kind of person you can love! This is a recipe for disaster.

What kinds of things do advertisers do to try to sell, using sexy-looking people? Write down a few of your thoughts.

The physical changes that take place during adolescence make it challenging to keep this all in perspective. The same hormones that are making both guys and girls look different - more manly or womanly, are the very hormones causing you to have an interest in those very qualities! It's healthy to be interested! These differences are natural, wonderful, and very special! It's normal to be curious when it comes to these body parts! Strong attraction is part of what makes marriage so wonderful! But, what makes humans different from the rest of the animal kingdom is the ability to exercise self-control, to think through consequences, and to act thoughtfully in order to honor loved ones, reach goals, and be the kind of person we all want to be.

It is actually that whole process that determines the kind of man or woman you will be and the kind of man or woman that will be attracted to you! It can be difficult, but the ways you handle these years have a lot to do with how your future will turn out. It is the struggle itself that creates character, personal responsibility, and an ethical foundation for the rest of your life. Have faith in yourself and always keep your future spouse in mind![407][408] Very few people at your age really understand what is happening to them, much less what is happening to other young men and women. Since they seem so different from you, it can be difficult to recognize the ways in which they are similar (hopes, dreams, goals, etc), the things you still have in common.

---

[407] Epstein, J. A., Griffin, K. W., & Botvin, G. J. (2001). Risk taking and refusal assertiveness in a longitudinal model of alcohol use among inner-city adolescents. *Prevention Science, 2*, 193-200.

[408] Tangney, J. P., Baumesiter, R. F., & Boone, A. L.(2004). High self-control predicts good adjustment, less pathology, better grades, and interpersonal success. *Journal of Personality, 72*, 271-322.

Remember... Objects are to be used; people are to be related to. Stereotypes are misleading. All people have thoughts, feelings, dreams, goals, families and past histories, just like you and your friends have! It is the struggle itself, and how you handle it, that develops you into a man or woman of character.

The Making of a Man

What do you think makes a man? Not anatomy, but qualities that earn respect.[409] List the qualities you think make a real man.

Did you say men like football? A lot of men like football, but could a "real man" not like football? Of course! There are some men who do not particularly like football, but like other sports. There are many that do not like any sports at all. But they may like something completely different – maybe working on computers or building houses or reading. It certainly is not football that makes a man a "real man."

Did you say that a real man has a lot of money? If your idea of what makes a man is the amount of things he has, how much does he have to have before he is considered a real man? Could a man who does not have very much be considered a real man based on the way he uses what he has? Could a rich man use his money selfishly or to hurt people? Is it more important how much a man has, or how he acquired and used his money? Do you know someone who does not have a lot but you consider him a real man?

Did you say men have muscles? Can men not have muscles? Even in the Olympics, the body builds of the athletes vary greatly, often depending on the sport in which they excel. And men who do not have interests that include muscle building may in every way be healthy and attractive, so that is not what makes a "real man."

Did you say a man has a fancy car? Could a man not have a fancy car? Could a "real man" have an old, not-so-fancy car? To some guys, an expensive car is a must. To others, the money would be better spent on electronic gadgets, golf equipment, or charities that are really helping others. Some of the richest people in America prefer to buy used cars, because they devalue after purchase. Surely it is not a fancy car that makes a man a "real man."

Did you say a man has sex with a lot of women?[410] Could a man not have sex with a lot of people? There are some men who go from person to person, starting

---

[409] Kindlon, D., & Thompson, M. (2000). *Raising Cain: Protecting the emotional life of boys.* (pp. 14-16, p. 197) New York: The Ballantine Publishing Group.

[410] Kindlon, D., & Thompson, M. (2000). *Raising Cain: Protecting the emotional life of boys.* (pp. 211 – 216, pp. 215-216) New York: The Ballantine Publishing Group.

families all over town and not loving or taking care of any of them. Others work hard to make sure their spouses are well cared for, and their babies have food and a place to live. Which is the "real man"? Many would say that a "real man" can control his sexual urges and wait for a person he commits to through marriage.[411] It is not sex with a lot of people that makes a man a "real man." That only proves his genitals work. Most men can claim this.

Obviously a man is not made up of those qualities. So, what do you think does make a man?

Add any other thoughts you may have now about what internal qualities you admire.

Manhood is measured by who he is (his character) and how he is (his actions).

Manhood is not measured by what you have.
Having a girlfriend does not make you a man.
Having a car does not make you a man.
Having money does not make you a man.

Manhood is not measured by how you compare to other people.
Being the best athlete does not make you a man.
Being the funniest or smartest or coolest guy does not make you a man.
Being the strongest or best looking or most popular does not make you a man.

A man is mentally strong. A man trains his mind and emotions to obey his will.

A man is respectful. A man treats all people with respect and treats his authorities with respect for their position. The way you treat people says more about you than it does about them.

A man is courageous. A man does what is right even when he is alone. The hardest time to be a man is when everybody is looking – or when nobody is looking.

A man protects. A man does not hurt people or allow them to be hurt, when it is within his power to help.

---

411 Kindlon, D., & Thompson, M. (2000). *Raising Cain: Protecting the emotional life of boys.* (pp. 215 – 216, pp. 215-216) New York: The Ballantine Publishing Group.

The Making of a Woman

What makes a woman?

What do you think makes a woman? Not anatomy, but actual qualities. List the qualities you think make a "real woman."

Are your answers true for every woman?

Did you say a woman likes shopping? Could a woman not like shopping? There are, in fact, many women who prefer to do other things and actually dread shopping, only going when it is absolutely necessary. Not to mention the fact that there are many women who just cannot afford to shop very much, but are fulfilled in so many other ways. And, consider women in high offices, who have responsibilities that keep them busy nearly all the time—or those who run companies that demand constant attention. Certainly, it is not shopping that makes a woman a "real woman."

Did you say a woman must wear the latest fashions? If so, consider the women you admire most. Chances are that some of the women most important to you personally do not wear the latest shoes or clothing. You probably know women who are strong, who have deeply integrated good character throughout all they have accomplished. Are they "real women?" And you most likely know girls who have all the latest fashion, but just don't exhibit the qualities you most value. Do you consider them to be "real women?"

Did you say a woman likes jewelry? Could a woman not like jewelry? In fact, there are many women who don't wear jewelry at all, even if they can afford the best. Some women simply don't like glitter and glamour and prefer a simpler appearance. Does that mean they are not "real women?" Certainly not! In fact, they may like fine music, sports or a number of other things besides jewelry. Jewelry does not make a person a "real woman."

Did you say that a real woman has sex with a lot of people? Could a woman not want to have sex with a lot of people? There are many women who do not have sex until they are married. They have decided they want sex to be a part of a relationship that is based on much more than just a physical relationship, and want to wait until they are married to have sex. Does that mean they are not a "real woman?" Not at all. In fact, many would say that it takes character, self-control and strong values to refuse to go along with a culture that promotes sex. Having sex with a lot of people does not define a "real woman."

If these qualities do not make up a "real woman," what does? Right down a few of your thoughts.

Now that you've given it more thought, list a few more internal qualities you admire.

A real woman is measured by who she is (her character) and how she is (her actions).

A real woman is not measured by what she has.
Having a boyfriend does not make you a woman.
Having the latest fashions does not make you a woman.
Having expensive jewelry does not make you a woman.

A real woman is not measured by how she compares to others.
Being the most fashionable does not make you a woman.
Being the funniest or smartest or coolest girl does not make you a woman.
Being the prettiest or most popular or having the best figure does not make you a woman.

A Real Woman knows herself.

A Real Woman takes time to find out who she is, who she wants to become and what she wants to accomplish.[412]

What do you like to do? What interests you? Who are your heroines? It takes a lot of time and thought to figure out the answers to these questions.

Give yourself time to grow and experience different things. Experiment! Read a book you are not sure you will like, listen to music that is not your usual type, make friends with someone outside of your regular group. You might surprise yourself.

Pay attention to your own thoughts and feelings. Writing is a great way to learn about yourself. If you do not know where to begin, try starting with "I think . . . " or "I feel . . . " or "I like . . . " and go from there. You are worth thinking about!

A Real Woman is confident.

---

[412] American Psychological Association, Task Force on the Sexualization of Girls. (2007). *Report of the APA task force on the sexualization of girls.* Washington, DC: American Psychological Association. Retrieved June 6, 2011from www.apa.org/women/programs/girls/report.aspx

A Real Woman will not forget herself to become the person other people want her to be.

Other people will always have ideas about how you should be, and their input can be valuable, but never try to squeeze yourself into someone else's mold. Never trade your dreams and goals for someone else's!

A Real Woman sends a clear message.

A Real Woman's speech, dress and behavior do not give people a wrong impression of who she is.[413]

Right or wrong, people sometimes make assumptions about what kind of person you are based on the way you look and the way you act. Choose your clothes, expressions and gestures carefully. Make sure the messages you send match your sexual values.

A Real Woman is caring.

A Real Woman reaches out to help others.

When you have confidence in who you are and where you are going, it is easier to keep your balance when life gets rough. When your balance is steady, you do not have to use all of your strength to keep from falling; you can reach out to help others.

---

[413] American Psychological Association, Task Force on the Sexualization of Girls. (2007). *Report of the APA task force on the sexualization of girls.* Washington, DC: American Psychological Association. Retrieved June 6, 2011from www.apa.org/women/programs/girls/report.aspx

SAFE Plan

State boundaries.

Establish boundaries. Everything covered by a modest bathing suit is off-limits.
Write boundaries. Fix boundaries clearly in the mind, which makes it easier to avoid compromise under pressure. Commit to maintaining boundaries.
Share boundaries. Verbalize your boundaries to friends and those you date, and accept help in maintaining those boundaries.

Avoid danger.

Stay away from dangerous situations that make it difficult to protect your boundaries, for sex and other risks, like drinking. Be firm, no compromise. Danger might be a friend who pressures you, a relationship that tempts you, or a time or place that offers opportunity (like a bedroom, an empty house, a party with drinking or drugs, etc.).

Firmly say, "No!"

Verbally
Use the word *no*; there is nothing clearer or more to the point.
Use strong words and a strong tone of voice; send your message loud and clear.
State what you are not going to do or what you want the other person not to do (i.e. "No. I'm not going upstairs with you," or "No. Do not put your hand on my butt.").
It's okay to state positive feelings about a person so they know it is the activity being rejected, not the person (i.e. "No. I think you are great, but I am NOT going to have sex with you.")
State reasons, but boundaries are not debatable. If someone pushes you to debate your boundaries, you must be ready to defend your position and not compromise.

Non-verbally
Say the same thing with your body that you are saying with your mouth.
Stiffen your body, sit up straight, fold your arms, hold up your palms to hold the other person away from you, or use other gestures to support what you are saying.
Use serious facial expressions and eye contact.

Exit
If all else fails, leave, which is the most definite, unmistakable non-verbal *no* you can give. This is your last line of defense; no matter how close you come to crossing your boundary, it is never too late to stop, get out of there, and keep safe. Also, know when to "exit" a relationship that may not be safe.

Boundaries

Write down some boundaries you want to keep in regards to the following risky behaviors. Discuss them with your parent (s) after you have finished.

Drugs –

Alcohol –

Smoking –

Violence –

Sexual activity outside of marriage (you might want to include dating) –

Imagine Your Wedding

Take a minute right now to imagine your own wedding.

Every person's wedding day is unique. What will your day be like?

Think about the people that will be there. Your parents? Your grandparents and other extended family? Will your brother or sister be in the wedding party? What do you think your loved ones will say to you on that day? How will you feel? What emotions do you hope to have? What emotions do you hope your family and friends will have for you?

Now focus on the person you have chosen to marry. Why are you marrying that person? Do they have the characteristics you thought about earlier in *Heritage Keepers®*? Think about the activity we did...what kind of person do you want to marry....does this person have the attributes you were looking for in a life-long relationship? Does this person respect you and your values, boundaries, and goals? Does this person treat you with dignity and respect and affirm your value and worth rather than compromising your value or worth?

Are you marrying a person you believe will be with you for the rest of your lifetime? What will it be like to grow old together? Possibly have children together? Will your dedication to finding the person that meets your standards be worth it?

On your wedding day, you are uniting with someone for a lifetime. Think about the fireplace that made sex safe. On this day, it all comes together. The social, familial, emotional and intellectual unions are all in place after this ceremony. Your commitment to each other has secured those unions. The physical union is now safe. Today you can combine love and intimacy. How does that feel? Think about the sex is like fire story. Do you feel safe? Do you feel loved? Take a second to contrast that feeling of intimacy and love with what you see today in the media about sex. How different are those two pictures? One is based on lust and using another person's body for your pleasure. The other is based on everything a human needs – intimacy within a secure and committed life-long relationship.

The choice to have this intimate lifelong relationship with someone is yours. I hope you will choose the best. No matter what your past has been, you can choose right now to make the best decisions for your future marriage—decisions that honor your marriage and honor yourself and your future spouse.

Your Commitment

The time has come for you to decide what you are going to do about abstaining from sexual activity outside of marriage. You have heard all the arguments people use – why young people should have sex before they are married. But, none of those arguments held up when the serious consequences were considered. You've learned the benefits of marriage, including the fact that those who wait report having the most satisfying sex,[414] and that those who don't are more likely to be unfaithful after marriage.[415]

You have had the opportunity to learn about sexually transmitted infections and the diseases that may develop as a result of sexual relationships outside of a mutually faithful marriage. And you've talked about the legal and financial responsibilities you will have for children you create, even if it is with someone you really never care to see again. But perhaps most important, you've had the opportunity to think about what is important to you, the people you love, the goals you have, and the kind of person you want to be. You've taken time to consider what genuine love is, and the way you want to be loved, for who you are deep inside. Finally, you have looked at what real love is. Sex is only a part of what bonds two people together. It is the intellectual, emotional, social and familial aspects of relationships, held together by the commitment of marriage, that makes a union safe for sex.[416][417]

Now it is time for you to make the commitment for the very best for yourself, to wait for the commitment of marriage to have sex. Once you make that commitment, you hold the power to not only hold out for that person you love enough to marry, but to be free of the consequences that are related to sex outside of marriage – free to reach your potential in life, and to become all you are meant to be! Make this commitment for yourself, those you love, and the ONE you marry. Do it for you, for them, for your hopes, dreams and goals, for your future family that deserves the very best! You will be glad you did!

Remember abstinence is...Not participating in any sexual activity outside of marriage.

Remember "recommitting to abstinence" is...Physically, mentally and emotionally recommitting to saving sex for marriage.

---

[414] Michael, R.T., Gagnon, J.H., Laumann, E.O., & Kolata, G. (1994). *Sex in America: A definitive survey* (p.1, p.131, p.225) Boston: Little, Brown and Company.

[415] Greeley, A. M. (1991). *Faithful attraction: Discovering intimacy, love, and fidelity in American marriage* (p. 244). New York: Tom Doherty Associates.

[416] Bearman, P. S., & Bruckner, H. (2001). Promising the future: Virginity pledges and first intercourse. *The American Journal of Sociology*, 106, 859-911.

[417] Rector, R. E., Johnson, K. A., & Marshall, J. A. (2004). *Teens who make virginity pledges have substantially improved life outcomes.* Center for Data Analysis Report #04-07. Retrieved June 11, 2011 from www.heritage.org.

Why Marriage Matters: 30 Conclusions, A Snapshot[418]

Family

1. Marriage increases the likelihood that fathers/mothers have good relationships with their children.
2. Cohabitation is not the functional equivalent of marriage.
3. Growing up outside an intact marriage increases the likelihood that children will themselves divorce or become unwed parents.
4. Marriage is a virtually universal human institution.
5. Marriage and a normative commitment to marriage, foster high quality relationships between adults, as well as between parents and children.
6. Marriage has important biosocial consequences for adults and children.
7. Children are most likely to enjoy family stability when they are born into a married family.
8. Children are less likely to thrive in complex households.

Economics

9. Divorce and unmarried childbearing increase poverty for both children and mothers.
10. Married couples seem to build more wealth on average than singles or cohabiting couples.
11. Marriage reduces poverty and material hardship for disadvantaged women and their children.
12. Minorities benefit economically from marriage also.
13. Married men earn more money than do single men with similar education and job histories.
14. Parental divorce (or failure to marry) appears to increase children's risk of school failure.
15. Parental divorce reduces the likelihood that children will graduate from college and achieve high-status jobs.

Physical Health and Longevity

16. Children who live with their own two married parents enjoy better physical health, on average, than do children in other family forms.
17. Parental marriage is associated with a sharply lower risk of infant mortality.
18. Marriage is associated with reduced rates of alcohol/substance abuse for both adults/ teens.
19. Married people, especially married men, have longer life expectancies than do otherwise similar singles.
20. Marriage is associated with better health and lower rates of injury, illness, and disability for both men and women.
21. Marriage seems to be associated with better health among minorities and the poor.

Mental Health and Emotional Well-Being

22. Children whose parents divorce have higher rates of psychological distress and mental illness.
23. Cohabitation is associated with higher levels of psychological problems among children.
24. Family breakdown appears to increase significantly the risk of suicide.
25. Married mothers have lower rates of depression than do single or cohabiting mothers.

Crime and Domestic Violence

26. Boys raised in non-intact families are more likely to engage in delinquent and criminal behaviors.
27. Marriage appears to reduce the risk that adults will be either perpetrators or victims of crime.
28. Married women appear to have a lower risk of experiencing domestic violence than do cohabiting or dating women.
29. A child not living with his or her own two married parents is at greater risk for child abuse.
30. There is a growing marriage gap between college-educated Americans and less-educated Americans.

---

[418] Institute for American Values (2005). *Why marriage matters: 26 conclusions from the social sciences.* (2nd ed)[Brochure]. Institute for American Values.

Bacterial STDs[419]

Bacterial Sexually Transmitted Diseases				
Common STDs	**Chlamydia**	**Gonorrhea**	**Syphilis**	**Trichomoniasis (Parasite)**
Where is it found?	Vagina, cervix, urethra, throat, discharge from penis, and rectum	Vagina, cervix, uterus, urethra, throat, and rectum	Genital area, mouth, skin, anus, and rectum	Vagina, cervix, and urethra
How can it be spread?	Oral, anal, and vaginal sex; mother to child	Oral, anal, vaginal sex; mother to child	Oral, anal, and vaginal sex; contact with sores; mother to child	Vaginal sex
What are the possible symptoms and complications?	May not have early symptoms, burning or pain with urination, discharge from penis and vagina, chronic low abdomen pain, pelvic inflammatory disease (PID) and infertility may result (mostly in females)	Males: often have no symptoms; may have burning or pain with urination. Females: often have no symptoms. May have vaginal discharge, may lead to pelvic inflammatory disease (PID) or infertility	Painless sore, untreated can spread to brain and/or heart, flu-like symptoms, damage to major body systems if untreated, can cause rash on infants' skin, birth defects and other problems with organs or possible stillbirth	Vaginal discharge and itching, burning during urination, males may have no noticeable symptoms but can cause temporary irritation in penis, may cause early delivery and low birth weight babies
Prevention	Abstain from sex; faithful marriage or mutually monogamous relationship with an uninfected partner; condoms used correctly and consistently reduce but do no eliminate the risk; testing and treatment	Abstain from sex; faithful marriage or mutually monogamous relationship with an uninfected partner; condoms used correctly and consistently reduce but do no eliminate the risk; testing and treatment	Abstain from sex; faithful marriage or mutually monogamous relationship with an uninfected partner; condoms used correctly and consistently reduce but do not eliminate the risk; testing and treatment	Abstain from sex; faithful marriage or mutually monogamous relationship with an uninfected partner; condoms used correctly and consistently reduce but do not eliminate the risk; testing and treatment
What are the treatments?	Antibiotics (permanent damage may have occurred prior to treatment)	Antibiotics (permanent damage may have occurred prior to treatment)	Antibiotics (permanent damage may have occurred prior to treatment)	Antibiotics (permanent damage may have occurred prior to treatment)

[419] 4Parents.gov. (2009, July 24). *Common sexually transmitted diseases (STDs).* Retrieved February 15, 2011 from http://www.4parents.gov/sexrisky/stds/common_std/common_std.html

Viral STDs[420]

Viral Sexually Transmitted Diseases

Common STDs	Genital Herpes: Herpes Simplex Virus	Human Papillomavirus (HPV)	Hepatitis B	HIV/AIDS
Where is it found?	Genitals and/or rectum	Vagina, cervix, penis, vulva, anus, scrotum, and other genital areas	Blood, semen, and vaginal fluid	Blood, semen, cervical and vaginal fluid, and breast milk
How can it be spread?	Oral, anal, and vaginal sex; contact with infected skin; rarely mother to child	Anal and vaginal sex; contact with infected skin; rarely mother to child	Oral, anal, and vaginal sex; IV drug use; mother to child	Oral, anal, and vaginal sex; IV drug use; mother to child
What are the possible symptoms and complications?	Often no symptoms are present, painful blisters or sores, fever, and swollen glands may occur, symptoms can recur throughout life, rarely serious infection can occur when passed to newborns	Most have no symptoms, but some can get genital warts, can cause cancer of the cervix, vulva, vagina, anus and penis	Often there are no obvious symptoms; jaundice, abdominal pain, loss of appetite, fatigue, joint pain; can lead to liver cancer and liver failure	No early symptoms or some flu-like symptoms that are often not noticed; rash; weakens immune system; multiple severe infections
Prevention	Abstain from sex; faithful marriage or mutually monogamous relationship with an uninfected partner; condoms used correctly and consistently reduce but do not eliminate the risk; testing and treatment	HPV vaccine (for some strains of HPV); abstain from sex; faithful marriage of mutually monogamous relationship with an uninfected partner; condoms used correctly and consistently reduce but do not eliminate the risk	Hepatitis B vaccine; abstain from sex; faithful marriage or mutually monogamous relationship with an uninfected partner; do not share needles; condoms used correctly and consistently reduce but do not eliminate the risk; testing	Abstain from sex; faithful marriage or mutually monogamous relationship with an uninfected partner; do not share needles; condoms used correctly and consistently reduce but do not eliminate the risk; testing
What are the treatments?	Symptom control that can help reduce recurrences, but no cure	No cure for infection, but medications can remove visible genital warts; regular Pap testing and follow-up medical treatment may deter development of cervical cancer.	Chronic infection can be treated with medication. No cure.	Symptom control with AIDS medicines (antiretroviral drugs); lifetime treatment is required; no cure

[420] 4Parents.gov. (2009, July 24). *Common sexually transmitted diseases (STDs).* Retrieved February 15, 2011 from http://www.4parents.gov/sexrisky/stds/common_std/common_std.html

Bibliography

4Parents.gov. (2009, July 24). *Common sexually transmitted diseases (STDs).* Retrieved February 15, 2011 from http://www.4parents.gov/sexrisky/stds/common_std/common_std.html

4parents.gov (2007). *State laws on age requirements and sex.* RetrievedJune 14, 2011, from http://www.4parents.gov/sexrisky/teen_sex/statelaws_chart/statelaws_chart.html

American Psychological Association, Task Force on the Sexualization of Girls. (2007). *Report of the APA task force on the sexualization of girls.* Washington, DC: American Psychological Association. Retrieved June 6, 2011from www.apa.org/women/programs/girls/report.aspx

American Social Health Association Panel (1998). *Sexually transmitted diseases in America: How many cases and at what cost?* American Social Health Association, Research Triangle Park, NC: Kaiser Family Foundation. Retrieved June 6, 2011 from http://www.kff.org/womenshealth/1447-std_rep.cfm

Bearman, P. S., & Bruckner, H. (2001). Promising the future: Virginity pledges and first intercourse. *The American Journal of Sociology*, 106, 859-911.

Begley, E., Crosby, R. A., Di Clemente, R. J. Wingood, G. M., & Rose, E. (2003). Older partners and STD prevalence among pregnant African American teens. *Sexually Transmitted Diseases*, 30, 211-213.

Bennett, N. G., Blanc, A. K., & Bloom, D. E. (1988). Commitment and the modern union: assessing the link between premarital cohabitation and subsequent marital stability. *American Sociological Review, 53*, 127–138.

Bingham, C. R., & Crockett, L. J. (1996). Longitudinal adjustment patterns of boys and girls experiencing early, middle, and late sexual intercourse. *Developmental Psychology, 32*, 647-658.

Borawski, E. A., Trapl, E. S., Lovegreen, L. D., Colabiachi, N., & Block, T. (2005). Effectiveness of abstinence-only intervention for middle school teens. *American Journal of Health Behavior*, 29, 423-434.

Brady, S. S., & Halpern-Felsher, B. L. (2007). Adolescents' reported consequences of having oral sex versus vaginal sex. *Pediatrics, 119*, 229-236.

Cabrera, N. J., Tamis-LeMonda, C. S., Bradley, R. H., Hofferth, S., & Lamb, M. E. (2000). Fatherhood in the twenty-first century. *Child Development, 71*, 127-136.

Centers for Disease Control and Prevention, (2005). *Trends in the prevalence of sexual behaviors.* National Youth Risk Behavior Survey. Washington, DC: Centers for Disease Control and Prevention. Retrieved June 6, 2011 from www.cdc.gov/HealthyYouth/yrbs/pdf/us_sexual_trend_yrbs.pdf

Cole, D. D., & Duran, M. G. (1998). *Sex and Character.* (p. 148) Dallas, TX: Foundation for Thoughts and Ethics

Coley, R. L. (1998). Children's socialization experiences and functioning in single-mother households: The importance of fathers and other men. *Child Development*, 69, 219-230.

Cooper, L. M., Shapiro, C. M., & Powers, A. M. (1998). Motivations for sex and risky sexual behavior among adolescents and young adults: A functional perspective. *Journal of Personality and Social Psychology, 75*, 1528-1558.

Cunningham, J. D., & Antill, J. K. (1994). Cohabitation and marriage: Retrospective and predictive comparisons. *Journal of Social and Personal Relationships, 11*, 77–93.

Duckworth, A. L., & Seligman, M. E. P. (2005). Self-discipline outdoes IQ in predicting academic performance of adolescents. *Psychological Science, 16*, 939-944.

Elmer-Dewitt, P. (1994, October 17). *Now for the truth about Americans and sex*. Time, p. 64-71.

Epstein, J. A., Griffin, K. W., & Botvin, G. J. (2001). Risk taking and refusal assertiveness in a longitudinal model of alcohol use among inner-city adolescents. *Prevention Science, 2*, 193-200.

Finger, R. Thelen, T., Vessey, J. T., Mohn, J. K., & Mann, J. R. (2003). Association of virginity at age 18 with educational, economic, social, and health outcomes in middle adulthood. *Adolescent & Family Health, 3*, 164-170.

Finkelhor, D., & Browne, A. (1985). The traumatic impact of child sexual abuse: A conceptualization. *American Journal of Orthopsychiatry.*

Goldscheider, F., Thornton, A., & Young-DeMarco, L. (1993). A portrait of the nest leaving process in early adulthood. *Demography, 30*, 683-699.

Goodman, B. (Director/Producer), & Dretzin, R. (Writer/Producer). (2001*). The merchants of cool* [Motion Picture]. United States: PBS Home Video.

Greeley, A. M. (1991). *Faithful attraction: Discovering intimacy, love, and fidelity in American marriage*. New York: Tom Doherty Associates.

Greeley, A. M. (1991). *Faithful attraction: Discovering intimacy, love, and fidelity in American marriage* (p. 244). New York: Tom Doherty Associates.

Hallfors, D. D., Waller, M. W., Bauer, D., Ford, C. A., & Halpern, C. T. (2005). Which comes first in adolescence-sex and drugs or depression? *American Journal of Preventive Medicine, 29*, 163-170.

Hsiu-Chen, Y., Lorenx, F. O., Wickrama, K. A. S., Conger, R. D., & Elder, G. H. (2006). Relationships among sexual satisfactin [sic], marital quality, and marital instability at midlife. *Journal of Family Psychology, 20*, 339-343.

Huang, C. C. (2005). Pregnancy intention from men's perspectives: Does child support enforcement matter? *Perspectives on Sexual and Reproductive Health, 37*, 119-124.

Institute for American Values (2005). *Why marriage matters: 26 conclusions from the social sciences.* (2nd ed)[Brochure]. Institute for American Values.

Jaffee, S., Caspi, A., Moffitt, T. E., Belsky, J., & Silva, P. (2001). Why are children born to teen mothers at risk for adverse outcomes in young adulthood? Results from a 20-year longitudinal study. *Development and Psychopathology, 13*, 377-397.

Johnson, T. J., & Stahl, C. (2004). Sexual experiences associated with participation in drinking games. *The Journal of General Psychology, 131*, 304-320.

Kahn, J. R., & London, K. A. (1991). Premarital sex and the risk of divorce. *Journal of Marriage and the Family, 53*, 845–855.

Kindlon, D., & Thompson, M. (2000). *Raising Cain: Protecting the emotional life of boys.* (pp. 14-16, p. 197) New York: The Ballantine Publishing Group.

Kindlon, D., & Thompson, M. (2000). *Raising Cain: Protecting the emotional life of boys.* (pp. 211 – 216, pp. 215-216) New York: The Ballantine Publishing Group.

Kim, H. K., & McKenry, P. C. (2000). The relationship between marriage and psychological well-being: A Longitudinal analysis. *Journal of Family Issues, 23*, 885-911.

Kline, G. H., Stanley, S. M., Markman, H. J., Olmos-Gallo, P. A., St. Peters, M., Whitton, S. W., et al., (2004). Timing is everything: Pre-engagement cohabitation and increased risk for poor marital outcomes. *Journal of Family Psychology, 18*, 311-318

Laumann, E. O., Gagnon, J. H., Michael, R. T., & Michaels, S. (1994). *The social organization of sexuality: Sexual practices in the United States* (p. 370, table 10.8). Chicago: University of Chicago Press.

Leitenberg, H., & Saltzman, H. (2003). College women who had sexual intercourse when they were underage minors (13-15). Age of male partners, relation to current adjustment, and statutory rape implications. *Sexual Abuse: A Journal of Research and Treatment, 15*, 135-147.

Loewenson, P. R., Ireland, M., & Resnick, M. D. (2004). Primary and secondary sexual abstinence in high school students. *Journal of Adolescent Health, 34*, 209-215.

Mademoiselle (1999). *Do you have HPV?* Mademoiselle, September, 112.

McIlhaney, J. S. & Bush, F. M. (2008). *Hooked: New science on how casual sex is affecting our children.* Chicago: Northfield Publishing.

Michael, R. T., Gagnon, J. H., Laumann, E. O., & Kolata, G. (1994). *Sex in America: A definitive survey.* (p. 1, p. 131, p. 225) Boston: Little, Brown, and Company.

Miller, H. G., Cain, V. S., Rogers, S. M., Gribble, J. N., & Tuner, C. F. (1999). Correlates of sexually transmitted bacterial infections among U.S. women in1995. *Family Planning Perspectives, 31*, 4-23.

Miller, K. S., Clark, L. F., Wendell, D. A., Levin, M. L., Gray-Ray, P., Velez, C. N., & Webber, M. P. (1997). Adolescent heterosexual experience: A new typology. *Journal of Adolescent Health, 20*, 179-186.

Mirowsky, J., & Ross, C. E. (2002). Depression, parenthood, and age at first birth. *Social Science and Medicine, 54*, 1281-1298.

Newcomb, M. D., & Bentler, P. M. (1980). Assessment of personality and demographic aspects of cohabitation and marital success. *Journal of Personality Assessment, 44*, 11–24.

Nichols, W. C. (2004) The first years of marital commitment (pp. 28-43). In Harway, M (Ed.) *Handbook of couples therapy.* Hoboken, New Jersey: John Wiley & Sons, Inc.

O'Donnell, L., O'Donnell, C. R., & Stueve, A. (2001). Early sexual initiation and subsequent sex-related risks among urban minority youth: the reach for health study. *Family Planning Perspectives, 33*, i268-275.

Rector, R. E., Johnson, K. A., & Marshall, J. A. (2004). *Teens who make virginity pledges have substantially improved life outcomes.* Center for Data Analysis Report #04-07. Retrieved June 11, 2011 from www.heritage.org.

Rector, R. E., Johnson, R. A., & Noyes, L. R. (2003). Sexually active teenagers are more likely to be depressed and to attempt suicide. Center for Data Analysis Report #30-04. Retrieved June 11, 2011 from www.heritage.org/ research/reports/2003/06/sexually_active_teeangers_are_more_likely_to_be_depressed.html

Rostosky, S. S., Regnerus, M. D., & Wright, M. L. C. (2003). Coital debut: the role of religiosity and sex attitudes in the Add Health Survey. *Journal of Sex Research, 40*, 358-367.

Schrof, J. M., & Wagner, B. (1994, October 17). *Sex in America*. U.S. News & World Report, pp. 74–81.

Sorensen, T. & Snow, B. (1991). How children tell: The process of disclosure in child sexual abuse. *Child Welfare, 70*, 3-15.

Sprecher, S., Barbee, A., & Schwartz, P. (1995). "Was it good for you, too?" Gender differences in the first sexual intercourse experiences. *Journal of Sex Research, 32*, 3-15.

Stanton, G. T. (1997). *Why marriage matters: Reasons to believe in marriage in postmodern society.* Colorado Springs: Pinon Press

Summit, R. C. (1983). The child sexual abuse accommodation syndrome. *Child Abuse & Neglect, 7*, 177-193.

Tamis-LeMonda, C. S., Shannon, J. D., Cabrera, N. J., & Lamb, M. E. (2004). Fathers and mothers at play with their 2- and 3- year-olds: contributions to language and cognitive development. *Child Development, 75*, 1806-1820.

Tangney, J. P., Baumesiter, R. F., & Boone, A. L.(2004). High self-control predicts good adjustment, less pathology, better grades, and interpersonal success. *Journal of Personality, 72*, 271-322.

Teachman, J. (2003). Premarital sex, premarital cohabitation, and the risk of subsequent marital dissolution among women. *Journal of Marriage and Family, 65*, 444-455.

Tiller, C. M. (2002). Chlamydia during pregnancy: Implications and impact on prenatal and neonatal outcomes. *Journal of Obstetric and Gynecologic, and Neonatal Nursing, 31*, 93-98.

Treas, J., & Giesen, D. (2000). Sexual Infidelity among married and cohabiting Americans. *Journal of Marriage and the Family, 62*, 48-60.

Van Bruggen, L. K., Runtz, M. G., Kadlec, H. (2006). Sexual revictimization: The role of sexual self-esteem and dysfunctional sexual behaviors. *Child Maltreatment, 11*, 131-145.

Waite, L. J., & Gallagher, M. (2000*). In sickness and in health. The case for marriage: Why married people are happier, healthier, and better off financially,* (pp. 63-64). New York: Doubleday.

Walsh, D. (2004). *Why do they act that way?* New York, NY: Free Press.

Whitehead, B. D., & Pearson, M. (2006). *Making a love connection: Teen relationships, pregnancy, and marriage.* Washington, DC: National Campaign to Prevent Teen Pregnancy.

Yllo, K., & Straus, M. A. (1981). Interpersonal violence among married and cohabiting couples. *Family Relations, 30*, 339–347.

Young, M., Denny, G., & Luquis, R. (1998). Correlates of the sexual satisfaction in marriage. *The Canadian Journal of Human Sexuality, 7*, 115-127.

Heritage Keepers Abstinence Education

Interested in having the *Heritage Keepers® Abstinence Education* program to share with others in your community? Become an advocate for getting the *Heritage Keepers® Abstinence Education* program in your child's school system.

Attitudes and behaviors are contagious, among teens and adults. Exposing others to a strong abstinence education program benefits not only them, but your teen as well. When the cultural environment is supportive of risk avoidance, young people are less likely to get involved in behaviors that can have consequences that put their futures in jeopardy.

Contact *heritage@heritageservices.org* with the subject line "Interested in Heritage program."

Healthy Family Formation Coalition

Sign up for the Healthy Family Formation Coalition, where you can get the latest information, including research findings, related to abstinence and marriage.

Visit *heritageservices.org* to sign up.

Media PSA's

Public Service Announcements are available for your local media. You can see these spots on *www.heritageservices.org*. Contact *heritage@heritageservices.org* with the subject line "PSA" to find out more.

Connect with Parents

Want to connect with other parents of pre-teens, teens and college-aged children?

Follow @abstinenceworks on Twitter and like Heritage Community Services on facebook!